Logical Problem Solving

Before the Flowchart

With C++ and Visual Basic Applications

Robert Lamey

Prentice Hall
Upper Saddle River, NJ 07458

Library of Congress Cataloging-in-Publication Data

Lamey, Robert.
   Logical problem solving before the flowchart with C++ and visual basic applications /
Robert Lamey.
     p. cm.
   ISBN 0-13-061882-9
     1. C++ (Computer program Language). 2. Microsoft Visual Basic. 3. Computer logic.
I. Title.

QA76.73.C153 L346 2002
005.13'3—dc21

                      2001021524

Vice President and Editorial Director, ECS: Marcia J. Horton
Senior Acquisition Editor: Petra J. Recter
Assistant Editor: Sarah Burrows
Vice President and Director of Production and Manufacturing, ESM: David Riccardi
Executive Managing Editor: Vince O'Brien
Managing Editor: David A. George
Production Services/Compositor/Art Studio: Prepare Inc.
Director of Creative Services: Paul Belfanti
Creative Director: Carole Anson
Cover Designer: Jayne Conte
Art Editor: Adam Velthaus
Manufacturing Manager: Trudy Pisciotti
Manufacturing Buyer: Lynda Castillo
Senior Marketing Manager: Jennie Burger
Editorial Assistant: Karen Shultz

© 2002 by Prentice-Hall, Inc.
Pearson Education
Upper Saddle River, NJ 07458

The author and publisher of this book have used their best efforts in preparing this book. These efforts include the development, research, and testing of the theories and programs to determine their effectiveness. The author and publisher make no warranty of any kind, expressed or implied, with regard to these programs or the documentation contained in this book. The author and publisher shall not be liable in any event for incidental or consequential damages in connection with, or arising out of, the furnishing, performance, or use of these programs.

Printed in the United States of America

10 9 8 7 6 5 4 3 2 1

ISBN 0-13-061882-9

Pearson Education Ltd., *London*
Pearson Education Australia Pty., Limited, *Sydney*
Pearson Education Singapore, Pte. Ltd
Pearson Education North Asia Ltd., *Hong Kong*
Pearson Education Canada, Ltd., *Toronto*
Pearson Educación de Mexico, S.A. de C.V.
Pearson Education Japan, *Tokyo*
Pearson Education Malaysia, Pte. Ltd.

Contents

Preface

PROBLEM SOLVING SKILLS

The issue would seem to be intractable. How do you solve a problem that you have never been taught to solve? Or, from an instructor's point of view, how do you teach someone else to develop new, creative solutions to previously unseen problems? Are such solutions the province of the exceptionally creative? Are creative solutions truly the marks of rare sparks of genius? Or, on the other hand, are there techniques that can be taught to anyone that lead to inventive approaches to daunting problems and ultimately to solutions.

Science, mathematics, and programming instructors constantly face this question. In each field the mechanics are straightforward consisting of principles and formulas. Teaching usually involves explaining the formulas, indicating what is to be memorized, and demonstrating how the mechanics are implemented. And, with varying amounts of effort, these mechanics and the accompanying calculations, can be learned by nearly all students. The calculations involved in determining the speed of a falling object, the balancing of chemical equations, the use of the quadratic formula, and the use of the pow() function in a C++ program represent implantations of formulas that are eminently learnable. These operations are sometimes called "plug and chug" because finding a solution involves choosing the appropriate a formula (or syntax), plugging in the proper numbers, and letting a calculator (or computer) chug until an answer appears on the display.

While this does involve one type of problem solving it limits students to solving problems that they have been taught to solve, problems that have a known algorithm for determining the solution to the problem. Unfortunately, in this electronic age, solving these types of problems is generally left to devices that work tirelessly, more reliably, and thousands of times faster than the most capable human. The execution of formulas has become the domain of computers. Those who only learn how to implement known formulas such as calculating a weighted average or the solution to two equations with two unknowns are preparing to compete directly with a computer. This is a competition that cannot be won.

However, computers fail when presented a novel problem for which there is no program available. Problem solving at this level requires creativity and the intervention of human thinking. Consequently determining creative solutions to previously unseen problems is a point of focus for mathematics, physics, economics, and numerous classes in the fields of technology and engineering.

This text concentrates on this higher level of problem solving and how it can be implemented by writing computer programs. That is, the expansion of basic principles and calculations to allow more complex problems to be solved. These are problems that involve the creative application of the more fundamental ideas rather than the mere resolution of a formula. For example, finding the solution to a quadratic equation is simple. Values for each tern are substituted into the quadratic formula and the resulting expression is evaluated. A more interesting and challenging problem is how to solve a fifth order equation. Since there is no algebraic solution for equations of order higher than four, this level of problem solving is not commonly taught. However, this seemingly difficult problem can be handled by combining the methods described in this text with the power of a personal computer.

This type of problem solving is difficult to learn and even more difficult to teach. However, in an age where calculators and computers have taken over most of the fundamental calculations and many not so fundamental calculations, it is important for students to learn to solve the problems that require the creative thinking that is (at least for the moment) beyond the abilities of electronic devices.

The formula for acceleration of a falling object can be read from a physics text and programmed into a calculator. Determining the velocity of a ball dropped from the top of a building after three seconds is as simple as entering a time value into the equation. Determining the speed required to keep a satellite in orbit is not so simple. Somewhere there is probably a formula that answers the question but because that formula is not readily available the problem becomes one of applying basic concepts from physics and mathematics in a creative fashion to determine a solution to the problem. This level of problem solving, finding answers to previously unseen problems, is still the realm of humans.

THE ROLE OF THE CALCULATOR

Approximately twenty-five years ago educators made the decision to introduce the use of calculators in the classroom. The goal was straightforward and seemed reasonable at the time. In the electronic age where a hand-held device could quickly, accurately, and reliably produce arithmetic answers, everyone should learn to use the new device.

In theory, the calculator would remove the tedium from the study of mathematics by making unnecessary the memorization of multiplication tables, decimal to fraction conversions, square root algorithms, and the standard constants, such as the number of feet in a mile. Students would benefit by the substitution of problem solving skills for the hours formerly spent practicing long division, dividing fractions, and calculating interest. Motivation would skyrocket as memorization and tedious practice was replaced with fascinating problems that appealed to students' imagination.

As the price of calculators plummeted and the capabilities expanded, calculators (and later computers) took over the tasks of solving equations, graphing functions, and calculating determinates. Again the use of calculators was justified from many directions. School should be fun and the tedium of arithmetic mechanics was not. The technology has become accepted in society and students must learn to make use of the most efficient tools. The memorization of formulas is irrelevant when the formulas can be programmed into the memory of the calculator. However, the primary rationalization was the increased time that could be devoted to problem solving once the mechanics were handled by electronic devices.

Unfortunately the promise of enhanced problem solving skill has failed to materialize. Some educators consider the skill to be innate and a given student either has the ability to think creatively or he does not. More commonly teachers acknowledge the difficulty in developing these problem-solving skills not to mention the unpopularity of "word problems", and choose to focus on more formula-based skills.

Fortunately the microprocessor that has made it unnecessary for people to determine a 15% tip or to calculate their taxes (which maybe handled by a computer program or it can be a truly creative exercise requiring teams of accountants and lawyers), offers expanded options in methods for attacking novel problems. Consider the daily compounding of interest for a bank account. The formula for daily compounding is not commonly known and no one would be interested in actually calculating interest on an account by adding the interest to the principle on a daily basis for perhaps five years. However it only takes minutes to program a computer to perform the thousands of calculations required. The end result is an answer to the problem despite the fact that the formula for compound interest is unknown.

THE CHANGING ROLE FOR STUDENTS

The reality of the calculator and the computer has fundamentally changed the role of the student in the problem solving process. Prior to the introduction of electronic calculating devices all calculations were made by hand and the student's role was to execute the algorithms. The teacher provided the plan of attack whether it was the method for multiple digit multiplication, the formula for compound interest, or the equations for calculating probabilities. Students memorized formulas and performed calculations.

The execution of algorithms has, for better or worse, become the domain of the machine. The number of people able to balance a checkbook, perform long division, or calculate a square root without a calculator is rapid diminishing. While the loss of basic numeric skills may be unfortunate and appears to be accompanied by the loss of understanding of fundamental arithmetic concepts, it is clear that the most adept human is no match for a computer in terms of speed, accuracy, or the ability to work for days on end without getting hungry, sleepy, or careless.

	Algorithm	Execution
Pre-Computer	Teacher	Student
Post-Computer	Student	Computer

However, if the student is no longer needed to manually make calculations, it becomes critical that he take on a new role previously filled by the teacher. It is the student who must develop creative solutions to problems previously unseen. That is, **students must learn to develop new algorithms without the aid of a teacher**, algorithms that may or may not be left to a computer to execute later. In short, problem-solving skills have become critically important.

The converse of this idea brings the concept into even higher relief. If students are only taught to execute algorithms then they are being prepared to compete directly with computers. This is an unnecessary and a futile contest. It is important that students learn to perform the higher functions that are beyond the abilities of computers.

PROBLEM SOLVING SKILLS

This returns us to the original problem. How can problem-solving skills be taught? How can insight into the resolution of an arbitrary problem be developed? How can the level of creative thinking be enhanced for the students in programming, science and mathematics classes? The problem is not intractable. There are two methods for developing precisely these skills.

The first step is to examine a set of approaches to problem solving. Because science and mathematics classes usually concentrate on individual principles and the applicable formulas, students often find that their first computer programming class is their first challenge in logical problem solving. In programming classes there is no way to avoid problem solving. Before anyone can write a program he must determine what to write. That is, there must be a plan for attacking the problem whether the program is to calculate square roots, calculate the number of days between widely separated dates, or determine the speed required to keep a satellite in orbit. For this reason many high schools, technical colleges, and universities are requiring classes in logical problem solving as a prerequisite for programming classes.

This is not to imply that mathematics classes are devoid of this level of problem solving. Algebra classes do contain word problems. Geometry classes require the proving of theorems. Trigonometry classes include the proving of trigonometric identities. However, these topics tend to be troublesome, unpopular with students, and difficult for teachers. Consequently far more time is spent on the mechanics of manipulating equations and the implementation of established algorithms, than on developing creative solutions. Similarly the proving trigonometric identities takes a back seat to calculating tangent function values. Geometry classes may not be required for graduation or the calculation of areas and volumes with their reliance on formulas may be substituted for the more creative, less structured, and more difficult task of proving theorems. In programming classes the student finds there is no way to avoid problem solving.

The traditional method for helping students learn to develop these plans is to have them first develop flowcharts or write pseudo-code that outlines the step-by-step procedure for solving the problem. The difficulty with this approach is that a flowchart is merely a description of a plan that is already developed. A student who does not know how to solve a problem will probably be unable to write a flow chart. In fact it is not uncommon for programming instructors who require the use of flowcharts to find that *students have written the program first and then constructed the flowchart from the program.* We could call this re-engineering at its worst.

This is not to minimize the value of flow-charting. Flow charting and the writing of pseudo-code are a useful tools for *clarifying* a plan before beginning to write code and will be used extensively in this text but they are of little help in *developing* the plan ***The intention of this text is to back-up one step from the flowchart and present a set of techniques for analyzing problems*** that leads to a plan for simultaneously answering the question of how to make the flowchart and how to write the program.

The second method for developing problem solving skills is to build a repertoire of problems that have already been solved. There is no substitute for experience in any endeavor and it is an unfortunate truth that no one starts out experienced. However experience in problem solving can be built by beginning with simple problems and building on the insight gained by each success. Clearly the problem of calculating the necessary speed to keep a satellite in orbit is not the place to begin developing problem-solving skills. It is more reasonable to begin with simple problems that can be solved by combining just a few well-known formulas or involve an easily followed train of logic. As experience grows new problems are often seen as mere variations or extensions of problems already solved.

Will readers who follow this book to its conclusion be able to solve the problems of planning a sustainable ecology, developing a clean energy source, and returning astronauts safely from Mars? Possibly not. But my experience in teaching computer programming over fourteen years makes me absolutely sure that anyone's problem solving abilities can be enhanced and that this enhanced ability is a valuable skill that pays dividends far beyond the confines of a programming class.

THE TEXT LAYOUT

Each of the following chapters explores a different method for solving problems and variations on the method for expanding its usefulness. The chapters begin with an explanation of the approach and then proceed through a series of examples that demonstrate the application of the approach. In general each example will add increased complexity and difficulty in implementing the method.

After the plan for attacking the problem has been described in detail, pseudo-code and a flowchart are developed to clarify the plan. Finally computer programs are written in C++ and Visual Basic to implement the plan and produce a solution to the problem. The important sections of the source code contain comments that relate the code to steps in the pseudo-code. While most readers will be learning or preparing to learn either C++ or BASIC, in general it is not necessary to be able to program to follow the implementation of the programs. Both C++ and BASIC computer code are sufficiently readable for non-programmer that the logic of the pseudo-code can be followed.

Those who are studying programming and/or have access to C++ or Visual Basic programming environment will want to duplicate the solutions to the problems presented. The C++ source code for this text has been generated using Visual C++ Ver. 6 but will run equally well on Turbo-C++ or on a UNIX system. The Visual Basic code was written using Visual Basic Ver. 6. Both Visual C++ and Visual Basic are included in Visual Studio Ver. 6

Consequently this text is intended for two groups. First, those who are attempting to expand their ability to solve problems by making use of the processing power of a computer. Commonly this would be a student in an introduction to programming logic class but might also might be a self-study individual attempting to maximize the usefulness of his computer. Second, students currently in a C, C++, or BASIC programming class should use this text as a supplement to their programming textbook in order to get the maximum utility from their study of programming.

Logical Problem Solving: Before the Flowchart is concerned with methods for discovering creative approaches and solutions for problems that the reader has never been taught to solve. It uses C++ and BASIC to implement those solutions and to demonstrate that the method leads to success and a solution. It is not a text for learning how to program or even how to create flowcharts or write pseudo-code but will effectively supplement programming books.

THE WEBSITE

To supplement this text Prentice-Hall has built a website to serve as a central repository for material that support and enhance this text. The URL for the website is `www.prenhall.com/lamey`.

For instructors using *Logical Problem Solving* as the core of a problem solving class, a sample syllabus is provided. For both problem solving classes and programming classes using the text as a supplemental work, the entire text has been converted to PowerPoint presentations. The problem solving lessons that are detailed in the following chapters are presented in outline form allowing instructors to add insight and explanation as the Rules and the problems are introduced.

Chapter objectives are posted as well as practice problems and Internet hyperlinks to problem solving related sites. Some of these sites address problem solving in general and some address the more traditional problems solved in this text. As might be expected there are often many ways to solve any particular problem.

THE RULES

The core of this text is the set of rules for solving problems. The rules represent a heuristic rather than an algorithm for problem solving. Obviously there is no formula that can be applied universally to every problem. Instead the rules represent a set of approaches and guidelines that can lead a problem solver in the direction of a solution.

For example, rule one states that it is critically important to be clear about the information that is available for solving the problem and exactly what the end point of the problem is. While this would appear obvious on the surface, ignoring this rule will usually leave the problem solver with inadequate information and no sure end where the problem can be considered solved. In many cases merely restating the problem can bring enough clarity that a solution becomes apparent. Better still, making a list of known facts about the problem can make clear valuable information that was less obvious in the original problem statement.

None of the rules or even all of them combined will create a guaranteed formula for solving any given problem. Creative thought cannot be reduced to an equation. However, the rules do represent a set of approaches that steer the problem solver to that critical moment of insight when a plan forms linking initial conditions to the problem solution.

EXPERIENCE

The second element in problem solving is the experience gained in previously solved problems. Everyone in every endeavor begins as a novice. Experience is accumulated slowly as progressively more difficult problems are encountered and solved. Experience includes the both the work of the problem solver and the problems that the problem solver has encountered that were solved by others. Sir Isaac Newton pointed out. "If I have seen farther (than you and Descartes), it is by standing upon the shoulders of Giants."[1]

Problem solving is similar to playing an instrument, playing a sport, or playing chess. One individual may have greater initial ability than another but practice and experience always bring improvement. Just as no one starts playing in a symphony orchestra or playing in the Olympics, problem solvers begin with simpler problems involving straightforward problems requiring few steps. With practice more complex problems can often be seen as adaptations or expansions of previously solved problems.

This text begins with simple problems that can be solved quickly by applying the most elemental rules. As experience in problem solving is gained more rules are introduced and the level of complexity of the problems increases. Already solved problems maybe used as a single steps in finding the solutions to larger or more general problems.

Many of the early problems are simplified versions of more general problems that were intentionally limited in order to find a partial solution. Partial solutions are often more useful than no solution at all. Chapter seven considers more general problems and is dedicated to removing the limits that were imposed on problem considered in earlier chapters.

THE BIG PICTURE

Problem solving is an accumulative effort. The more the skill is practiced the greater it grows. To keep the examples simple, i.e. short, many of the examples in this book were taken from the fields of mathematics, physics, and data acquisition. But problem solving is a general skill that, once learned and practiced, pays dividends in almost every field.

Biologists need to know why a given cell will not multiply in a given culture or how the three-dimensional structure of a protein can be determined. Bankers need to determine whether the value of a loan can be recovered if a company fails. Any one who ever takes a chance would like to have some idea what the odds for success are. Truck drivers need to know how to minimize time and cost, and maximize their profit. For some problems the solution is a matter of experience rather than a computer program but the problem solving, maybe through trial and error, is the same.

Learning the rules presented in the following chapters and analyzing the problems presented will lead the reader to a general and valuable skill. It is a skill that will stay with you and pay dividends in widely diverse areas and in unexpected places. Good luck and go forward.

[1]Letter from Newton to Robert Hooke, Feb. 5, 1675/1676

Acknowledgments

It is reasonable and proper to acknowledge several individuals who have contributed insight, effort, or support to the creation of this text.

David Wilhelm of the University of California provided the necessary skill at integral calculus for the creation of Appendix C. His integration of the ellipse described in Problem 6.6 is clear, complete, and creative.

My technical assistants, Brett Jungels and Jie Chi of Purdue University, saved me hours of work by translating a significant number of my C++ solutions into Visual Basic.

Jamie Van Landuyt and Trina Zimmerman showed extraordinary patience, supporting this project through more years than it should have taken. For their endurance through numerous, unavoidable interruptions, they have my thanks.

My special thanks belongs to Bob Wilhelm whose late night discussions contributed so much insight to the formulation of this text. Tapping into his 30 years of teaching experience led to the formulation of Chapter 9 and Rule Zero.

Finally, I would like to thank the reviewers of this text: C. Robert Putnam, *California State University Northridge,* Mary Veronica Kolesar, *Utah State University,* Lynn Kelly, *New Mexico State University.*

CHAPTER 1

Understanding the Problem

1.1 IN THE BEGINNING

If a problem is stated in the form of an equation, the solution requires nothing more than executing a set of well-known algorithms. However, real problems are expressed in words rather than algebraic symbols. We may need to know how much cement is required for the backyard basketball court, how much money must be saved each week to provide a millionaire's retirement by age 50, or how fast a satellite must go in order to remain in orbit. The problem is how to get started on the path that leads from the conditions given in the problem to the solution to the problem (and possibly that wealthy early retirement).

Understanding the problem would seem to be the perfectly obvious first step in finding a solution to the problem. Yet, this first and absolutely crucial step is so often overlooked that it deserves special consideration. In fact, it is often the case that merely taking the time to examine the problem in detail provides the insight that leads to a solution.

There are two extremely important elements in understanding the problem. These two elements are summarized in Rule 1.

> **Rule 1   The Clarity Rule**
> 1. Be clear about what information you have to work with.
> 2. Be clear about what information you are trying to discover.

The solution to every problem can be represented graphically by three boxes.

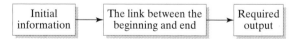

Following chapters will focus on the center box and how the link is discovered when merely examining the conditions of the problem does not make the solution apparent. In this chapter the focus will be on problems in which the link that relates the beginning to the end can be discovered by following the clarity rule. It will be come clear later that even when more clever approaches need to be applied to determine the link, this rule will still be critically important. Keep in mind that if Rule 1 is ignored there is little chance of ever finding a solution to the problem.

When the statement of a problem becomes more complex, it is often worthwhile to make an itemized list of the information given in the problem description so that no piece of useful data is overlooked or misunderstood. Similarly, restating exactly what information the solution requires can make the end point of the problem more apparent. In Problem 1.1 the information supplied in the problem and the solution required are apparent. The list is supplied to illustrate the technique. In later problems the information will not be nearly so obvious and the list will be seen to be of considerable value.

PROBLEM 1.1   *If a man is 6′ 1.5″ tall, what is his height in centimeters?*

Initial Data: The man's height is a physical distance of 6′ 1.5″.

Objective: Find the metric equivalent in centimeters of 6′ 1.5″.

The initial information concerning the man's height is given in feet and inches. Since most of the world uses the metric system and height is commonly measured in meters or centimeters this represents a real-world problem. Because conversion factors do not handle compound units, e.g. feet and inches, the first step is to change the man's height into a total number of inches. The second step is to use the commonly known conversion factor of 2.54 cm/in. Multiplying the total number of inches by this conversion factor solves the problem. An alternative approach would have been to convert 6′ 1.5″ in to feet; however, the conversion from feet to centimeters is not commonly known and that approach would not bring us closer to a solution.

Once this two-step plan for solving the problem has been developed, writing pseudocode or creating a flowchart helps to organize the process before making the conversion to computer code. Pseudocode is a natural language version of computer code. There is no formal syntax and pseudocode cannot be compiled into a computer program. The purpose in writing pseudocode is to organize and order the steps for the solution to the problem in order to eliminate confusion when the C++ or Visual Basic code is written. Pseudocode for the solution to the problem can be written in the following steps.

Pseudocode Solution

1. Begin
2. Convert 6 feet to inches by multiplying by 12.
3. Calculate the man's height by adding 1.5 inches to the number of inches calculated in step 1.
4. Convert the man's height to centimeters by multiplying the total number of inches calculated in step 2 by 2.54 cm/in.
5. Display the results.
6. End

A second method for organizing the plan is to create a flowchart. A flowchart is a graphical representation of the solution process. It is slightly more formal than writing pseudocode in that the symbols used have specific meanings. In general pseudocode is preferred by programmers and flowcharting is more useful in designing systems. However, flowcharts provide a more visual representation of the code that needs to be written and can be useful to those new to structured programming.

The rounded rectangle is used to indicate the beginning and the end of the program. Processes are represented by rectangles and arrows are used to show the "flow" of the logic. User input and program output are written in parallelograms. In later problems diamonds will be added to indicate decision points.

Flowchart

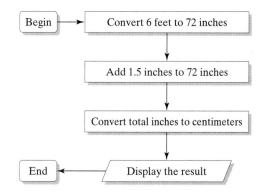

After the plan for solving the problem is devised and organized using pseudocode or a flowchart, the next step is to describe the plan in a manner that can be understood by a computer. The most common computer languages currently in use are C++ and Visual Basic. Visual Basic provides beginning programmers an easy-to-learn environment that quickly produces programs that run in a familiar "window." C++ is the preferred language when power, speed, and access to the hardware are important. Solutions will be provided in both languages.

Solution Implemented in C++

```
1   // Problem1_1.cpp
2   #include <iostream.h>   // Makes available standard input/output routines
3
4   int main(void)
5   {
6      int feet = 6;
7      float inches = 1.5, total_inches, centimeters;
8                        // Declaration and initialization of variables.
9
10     total_inches = feet * 12.0 + inches;  // Steps 1 & 2 of the pseudocode
11     centimeters = total_inches * 2.54;    // Step 3 of the pseudocode
12
13     cout.setf (ios::fixed|ios::showpoint); // Formatting commands
14     cout.precision(2);        // Set the number of decimal places to 2.
15
16     cout << "A height of " << feet << " feet " << inches
17        << " inches is " << centimeters << " centimeters." << endl;
18                        // Output the results - Step 4
19     return(0);
20 }
```

The line numbers are not part of the C++ program and have been added to the programs in this text only for reference purposes. In every problem the first line will be reserved for the name of the problem to be solved. Here the problems are named by chapter and problem number but more commonly a descriptive name is used. The double slash is used in C++ to indicate a comment line. Everything following // to the end of the line is ignored by the compiler. Similarly white space is ignored and is included in the program only to make the program more readable by humans.

The include statement on line 2 makes available the output routines that display the results of the calculation and format it using the parameters specified on lines 13 and 14. These indicate that the numeric results for floating-point numbers should be displayed in decimal notation to a precision of two decimal places and that trailing zeros should be displayed.

Line 4 begins the main function of the program. C++ programs have one and only one main function. `int main(void)` tells the compiler that the program requires no information from the operating system and will return an integer to the operating system when the program terminates. The returned value is specified on line 19 and is zero. The program would run correctly without the return value but for reasons beyond the scope of this book the return is included. If line 19 is eliminated, the program should be begun with `void main(void)` informing the compiler that no information will be returned to the operating system.

The variables used in the program are declared and initialized on lines 6 and 7. Calculations are made on lines 10 and 11.

Output of the C++ Program

```
A height of 6 feet 1.50 inches is 186.69 centimeters.
```

Because the focus of this book is on the logic required to solve a problem, many of the details involved in creating the interface for the Visual Basic program have been ignored. The following is the actual code written to implement the calculations and the display of the results.

Solution Implemented in Visual Basic

```
1  Option Explicit
2     'When Calculate button is clicked
3     '   Declare centimeter variable, calculate value for
4     '   centimeter and display the result
5  Private Sub cmdCalculate_Click()
6     Dim centimeters As Double
7     centimeters = (6 * 12 + 1.5) * 2.54      'Find the total number of inches
8                                              '  and convert to centimeters
9     lblOutput.Caption = centimeters & " centimeters"
10 End Sub
11          'Load introductory message
12 Private Sub Form_Load()
13          lblInput.Caption = "The height of a 6'1"" " & _
14          vbCrLf & "man in centimeters is"
15 End Sub
```

The `Option Explicit` statement is not necessary in Visual Basic programs. It is used to require the programmer to declare variables by type before they are used. In this program the variable "centimeters" is declared to be a double-precision, floating-point number on line 6. The calculations that convert 6′ 1.5″ to centimeters have been reduced to a single assignment statement on line 7.

The initial message to the user is created on lines 13 and 14 and displayed when the form is loaded. The calculated value for "centimeters" is displayed in the output box by line 7. Comment lines have been included in the programming by using the apostrophe.

Output of the Visual Basic Program

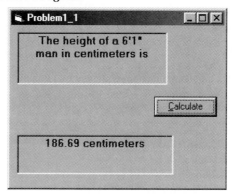

1.2   INCLUDING COMMON INFORMATION

Usually problems are more involved than merely converting feet to inches and inches to centimeters. When this is the case, the list of initial information given in the problem should be expanded to include commonly known relevant information.

PROBLEM 1.2   *How much does 50 gallons of water weigh?*

This problem would be trivial if the weight of one gallon of water were known; however, this not a commonly available number in the English system. On the other hand, the equivalent problem of converting fluid volume to mass is simple in the metric system. One approach to solving the problem would be to search the Internet for a conversion factor that would convert gallons of water to pounds. However, the challenge is not to find someone else who has solved the problem for us but to discover a train of logic that leads from the initial condition to the solution using commonly known information. This leads us to add a few well-known facts to our list of initial data.

Initial Data: **1.** 50 gallons of water to be weighed

2. 3.785 liters in a gallon (listed on every 1-gallon milk container)

3. 1 liter has a volume of 1000 cm^3

4. 1 cm^3 of water has a mass of 1 gram

5. 1000 grams equals 1 kilogram

6. At certain standard conditions, 1 kg of water weighs 2.2 pounds

Objective: Find the weight of 50 gallons of water.

Notice that this problem involves liquid volume and weight. By merely writing down commonly known information about volume and weight we can trace a path from the 50 gallons of water given in the problem to a number representing the weight of the water. This leaves only the implementation of the five conversions in data items 2 through 6. The implementation brings us to Rule 2.

Rule 2   The Units Rule

Pay attention to units. If the unit of measurement is kept with each number, the mathematical operation to be performed will be apparent without the knowledge of any formula. Correct operations will lead to units that cancel. Incorrect operations will lead to units that compound and confound.

Pseudocode Solution

1. Begin

2.   Convert 50 gallons to liters.

50 gallons * 3.785 liters/gallon

3.   Convert liters to cm^3.

189.25 liters * 1,000 cm^3/liter

4.   Convert cm^3 of water to grams.

189,250 cm^3 * 1 g/cm^3

5.   Convert grams to kilograms.

189,250 g * 1 kg/1,000 g

6.   Convert kilograms to pounds.

189.25 kg * 2.2 lbs/kg

7.   Display the answer.

8. End

In step two multiplication of 50 gallons by 3.785 liters/gallon leads to the cancellation of gallons, and liters remains as the only unit. This step not only illustrates Rule 2 but also Rule 1. Being clear about what you are trying to calculate is not only true for the entire problem but also applies to each step. In this case the objective of step 1 was to calculate a number of liters. Multiplication by 3.785 liters/gallon accomplished that goal.

Notice that 3.785 liters/gallon and 1 gallon/3.785 liters are both valid conversion units. However, multiplying 50 gallons by 1 gallon/3.785 liters would result in 13.2 $gallons^2$/liter, which makes no sense. Similarly, dividing 50 gallons by 3.785 liters/gallon would result in the same nonsense units. The operation to be performed and the conversion factor to be used will always be obvious if the units are kept with the numeric values.

The same logic applies for each succeeding step in the problem and will always apply anytime conversion of units is involved. Always perform arithmetic operations with the units.

In this problem the difference between mass and weight was ignored. While such shortcuts lack mathematical purity, the equivalence between 2.2 pounds and one kilogram is a fair conversion on earth at sea level. Remember the objective is to get a reasonable answer to a problem. Fifty gallons of water would have the same mass but a different weight on the moon but we're not on the moon. If we were, a different conversion factor would be needed.

Flowchart

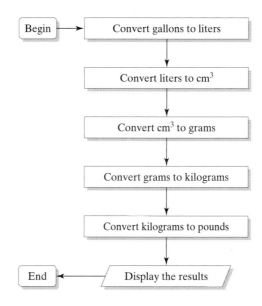

Solution Implemented in C++

```
1   //   Problem1_2.cpp
2   #include <iostream.h> // Makes available standard input/output routines
3   int main(void)        // The program gets no information from the operating
4   {                     //   system and returns an integer
5       float gallons = 50;
6       float liters, cu_centimeters, grams, kilograms, pounds;
7                         //   Variables for each step of the problem
8       liters = gallons * 3.785;          // Step 2 of the pseudocode
9       cu_centimeters = liters * 1000;    // Step 3 of the pseudocode
10      grams = cu_centimeters;            // Step 4 of the pseudocode
11      kilograms = grams / 1000;          // Step 5 of the pseudocode
12      pounds = 2.2 * kilograms;          // Step 6 of the pseudocode
13      cout << "50 gallons of water weighs " << pounds << " pounds." << endl;
14                        //Display the results
15      return(0);
16  }
```

The implementation of the routine for determining the weight of 50 gallons of water made one conversion on each line of the program. This raises the question of whether several or all of the steps could have been accomplished in a single, complex mathematical operation. The answer is that a single line such as

```
pounds  = gallons * 3.785 liters/gallon * 1000 cm³/liter * 1 gram/cm³
                 * .001 kg/gram * 2.2 pounds/kg;
```

could have been used and the program would have yielded the same result. Notice that gallons, liters, cm³, grams, and kilograms all cancel out leaving pounds as the only unit. However, the objective here is not to write the most compact source code but to be clear about every step of the logic used to solve the problem.

To implement the more compact logic, lines 8 through 12 would be replaced by the single line

```
pounds = gallon * 3.785 * 1000 * 1 * .001 * 2.2;
```

Of course, the algebra could be further simplified by eliminating the third, fourth, and fifth factors, which when combined are equivalent to the multiplicative identity, i.e. one. The only problem with making such simplifications is that the code becomes rather removed from the logic that it represents. In the absence of appropriate commenting this makes the code more difficult to troubleshoot if an error is made in writing the computer code.

Output of the C++ Program

```
50 gallons of water weighs 416.35 pounds.
```

It should also be noted that liberties have been taken with the normal rules for significant figures. The number 50 in 50 gallons of water has only one significant figure. The solution to the problem should be rounded to 420 pounds. Proper rounding will be included in later problems. For now the focus is confined to the logic involved in solving the problem.

Solution Implemented in Visual Basic

```
1     Option Explicit
2     Private Sub cmdConvert_Click()
3         Dim gallons As Double
4         Dim liters As Double
5         Dim cu_centimeters As Double
6         Dim grams As Double
7         Dim kilograms As Double
8         Dim pounds As Double
9
10        gallons = 50
11        lblLiters.Caption = gallons * 3.785 & " liters " & _
12            vbCrLf & "with a volume of"
13        liters = gallons * 3.785
14        lblCuCentimeters.Caption = liters * 1000 & _
15            " cubic centimeters with a mass of"
```

```
16        cu_centimeters = liters * 1000
17        lblGrams.Caption = cu_centimeters & " grams or"
18        grams = cu_centimeters
19        lblKilograms.Caption = grams / 1000 & " kilograms" & _
20            vbCrLf & "and a weight of"
21        kilograms = grams / 1000
22        lblPounds.Caption = kilograms * 2.2 & " pounds"
23    End Sub
24
25    Private Sub Form_Load()
26        frmProblem1_2.Top = (Screen.Height - _
27            frmProblem1_2.Height) / 3
28        frmProblem1_2.Left = (Screen.Width - _
29            frmProblem1_2.Width) / 3
30        lblInput.Caption = "50 gallons of water equals"
31    End Sub
```

The Visual Basic program has been expanded (lines 11 through 22) to display the intermediate values for the fluid volume of the water in liters, the volume of the water in cubic centimeters, the mass of the water in grams and kilograms, and finally the weight of 189.25 kilograms of water.

Lines 26 through 29 merely size and center the window that contains the initial statement and, after the Convert button has been pressed, the output information. While a few extra lines of code have been included for formatting purposes, the logic of the Visual Basic program is identical to the C++ program.

Output of the Visual Basic Program

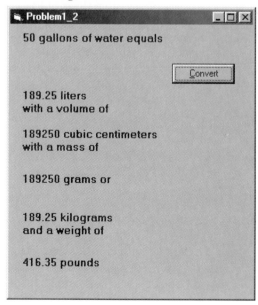

1.3 INCLUDING UNCOMMON INFORMATION

If the information contained in the problem appears to have a simple link to the required result but the link is unknown, there are two options left to the problem solver.

1. Find the link. That is, look up the formula, conversion factor, or relationship in a physics book, a conversion table, or on the Internet.

2. Derive the relationship.

The second option is the more interesting in that it creates a problem within a problem. The original problem cannot be solved until the link (possibly a formula) between the initial data and the outcome is available. The second problem is how to invent the link from other information.

PROBLEM 1.3   *What Celsius temperature is equivalent to a given Fahrenheit temperature?*

The solution to this problem requires knowing the relationship between Celsius and Fahrenheit temperatures. However, this is not a formula that the average person has memorized. On the other hand, it is not obscure information and could be found easily from many different sources. If the problem solver chooses to look up the equation, the problem collapses to one of plugging values into a formula and becomes a one-step problem similar to Problem 1.1.

However, not all formulas are so readily available. For the sake of practicing problem-solving skills, let's assume that there is no resource available that will provide the needed formula. The intention is to show that a problem is not intractable just because a formula is not known. The problem within the problem is reflected in Problem 1.3a.

PROBLEM 1.3A   *What is the relationship between the Celsius and Fahrenheit scales?*

This problem is solved by applying Rule 1. The question to ask is, what information is available relevant to the problem? What do we know that might be useful? In this case there are a couple of commonly known facts that will allow the problem to be resolved. These should be listed as initial data for the problem.

Initial Data: 1. The freezing point of water is 32°F or 0°C.
              2. The boiling point of water is 212°F or 100°C.

Outcome: Find the formula relating Celsius and Fahrenheit temperatures.

By merely writing down this information, more information becomes apparent. Drawing a picture makes the situation even clearer. Celsius degrees are bigger than Fahrenheit degrees. To span the temperature range from the freezing point of water to the boiling point requires only 100 degrees on the Celsius scale. The same range on the Fahrenheit scale requires 180 degrees (212° − 32°).

°C	0	← 100 →	100
°F	32	← 180 →	212

This observation leads to the scaling relationship:

$$100°C = 180°F$$
$$1 = 100°C/180°F$$
$$1 = 5°C/9°F$$

All conversions involve multiplication by the multiplicative identity, that is, one. In this case, the useful form of one is $1 = 5°C/9°F$.

The next issue is that the two scales fail to zero at the same place. Before the scaling factor can be used, 32° must be subtracted from the Fahrenheit temperature. This effectively slides the Fahrenheit scale 32° to the right making the zero points of the two scales align. Zeroing the two scales and then applying the scaling factor lead to the mathematical equation:

$$°C = \frac{5°C}{9°F}(°F - 32°F)$$

The formula can be tested by substituting known true values for the Celsius and Fahrenheit temperatures, namely, $0°C = 32°F$ and $100°C = 212°F$. Both of these substitutions yield true statements. Notice that the units for the degrees Fahrenheit cancel out.

The relationship between Celsius and Fahrenheit temperatures was derived by noting only two commonly known equivalent temperatures. Even though little was known initially about the relationship between Celsius and Fahrenheit temperatures, by writing it down, being clear about the information, and being careful with the units the relationship between the temperature scales was discovered.

At this point the original problem becomes trivial.

Initial Data: **1.** Fahrenheit temperature supplied by the user.
                 2. The derived (or researched) formula.

Objective: Convert a user-supplied Fahrenheit temperature to Celsius degrees.

Pseudocode Solution

1. Begin
2.   Get the Fahrenheit temperature from the user.
3.   Calculate the Celsius temperature using the derived formula.
4.   Display the result.
5. End

Flowchart

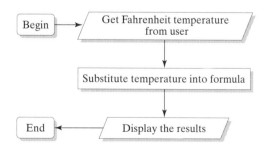

Solution Implemented in C++

```
1   // Problem1_3.cpp
2   #include <iostream.h>
3   #include <iomanip.h>
4
5   int main(void)
6   {
7       float Ftemp, Ctemp;
8       cout << "Enter the Fahrenheit temperature to be converted"
9           << "\n\n\tto its equivalent Celsius temperature -->    ";
10      cin >> Ftemp;
11      Ctemp = 5 / 9.0 * (Ftemp - 32);      // 9.0 is used to avoid
12                                           //    integer division
13      cout << "\n" << Ftemp << " degrees Fahrenheit is equal to "
14          << setiosflags(ios::fixed) << setprecision(2)
15          << Ctemp  << " degrees Celsius.\n\n";
16                          // output precision is set to two decimal
17                          // places
18      return(0);
19  }
```

The second `include` statement on line 3 allows the use of the `setiosflags()` function found on line 14. The combination of the `fixed` flag and the `setprecision()` function causes the output to be displayed with two decimal places.

The capitalization in the variables `Ftemp` and `Ctemp` is not required but seems appropriate for variables derived from the proper names Gabriel Fahrenheit and Anders Celsius. The use of uppercase letters provides an opportunity to note that C++ (like C) is case sensitive and, once `Ftemp` and `Ctemp` have been declared using capital letters, all subsequent references to these variables must be spelled with the first letter capitalized.

`Ftemp` and `Ctemp` have been declared to be floating-point values so that a fraction of a degree can be entered and displayed. They could have been declared to be `doubles` but there is seldom reason to calculate temperatures to greater accuracy than seven significant figures.

Line 11 makes the conversion from Fahrenheit degrees to Celsius degrees. The use of 9.0 in the conversion factor is critical to the conversion. Because C++ performs integer division if both the numerator and denominator of a fraction are integers, the value of 5/9 is zero. To evaluate the fraction to its proper value of .555555... either (or both) the nominator or denominator must be converted to a floating-point number. This can be accomplished by expressing the fraction in any of the three following forms:

$$5 \ / \ (\text{float}) \ 9$$
$$5 \ / \ \text{static\_cast<float>}(9)$$
$$5 \ / \ 9.0$$

The first option of using the (float) type cast operator will work but is a remnant of the C language and is generally not used in C++. Lines 13 through 15 produce the output message formatted to two decimal places.

Output of the C++ Program

```
Enter the Fahrenheit temperature to be converted
     to its equivalent Celsius temperature --> 78
78 degrees Fahrenheit is equal to 25.56 degrees Celsius.
```

Solution Implemented in Visual Basic

```
1    Option Explicit
2    Private Sub cmdConvert_Click()
3        Dim Ftemp As Double            'Declare the variables
4        Dim Ctemp As Double
5        Ftemp = Val(txtInput.Text)
6        Ctemp = 5 / 9 * (Ftemp - 32)   'Calculate the Celsius temperature
7        lblOutput.Caption = Ftemp & " degrees Fahrenheit " & _
8            " equals " & Format(Ctemp, "0.00") & " degrees Celsius"
9    End Sub
10
11   Private Sub Form_Activate()
12       txtInput.SetFocus                'Set the cursor in the input box
13   End Sub
14   Private Sub Form_Load()              'Position the program window
15       frmProblem1_3.Top = (Screen.Height - frmProblem1_3.Height) / 3
16       frmProblem1_3.Left = (Screen.Width - frmProblem1_3.Width) / 3
17                                        'Message to the user
18       lblInput.Caption = "Enter the Fahrenheit" & _
19           " temperature to be converted" & _
20           " into degrees Celsius."
21   End Sub
```

Line 2 begins the conversion process when the command button is clicked. Line 5 reads the text in the text box called txtInput, converts it to a numeric value, and stores it in the variable Ftemp. The conversion process takes place on line 6. Notice that in Visual Basic 5/9 is not calculated as integer division. Visual Basic uses a different operator, the backslash, for integer division. Line 7 creates the output message and formats the Celsius value to use two decimal places.

As in the previous Visual Basic program, the Form_Load() subroutine sizes and centers the window and displays the initial message to the user. Lines 11 and 12 combine to place the initial cursor position in the txtInput box.

Output of the Visual Basic Program

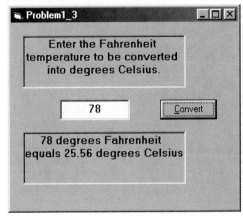

PROBLEM 1.4   *What is the area of a user-defined trapezoid?*

Finding the area of a trapezoid is similar to converting temperatures. A formula for the conversion would make the problem trivial but again there is no need to search math books or the Internet for the formula. Deriving the formula is simple and, as in the temperature conversion problem, constitutes a problem within the problem.

For this problem we can benefit from the experience of working the Fahrenheit to Celsius conversion. Generating the formula $°C = \dfrac{5.0\ °C}{9.0\ °F} * (°F - 32°F)$ was simple after the need for clarity led us to create a number line. When dealing with geometric figures, a picture can be a great aid in solving a problem, which is restated as Rule 3.

> **Rule 3   The Picture Rule**
> Whenever possible draw a picture.

In this case the issue that requires clarity is "What is a trapezoid?" It's simple to picture a trapezoid in your mind but, if time is taken to draw a trapezoid on paper, an interesting fact becomes apparent that was not obvious in a mental picture. The addition of two lines to the trapezoid adds information that is critical to the solution to the problem. A trapezoid is a combination of simpler shapes and the areas of these simpler shapes have well-known formulas. By adding the areas of two triangles and a rectangle, we have the area of the trapezoid.

The initial information given in the problem should be listed as:

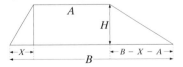

Initial data: **1.** The area of the trapezoid is the sum of the end triangles and the center rectangle.

2. Values for the length of the top (A), the bottom (B), and the height (H) will be provided.

3. The length of the base of the left-hand triangle is unknown and will be called X.

4. The base of the right-hand triangle is unknown but can be expressed as $B - A - X$, that is, the total length of the bottom of the trapezoid minus A (the top and the bottom of the rectangle both have a section of length of A) minus the base of the left-hand triangle (X).

Objective: Find the area of the trapezoid or,

Find the area of the rectangle and the triangles or,

Calculate:

$$\text{Area of Trapezoid} = \text{Area of Left-Hand Triangle} + \\ \text{Area of Right-Hand Triangle} + \\ \text{Area of Rectangle}$$

Fortunately, resolving the algebraic equation causes the lone unknown (X) to vanish, leaving nothing but constants on the right side of the equation.

$$\text{Area} = \text{Area\_of\_Left} + \text{Area\_of\_Right} + \text{Area\_of\_Rect}$$
$$\text{Area} = .5HX + .5H(B - A - X) + AH$$
$$\text{Area} = .5HX + .5HB - .5HA - .5HX + AH$$
$$\text{Area} = .5HB + .5HA$$
$$\text{Area} = .5H(B + A)$$

By drawing a picture of the rectangle, labeling the values to be supplied by the user (the height, the length of the top, and the length of the bottom), and adding the areas of the elementary figures, the problem resolved itself. Admittedly using a single variable (X) to express the base length of both triangles was slightly clever, but this is precisely the type of insight that comes with practice at solving problems. In general, the fewer unknowns used to express the values in a problem the better.

Once the inner problem has been solved, writing the pseudocode and creating the flowchart are trivial issues.

Pseudocode Solution

1. Begin

2.   Message to the user to supply values for height and both bases.

3.   Calculate the trapezoid area using the derived formula.

4.   Display the results.

5. End

Flowchart

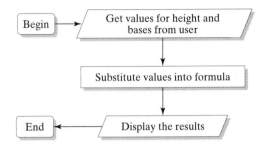

Solution Implemented in C++

```
1    // Problem1_4.cpp
2    #include <iostream.h>
3    #include <iomanip.h>
4
5    int main(void)
6    {
7         float top, bottom, height, area;
8         cout << "This program calculates the area of a trapezoid" << endl;
9         cout << "\tEnter the top     " << flush;
10        cin >> top;
11        cout << "\tEnter the bottom  " << flush;
12        cin >> bottom;
13        cout << "\tEnter the height  " << flush;
14        cin >> height;
15        area = .5 * height * (bottom + top);
16        cout << "\n\nThe area of the trapezoid is "
17             << setiosflags(ios::fixed|ios::showpoint)
18             << setprecision(2) << area << endl;
19        return(0);
20   }
```

The message to the user and the prompts for information about the trapezoid are handled on lines 8 through 14. It is worth pointing out that the notation on line 15 differs from standard algebraic notation. On this line both of the multiplication symbols (*) and the parentheses are required for the correct calculation of the area and to avoid a syntax error from the compiler.

Output of the C++ Program

```
This program calculates the area of a trapezoid
     Enter the top 10
     Enter the bottom 40
     Enter the height 5

The area of the trapezoid is 125.00
```

Solution Implemented in Visual Basic

```
1    Private Sub cmdCalculate_Click()
2        Dim top As Double, bottom As Double
3        Dim height As Double, area As Double
4        top = Val(txtInput1.Text)
5        bottom = Val(txtInput2.Text)
6        height = Val(txtInput3.Text)
7        area = 0.5 * height * (bottom + top)
8        lblOutput.Caption = "The area of the trapezoid is " & _
9            area
10   End Sub
11
12   Private Sub Form_Activate()
13       txtInput1.SetFocus
14   End Sub
15
16   Private Sub Form_Load()
17       frmProblem1_4.top = (Screen.height - _
18               frmProblem1_4.height) / 3
19       frmProblem1_4.Left = (Screen.Width - _
20               frmProblem1_4.Width) / 3
21       lblMessage.Caption = "This program calculates the " & _
22           "area of a trapeziod."
23       lblInput1.Caption = "Enter the top of the trapezoid"
24       lblInput2.Caption = "Enter the bottom of the trapezoid"
25       lblInput3.Caption = "Enter the height of the trapezoid"
26   End Sub
```

Output of the Visual Basic Program

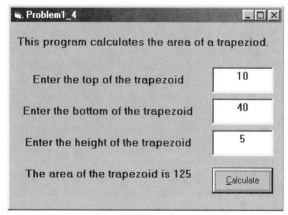

There is a second way to approach the trapezoid problem that is slightly more graphical and slightly less mathematical. Consider a line *MN* drawn from the center of the left side M to the center of the right side N. The length of the line would be half of X plus half of Y shorter than the bottom and half of X plus half of Y longer than the top of the trapezoid. If a line is drawn from M perpendicular to the bottom it creates a new triangle that can be pivoted $180°$ around point M. If the same operation is performed with the right-hand triangle rotating around point N, a rectangle is created of length MN and height H.

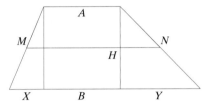

In simpler terms MN is seen to be the average of the top and the bottom. Notice that the base of the right-hand triangle has been listed as Y. For this solution its relation to X is no longer relevant. The length of MN can be expressed as a function of the top and the bottom of the trapezoid or:

$$MN = A + .5X + .5Y$$
$$MN = B - (.5X + .5Y)$$
$$2MN = A + B$$
$$MN = .5(A + B)$$
$$\text{Area} = .5H(A + B)$$

By adding the first two equations the X and Y terms sum to zero, leaving MN defined only in terms of A and B. The area of the new rectangle, which has the same area as the trapezoid, is found by merely multiplying the value of MN by H or multiplying half of A plus B by the height.

While considering the inclusion of uncommon information, it is interesting to examine a problem that dispels the erroneous common knowledge that astronauts aboard the space shuttle float because there is no gravity "way out in space."

PROBLEM 1.5   *Calculate the pull of gravity on an astronaut aboard the space shuttle.*

There is little data given in the problem besides the fact that there is an astronaut and he presumably has some positive weight. In this case a scaled drawing helps dispel the "no gravity" myth. The needed information that is not commonly known is that the radius of the earth is approximately 3,960 miles, give or take a few miles, depending on where you are standing at the moment.

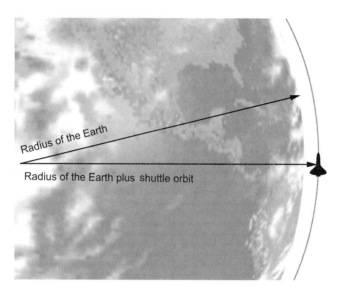

The image makes it clear that a typical shuttle orbit of 200 miles is not very high above the earth's surface compared to the radius of the earth. Gravity certainly wouldn't disappear in such a short distance. In fact, gravity decreases in an inverse square ratio, which is a piece of information that may or may not be remembered from high school physics.

Initial Data: **1.** The weight of the astronaut at sea level is supplied by the user.

2. The height of the shuttle orbit must also be supplied by the user.

3. Gravity decreases as the square of the distance from the center of mass increases or, if the shuttle is 200 miles above the earth, then the correction factor for the pull of gravity on the astronaut is:

$$\frac{\text{orbital\_weight}}{\text{sea\_level\_weight}} = \left(\frac{\text{radius\_of\_the\_earth}}{\text{radius\_of\_the\_orbit}}\right)^2$$

$$\text{orbital\_weight} = \text{sea\_level\_weight} \times \frac{3960^2}{(3960 + 200)^2}$$

Output: Determine the pull of gravity on an astronaut in orbit aboard the space shuttle.

Pseudocode Solution

1. Begin

2.   Declare variables.

3.   Message to the user about the purpose of the program.

4.   Prompt the user to enter information about the height of the orbit and the weight of the astronaut.

5.   Make calculations based on the inverse square law.

6.   Display results.

7.   End

Flowchart

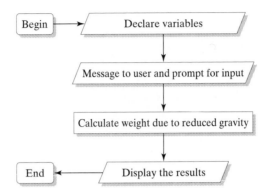

Solution Implemented in C++

```
1    // Program1_5.cpp
2    #include <iostream.h>
3
4    void main(void)
5    {
6        double sea_level_weight, orbital_weight, altitude;
7        cout.setf(ios::fixed|ios::showpoint);
8        cout.precision(1);
9        cout << "This program calculates the pull of gravity\n"
10            << "\ton an astronaut while flying on the\n"
11            << "\t\tspace shuttle.\n\n";
12        cout << "Enter the astronaut's weight at sea level . .   ";
13        cin >> sea_level_weight;
14        cout << "Enter the altitude of the space shuttle . .    ";
15        cin >> altitude;
16        orbital_weight = sea_level_weight * (3960 * 3960) /
17                ((3960 + altitude) * (3960 + altitude));
18        cout << "The pull of gravity on an astronaut aboard the space shuttle "
19            << "\n\n\tis " << orbital_weight << " pounds." << endl;
20   }
```

Lines 16 and 17 make the calculations using the radius of the earth squared in the numerator of the fraction and the radius plus height of the orbit squared in the denominator. Two items are worth special notice on these lines. First, the units for the numerator and the denominator of the fraction are miles squared and they cancel. This leaves pounds (the units for sea_level_weight) as the only remaining unit on the right side of the equal sign. Second, both sets of parentheses are required in the denominator in order for the operations to be carried out in the correct order.

Output of the C++ Program

```
This program calculates the pull of gravity
        on an astronaut while flying on the
                space shuttle.

Enter the astronaut's weight at sea level . .    200
Enter the altitude of the space shuttle . .      200
The pull of gravity on an astronaut aboard the space shuttle

        is 181.2 pounds.
```

If a 200-pound man in the space shuttle orbiting the earth at an altitude of 200 miles still experiences a gravitational pull of 181 pounds, why does he float? The answer is in the incredible speed of the space shuttle. The astronauts and the shuttle itself are in free fall. They are both traveling so fast that they are literally falling over the edge of the earth. Since the earth is round, as the surface falls away, the shuttle falls exactly the same amount in order to maintain a constant distance from the ground. How fast must the shuttle and astronauts travel to achieve this equilibrium? The solution is in Chapter 7 in which old solutions are expanded to provide new answers to more complex problems.

Solution Implemented in Visual Basic

```
1    Option Explicit
2    Private Sub cmdCalculate_Click()
3        Dim orbital_weight As Double
4        Dim sea_level_weight As Double
5        Dim altitude As Double
6        sea_level_weight = Val(txtInput1.Text)
7        altitude = Val(txtInput2.Text)
8        orbital_weight = sea_level_weight * (3960 ^ 2) / _
9            (3960 + altitude) ^ 2
10       lblOutput.Caption = "The pull of gravity on an " & _
11           "astronaut aboard the space shuttle is " & _
12           Format(orbital_weight, "0.0") & " pounds."
13   End Sub
14   Private Sub Form_Activate()
15       txtInput1.SetFocus
16   End Sub
17   Private Sub Form_Load()
18       lblMessage.Caption = "This program calculates the " & _
19           "pull of gravity on an astronaut while flying on " & _
20           "the space shuttle."
21       lblInput1.Caption = "Enter the astronaut's weight " & _
22           "at sea level."
23       lblInput2.Caption = "Enter the altitude of the space " & _
24           "shuttle."
25   End Sub
```

Generally C++ programmers don't expect that the features of C++ will work in Visual Basic. And Visual Basic programmers don't expect Visual Basic features to work in C++, except for the one item used on line 8. Programmers who learn Visual Basic first and then move to C++ often expect the caret ($\wedge$) to indicate that some base should be raised to a power. Expressions such as $3960 \wedge 2$ meaning 3960^2 are valid only in Visual Basic. C++ uses the pow() function to accomplish raising numbers to a power.

If the formatting function used on line 12 is omitted, the calculations will be made properly except that the answer will be displayed with many decimal places. This creates the illusion of accuracy that doesn't exist. If the astronaut's weight is only known to the nearest pound or possibly the nearest quarter pound on Earth, then these three (or at best four) significant figures set the limit for accuracy in all calculations using that number. Even though a computer or calculator may produce a solution with many decimal places, that doesn't imply there is any meaning to the numbers. It is up to the human to understand the accuracy limits to the calculation and, in this case, limit the display to one decimal place at best.

Output of the Visual Basic Program

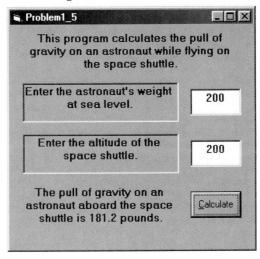

1.4   WORKING BACKWARD

Not all people think in exactly the same way. An explanation that is perfectly clear to one person may be meaningless to another. A line of reasoning may be obvious to one person and unclear to another. It is not a matter of intelligence (whatever that may be). Different people think differently.

It is not merely a difference between people. A single individual may hear an explanation that is unclear and confusing one day and then suddenly several days later (or possibly in the middle of the night) the concept is so apparent that he can't understand why the idea was not obvious before.

A great deal has been written about this ethereal quality that is commonly called insight. In problem solving there is the hope that the problem solver will spontaneously get some insight into how the problem might be solved. This text focuses on techniques that will foster insight. Working backward is sometimes an effective technique.

Rule 4   Working Backward Rule
Instead of working from the beginning of a problem asking what is the first step toward the end, start at the end and ask what is needed to perform the last step. From there examine what is necessary for the second to last step and work toward the beginning.

Problem 1.6 is an example of a problem that solves more easily backward.

PROBLEM 1.6   *Calculate the number of molecules in a certain amount of chemical compound. There are 6.02×10^{23} molecules in one mole of any compound. A mole has the same weight in grams as one molecule of the compound weights in Atomic Mass Units (AMUs).*

At first glance it would appear that the solution to this problem requires some knowledge of chemistry. In fact, beyond the idea that molecules are very small things that comprise materials, no knowledge of chemistry is needed. Instead, a careful reading of the information provided in the problem is all that is necessary.

To begin analyzing the problem apply the clarity rule and make a list of the information given in the problem and the objective.

Initial Data: **1.** The mass of the material is known (supplied by the user).

2. The weight of one molecule is known (supplied by the user).

3. Whatever a mole might be, it is a unit that contains 6.02×10^{23} molecules of the compound. This constant is Avogadro's number. However, leaving Avogadro's number written in this fashion would violate Rule 2 concerning numbers and their units. Avogadro's number should be written 6.02×10^{23} molecules/mole.

4. The mass of one mole (measured in grams) is equal to the weight of one molecule (measured in AMUs). This information is easily overlooked but is critically important to solving the problem.

Objective: Find the number of molecules in a given amount of compound.

To solve this problem backward start with the objective and ask the question, "What is needed to calculate the number of molecules?" With this in mind search for information relating molecules to something else. Item 3 on the Initial Data list provides Avogadro's number relating molecules to moles. It is not necessary to know what moles are. It is the relationship between molecules and moles that is important. If we have the number of moles and the number of molecules/mole, the number of molecules can be calculated. That is,

$$\text{Molecules} = \text{Moles} \times \text{Molecules/Mole}$$

This formula constitutes the last calculation of the problem. The number of molecules per mole is given in the problem (Avogadro's number) so the next step is to find the number of moles. Again, examining units leads to the observation that the number of moles must equal the mass of compound divided by the mass of one mole or

$$\text{Moles} = \text{Mass of Compound} \div \text{Mass per One Mole}$$

or

$$\text{Moles} = \text{Mass} \times \text{One Mole/Mass}$$

Notice that the mass units (grams) cancel out on the right side of the equation, leaving a number of moles, which is exactly what was needed. Now, to restate, we can find the number of **molecules** if we have the number of moles and the number of molecules per mole. We can find the number of **moles** if we have the mass of the compound and the mass of one mole. But we do have the mass of the compound; it is a user-supplied number. We also have the mass of one mole. The fourth data item on our list states that the mass of one mole is the same as the weight of one molecule and Atomic Mass Units, which is user supplied.

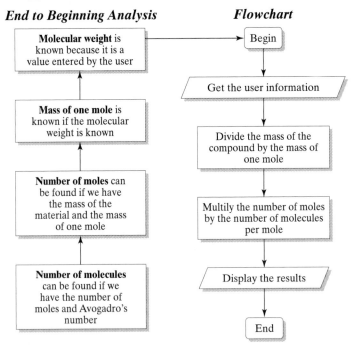

End to Beginning Analysis   *Flowchart*

Pseudocode Solution

1. Begin

2. Get the necessary information from the user.

3.   Recognize that the weight of a molecule (AMUs) is the same as the mass of one mole.

4.   Divide the mass of the compound by the mass of one mole. Notice that the units "grams" cancel, leaving only the number of moles.

5.   Multiply the number of moles by the number of molecules per mole. Notice that the units "moles" cancel leaving only the number of molecules.

6.   Display the results.

7.   End

Even though the problem has been analyzed from back to front, the flowchart and the pseudocode are written from beginning to end. Programs represent a series of operations that the microprocessor of the computer must perform. To perform those operations each symbol must have a value. The backward analysis considered what could be calculated if only certain values were available. For the processor, those values must be known so it is necessary to begin with the values supplied by the user.

Solution Implemented in C++

```
1     // Program1_6.cpp
2     #include <iostream.h>
3     #include <iomanip.h>
4
5     int main(void)
6     {
7             double compound, mol_weight, moles, molecules;
8             const double AvNum = 6.02e23;
9                         // Avogadro's Number defined as a constant variable
10            cout << "This program calculates the number of molecules in"
11                << "\n\ta specified amount of mass." << endl;
12                        // Get input from the user
13            cout << "\n\n\tEnter the mass of the compound -> ";
14            cin >> compound;
15            cout << "\tEnter the molecular weight for the compound --> ";
16            cin >> mol_weight;
17                        // Make the calculations
18            moles = compound / mol_weight;
19            molecules = moles * AvNum;
20            cout.setf(ios::scientific|ios::showpoint|ios::fixed);
21            cout << "\n\nThere are " << setprecision(3) << molecules
22                << " molecules in ";
23                        // Change to exponential notation
24            cout.unsetf(ios::scientific);
25            cout << setprecision(2) << compound << " grams of compound.\n";
26            return(0);
27    }
```

After the user has been informed of the purpose of the program and has been prompted to enter values for the mass of the compound and its molecular weight (lines 10 through 16), the calculations begin on line 18. Line 18 determines the number of moles in the sample and line 19 calculates the number of molecules in that number of moles. These two lines correspond to steps 4 and 5 in the pseudocode. The display is formatted by lines 20 through 25. Notice there is not only a change in the precision for the displayed values but molecules is displayed as a floating-point number while compound is written in exponential notation (line 24).

The value for Avogadro's number is stored in AvNum on line 8. Notice that the double-precision variable was defined to be a constant variable (a regrettable oxymoron). This is a good programming practice. Values that should not change during the execution of the program should be prevented from changing by using the const keyword when the variable is declared.

Output of the C++ Program

```
This program calculates the number of molecules in a specified amount of
mass.

Enter the mass of the compound -->    100
Enter the molecular weight for the compound -->    25

There are 2.41e+024 molecules in 100.00 grams of compound.
```

Solution Implemented in Visual Basic

```
1   Option Explicit
2   Private Sub cmdCalculate_Click()
3       Dim MolWeight As Double
4       Dim Mass As Double
5       Dim Moles As Double
6       Dim Molecules As Double
7       Mass = Val(txtMass.Text)
8       MolWeight = Val(txtMolWeight.Text)
9       Moles = Mass / MolWeight
10      Molecules = Moles * 6.02E+23
11      lblOutput.Caption = "There are " & Molecules & _
12          " molecules in " & Mass & " grams of the compound."
13  End Sub
14  Private Sub Form_Activate()
15      txtMass.SetFocus
16  End Sub
17  Private Sub Form_Load()
18     frmProblem1_6.Top = (Screen.Height -
19     frmProblem1_6.Height) / 3
20     frmProblem1_6.Left = (Screen.Width -
21         frmProblem1_6.Width) / 3
22     lblMessage.Caption = "This program calculates the " & _
23         " number of molecules in a specified amount of mass."
24     lblInput1.Caption = "Enter the mass of the compound."
25     lblInput2.Caption = "Enter the molecular weight of " & _
26         "the compound."
27  End Sub
```

As in previous problems, the user information is entered into a text box and converted to double-precision, floating-point numbers by the Val function (lines 7 and 8). The calculations that determine the number of Moles and Molecules are carried out on lines 9 and 10. The formatted output is sent to the Output label box in lines 11 and 12. Lines 14 to 21 are not involved in the logic of the problem but merely size, position, and set the focus for the initial window. The remaining lines of the program display messages in the label boxes.

Output of the Visual Basic Program

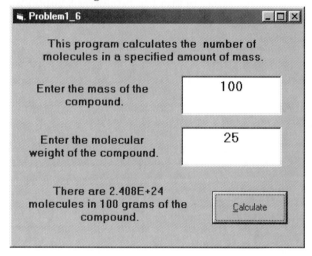

1.5   WORKING BACKWARD—A BALL IS DROPPED FROM A TALL BUILDING

In a structured programming environment in which the program must necessarily run from the beginning to the end, the use of backward logic may seem counterintuitive. However, one of the by-products of learning to solve problems logically is the ability to troubleshoot situations that are not performing as expected.

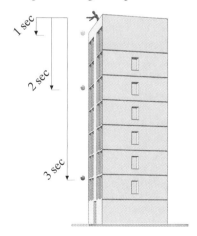

The troubleshooting may involve debugging a program, possibly zeroing in on a fault in an electrical circuit, or discovering the reason the bridge collapsed. In each case the beginning of the search for the error is at the end point. The program does not produce the desired outcome; the circuit delivers a distorted waveform, or the bridge is in rubble. From the end point we move backward, asking what might have caused the poor outcome. Or, thinking in terms of cause and effect, what cause might have produced the observed effect?

In solving problems, there is no already existing solution to perform badly but the logical process is the same. In order to produce a solution we can ask what must be in place for the last step to occur, and then what is needed for the second to last step, and then for the third to last, and so on.

Having already mentioned the carelessly discarded ball, it is reasonable to form it into Problem 1.7.

PROBLEM 1.7   *If a ball is dropped from a tall building, how far does it travel in the first second, the second second, the third second, and the fourth second? For the sake of simplicity we will ignore the effects of updrafts, air resistance, altitude, and migrating geese. The ball falls at a rate solely dependent on gravity, which produces an acceleration of ~32 ft/sec². Imagine the ball falling in a very tall, very thin vacuum chamber. In reality this is equivalent to isolating the effect of one force (gravity) on the ball and leaving consideration of other forces until later.*

Working backward from the end, it is clear that before we can determine the distance traveled during each of the first four seconds, we must know the position of the ball after each second, counting the instant it is dropped as time zero. Then, for example, the distance traveled during the third second is the difference between the positions of the ball at $t = 3$ seconds and $t = 2$ seconds. If calculating the difference is the last step, then calculating the ball position at one-second intervals from the time it was dropped is the second to last step. To do this, as in the Fahrenheit conversion problem, we either look up a formula or take the more interesting route and derive the formula using the calculus.

Given that the acceleration due to gravity is 32 ft/sec², integration produces the velocity at any time and a second integration produces the distance an object travels under the influence of gravity.

$$a = 32 \text{ ft/sec}^2$$
$$v = \int 32 \text{ ft/sec}^2 \, dt = 32t \text{ ft/sec}$$
$$d = \int 32t \text{ ft/sec} \, dt = 16t^2 \text{ ft}$$

That is, the distance traveled in feet at any time can be found by squaring the number of seconds and multiplying by 16.

Two important items should be noted in making the preceding calculations. First, 32 ft/sec^2 is not a universal constant and depends on the altitude, latitude, the density of the Earth in the vicinity of the falling object, and several other factors. At sea level and at 45° north latitude, 32.1740 ft/sec^2 is considered accurate. Second, following Rule 2, care was taken to keep the units with each number. Velocity is $32t$ ft/sec because the unit for t (time) is seconds, which cancels out one of the seconds in the denominator of 32 ft/sec^2. Similarly, distance is $16t^2$ ft because t^2 provides units of $\sec^2$ in the numerator to cancel out the $\sec^2$ in the denominator. Units should never be ignored.

Initial Data: **1.** The ball is stationary at time zero.

   2. A ball is dropped and falls under the influence of gravity.

   3. The fall is not affected by any other forces.

   4. Calculated relevant information: For a given amount of time t, a falling object travels $16t^2$ ft.

Objective: Find the distance traveled in each of the first four seconds of free fall.

Pseudocode Solution

   1. Begin
   2.   Calculate d_1, the distance after 1 sec.
   3.   Calculate d_2, the distance after 2 sec.
   4.   Calculate d_3, the distance after 3 sec.
   5.   Calculate d_4, the distance after 4 sec.
   6.   Display the results.
   7.   Calculate $d_2 - d_1$.
   8.   Calculate $d_3 - d_2$.
   9.   Calculate $d_4 - d_3$.
   10.   Display the results.
   11. End

Flowchart

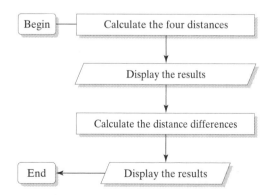

Solution Implemented in C++

```
1    // Problem1_7.cpp
2    #include <iostream.h>
3
4    int main (void)
5    {
6        double time1 = 1, time2 = 2, time3 = 3, time4 = 4;
7        double dist1, dist2, dist3, dist4;
8
9        dist1 = 16 * time1 * time1;   // Distance calculations for
10       dist2 = 16 * time2 * time2;   //    each second
11       dist3 = 16 * time3 * time3;
12       dist4 = 16 * time4 * time4;
13       cout << "This program calculates distances traveled by a falling"
14               <<"ball.\n\n" << endl;
15       cout << "After " << time1 << " second the ball has fallen "
16               << dist1 << " feet." << endl;
17       cout << "After " << time2 << " seconds the ball has fallen "
18               << dist2 << " feet." << endl;
19       cout << "After " << time3 << " seconds the ball has fallen "
20               << dist3 << " feet." << endl;
21       cout << "After " << time4 << " seconds the ball has fallen "
22               << dist4 << " feet.\n" << endl;
23
24       cout << "During the first second the ball fell "
25               << dist1 << " feet." << endl;
26       cout << "During the second second the ball fell "
27               << dist2 - dist1 << " feet." << endl;
28       cout << "During the third second the ball fell "
29               << dist3 - dist2 << " feet." << endl;
30       cout << "During the fourth second the ball fell "
31               << dist4 - dist3 << " feet.\n" << endl;
32       return(0);
33   }
```

It is clear that this program could have been written in a more compact fashion using for() loops and an array to store the distances. These programming features will be used in subsequent chapters. However, this chapter is about clarity. Consequently, shortcuts have been avoided and each operation has been spelled out.

Problem 1.7 is divided into three sections. The first section (lines 9 through 12) calculates the distance the ball has fallen after each of the first four seconds of free fall. Lines 15 through 22 display the results of those calculations. Lines 24 through 31 calculate the distance fallen during each second and display the results as the calculations are made. Later these logical groupings will be written as functions but for now clarity is the key.

Output of the C++ Program

This program calculates distances traveled by a falling ball.

After 1 second the ball has fallen 16 feet.
After 2 seconds the ball has fallen 64 feet.
After 3 seconds the ball has fallen 144 feet.
After 4 seconds the ball has fallen 256 feet.

During the first second the ball fell 16 feet.
During the second second the ball fell 48 feet.
During the third second the ball fell 80 feet.
During the fourth second the ball fell 112 feet.

Solution Implemented in Visual Basic

```
1    Option Explicit
2    Dim distance(1 To 4) As Double
3
4    Private Sub cmdFourSec_Click(Index As Integer)
5        lblOutput1.Caption = "After four seconds the ball " & _
6            "has fallen " & distance(4) & " feet."
7        lblOutput2.Caption = "During the fourth second " & _
8            "the ball fell " & distance(4) - distance(3) & _
9            " feet."
10   End Sub
11   Private Sub cmdOneSec_Click(Index As Integer)
12       lblOutput1.Caption = "After one second the ball " & _
13           "has fallen " & distance(1) & " feet."
14       lblOutput2.Caption = "During the first second " & _
15           "the ball fell " & distance(1) & " feet."
16   End Sub
17   Private Sub cmdThreeSec_Click(Index As Integer)
18       lblOutput1.Caption = "After three seconds the ball " & _
19           "has fallen " & distance(3) & " feet."
20       lblOutput2.Caption = "During the third second " & _
21           "the ball fell " & distance(3) - distance(2) & _
22           " feet."
23   End Sub
24   Private Sub cmdTwoSec_Click(Index As Integer)
25       lblOutput1.Caption = "After two seconds the ball " & _
26           "has fallen " & distance(2) & " feet."
27       lblOutput2.Caption = "During the second second " & _
28           "the ball fell " & distance(2) - distance(1) & _
29           " feet."
30   End Sub
31   Private Sub Form_Load()
32       lblMessage.Caption = "This program calculates the " & _
33           "distance traveled by a falling ball after " & _
34           "one, two, three, and four seconds."
35       distance(1) = 16 * 1 * 1
36       distance(2) = 16 * 2 * 2
37       distance(3) = 16 * 3 * 3
38       distance(4) = 16 * 4 * 4
39   End Sub
```

As in the C++ program, the use of a looping structure was avoided in favor of a specific line of code for each operation. The initialization of the four distance variables is written in lines 35 through 38. At runtime these operations are performed as the form is loaded. Both the display of the information and the calculations and display for the distance fallen during each second occur in response to the click of a command button. While this does not strictly follow the flowchart, the logic is intact and the program is more in line with the event-driven nature of Visual Basic.

There is a critical Visual Basic element that should be noted in creating each of the command buttons. The Index property in the Properties Box must have the correct index for the distance array. Command button cmdOneSec needs the index 1; command button cmdTwoSec needs the index 2; and so on for the remaining buttons.

Output of the Visual Basic Program

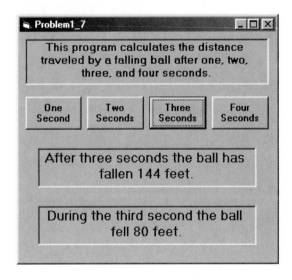

It is apparent that while the approach to the problem of the falling ball is effective, the implementation is rather inefficient. The obvious question is how many calculations would have to be made and how much code would have to be written if a table of data were required for the first 200 seconds of free fall. There is no avoiding making the calculations if a massive amount of data is required; however, the number of calculations is generally irrelevant in an age of high-speed personal computers. Of greater concern is the number of instructions that must be written by the programmer in order to make those calculations.

Clearly, what is needed in a programming language is a construction that will conveniently tell a computer to repeat an operation, possibly with small variations for each cycle. For the problem solver a new tool in his set of skills is needed. To harness the power of a computer the problem solver must look for repeatable operations. Difficult problems can often be solved by a simple operation that is repeated many times. This is the topic for the next chapter.

CHAPTER 2

Repetition

2.1 THE POWER OF THE PERSONAL COMPUTER

Gordon Moore, the cofounder of Intel Corp., observed in 1965 that the density of transistors was doubling every year. That rate has slowed slightly and the transistor density is currently doubling every 18 months. However, transistor density is only one factor determining the processing power of a personal computer. Increased clock speed, caching, and improved instruction sets along with many other advances have produced personal computers with amazing capabilities.

A $1,500 personal computer purchased today has processing power that would put it in the category of a supercomputer just ten years ago. Using computers for e-mail, word processing, and tracking finances is a tremendous convenience but these tasks do not come close to utilizing all the processing power available. Combining this processing power with problem-solving skills can generate solutions to problems that would otherwise either take years to calculate or considerable training in a specialized field.

Fermat's Last Theorem provides a good example. In the seventeenth century Pierre de Fermat asserted that the equation $x^n + y^n = z^n$ has no nonzero integer solutions for values of $n > 2$. He claimed to have an elegant proof for the assertion but no room in the margin of the manuscript he was writing to include it. For over 360 years that proof eluded the best mathematicians until Andrew Wiles of Princeton announced a solution to the theorem. After some revision, the proof was accepted as correct in 1994.

More interesting, from the point of view of using computers to solve problems, is the fact that long before there was a correct theoretical solution mathematicians were sure that the theorem (actually a conjecture) was correct. Computer simulations had been run for values of n from 3 to over 100,000 without discovering integer values for x, y, and z that satisfy the equation. Although the simulations did not prove the theorem, they did make mathematicians very, very sure that the theorem was true.

The ability of a computer to perform an operation or a series of operations many times, reliably, and at amazing speeds provides new methods of problem-solving for the problem solver's arsenal.

Rule 5   The Repetition Rule
When approaching a problem, look for repeated operations. Computers can repeat operations millions of times very quickly.

2.2   THE FALLING BALL

Problem 2.1 returns to the discussion of the falling ball. In this case calculations must be made for the first 20 seconds. The calculations for each second could be coded individually but this would quickly become tedious. In this case it is better to consider which operations are repeated and to incorporate that information into our problem-solving logic.

PROBLEM 2.1   *If a ball is dropped from a sufficient height, how far does it travel each second and what is its speed at the end of each second for the first 20 seconds? Again it is necessary to assume that no other forces beside gravity affect the motion of the ball.*

The initial data is the same as Problem 1.7, namely, that gravity accelerates any falling object near the Earth's surface at ~ 32 ft/sec^2. In addition we have the relevant formulas derived in Chapter 1 for the velocity and the distance traveled in each second.

Initial Data: **1.** Value for acceleration due to gravity: 32 ft/sec^2

2. Derived formulas for velocity and distance

$$v = 32 \text{ ft/sec} * \text{time}$$

$$d = 16 \text{ ft} * \text{time} * \text{time}$$

3. The operations for calculating velocity and distance must be repeated 20 times.

4. Output is required each time velocity and distance are calculated.

Objective: Tabled results for velocity, total distance, and interval distance during the first 20 seconds of free fall.

With the addition of repeated operations in the logic, the solution simplifies while the pseudocode and flowchart become slightly more involved. The important item when programming loops is determining what actions or calculations occur only once and belong outside the loop, and which actions or calculations are repeated and belong inside the loop.

Rule 6   The Clarity in Loops Rule

When a problem involves repeated operations, be clear about which operations are repeated and belong inside the looping structure and which operations occur only once and should be outside of the loop.

Notice that the same calculations are made for 20 different values of time (time = 1 second to time = 20 seconds). Time is the independent variable. All other values depend on time. For each one-second interval the same calculations are made for velocity, total distance, and one-second interval distance. This suggests setting up a loop in which the necessary calculations are made for one value of time and then repeated for each new value until the value of time reaches the terminal value of 20 seconds. By using a loop, the calculations to be made are described only once but are performed many times, each time using a new value for time.

Notice in the following pseudocode that, in accordance with the clarity in loop rule, the declaration and the initialization of the variables only occur once and are listed before the loop begins. The calculations for velocity, total distance, and interval distance must be repeated for each cycle of the loop, that is, for each value of time, and are placed within the loop. For the same reason the display of the calculated information, the saving of the distance calculated for the current cycle (to be used in the following cycle), and the incrementing of the variable time all are within the loop.

Pseudocode

1. Begin
2.   Declare variables for time, velocity, total distance, previous distance, and interval distance.
3.   Print the opening messages.
4.   Repeat 20 times (once for each value of time).
5.   Calculate the velocity.
6.   Calculate the total distance.
7.   Calculate the one-second interval distance.
8.   Display the information.
9.   Save the total distance in the `previous_distance` variable to be used in the next cycle.
10.   Increment the value of time by one second.
11.   Test for 20 cycles; if true, end loop.
12. End

Steps 5 through 11 describe the operations to be repeated and are indented from step 4, which indicates the number of repetitions and the variable that tracks the number of repetitions. This indentation is important and provides clarity to the pseudocode. The same indentation should also be used in writing the C++ and the Visual Basic code.

The logic in the pseudocode is straightforward except for step 9. In order to calculate the distance the ball traveled in any second two things must be known: the distance traveled up to time t and the distance traveled up to time $t - 1$. That is, the distance traveled during the fifth second is the distance traveled in the first five seconds minus the distance traveled in the first four seconds. For each cycle it is necessary to have the total distance value from the previous cycle. This value is stored in the `previous_distance` variable.

Flowchart

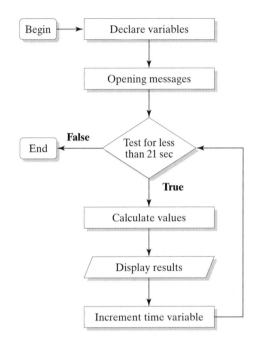

Solution Implemented in C++

```
1    //Problem2_1.cpp
2    #include <iostream.h>
3    #include <iomanip.h>
4
5    void main (void)
6    {
7        double time, total_distance, previous_distance = 0;
8        double interval_distance, velocity;
9
10       cout << "This program calculates rate of descent and the distance "
11           << "\ntraveled by a falling ball at intervals of one second.\n\n"
12           << endl;
13
14       cout << "Second     Descent Rate     Total Distance     Interval "
15           << "Distance\n" << endl;
16       for (time = 1; time <= 20; time++)
17       {
18           velocity = 32 * time;  // velocity at the end of interval
19           total_distance = 16 * time * time;  // total distance traveled
20           interval_distance = total_distance - previous_distance;
21                                   // interval distance
22           cout << setw(4) << time << setw(11) << velocity << " feet/sec"
```

```
23                  << setw(12) << total_distance << " feet"
24                  << setw(12) << interval_distance << " feet" << endl;
25          previous_distance = total_distance;  // save the total distance for
26                                               // calculations in next cycle
27     }
28  }
```

The opening message to the user, the declaration of the variables, and the column headings are described in lines 7 through 15. The description of the loop based on the loop counter, `time`, and the number of cycles is on line 16. The loop counter can be any variable that will change from the starting value to the terminal value in the required number of steps. The counter may count up, count down, or count in multiples as long as it reaches the terminal count in 20 cycles. In this case the counter is used for two purposes. It not only counts cycles but also indicates the number of seconds the ball has fallen up to that cycle and can be used in the output in the column that lists the number of seconds.

Lines 18 and 19 make the necessary calculations based on the derived formulas for velocity and distance. There are two important issues in line 20. First, it is extremely important when programming to give variables descriptive names. Since `interval_distance` describes the distance fallen during any given second, `total_distance` describes the distance fallen up to that time, and `previous_distance` describes the distance fallen prior to that second, the meaning of

```
20          interval_distance = total_distance - previous_distance;
```

is clear. Using algebra-style variable names such as *x*, *y*, and *z* is a recipe for confused logic and makes troubleshooting programming errors a nightmare.

Second, `previous_distance` is initialized to zero on line 7 and its value is updated on line 25. The initialization to zero indicates that prior to falling for the first second the ball was stationary. For each cycle the current value of `previous_distance` is the `total_distance` from the previous cycle. Therefore, the last operation in the loop is to set

```
25          previous_distance = total_distance;  // save the total distance for
26                                               // calculations in next cycle
```

Output of the C++ Program

```
This program calculates rate of descent and the distance traveled by a
falling ball at intervals of one second.
```

Second	Descent Rate	Total Distance	Interval Distance
1	32 feet/sec	16 feet	16 feet
2	64 feet/sec	64 feet	48 feet
3	96 feet/sec	144 feet	80 feet
4	128 feet/sec	256 feet	112 feet
5	160 feet/sec	400 feet	144 feet
6	192 feet/sec	576 feet	176 feet

7	224 feet/sec	784 feet	208 feet
8	256 feet/sec	1024 feet	240 feet
9	288 feet/sec	1296 feet	272 feet
10	320 feet/sec	1600 feet	304 feet
11	352 feet/sec	1936 feet	336 feet
12	384 feet/sec	2304 feet	368 feet
13	416 feet/sec	2704 feet	400 feet
14	448 feet/sec	3136 feet	432 feet
15	480 feet/sec	3600 feet	464 feet
16	512 feet/sec	4096 feet	496 feet
17	544 feet/sec	4624 feet	528 feet
18	576 feet/sec	5184 feet	560 feet
19	608 feet/sec	5776 feet	592 feet
20	640 feet/sec	6400 feet	624 feet

As the table grows, the error introduced by considering only gravity and ignoring the effect of wind resistance also grows until it reaches the terminal velocity for the object. This leads to Rule 7.

> **Rule 7   The Limit the Problem Rule**
>
> When a problem is too difficult to solve, consider limiting the problem to find a special-case solution.

Limiting the problem can take many forms. In Problem 2.1 only one force acting on the falling ball was considered. In this case the limitation leads to a poor solution to the problem because the effect of wind resistance quickly becomes greater than the force of gravity. On the other hand, the program provides a good indication of the vector force exerted on the ball by gravity and is, therefore, a good solution within the limits set by the problem. A problem may also be limited by finding solutions to a limited accuracy or for only positive values of a variable. It is often the case that a partial solution is better than no solution at all.

A second advantage to limiting a problem is that in solving the special-case problem, insight is often gained into a more general solution or at least one that considers a greater number of factors and, therefore, more accurately describes the real-world problem. Rule 7 is examined extensively in Chapter 7.

Solution Implemented in Visual Basic

```
1   Private Sub cmdCalculate_Click()
2       Dim time As Double
3       Dim total_distance As Double, previous_distance As Double
4       Dim interval_distance As Double, velocity As Double
5       previous_distance = 0
6       msgTable.Rows = 22
7       For time = 1 To 20
```

```
8              velocity = 32 * time
9              total_distance = 16 * time * time
10             interval_distance = total_distance - previous_distance
11             msgTable.Row = time + 1
12             msgTable.Col = 0
13             msgTable.Text = Format(time, "@@@@@@@@@@")
14             msgTable.Col = 1
15             msgTable.Text = Format(velocity, "@@@@@@@@@@") & _
16                 "  feet/sec"
17             msgTable.Col = 2
18             msgTable.Text = Format(total_distance, "@@@@@@@@@@@@") & _
19                 "  feet"
20             msgTable.Col = 3
21             msgTable.Text = Format(interval_distance, "@@@@@@@@@@@@@@") & _
22                 "  feet"
23             previous_distance = total_distance
24         Next time
25     End Sub
26
27     Private Sub Form_Load()
28         lblMessage.Caption = "This program calculates the distance traveled " & _
29             " by a falling ball for the first 20 seconds of free fall."
30         msgTable.Cols = 4
31         msgTable.ColWidth(0) = 1000
32         msgTable.ColWidth(1) = 1800
33         msgTable.ColWidth(2) = 1800
34         msgTable.ColWidth(3) = 1800
35         msgTable.Row = 0
36         msgTable.Col = 0
37         msgTable.Text = "Seconds"
38         msgTable.Col = 1
39         msgTable.Text = "Descent Rate"
40         msgTable.Col = 2
41         msgTable.Text = "Total Distance"
42         msgTable.Col = 3
43         msgTable.Text = "Interval Distance"
44     End Sub
```

The logic involved in the Visual Basic solution to the problem is identical to the
C++ implementation. The extra code in the Visual Basic program is to handle the tabled
display of the output data.

The loop structure is contained in lines 7 through 24 with the variable time used
as both loop counter and the number of seconds in the output display. Lines 8 and 9 use
the derived formulas to calculate velocity and distance. As in the C++ program
descriptive names are used for the variables involving distance. Line 10 relates the
interval_distance to the total_distance and the previous_distance.

```
10             interval_distance = total_distance - previous_distance
```

Always resist the temptation to use x, y, and z for variable names. The few keystrokes saved are not worth the confused logic that poorly named variables produce. The critical term is `previous_distance`. It was initialized on line 5 to zero, indicating that the ball was at rest and immobile at the start of the problem, and is updated each cycle on line 23.

Visual Basic provides a FlexGrid for tabling data. The FlexGrid is not an ordinary element of the toolbox displayed by default on the left side of the project area and must be added before the program is run. To add the FlexGrid to the toolbox, click the Projects pull-down menu and then choose the Components option. When the Components window appears, scroll down the list of components to Microsoft FlexGrid Control 6.0 and click the check box as shown in the following screen. Finally, click OK and the icon for the FlexGrid will appear in the toolbox. The FlexGrid can be added to the Form and sized in the same manner as any other item in the toolbox.

Lines 30 through 34 set the number of columns and the size of the columns in the FlexGrid. The column headings are set in lines 35 through 43. The majority of the code inside the for loop beginning on line 7 is used to place the output in the proper cells of the FlexGrid. The calculations for the distances and velocity require only lines 8 to 10.

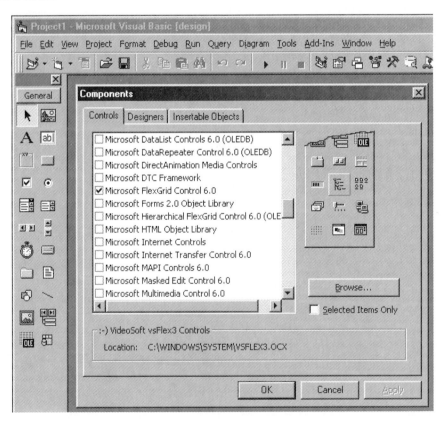

Output of the Visual Basic Program

Problem2_1				_ □ ×

This program calculates the distance traveled by a falling ball for the first 20 seconds of free fall.

Calculate

Seconds	Decent Rate	Total Distance	Interval Distance	▲
1	32 feet/sec	16 feet	16 feet	
2	64 feet/sec	64 feet	48 feet	
3	96 feet/sec	144 feet	80 feet	
4	128 feet/sec	256 feet	112 feet	
5	160 feet/sec	400 feet	144 feet	
6	192 feet/sec	576 feet	176 feet	
7	224 feet/sec	784 feet	208 feet	
8	256 feet/sec	1024 feet	240 feet	
9	288 feet/sec	1296 feet	272 feet	
10	320 feet/sec	1600 feet	304 feet	
11	352 feet/sec	1936 feet	336 feet	
12	384 feet/sec	2304 feet	368 feet	▼
13	416 feet/sec	2704 feet	400 feet	

2.3   THE PENNY PROBLEM

The penny problem not only illustrates the computational power of the personal computer but also the amazing numeric growth that occurs when a number is repeatedly doubled. The traditional problem asks the question, "Is it better to be paid $ 1,000,000 today or to be paid one penny today, two pennies tomorrow, four pennies the third day, and to continue doubling the payment every day for one month?" We'll consider a variation on this question.

PROBLEM 2.2   *What is the value, mass, and volume of a stack of pennies that accumulates at the rate of one penny the first day, two pennies the second day, and doubling every day after for a given number of days? A penny weighs approximately 2.5 grams and has a volume of 0.4 cm³.*

As always the first step is to be clear about the information given in the problem and the objective. In this problem the information most often overlooked is given in item three of the initial data. We are interested in the accumulated value, mass, and volume of the pennies at the end of each day, not merely the pennies of that day. At the end of day two we have three pennies, two pennies from day two and one penny from all previous days, specifically day one. At the end of three days, we have seven pennies, four pennies from day three and three more from days one and two.

Initial Data: **1.** The number of days is the number of cycles for the repeated operations and is provided by the user.

2. The number of pennies doubles each day.

3. The number of pennies accumulated after a given number of days is the number of pennies from the last day plus all the pennies from the previous days.

4. One penny has a mass of 2.5 grams.

5. The volume of one penny is 0.40 cm^3.

Objective: Create a table for the accumulated values for the monetary value of the pennies, the mass of the pennies, and the volume of the pennies at the end of each day.

To solve the problem it is necessary to create a repeated operation that will:

1. Calculate the number of pennies added to the pile each day.

2. Determine the value, mass, and volume of each day's pennies.

3. Add those amounts to the amounts accumulated up until that day.

Notice that the preceding operations must occur every day, that is, for every cycle of the loop. Therefore, these operations are programmed inside the loop.

The addition of each day's numbers to those already accumulated involves the idea of the running sum. In a running sum two numbers represented by variables are added and the sum is stored in one of the original variables. In this problem the total mass of the pennies for any day is the total mass from the previous day plus the mass of the current day's pennies. The code

```
total_mass = total_mass + penny_mass * pow( 2, day);
```

should be read, "The new total mass is equal to yesterday's total mass plus the mass of one penny multiplied by the number of pennies for that day." For any given day the number of pennies is equal to 2^{day} or 2 raised to the "day" power. The monetary value of the stack of pennies and the volume of the pennies use similar running sums. When using running sums, it is important to initialize the variables holding the totals to zero when the variables are declared.

The initialization to zero (the additive identity) occurs only once and is outside of the loop. Similarly, the opening message, the user input for the number of days the calculations will be made, and the setting of the formatting parameters are operations that occur only once and are also handled before the loop begins.

Pseudocode

1. Begin
2. Declare variables for the total number of days, the weight of one penny, the volume of one penny, the total mass of the pennies, the total volume of the pennies, and the value of the pennies.
3. Initialize the appropriate variables.
4. Output the opening message to the user.
5. Get the total number of days for which the program will run.
6. Set the formatting parameters for two decimal places.
7. Run loop for as many days as the user specifies.
8. Calculate total mass of pennies.
9. Calculate total volume of pennies.
10. Calculate value of pennies.
11. After 20 days, change the units to kilograms and cubic meters.
12. After 34 days, change to exponential notation to accommodate large numbers.
13. End loop after the specified number of days.
14. End

The pseudocode clearly identifies which operations occur only once and which operations occur for each cycle of the loop. Repeated operations are listed under step 7 and are indented to indicate their membership in the loop. Step 7 also identifies the number of days entered by the user as the terminal count for the loop.

Steps 11 and 12 illustrate the iterative nature of programming. The first listing of the pseudocode might not have contained these lines that alter the formatting of the output. After all, the formatting does not impact the logic followed in finding the solution. However, after the problem is solved, coded, and the program is run, we might find that the output is more readable if certain formatting adjustments are made. Following the first run of the program, it was discovered that after 20 days the values for mass and volume became sufficiently large as to merit a change in units. After 34 days, the units of kilograms and cubic meters became inadequate and the formatting was changed to exponential notation. The need for these formatting items might have been anticipated by an experienced programmer, but it is more likely they would not have been noticed when the focus was on the logic used to solve the problem.

Flowchart

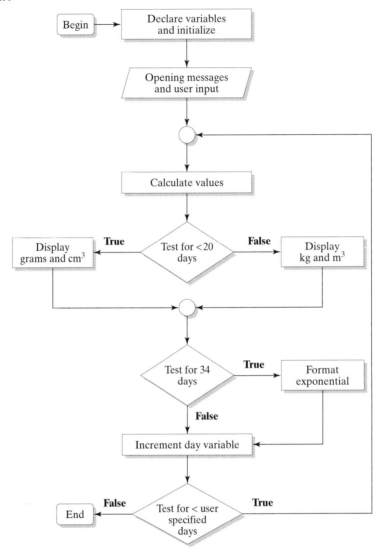

Solution Implemented in C++

```
1    //Problem2_2.cpp
2    #include <iostream.h>
3    #include <iomanip.h>
4    #include <math.h>
5
6    void main(void)
7    {
8        int day, total_days;
```

```
 9      const double penny_mass = 2.5, penny_volume = .40;
10      double total_mass = 0, total_volume = 0, value = 0;
11
12      cout << "This program calculates the mass, volume,"
13          << "\nand value of a pile of pennies if one penny is"
14          << "\nadded the first day and double the previous day's"
15          << "\npennies is added on each subsequent day.\n"
16          << "\n\tEnter the number of days      ";
17      cin >> total_days;
18      cout.setf(ios::fixed|ios::showpoint);
19      cout.precision(2);
20      cout << "\nDay        Value          Mass          Volume" << endl;
21      for (day = 0; day < total_days; day++)
22      {
23          value = value + pow(2, day);
24          total_volume = total_volume + penny_volume * pow( 2, day);
25          total_mass = total_mass + penny_mass * pow( 2, day);
26          if (day <= 20)
27              cout << setw(3) << day + 1
28                  << "  $" << setw(13) << (value / 100)
29                  << setw(15) << total_mass << " g"
30                  << setw(15) << total_volume << "cu. cm." << endl;
31          else
32              cout << setw(3) << day + 1
33                  << "  $" << setw(13) << (value / 100)
34                  << setw(15) << (total_mass) / 1000 << " kg"
35                  << setw(15) << (total_volume / 1000000)
36                  << "cu. meters" << endl;
37          if (day >= 34)
38          {
39              cout.setf(ios::scientific|ios::showpoint);
40              cout.precision(4);
41          }
42      }
43  }
```

Line 21 controls the looping structure using day for the counter variable. The value of `total_days`, supplied by the user, is the terminal count. The loop could start with day set equal to one and continue until the terminal count is exceeded. However, in this problem it is more convenient to set day equal to zero and to end the loop when the terminal count is reached rather than exceeded. Notice the lack of an equal sign in the test condition. The advantage of starting the loop counter at zero is seen on lines 23 through 25. In these calculations the loop counter is used as a multiplication factor based on powers of two. Since two raised to the zero power is one, which is the number of pennies on the first day, zero is the preferred starting count for the loop.

The number of pennies is calculated on line 23 as two raised to the power of the loop counter. In the first cycle day is equal to zero and two raised to the zero power is one, the number of pennies for the day. In the second cycle day is equal to one and two raised to the first power is two, the number of pennies for the second day. The second day's pennies are added to all previous day's pennies (one on this cycle) for a total of three pennies after the second day. Similarly, on the third cycle the value of day is two and two raised to the second power is four, the number of pennies for the third day. Those four pennies are added to all previous day's pennies for a total of seven pennies after three days.

Lines 24 and 25 calculate the total_volume and total_mass, respectively. These values are based on the same exponentially increasing number of pennies that were calculated on line 23. The only difference is that the number of pennies is multiplied by either the volume or the mass of a single penny.

Output of the C++ Program

```
This program calculates the mass, volume,
and value of a pile of pennies if one penny is
added the first day and double the previous day's
pennies is added on each subsequent day.

Enter the number of days      30

Day          Value            Mass               Volume
 1   $         0.01           2.50 g             0.40 cu. cm
 2   $         0.03           7.50 g             1.20 cu. cm
 3   $         0.07          17.50 g             2.80 cu. cm
 4   $         0.15          37.50 g             6.00 cu. cm
 5   $         0.31          77.50 g            12.40 cu. cm
 6   $         0.63         157.50 g            25.20 cu. cm
 7   $         1.27         317.50 g            50.80 cu. cm
 8   $         2.55         637.50 g           102.00 cu. cm
 9   $         5.11        1277.50 g           204.40 cu. cm
10   $        10.23        2557.50 g           409.20 cu. cm
11   $        20.47        5117.50 g           818.80 cu. cm
12   $        40.95       10237.50 g          1638.00 cu. cm
13   $        81.91       20477.50 g          3276.40 cu. cm
14   $       163.83       40957.50 g          6553.20 cu. cm
15   $       327.67       81917.50 g         13106.80 cu. cm
16   $       655.35      163837.50 g         26214.00 cu. cm
17   $      1310.71      327677.50 g         52428.40 cu. cm
18   $      2621.43      655357.50 g        104857.20 cu. cm
19   $      5242.87     1310717.50 g        209714.80 cu. cm
20   $     10485.75     2621437.50 g        419430.00 cu. cm
21   $     20971.51     5242877.50 g        838860.40 cu. cm
22   $     41943.03       10485.76 kg            1.68 cu. meters
23   $     83886.07       20971.52 kg            3.36 cu. meters
24   $    167772.15       41943.04 kg            6.71 cu. meters
25   $    335544.31       83886.08 kg           13.42 cu. meters
26   $    671088.63      167772.16 kg           26.84 cu. meters
27   $   1342177.27      335544.32 kg           53.69 cu. meters
28   $   2684354.55      671088.64 kg          107.37 cu. meters
29   $   5368709.11     1342177.28 kg          214.75 cu. meters
30   $  10737418.23     2684354.56 kg          429.50 cu. meters
```

The results from running the program show that after 30 days the value of the pile of pennies is in excess of $10 million. The more unfortunate result is that the pile weighs almost 3,000 tons (the conversion is left to the reader) and is large enough to fill several classrooms to the ceiling.

Since the number of days is input provided by the user, we can run the program for a little over three months and get an even more fascinating result.

Second Output Based on 94 Cycles of the Program

```
This program calculates the mass, volume,
and value of a pile of pennies if one penny is
added the first day and double the previous day's
pennies is added on each subsequent day.

Enter the number of days      94
```

Day		Value	Mass	Volume
1	$	0.01	2.50 g	0.40 cu. cm
88	$	3.095e+024	7.737e+023 kg	1.238e+020 cu. meters
89	$	6.190e+024	1.547e+024 kg	2.476e+020 cu. meters
90	$	1.238e+025	3.095e+024 kg	4.952e+020 cu. meters
91	$	2.476e+025	6.190e+024 kg	9.904e+020 cu. meters
92	$	4.952e+025	1.238e+025 kg	1.981e+021 cu. meters
93	$	9.904e+025	2.476e+025 kg	3.961e+021 cu. meters
94	$	1.981e+026	4.952e+025 kg	7.923e+021 cu. meters

The incredible number here is not the value of the pennies, which is, in fact, unfathomable, but the values for mass and volume. After 94 days, the pile of pennies would be just slightly less massive than the earth. If we assume the copper had to be mined from other planets and asteroids and brought to the earth for minting, we are faced with the question of what effect the extra mass would have on the earth's orbit.

The size of the pile is no longer a relevant issue. The volume of 7.923e+21 cubic meters would cover the earth, increasing the radius of the earth from 4,000 miles to over 11,400 miles. Again other factors make this number invalid. Such a large volume of metal would experience gravitational forces that would cause changes in the density of the copper. Of course, people who managed to avoid being buried by the pennies would experience a similar unfortunate increase in gravitational attraction.

This is not the only source of error in the program. Ignoring the massive forces of gravity is an easy error to spot when the pile becomes significantly large. The more subtle error is evident even in the first two weeks. Since the mass and volume for a penny have only been measured to two significant figures, each answer is only accurate to two significant figures. After 30 days, the value of $10,737,418.23 is accurate but the mass of 2,684,354.56 kg should be rounded to 2.7×10^6 kg. Similarly, the volume should be rounded to 430 cubic meters.

The conclusion to the problem is that if an offer is made for $1,000,000 or a penny the first day and double the previous day's pennies for the next 94 days, take the $1,000,000 rather than destroy the earth. As you might expect, verification of the value for the increase in the radius of the Earth is left as an exercise for the reader.

Implementation in Visual Basic

```
1   Option Explicit
2
3   Private Sub cmdEnd_Click()
4       Unload frmProblem2_2
5   End Sub
6
7   Private Sub Form_Activate()
8       txtInput.SetFocus
9
10  End Sub
11
12  Private Sub Form_Load()
13      lblInputMessage.Caption ="Enter the number" & vbCrLf & _ "of days"
14      lblMessage.Caption="This program calculates the mass" & _
15          ", volume, and value of a pile of pennies if one penny"& _
16          " is added the first day and double the previous" & _
17          " day's " & _
18          "pennies is added on each subsequent day."
19      msgTable.ColWidth(0) = 500
20      msgTable.ColWidth(1) = 2500
21      msgTable.ColWidth(2) = 2100
22      msgTable.ColWidth(3) = 2600
23      msgTable.Row = 0
24      msgTable.Col = 0
25      msgTable.Text = "Day"
26      msgTable.Col = 1
27      msgTable.Text = "Value"
28      msgTable.Col = 2
29      msgTable.Text = "Mass"
30      msgTable.Col = 3
31      msgTable.Text = "Volume"
32
33  End Sub
34
35  Private Sub txtInput_Change()
36      Dim total_days As Integer
37      total_days = Val(txtInput.Text)
38      msgTable.Rows = total_days + 2
39      Dim day As Long
40      Dim penny_mass As Double
41      Dim penny_volume As Double
```

```
42     Dim total_mass As Double
43     Dim total_volume As Double
44     Dim value As Double
45     penny_mass = 2.5
46     penny_volume = 0.40
47     value = total_mass = total_volume = 0
48     For day = 1 To total_days
49         msgTable.Row = day + 1
50         msgTable.Col = 0
51         msgTable.Text = Str(day)
52         msgTable.Col = 1
53         value = value + (2 ^ (day - 1)) / 100
54         msgTable.Text = Format(FormatCurrency(value, 2), _
55             "@@@@@@@@@@@@@@@@@@@@@@@@@@@@@@@@")
56         msgTable.Col = 2
57         If day < 22 Then
58             total_mass = total_mass + penny_mass * 2 ^ (day - 1)
59             msgTable.Text = Format(FormatNumber(total_mass, 2), _
60                 "@@@@@@@@@@@@@@@@@@@@@@@@@@@@@@") & " g"
61             msgTable.Col = 3
62             total_volume = total_volume + penny_volume * 2 ^ (day - 1)
63             msgTable.Text = Format(FormatNumber(total_volume, 2),
64                 "@@@@@@@@@@@@@@@@@@@@@@@@@@@@@@@@") & " cu. cm."
65         Else
66             total_mass = total_mass + penny_mass * 2 ^ (day - 1)
67             msgTable.Text = Format(FormatNumber(total_mass / _
68                 1000, 2), "@@@@@@@@@@@@@@@@@@@@@@@@@@") & " kg"
69             msgTable.Col = 3
70             total_volume = total_volume + penny_volume * _
71                 2 ^ (day - 1)
72             msgTable.Text = Format(FormatNumber(total_volume / _
73                 1000000, 2), "@@@@@@@@@@@@@@@@@@@@@@@@@@") & " cu. meters."
74         End If
75
76     Next day
77     txtInput.SetFocus
78 End Sub
```

The logic for the implementation in Visual Basic is the same as in the C++ program except the code for the calculations is more spread out to allow for the greater formatting requirements of the FlexGrid display.

Line 48 describes the loop required for the number of days requested by the user. The running sums for the value of the pennies and their mass and volume are handled on lines 53, 58, and 62, respectively.

The initial focus for the program is described on line 77 and the output table upgrades for each change to the input text box.

Output of the Visual Basic Program

Day	Value	Mass	Volume
15	$327.67	81,917.50 g	13,106.80 cu. cm.
16	$655.35	163,837.50 g	26,214.00 cu. cm.
17	$1,310.71	327,677.50 g	52,428.40 cu. cm.
18	$2,621.43	655,357.50 g	104,857.20 cu. cm.
19	$5,242.87	1,310,717.50 g	209,714.80 cu. cm.
20	$10,485.75	2,621,437.50 g	419,430.00 cu. cm.
21	$20,971.51	5,242,877.50 g	838,860.40 cu. cm.
22	$41,943.03	10,485.76 kg	1.68 cu. meters.
23	$83,886.07	20,971.52 kg	3.36 cu. meters.
24	$167,772.15	41,943.04 kg	6.71 cu. meters.
25	$335,544.31	83,886.08 kg	13.42 cu. meters.
26	$671,088.63	167,772.16 kg	26.84 cu. meters.
27	$1,342,177.27	335,544.32 kg	53.69 cu. meters.
28	$2,684,354.55	671,088.64 kg	107.37 cu. meters.
29	$5,368,709.11	1,342,177.28 kg	214.75 cu. meters.
30	$10,737,418.23	2,684,354.56 kg	429.50 cu. meters.

2.4   GRADE POINT AVERAGE

Problem 2.3 involves the calculation of a student's grade point average (GPA). The problem itself is rather simple; however, it not only illustrates the value of being able to perform repeated operations but it also introduces the concept of weighted values or what is sometimes called a weighted average. College grades are weighted by the number of credit hours assigned to each class. Similarly, number systems weight digits by their position in the number. Just as a five-hour class is weighted more heavily when calculating a GPA, the 5 in the number 654 is weighted more heavily than the 4 and less heavily than the 6, in both cases, by a factor of 10. In the next section we'll look more closely at the weighting of decimal and binary number systems, but first a simpler problem.

PROBLEM 2.3   *What is the grade point average for a given set of grades?*

In this problem we will allow the user to continuously enter grades until hitting the <Esc> key.

Initial Data: **1.** Scale of grades: A = 4, B = 3, C = 2, D = 1, F = 0.
            2. User supplies the grade.
            3. User supplies the number of credit hours for each grade.

4. The credit hours represent the weighting for each grade.

5. Quality points for each class are the class credit hours multiplied by the scaled value for the grade received.

6. GPA equals total quality points divided by total credit hours.

Outcome: Provide running account of credit hours, quality points, and GPA.

After the problem information has been listed, it is important to be clear about what exactly the grade point average is (Rule 1 – clarity). To calculate most averages it is necessary to sum all the values to be averaged and then divide by the number of values added. The average of 20 test scores is the sum of those scores divided by 20. In this case all the test scores count equally in calculating the average, i.e., each score has the same weight as every other score.

On the other hand, a grade point average is a *weighted* average, which means that each grade must be multiplied by a weight value. In the case of a GPA, that weight is the number of credit hours for the class. The product of the credit hours and the point value of the grade is the number of quality points. It is actually the quality points that are averaged by dividing the total number of quality points by the total credit hours. This results in a weighted average grade per credit hour.

The next step in solving the problem is to identify which operations occur only once and which should be part of the loop (Rule 6 – clarity in loops). In this case the message to the user explaining the purpose of the program is the only item that is not repeated. The prompts for the grade and the number of credit hours for the class are repeated for every class included in calculating the grade point average. Of course, the calculations based on the user-supplied information and the display of the updated information are also recurrent and are included inside the loop.

The logic in solving the problem is straightforward. For each grade the point value of the grade is multiplied by the weighted value, which is the number of credit hours. This weighting causes a five-credit hour A to impact the total GPA more than a two-credit hour D. The multiplication of credit hours and the numeric value of the grade provides the number of quality points for the class. Running sums of the total hours and the total number of quality points are stored and used to calculate the current GPA, which is the current value for total quality points divided by the credit hours. Then the quality points, total hours, and the GPA are displayed for each cycle.

As a programming note, the number of hours is read into the programs as a character rather than an integer. This necessitates the conversion to an integer before arithmetic is performed but it allows for the escape key to be recognized for the program termination. Because characters are read into the program by their ASCII values, the conversion merely requires the subtraction of 48 from the character input. Another option would be to read in the credit hours as a string and use a conversion function to determine the number of credit hours.

Pseudocode

1. Begin

2.   Declare and initialize variables.

3.   Display message to user.

4.   Begin data entry and display loop.

5.   Prompt for course credit hours and grade.

6.   Check hours for end of data entry.

7.   Convert character hours to integer hours and add to total hours.

8.   Increase quality points based on grade.

9.   Check grade for end of data entry.

10.   Calculate GPA.

11.   Display quality points, total hours, and GPA.

12.   Branch always to beginning of loop.

13. End

Flowchart

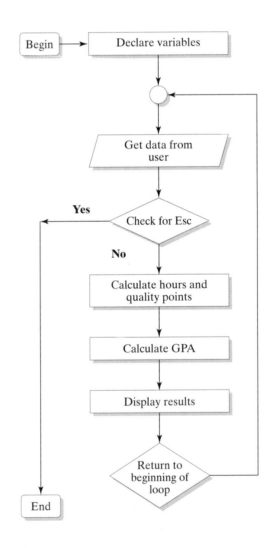

Implementation in C++

```cpp
1   //Problem2_3.cpp
2   #include <iostream.h>
3   #include <conio.h>
4
5   void main(void)
6   {
7       int quality_points = 0, total_hours = 0, counter = 1;
8       double GPA;
9       char grade, hours, flag = 0;
10
11      cout << "This program provides a running output for quality "
12          << "points and GPA\n";
13      cout << "\n\tHit <Esc> to end program \n" << endl;
14      do
15      {
16          cout << "Course " << counter++ << ":  Enter cr. hrs. " << flush;
17          hours = getche();
18          if (hours == 27)
19              break;
20          cout << "   Enter grade   " << flush;
21          grade = getche();
22          hours = hours - 48;
23          total_hours += static_cast<int>(hours);
24          switch (grade)
25          {
26              case 'A':
27              case 'a':
28                  quality_points += hours * 4;
29                  break;
30              case 'B':
31              case 'b':
32                  quality_points += hours * 3;
33                  break;
34              case 'C':
35              case 'c':
36                  quality_points += hours * 2;
37                  break;
38              case 'D':
39              case 'd':
40                  quality_points += hours * 1;
41                  break;
42              case 'F':
43              case 'f':
44                  break;
45              case 27:
46                  flag = 1;
47                  break;
48              default:
49                  cout << "\nInvalid grade -- re-enter\n";
```

```
50                        total_hours -= static_cast<int>(hours);
51                        break;
52              }
53          if (flag == 1)
54              break;
55          GPA = quality_points / static_cast<double>(total_hours);
56          cout << "\nQuality points = " << quality_points << "  Total hours  "
57              << total_hours << "   GPA = " << GPA << endl;
58      }while (1);
59  }
```

By using a while loop with a test condition that is always true, line 58, the loop is made to run continuously. This allows a little more flexibility in the loop by putting the exit condition at a particularly convenient spot rather than at the beginning of the loop, as in a while statement, or at the end, as in a do/while. In this case the exit condition for the loop is placed on line 18 and tests the input for the number of credit hours. If the <Esc> key is pressed instead of a number of credit hours, the loop is ended and the displayed GPA is based on the last valid entry. There is also a second exit opportunity. If the <Esc> key is pressed instead of a grade for a class, the terminating input is detected on line 45, which causes a flag to be set. Line 53 tests the flag and if it has been set to one the loop is ended.

The conversion of the letter grade to its numeric equivalent is handled on line 22 by subtracting 48 from the ASCII value for the number. The running total of the credit hours is calculated on line 23 and the quality points are tallied in the body of the switch statement. Again, it is worth noting that variable names such as `quality_points` and `total_hours` provide clarity that makes the extra keystroke worthwhile.

After values for `total_hours` and `quality_points` have been determined, the GPA is calculated on line 55. Because `total_hours` and `quality_points` are both integers, it is necessary to convert at least one of them to a floating-point number to avoid loosing the decimal portion of the GPA when the division is performed. In C++ the `static_cast<double>()` operator is preferred over the C-style type cast operator (`double`).

Output of C++ Program

```
This program provides a running output for quality points and GPA

Hit <Esc> to end the program

Course 1:  Enter cr. hrs. 4    Enter grade   A
Quality points = 16    Total hours  4    GPA = 4
Course 2:  Enter cr. hrs. 3    Enter grade   A
Quality points = 28    Total hours  7    GPA = 4
Course 3:  Enter cr. hrs. 3    Enter grade   B
Quality points = 37    Total hours  10    GPA = 3.7
Course 4:  Enter cr. hrs. 3    Enter grade   C
Quality points = 43    Total hours  13    GPA = 3.30769
Course 5:  Enter cr. hrs. 1    Enter grade   A
Quality points = 47    Total hours  14    GPA = 3.35714
Course 6:  Enter cr. hrs.
```

It should be noted that the rules involving significant figures do not apply in calculating a grade point average. The numbers involved in the calculations are not measurements but are pure, i.e., exact, numbers. Three credit hours are exactly three hours or 3.000000 with as many trailing zeros as the programmer desires. Similarly, the four points for a grade of A are exactly four or 4.0000000, again with an arbitrary number of zeroes.

Implementation in Visual Basic

```
1    Option Explicit
2        Dim quality_points As Double
3        Dim total_hours As Integer
4        Dim GPA As Double
5        Dim counter
6    Private Sub cmdCalculate_Click()
7        Dim value As Integer, hours As Integer
8        If txtGrade.Text = "a" Or txtGrade.Text = "A" Then
9            value = 4
10       Else
11           If txtGrade.Text = "b" Or txtGrade.Text = "B" Then
12               value = 3
13           Else
14               If txtGrade.Text = "c" Or txtGrade.Text = "C" Then
15                   value = 2
16               Else
17                   If txtGrade.Text = "d" Or txtGrade.Text = "D" Then
18                       value = 1
19                   Else
20                       If txtGrade.Text = "f" Or txtGrade.Text = "F" Then
21                           value = 0
22                       Else
23                           txtGrade.Text = ""
24                           txtGrade.SetFocus
25                       End If
26                   End If
27               End If
28           End If
29       End If
30       If txtCredits.Text = "1" Or txtCredits.Text = "2" _
31           Or txtCredits.Text = "3" Or txtCredits.Text = "4" _
32           Or txtCredits.Text = "5" Or txtCredits.Text = "6" Then
33               hours = Val(txtCredits.Text)
34       Else
35           txtCredits.Text = ""
36           txtCredits.SetFocus
37       End If
38       quality_points = quality_points + value * hours
39       total_hours = total_hours + hours
40       GPA = quality_points / total_hours
41       txtPoints = Str(quality_points)
42       txtHours = Str(total_hours)
```

```
43        txtGPA = Str(GPA)
44        txtGrade.Text = ""
45        txtCredits.Text = ""
46        txtGrade.SetFocus
47        counter = counter + 1
48        lblGrade.Caption = "Enter Grade (Class " & _
49            Str(counter) & ")"
50    End Sub
51
52    Private Sub cmdEnd_Click()
53        Unload frmProblem2_3
54    End Sub
55
56    Private Sub cmdRestart_Click()
57        txtGrade.Text = ""
58        txtCredits.Text = ""
59        txtPoints.Text = ""
60        txtHours.Text = ""
61        txtGPA.Text = ""
62        txtGrade.SetFocus
63        counter = 1
64        quality_points = 0
65        GPA = 0
66    End Sub
67
68    Private Sub Form_Activate()
69        txtGrade.SetFocus
70    End Sub
71
72    Private Sub Form_Load()
73        frmProblem2_3.Top = (Screen.Height - _
74                             frmProblem2_3.Height) / 3
75        frmProblem2_3.Left = (Screen.Width - _
76                             frmProblem2_3.Height) / 3
77        lblMessage.Caption = vbCrLf & "This program " & _
78            " provides a running output for quality-points " & _
79            " and GPA."
80        lblGrade.Caption = "Enter Grade (Class 1)"
81        lblCredits.Caption = "Enter Credit-Hours"
82        lblPoints.Caption = "Quality Points"
83        lblHours.Caption = "Total Hours"
84        lblGPA.Caption = "Grade Point Average"
85        quality_points = 0
86        GPA = 0
87        counter = 1
88    End Sub
89
90    Private Sub txtGrade_LostFocus()
91        txtCredits.SetFocus
92    End Sub
```

Output of the Visual Basic Program

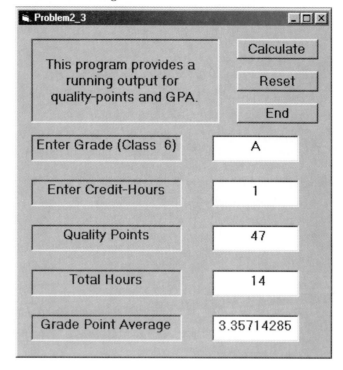

2.5   BINARY CONVERSION

We take our use of a decimal-based system for counting and arithmetic for granted but the choice to use base 10 is in fact quite arbitrary. A system based on powers of eight instead of ten would be just as valid. If humans had evolved to have eight fingers instead of ten, base 8 would probably be in use and considered more natural.

Consider the number 432. The number is sufficiently familiar that there is no need to examine its parts to understand its value. But if we do look more closely we find that it is really the sum of three weighted numbers: 4 multiplied by a weight of 100, plus 3 multiplied by a weight of 10, plus 2 multiplied by 1. Expressed mathematically:

$$432 = 4 \times 10^2 + 3 \times 10^1 + 2 \times 10^0$$

The use of decimal numbers is only a matter of convenience and if another base were to be found more convenient for a special purpose there is no reason not to leave base 10 (decimal) and use the more convenient system. This is exactly the choice that was made with the advent of digital computers. Computers were originally analog devices but the analog computers have been completely supplanted by computers whose transistors can take only one of two states, either completely closed or completely open. (Note: Before the age of transistors, it was vacuum tubes or relays that either conducted current or didn't.) This open or shut condition can be best represented by a 1 or a 0. Just as if computers had only two fingers, it was more natural to use a number system with only two characters, i.e., a base 2 or binary system.

This leads to the need to convert numbers from one system to another, namely, Problem 2.4.

PROBLEM 2.4 *How can an arbitrary positive integer be converted from decimal (base 10) to binary (base 2)?*

There is a clever algorithm for making this conversion that lends itself well to implementation on computer called casting out twos. However, this would entail knowing the algorithm. If the algorithm is known, there is no problem solving involved, merely algorithm execution. We will start by assuming that very little is known about binary numbers beyond the fact that the position of each digit or bit indicates its weight. It is simple to state that the value of a binary number is based on weighted values with each position representing a power of two. It is a bit more difficult to grasp the meaning of a binary number such as 110101000100_2. In these cases there are advantages in considering a specific case and, after that specific case is completely understood, attempting to generalize to a procedure that will work for all cases.

> **Rule 8   The Concrete Example Rule**
>
> When examining a general problem, it is often more illuminating to work with a specific instance. An example with specific numeric values is always easier to understand than the general case.

In this case we'll consider the arbitrary number 54 for conversion to binary, keeping in mind that developing a method that will work on any number is the final goal. As always it is critically important to be clear about what initial information we have to work with. While little information is specifically provided in the problem, the term *base 2* provides all the information that is necessary.

Initial Data: **1.** Binary numbers are composed of 1s and 0s.

2. The binary number system uses powers of two in exactly the same manner as the decimal system uses powers of ten. That is, the rightmost bit (character) in a binary number has a weighted valued of 2^0 or 1. Moving leftward the bits have weighted values of 2^1 or 2, 2^2 or 4, 2^3 or 8, 2^4 or 16, 2^5 or 32, and so on.

3. The decimal number
$$432 \text{ means } 4 \times 10^2 + 3 \times 10^1 + 2 \times 10^0$$

4. The binary number.
$$101 \text{ means } 1 \times 2^2 + 0 \times 2^1 + 2 \times 2^0$$

Objective: Find the binary equivalent of the example number in a manner that will apply to all positive integers.

Notice that in stating the objective as limited to positive integers Rule 7 was applied to simplify the problem. The general case that includes the conversion of negative numbers and fractions is explored fully in Chapter 7 as Problem 7.2.

This problem represents another example in which insight can be gained by working backward (Rule 4 Working Backward). Consider the opposite problem of converting binary to decimal. It is a simple problem to convert a binary number such as 110110 to decimal by summing the weighted values of each of the bits. The rightmost bit, zero, indicates we have no bit weighted at 1. The bit second from the right indicates that there is a one weighted at 2. Continuing:

$$0 \times 2^0 = \qquad 0$$
$$1 \times 2^1 = \qquad 2$$
$$1 \times 2^2 = \qquad 4$$
$$0 \times 2^3 = \qquad 0$$
$$1 \times 2^4 = \qquad 16$$
$$1 \times 2^5 = \qquad 32$$
$$110110 = \qquad 54$$

If the decimal number of 54 were to be converted to binary, it is clear that the first bit (the most significant bit on the left) would represent the highest power of 2 that is not greater than the number to be converted. That is, the most significant bit would represent 2^5 or 32. Because 2^6 (64) is larger than 54, it cannot be the weighted value of the first bit. This tells us how many bits are in the final binary number. The foregoing example shows that if the first bit represents the fifth power of 2 there must be six bits in the final binary number. Because the powers of 2 begin with 0 ($2^0 = 1$), there will always be one more bit than the highest power of 2 that is less than the number to be converted.

This means that the first step in converting a number such as 54354 or any other positive decimal integer is to find the largest power of 2 that is not larger than the number. This can be accomplished by repeatedly performing integer division by two on the number until the result is zero. This results in the loss of the original number so it's important to perform the division on a copy of the number. The count of the number of divisions is one greater than the highest power of two contained in the number.

Alternatively we could compare the original number to incrementing powers of two. This does not require a copy of the original number and is the method used in the following solution. In this solution the `while` loop causes the `power` variable to be incremented past the highest power of two in the number so `power` is reduced by two after the loop ends. Subtracting two is necessary because after the loop has found the power of two greater than the number, power is incremented by the postincrement operator once more as the loop ends.

Once the highest power of two less than the number to be converted has been identified, a second loop is begun. **This loop performs the opposite operation of the**

binary to decimal conversion shown previously. Instead of adding the values of each bit together to find the decimal equivalent of a binary number, the value of each bit is subtracted from the original number to find the bit pattern. This loop begins by dividing the original number, decimal, by the highest power of two. This will always result in a quotient of 1. The fraction is truncated in integer division. To store the 1 in the character array binary, 48 is added to 1 to convert the number 1 to the ASCII character 1. Then the power of two is subtracted from the original number.

If 54 is to be converted to binary, the highest power of two is 32. First, integer division is performed to determine whether the first bit is 0 or 1. For the first cycle this will always be 1 but for other cycles it could be a 0 or a 1. The first bit is stored in the first space in the binary array. Then 32 is subtracted from 54 leaving 22 and making 22 the new value of decimal. Before the loop begins its next cycle, power is decremented and counter, the index for the binary array, is incremented.

The last line of the loop places a space in the character array (ASCII 32) if power is evenly divisible by four. This separates the resulting binary number into nibbles (groups of four bits) to make the resulting binary number easier to read.

The plan developed to convert 54 into binary is generalized in the pseudocode.

Pseudocode

1. Begin
2. Declare variables.
3. Get the number to be converted from the user and store in decimal.
4. Determine the highest power of two that is less than the input number.
5. Initialize power to highest power of two that is less than the input number.
6. Begin conversion loop.
7. Divide decimal by two raised to power.
8. Store the integer quotient (1 or 0) in the binary character array.
9. If the integer result is 1, create new value for decimal equal to decimal -2^{power} raised to power.
10. If power is evenly divisible by four, add a space to the binary array to separate nibbles.
11. Decrement power.
12. Increment index for binary array.
13. Continue if power is greater than or equal to zero.
14. Display the result.
15. End

Flowchart

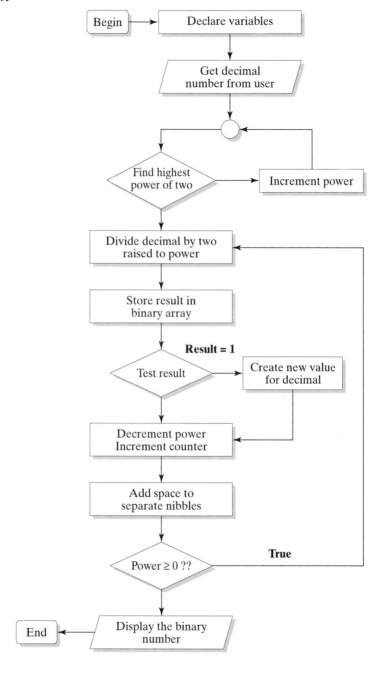

Implementation in C++

```
1    //Problem2_4.cpp
2    #include <iostream.h>
3    #include <math.h>
4
5    void main(void)
6    {
7        unsigned long decimal;
8        int counter = 0, power = 0;
9        char binary[100] = {0};
10
11       cout << "Enter the positive decimal integer to be converted to "
12           << "binary\n\n\tThe number must be less than 4.2 billion --> ";
13       cin >> decimal;                // Get number from user
14       while ( pow(2,power++) < static_cast<float>(decimal));
15                        // Find the power of 2 one greater
16                        //   than the decimal number
17       power = power - 2;      // Subtract 2 because of the post incrementing
18       do                 // of power at the end of the first loop
19       {
20          binary[counter++] = decimal / pow(2, power) + 48;
21                        // Determine whether binary[counter] is 1 or 0
22          if (binary[counter - 1] == '1')
23             decimal = decimal - pow(2, power);
24                        // If bit is 1 reduce decimal appropriately
25          if (power % 4 == 0)
26               binary[counter++] = 32;
27                        // Place space between nibbles
28       }while (--power >= 0);
29       cout << "\n\n\tBinary -->    " << binary << endl;
30   }
```

Many of the problem-solving rules listed in this text have been used in solving the binary conversion problem. The information given in the problem was listed. Additional information about weighted values was added to the list. The problem was worked backward to gain insight as to how the conversion could be accomplished. And a concrete example, the number 54, was explored before the general case as attacked.

The problem was also limited in scope before the pseudocode or the C++ code was written. The numbers to be converted were confined to the set of integers that would fit in an unsigned integer variable, namely, integers between zero and approximately 4.3 billion. The algorithm will not work for floating-point numbers such as 4.25. If negative numbers were included, decisions would have to be made as to whether the negative binary number would be expressed with a negative sign or would be expressed as a twos complement number. The latter option represents the method used for storing negative numbers in computer memory.

Two programming features should be noted on line 14. The first is the semicolon at the end of the `while` statement. Typically there is no punctuation here but when a semicolon is used it tells the compiler that the line beginning with `while` is the only line in the loop. This means there is no body of code that is repeated except the code within the parentheses, namely, the test condition and the addition of one to the value stored in the variable power.

```
14      while ( pow(2,power++) < static_cast<float>(decimal));
```

Power, which was initialized to zero, counts how many cycles of the loop are required before the power of two exceeds the value of decimal. After the first test condition is evaluated, power is incremented in preparation for the next cycle. When the power variable is sufficiently large, making the test condition fail, power is incremented once more before line 17 is executed. That is, the value of power is two greater than the power of two represented by the first bit in the equivalent binary number. Consequently, power must be reduced by two on line 17 before it can be used in the do loop that creates the binary number.

As the value of bits are determined, the counter variable places each bit in the correct place in the output character array. In the first cycle of the do loop the most significant bit is determined and, because counter equals zero, the ASCII value of the bit is placed in the first position of the binary array. If the value of the bit is one, then the value of decimal is appropriately reduced by line 23.

Lines 25 and 26 do not affect the logic of the program and are only used to format the binary number. Long strings if 1s and 0s are difficult to read. These lines cause spaces to be inserted into the binary number to divide it into nibbles (sets of four bits).

There is one more subtle feature to the program. Line 29 outputs the binary number as a string. For this to happen there must be a terminating NULL (ASCII zero) at the end of the string. The NULL could have been added to the next position in the binary array after the do loop terminated. However, this was not necessary because all positions in the array were set to zero when the array was declared on line 9. As each bit was added to the array, the NULL in its position was overwritten. After the final bit was added, the next position already held a NULL.

Output of C++ Program

```
Enter the positive decimal integer to be converted to binary

    The number must be less than 4.2 billion -->   54354

    Binary -->   1101 0100 0101 0010
```

Implementation in Visual Basic

```
1    Option Explicit
2    Private Sub cmdConvert_Click()
3        Dim binary(0 To 100) As Byte
4        Dim number As Long
5        Dim counter As Integer
6        Dim power As Integer
7        txtOutput.Text = ""
8        number = Val(txtInput.Text)
9        counter = 0            'Set to first position in binary array
```

```
10      power = -1              'Set so first test of 2^power = 1
11      Do
12          power = power + 1
13      Loop While (2 ^ power) <= number
14      power = power - 1
15      Do
16          binary(counter) = Int(number / 2 ^ power)
17          If binary(counter) = 1 Then
18              number = number - 2 ^ power
19          End If
20          counter = counter + 1
21          power = power - 1
22      Loop While power >= 0
23      For power = 0 To counter - 1
24          txtOutput = txtOutput & Trim(Str(binary(power)))
25          If ((counter - 1) - power) Mod 4 = 0 Then
26              txtOutput = txtOutput & " "
27          End If
28      Next power
29  End Sub
30
31  Private Sub cmdEnd_Click()
32      Unload frmProblem2_4
33  End Sub
34
35  Private Sub Form_Activate()
36      txtInput.SetFocus
37  End Sub
38
39  Private Sub Form_Load()
40      lblMessage.Caption = "Enter the decimal integer to be converted " & _
41          "to binary." & vbCrLf & "The number must be less " & _
42          "2.1 billion."
43  End Sub
44  Private Sub txtInput_GotFocus()
45      txtInput.Text = ""
46  End Sub
```

While the logic is the same in both the C++ and the Visual Basic programs, the implementation is slightly different due to differences in the languages. The most noticeable difference is the upper limit on values that can be entered by the user. Both languages use 32-bit-long integers, but only C++ allows unsigned longs that use all 32 bits to store the value of the variable. The signed longs of Visual Basic use 31 bits to store the magnitude of the number and the most significant bit to store the sign. Consequently, the upper limit for the user input is only half as large in Visual Basic.

Line 3 in which the character array binary is declared does not indicate that initial values for the elements of the array should be zero. Initialization to zero is performed automatically in Visual Basic.

After the do loop on lines 11 to 13 is complete, only one is subtracted from the value of power on line 14 compared to two that was subtracted in the C++ program. In C++ the postincrement operator incremented power one additional time after the test condition failed. When the test fails in Visual Basic, the loop ends and there is no extra incrementing.

The building of the binary output takes place on line 24. On this line individual bits are concatenated on to the previous output. Because Visual Basic adds a space before displaying strings, the `trim()` function is used to eliminate the unwanted spaces from the output.

Output of the Visual Basic Program

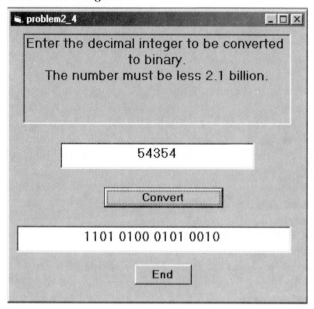

2.6   DAILY COMPOUNDED INTEREST

In many cases the logic required to solve a problem is not very difficult but implementing the logic entails an extremely large amount of work. Fortunately, we have computers to perform the manual labor but it is necessary for the designer of the solution to create a plan based on repeated operations. The key to designing looping operations is determining what operations are to be performed once (and are, therefore, outside of the loop) and which operations are performed many times (and are placed within the loop.)

PROBLEM 2.5   *Determine the value of a savings account for an unspecified initial principle, interest rate, and number of years interest is accrued. The interest is to be compounded daily and displayed yearly.*

Of course, there does exist a nice formula for this calculation. However, plugging numbers into a formula is merely the execution of logic developed by someone else. The purpose here is not to practice execution but to develop logic.

Initial Data: **1.** Principle, interest rate, and number of years supplied by the user.

2. The number of days interest is drawn on the account is the number of years multiplied by 365.

3. The daily interest rate is the annual rate divided by 365.

4. Each day the principle will be larger than the day before by the amount of interest earned the previous day.

Output: Display the principle at the end of each year and at the end of the period specified by the user.

Notice that a simplifying assumption has been made for this problem. The time for which an account accrues interest is generally specified as the number of days between two dates, not a number of years. Furthermore, no year really has 365 days. Any given year has 365 or 366 days depending on whether it is a leap year. There are ways to calculate the exact number of days between two dates but that is another problem in itself. In this case the use of 365 days in a year would be unsatisfactory for banks that require to-the-penny accuracy for their accounts. However, for the account holder looking to have an idea of what kind of return he or she can expect on $10,000 after 10 years, the program will serve.

The next step is to be clear what will be calculated once and what will be calculated many times. The number of days the account will draw interest and the daily interest rate should be calculated once before the repeated operations begin. Because interest is calculated daily, each day there is a new principle for the account. The number of days determines how many times the loop should repeat. The calculation of the interest and the addition of the interest to the principle occur every day and are, therefore, repeated operations and belong inside the loop.

The display for the principle at the end of each year is also a repeated operation and should be within the loop. However, during most days (cycles) the principle is not displayed. Only during cycles that are evenly divisible by 365 and represent the end of a year is the display routine called.

The logic of the problem involves the repeated use of the formula:

$$\text{Interest} = \text{Principle} \times \text{Rate} \times \text{Time}$$

The rate is the interest per day and the time is one day. Notice that the day unit cancels. If the units rule is ignored, it is easy to make the mistake of using an annual rate with a daily compounding, which leads to units of (dollar $\times$ days)/year. After the day's interest is calculated, it is added to the old principle to create a new principle to be used in the next day's calculations.

Pseudocode

1. Begin

2. Declare variables.

3. Get information from the user.

4. Calculate the number of days.

5. Calculate the daily interest rate.

6. Begin loop.

7. Calculate daily interest.

8.   Calculate daily principle.

9.   Display result at the end of each year and at the end of the loop.

10. End loop after the required number of days.

11. End

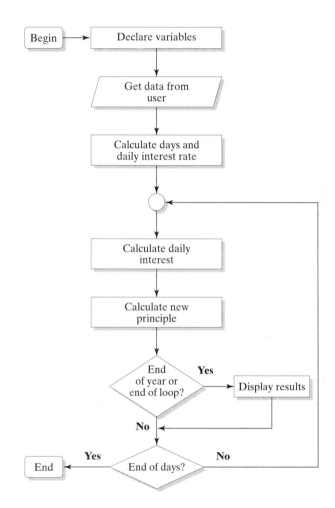

Solution Implemented in C++

```
1    //Problem2_5.cpp
2    #include <iostream.h>
3    #include <iomanip.h>        // for setw() function
4
5    void main(void)
6    {
7        double years, annual_rate, daily_rate, daily_interest, principle;
8        long days, counter = 1;
```

```
9
10        cout << "This program calculates the annual interest "
11           << "\n\tand principle for a savings account."
12           << "\n\nEnter the starting principle                $ " << flush;
13        cin >> principle;
14        cout << "\nEnter the annual interest rate as a percent   " << flush;
15        cin >> annual_rate;
16        cout << "\nEnter the number of years                   " << flush;
17        cin >> years;
18        cout.setf(ios::fixed|ios::showpoint);    //
19        cout.precision(2);
20        days = static_cast<long>(years * 365);   // number of days for loop
21        daily_rate = annual_rate / 100 / 365;   // daily rate expressed as a
22                                      // decimal rather than a percent
23        cout << "\n\n    Year            Principle\n" << flush;
24        do
25        {
26           daily_interest = daily_rate * principle;
27           principle += daily_interest;
28           if (counter % 365 == 0 || counter == days)
29              cout << setw(7) << counter / 365.00 << setw(20) << principle
30                 << endl;
31        }while (counter++ <= days);
32  }
```

In order to simplify the programming and to avoid getting bogged down in error checking, each of the problems in this text makes the assumption that the user will input reasonable numbers. This is not a very real-world scenario and users often hit inappropriate keys. The input "1234" can easily become "12f34" if fingers are left on the keyboard while numbers are entered by the numeric keypad. A well-written program should check for such irregularities in the input and prompt the user to reenter the data if an error is detected.

In the preceding program the presumption is that the user will enter the annual interest rate as a percent, e.g., 6.5 percent APR would be entered as 6.5. If the user instead enters .065, the program becomes wildly inaccurate. Line 21 makes the conversion from an annual percentage rate to decimal factor by dividing by 100 and then to a daily decimal factor by dividing again by 365.

After the `daily_interest` is calculated on line 26 by multiplying the `daily_rate` by the `principle`, a revised `principle` is created on line 27 by adding the `daily_interest` to the `principle`. It is worth reiterating the importance of using meaningful names for variables. An easy problem can be made much harder by using a, b, c, and d for variable names.

Output of C++ Program

```
This program calculates the annual interest
          and principle for a savings account.

Enter the starting principle               $ 10000
Enter the annual interest rate as a percent    6.3
Enter the number of years                    10.95
```

Year	Principle
1.00	10650.21
2.00	11342.70
3.00	12080.21
4.00	12865.68
5.00	13702.22
6.00	14593.15
7.00	15542.02
8.00	16552.57
9.00	17628.84
10.00	18775.09
10.95	19930.40

By compounding the interest daily the account value increases more rapidly than if the interest were calculated only once at the end of the year. At 6.3 percent the interest on $10,000 would be $630 dollars using this annual calculation scheme. Daily compounding results in an extra $20 at the end of the first year and the difference between the values calculated by the two methods grows each year. After 11 years, the value of the account has doubled using daily compounding. How long it would take to double the account value using the once-a-year method is an exercise left to the reader.

Solution Implemented in Visual Basic

```
1    Option Explicit
2    Private Sub cmdCalculate_Click()
3       msgTable.SetFocus
4    End Sub
5
6    Private Sub cmdEnd_Click()
7       Unload frmProblem2_5
8    End Sub
9
10   Private Sub cmdReset_Click()
11      lblRate.Caption = ""
12      lblYears.Caption = ""
13      txtPrinciple.Text = ""
14      txtYears.Text = ""
15      txtRate.Text = ""
16      msgTable.Rows = 1
17      txtPrinciple.SetFocus
18   End Sub
19
20   Private Sub Form_Activate()
21      txtPrinciple.SetFocus
22   End Sub
23
24   Private Sub Form_Load()
25      frmProblem2_5.Top = (Screen.Height - _
26                           frmProblem2_5.Height) / 3
27      frmProblem2_5.Left = (Screen.Width - _
28                           frmProblem2_5.Width) / 3
```

```
29      lblMessage.Caption = "This program calculates" & _
30          " the annual interest and principle for a " & _
31          "savings account."
32      lblPrinciple.Caption = "Enter the starting principle"
33  End Sub
34
35  Private Sub msgTable_GotFocus()
36      msgTable.Rows = Int(Val(txtYears.Text)) + 3
37      msgTable.FixedRows = 1
38      msgTable.ColWidth(0) = 2500
39      msgTable.ColWidth(1) = 2500
40      msgTable.Row = 0
41      msgTable.Col = 0
42      msgTable.Text = Format("Year", "@@@@@@@@@@@@@@@@@@@@")
43      msgTable.Col = 1
44      msgTable.Text = Format("Principle", _
45          "@@@@@@@@@@@@@@@@@@@@@@@@@@")
46      Dim days As Long
47      days = Val(txtYears.Text) * 365
48      Dim counter As Long
49      counter = 1
50      Dim daily_rate As Double
51      daily_rate = Val(txtRate.Text) / 100 / 365
52      Dim interest As Double
53      Dim principle As Double
54      principle = Val(txtPrinciple.Text)
55      Do While counter <= days
56          interest = daily_rate * principle
57          principle = principle + interest
58          If counter Mod 365 = 0 Or counter = days Then
59              msgTable.Row = counter \ 365 + 1
60              If counter = days And days Mod 365 <> 0 Then
61                  msgTable.Row = counter \ 365 + 2
62              End If
63              msgTable.Col = 0
64              msgTable.Text = Format(FormatNumber(counter / _
65                  365, 2), "@@@@@@@@@@@@@@@@@@@@")
66              msgTable.Col = 1
67              msgTable.Text = Format(FormatCurrency(principle,2), _
68                  "@@@@@@@@@@@@@@@@@@@@")
69          End If
70          counter = counter + 1
71      Loop
72  End Sub
73
74  Private Sub txtPrinciple_LostFocus()
75      lblRate.Caption = "Enter the interest rate"
76      txtRate.SetFocus
77  End Sub
```

```
78
79  Private Sub txtRate_LostFocus()
80      lblYears.Caption = "Enter the years"
81      txtYears.SetFocus
82  End Sub
83
84  Private Sub txtYears_LostFocus()
85      msgTable.SetFocus
86  End Sub
```

A great deal of the Visual Basic code in the preceding program is concerned with creating text boxes, control buttons, and output formatting. The core of the logic is contained in just a few lines of the code. Line 51 makes the crucial conversion from an annual percentage rate to a decimal representing the daily interest rate (daily_rate). Lines 56 and 57 perform the calculations for the daily_interest and the current principle. Most of the do loop that operates from lines 55 to 71 controls the formatting of the output into the proper lines and columns of the output table.

Output of Visual Basic Program

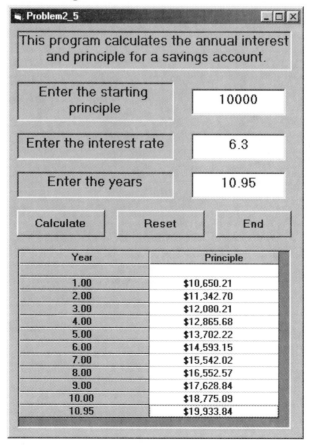

2.7 THE WALL PROBLEM

The summing of an infinite series of numbers can be a rather challenging mathematical operation. Even if the summation behaves nicely and converges to a definite answer rather than becoming infinite, finding the sum without performing an infinite number of additions can require uncommon mathematical talent.

Although computers are not able to perform an infinite number of calculations, they can perform very many calculations very quickly. In almost all cases performing very many calculations leads to a clear indication of the correct answer for an infinite sum even though it stops short of the certainty provided by an infinite number of additions.

Consider the paradox involved in walking to a wall that is 1 meter away. Before you can get to the wall, you have to get halfway to the wall, leaving half the distance. Next you have to travel half the remaining distance, leaving one quarter of the original distance to the wall. Again, you must travel half of the remaining distance before getting to the wall but at that point one eighth of the distance is left. No matter how many approaches to the wall are made there is always a distance equal to the last step that remains. Apparently it is impossible to ever reach the wall.

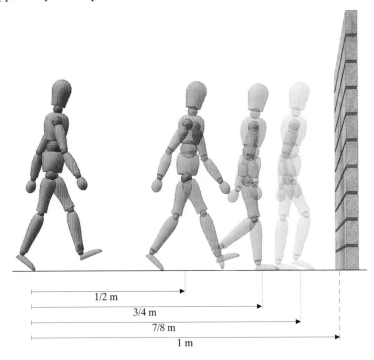

The sum of the distances traveled in meters is

$$\text{Distance} = \frac{1}{2} + \frac{1}{4} + \frac{1}{8} + \frac{1}{16} + \frac{1}{32} + \frac{1}{64} + \cdots$$

Expressed in summation notation, the equation collapses to

$$\text{Distance} = \sum_{n=1}^{\infty} \frac{1}{2^n}$$

While we know in our hearts that we can reach the wall and the distance traveled will be 1 meter, there is still that nagging little distance that can't be accounted for without summing an infinite number of terms. Even when the distance remaining becomes microscopic or subatomic, our sum leaves us short of the correct answer by a distance equal to the last step taken toward the wall.

On the other hand, we can ask how many terms of the sum would we have to add before we were quite sure that the infinite sum would equal 1? Would 100 terms do the job, or 1,000 terms, or 1,000,000? The answer is that it doesn't matter. With a computer doing the work we can command the addition of as many terms as is necessary to make us comfortable with the answer. Is a million terms added together sufficient to prove that we have found the correct sum? No, but it really doesn't matter. We're not mathematicians looking for numeric purity. We just want an answer we can be confident about.

This is one more form of limiting the problem. Rather than limiting the number of factors in play as we did in the falling ball problem, or limiting the domain to positive integers as we did in the binary conversion problem, here we limit the amount of time and effort we are willing to spend on the problem. Again we sacrifice a bit of mathematical purity for the sake of getting a reasonable answer to the problem.

PROBLEM 2.6   *Is it possible to walk to a wall?*

To solve the problem we'll limit the number of steps to the wall to 50. That will leave us short of the wall but the solution will likely be instructive. If we are satisfactorily close to the wall, the problem is solved. If not, the program can be adjusted to make many more steps toward the wall. It might also be worthwhile to consider how much time is required for each step toward the wall. To keep the example concrete we'll assume the walker begins 1 meter from the wall and is moving at a continuous pace of 1 meter per second.

Initial Data: **1.** The initial position is 1 meter from the wall.
　　　　　　　　2. Each step covers one half of the remaining distance to the wall.
　　　　　　　　3. Motion toward the wall is at the rate of 1 meter per second.
　　　　　　　　4. Fifty steps are made toward the wall.

Output:　　　Determine how close the walker is to the wall after 50 steps.

Rule 9   The Successive Approximation Rule
When an exact solution is too difficult to calculate, an approximate answer of arbitrary accuracy can often be found by adding terms that make a partial solution come ever closer to the true solution.

Since it is apparent that there is a repeated operation involved, namely, stepping toward the wall, the first task is to separate the actions to be performed once from the actions to be performed repeatedly. A running sum is involved to track the distance traveled. This implies that there must be a variable to store the sum and it must be initialized to zero. We also need a step variable that is defined and initialized outside the loop.

The loop must cycle 50 times representing 50 steps. For each step the step distance must be added to the sum variable and a new step size created that is one half of the previous step. Knowing exactly how many times the loop will cycle suggests the use of a `for` loop.

Pseudocode

   1. Begin

   2.   Declare variables.

   3.   Initialize the step size to 1 meter and the running sum to 0.

   4.   Message to the user and column headings.

   5.   Begin loop for 50 cycles.

   6.   Create the new step equal to half the previous step.

   7.   Add the step to the running sum.

   8.   Display step and sum for each cycle.

   9.   End loop.

  10. End

Flowchart

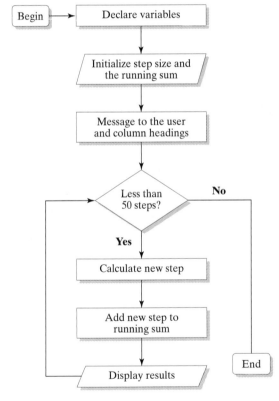

```
1    //  Problem 2.6 --  The Wall
2    #include <iomanip.h>
3    #include <iostream.h>
4
5    void main(void)
6    {
7        double step = 1, sum = 0;
8        int counter;
9        cout.precision(15);
```

```
10        cout.setf(ios::showpoint);
11        cout << "This program calculates the distance traveled toward a wall"
12             << "\n\tbeginning one meter from the wall and covering half the"
13             << "\n\tdistance to the wall with each step.\n" << endl;
14        cout << " Step        Step Distance         Total Distance\n  " << endl;
15        for (counter = 1; counter <= 50; counter++)
16        {
17            step /= 2;        // Reduce the size of the step
18                              //    to half of the previous step
19            sum += step;      // Generate a running sum of all steps
20            cout << setw(4) << counter << setw(23) << step
21                 << setw(24) << sum << endl;
22        }
23    }
```

While the logic for this problem is straightforward, there are two equally efficient methods for implementing the logic. In the preceding code the variable step was initialized to one but inside the loop step was divided by two, creating a value of one half before it was added to the running sum. The initial value for step is determined by the order of lines 17 and 19. If these lines are reversed, then step would need to be initialized to one half instead of one.

```
This program calculates the distance traveled toward a wall
        beginning one meter from the wall and covering half the
        distance to the wall with each step.
```

Step	Step Distance	Total Distance
1	0.500000000000000	0.500000000000000
2	0.250000000000000	0.750000000000000
3	0.125000000000000	0.875000000000000
4	0.0625000000000000	0.937500000000000
5	0.0312500000000000	0.968750000000000
6	0.0156250000000000	0.984375000000000
7	0.00781250000000000	0.992187500000000
8	0.00390625000000000	0.996093750000000
9	0.00195312500000000	0.998046875000000
10	0.000976562500000000	0.999023437500000
11	0.000488281250000000	0.999511718750000
12	0.000244140625000000	0.999755859375000
13	0.000122070312500000	0.999877929687500
⋮	⋮	⋮
40	9.09494701772928e-013	0.999999999999091
41	4.54747350886464e-013	0.999999999999545
42	2.27373675443232e-013	0.999999999999773
43	1.13686837721616e-013	0.999999999999886
44	5.68434188608080e-014	0.999999999999943
45	2.84217094304040e-014	0.999999999999972
46	1.42108547152020e-014	0.999999999999986
47	7.10542735760100e-015	0.999999999999993
48	3.55271367880050e-015	0.999999999999996
49	1.77635683940025e-015	0.999999999999998
50	8.88178419700125e-016	0.999999999999999

After the fiftieth step is taken, the distance remaining is less than 1 femtometer or approximately the width of a proton. Obviously at this point the term *close to the* wall has lost its meaning. For all practical purposes we reached the wall long before the fiftieth step.

There is one more piece of information that can be gleaned from the output of this program. If the walker is assumed to move at 1 meter per second, then the second column is the numeric value of the time for each step and the third column is the total elapsed time with both columns measured in seconds. As the distance for each step becomes vanishingly small, the time required for the step becomes equally small.

From this point it becomes apparent that not only will the distance become exactly 1 meter if an infinite number of steps are taken but also the time required for the infinite number of steps will be 1 second. Now the real resolution of the paradox becomes clear. The reason we can walk to a wall is because it is possible to make an infinite number of steps in a finite amount of time, if the time required for the steps becomes vanishingly small.

Solution Implemented in Visual Basic

```
1    Option Explicit
2    Private Sub cmdCalculate_Click()
3        Dim step As Double, sum As Double
4        Dim counter As Integer
5        step = 1
6        sum = 0                  'Initialize variables
7        For counter = 1 To 50
8            step = step / 2
9            sum = sum + step
10           msgTable.Row = counter + 1
11           msgTable.Col = 0
12           msgTable.Text = Format(counter, "@@@@")
13           msgTable.Col = 1
14           msgTable.Text = Format(FormatNumber(step, 15), _
15               "@@@@@@@@@@@@@@@@@@@@@@@@@")
16           msgTable.Col = 2
17           msgTable.Text = Format(FormatNumber(sum, _
18               15), "@@@@@@@@@@@@@@@@@@@@@@@@@")
19       Next counter
20   End Sub
21
22   Private Sub Form_Load()
23       lblMessage.Caption = "This program calculates the " & _
24           "distance traveled toward a wall beginning one meter" & _
25           " from the wall and coverring half the distance to the" & _
26           " wall with each step."
27       msgTable.Rows = 52
28       msgTable.ColWidth(0) = 600
29       msgTable.ColWidth(1) = 2500
30       msgTable.ColWidth(2) = 2500
31       msgTable.Row = 0
32       msgTable.Col = 0
33       msgTable.Text = "Step"
34       msgTable.Col = 1
35       msgTable.Text = "Step Distance"
36       msgTable.Col = 2
37       msgTable.Text = "Total Distance"
38   End Sub
```

The important code for implementing the logic of the solution is found on lines 7 to 9. Line 7 controls the required 50 cycles. Line 8 creates the steps and line 9 calculates the running sum. The rest of the program is formatting.

Output of Visual Basic Program

Step	Step Distance	Total Distance
1	0.500000000000000	0.500000000000000
2	0.250000000000000	0.750000000000000
3	0.125000000000000	0.875000000000000
4	0.062500000000000	0.937500000000000
5	0.031250000000000	0.968750000000000
6	0.015625000000000	0.984375000000000
7	0.007812500000000	0.992187500000000
8	0.003906250000000	0.996093750000000
9	0.001953125000000	0.998046875000000
10	0.000976562500000	0.999023437500000
11	0.000488281250000	0.999511718750000

This program calculates the distance traveled toward a wall beginning one meter from the wall and covering half the distance to the wall with each step.

2.8 SUPERFLY

Consider Superfly. Superfly came to earth with powers far beyond those of ordinary flies. Not only could Superfly fly at 120 miles per hour, Superfly was capable of instant acceleration and deceleration. Unfortunately, Superfly was not invulnerable and could be destroyed by being squashed between two speeding trains. Worse, Superfly was not very smart and his only response to an oncoming train was to fly away directly in front of the train.

One day two trains were speeding toward each other on the same track, each train traveling at 60 miles per hour. When the trains were exactly 1 mile apart, Superfly found himself sitting on the front of Train A and immediately took flight, flying directly toward Train B at 120 miles per hour. As soon as he touched Train B, Superfly turned around and flew back toward Train A. When he reached Train A, he again turned around and flew toward Train B. This ping-pong-ball flight plan continued until the collision of the trains and the demise of Superfly. The question is, "How far did Superfly fly between the trains?" Morbid as these calculations might be, the task was given to a programming student at a local community college so an accurate obituary could be written.

PROBLEM 2.7   *How long was Superfly's last flight?*

The student was faced with summing an infinite series with the terms of the series representing the distances of the laps flown between the trains. Because Superfly could travel at twice the speed of the trains, in any given amount of time he would travel twice as far. Since the trains were initially 1 mile apart, and Superfly traveled twice as far as Train B, Superfly would have traveled 2/3 of a mile compared to 1/3 of a mile for Train B before the first turnaround. Or listed more carefully:

Initial Data: **1.**   The trains begin 1 mile apart.

2.   The trains each travel 1 mile per minute.

3.   Superfly travels 2 miles per minute.

4.   In any given amount of time Superfly travels twice as far as either train.

5.   During the first lap, the Superfly distance plus the distance traveled by Train B must equal 1 mile.

6.   During the first lap, Superfly travels 2/3 mile and each train travels 1/3 mile based on the following algebra.

$$1 \text{ mile} = \text{Train B Distance} + \text{Superfly Distance}$$
$$1 \text{ mile} = \text{Train B Distance} + 2 \times \text{Train B Distance}$$
$$1 \text{ mile} = 3 \times \text{Train B Distance}$$
$$1/3 \text{ mile} = \text{Train B Distance}$$
$$2/3 \text{ mile} = \text{Superfly Distance}$$

7.   After the first lap, the distance between the trains has collapsed to 1/3 of a mile.

The first two laps can be represented graphically as:

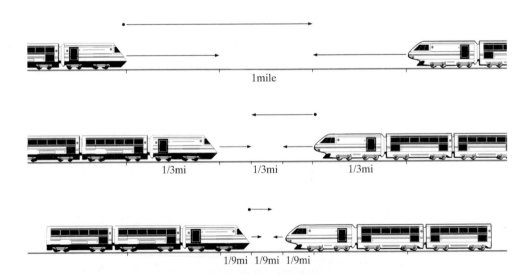

1mile

1/3mi   1/3mi   1/3mi

1/9mi 1/9mi 1/9mi

8. After the turnaround, Superfly faced the same situation except the initial distance was 1/3 of a mile instead of 1 mile. Regardless, Superfly raced toward Train A at 120 miles per hour, covering 2/3 of the 1/3 of a mile in the time that Train A covered 1/3 of the 1/3 of a mile. Train B also traveled 1/3 of the 1/3 of a mile, making the distance left after two trips equal to 1/9 of a mile.

9. Clearly, the distance left between the trains after each segment of Superfly's flight is 1/3 of the distance of the previous segment. The distance between the trains can be expressed as:

Distance 1 = 1 mile	or	$1/3^0$ mile
Distance 2 = 1/3 mile	or	$1/3^1$ mile
Distance 3 = 1/9 mile	or	$1/3^2$ mile
Distance 4 = 1/27 mile	or	$1/3^3$ mile
Distance 5 = 1/81 mile	or	$1/3^4$ mile

And so on.

10. It is also clear that each trip made by Superfly will be 2/3 of the distance between the trains. Superfly's travel log would show:

Trip 1	2/3 of Distance 1
Trip 2	2/3 of Distance 2
Trip 3	2/3 of Distance 3
Trip 4	2/3 of Distance 4
Trip 5	2/3 of Distance 5

And so on.

11. The total distance traveled by Superfly is then the sum of all of the preceding trips. This is more easily expressed mathematically by factoring out the 2/3 factor or,

$$\text{Superfly Distance} = \frac{2}{3}\,(\text{Distance 1} + \text{Distance 2} + \text{Distance 3} + \cdots)$$

Output: Determine the total distance flown by Superfly until the trains are one millionth of an inch apart.

For this problem the list of initial data is really an expanded list of information given in the problem plus information that represents logical conclusions based on the problem description. Item 4, that on each leg Superfly traveled twice as far as either train follows logically from the fact that Superfly traveled twice as fast.

Items 5 through 10 can be calculated or read directly from the graphical representation of the flight. Item 11 merely states that the total trip distance is equal to the sum of all the individual legs of the flight.

This still leaves the question of how many trips are required before we are sure we know the correct total distance. In this case it is better to rephrase the question. Rather than telling the computer to simulate a certain number of trips we can have the computer continue its calculations until the distance between the trains is so small that an additional trip would seem to no longer appreciably add to the total distance. This is an arbitrary number but remember we're not looking for ultimate truth. We only want an answer to the problem. Let's stop calculating when the distance between the trains is $1/1,000,000$ of an inch (roughly a couple hundred hydrogen atoms.) At this point Superfly is in grave trouble.

Pseudocode

1. Begin
2.   Declare and initialize variables.
3.   Declare terminal constant $= 1/1,000,000$ inch as a fraction of a mile.
4.   Message to the user.
5.   Set output parameters.
6.   Begin loop—Terminate when distance is less than $= 1/1,000,000$ inch
7.   Calculate running sum for Superfly distance.
8.   Display results.
9.   Calculate distance between trains for next cycle.
10.   End loop.
11. End

Flowchart

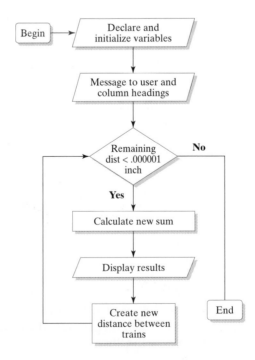

Solution Implemented in C++

```
1    // Problem2_7.cpp   -- Superfly
2    #include <iostream.h>
3    #include <iomanip.h>
4
5    void main(void)
6    {
7        int trip = 1;
8        double between_distance = 1, Superfly_distance = 0;
9        const double TERMINATION =  1E-6 / 5280 / 12;
10
11       cout << "This program calculates the distance flown by Superfly"
12           << "\n\ton his last flight\n" << endl;
13       cout << "  Trip     Distance between trains      Total Superfly"
14           << " distance\n" << endl;
15       cout.precision(14);
16       cout.setf(ios::fixed|ios::showpoint);
17       while (distance > TERMINATION / 3)
18       {
19           Superfly_distance += between_distance * 2/3.0;
20           cout << setw(5) << trip++ << setw(25) << distance
21               << setw(30) << Superfly_distance << endl;
22           between_distance /= 3.0;
23       }
24   }
```

Implementing the pseudocode as a computer program is straightforward, but there are a few items that deserve comment. Line 9 contains three important features.

```
9    const double TERMINATION =  1E-6 / 5280 / 12;
```

The TERMINATION distance for the problem is described as one millionth of an inch between the trains. First, the units rule is critical. All other distances in the problem are fractions of a mile. Either the distances calculated for Superfly and the trains must be converted to inches or the one millionth of an inch between the trains must be converted to a fraction of a mile. Including the units for line 9 yields:

$$\text{TERMINATION} = 1E{-}6 \text{ inches} \times \frac{1 \text{ mile}}{5{,}280 \text{ feet}} \times \frac{1 \text{ foot}}{12 \text{ inches}}$$

Inches and feet cancel leaving the desired units of miles for the TERMINATION distance.

Second, the variable TERMINATION is a constant. Placing the keyword const before the variable type ensures that the value of TERMINATION cannot be changed later in the program. By convention, constants are typically written in all uppercase letters in C++.

The third item to note is that numbers expressed in exponential notation are considered to be double precision floating-point numbers. If this were not the case, the division used to create the TERMINATION constant would involve integer division and the value of TERMINATION would be zero. Interpreting exponential notation as floating point numbers is not surprising since 1E-6 is equal to .000001. However, it would be important if the first factor were an integer value, e.g. 1E+2 equal to 100.

Superfly's distance (for the current leg of his flight) is calculated to be two thirds of the distance between the trains on line 19. There is a potential integer division problem in the fraction 2 / 3. Again, the value of two divided by three is zero if both numbers are integers. On line 19 two thirds has been expressed as 2 / 3.0 to make the denominator a floating-point number avoiding the integer division problem.

The use of 3.0 for the denominator was not necessary on line 22. In this case the numerator, `between_distance`, has been defined as a double-precision float; 3.0 was used only to make the floating-point division more apparent.

The precision was set to 14 decimal places on line 15 in order to achieve better than one millionth of an inch accuracy and still not exceed the limit of 15 significant figures for a double-precision float.

Output of C++ Program

```
This program calculates the distance flown by Superfly
   on his last flight


Trip      Distance between trains      Total Superfly distance

  1           1.00000000000000            0.66666666666667
  2           0.33333333333333            0.88888888888889
  3           0.11111111111111            0.96296296296296
  4           0.03703703703704            0.98765432098765
  5           0.01234567901235            0.99588477366255
  6           0.00411522633745            0.99862825788752
  7           0.00137174211248            0.99954275262917
  8           0.00045724737083            0.99984758420972
  9           0.00015241579028            0.99994919473657
 10           0.00005080526343            0.99998306491219
 11           0.00001693508781            0.99999435497073
 12           0.00000564502927            0.99999811832358
 13           0.00000188167642            0.99999937277453
 14           0.00000062722547            0.99999979092484
 15           0.00000020907516            0.99999993030828
 16           0.00000006969172            0.99999997676943
 17           0.00000002323057            0.99999999225648
 18           0.00000000774352            0.99999999741883
 19           0.00000000258117            0.99999999913961
 20           0.00000000086039            0.99999999971320
 21           0.00000000028680            0.99999999990440
 22           0.00000000009560            0.99999999996813
 23           0.00000000003187            0.99999999998938
 24           0.00000000001062            0.99999999999646
```

After running the program, there are a number of items in the output that are worth special notice. In just 24 trips the distance between the trains goes from 1 mile to a microscopic distance better measured in nanometers than miles. On the other hand, this should not be a surprise. The idea is to gain experience, insight, and intuition from each of these problems. The penny problem demonstrated how quickly numbers grow large for increasing powers of two. In the Superfly problem distances quickly become very small for increasing powers of one third.

The second item is the use of TERMINATION / 3 in the test condition of the while loop. One of the trickier points of using loops is making them run for the correct number of cycles. The final distance between the trains after 24 cycles is 1.062E-11 miles, which is less than the required 1.578E-11 miles (one millionth of an inch). In this case we don't want the loop to stop when the terminal distance is detected. We want the loop to cycle one more time after the terminal distance so the output routine will print the information of the terminal cycle. During that cycle, the distance will once more be divided by three. This makes the distance to be used for stopping the loop one third of the TERMINATION distance.

Solution Implemented in Visual Basic

```
1    Option Explicit
2    Private Sub cmdCalculate_Click()
3        Dim trip As Integer
4        Dim distance As Double, Superfly_distance As Double
5        Dim TERMINATION As Double
6        TERMINATION = 0.000001 / 5280 / 12
7        trip = 1
8        distance = 1
9        Superfly_distance = 0    'Initialize Variables
10       Do While distance > TERMINATION / 3
11           Superfly_distance = Superfly_distance + distance * 2 / 3
12           msgTable.Row = trip + 1
13           msgTable.Col = 0
14           msgTable.Text = Format(trip, "@@@@")
15           msgTable.Col = 1
16           msgTable.Text = Format(FormatNumber(distance, 14), _
17               "@@@@@@@@@@@@@@@@@@@@@@")
18           msgTable.Col = 2
19           msgTable.Text = Format(FormatNumber(Superfly_distance, _
20               14), "@@@@@@@@@@@@@@@@@@@@@@")
21           trip = trip + 1
22           distance = distance / 3    'Set trip and distance values
23                                      ' for the next cycle
24       Loop
25   End Sub
26
27   Private Sub Form_Load()
28       lblMessage.Caption = "This program calculates the " & _
29           "distance flown by Superfly on his last flight."
30       msgTable.Rows = 28
31       msgTable.ColWidth(0) = 600
32       msgTable.ColWidth(1) = 2500
33       msgTable.ColWidth(2) = 2500
```

```
34     msgTable.Row = 0
35     msgTable.Col = 0
36     msgTable.Text = "Trip"
37     msgTable.Col = 1
38     msgTable.Text = "Distance Between Trains"
39     msgTable.Col = 2
40     msgTable.Text = "Total Superfly Distance"
41  End Sub
```

Output of the Visual Basic Program

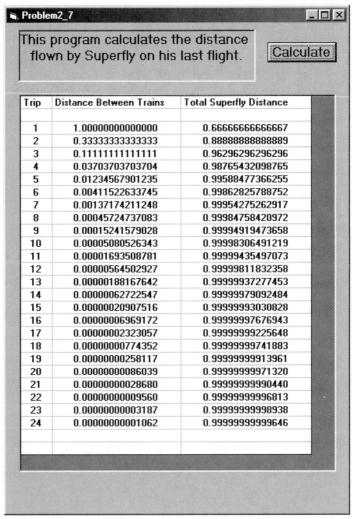

2.9   MACLAURIN SERIES EXPANSION

While this text is dedicated to creative thinking and methods for discovering novel methods for solving problems, that doesn't imply that every algorithm must be developed from first principles. Problem 1.4 developed the method for finding the area of a trapezoid. The idea was to avoid merely plugging numbers into the formula for the area of a trapezoid and to use reason to derive a method. In doing this we assumed that the formulas for the area of a rectangle and triangle were already known. No effort was made to discover formulas for the area of a rectangle or triangle. There are times when it is necessary to make use of the techniques discovered by others in order to progress to the solutions to more difficult problems.

Problems 2.6 and 2.7 (the walk to the wall and the Superfly problems) were examples of using repetiton to calculate the approximate sum of an infinite series. This type of summation has been used by mathematicians to determine the values for trigonometric and logarithmic functions. The MacLaurin Series expansion, an application of the more general Taylor series expansion, is an example of a more sophisticated use of an infinite series and provides an opportunity to examine the generation of factorials as a problem within the problem.

Understanding how the Taylor series expansion was developed is unnecessary. Its proof requires some knowledge of mathematics far beyond that required to use this text. Instead it should be considered a starting point from which new discoveries can be made. The Taylor series expansion is:

$$f(x) = f(h) + \sum_{n=1}^{\infty} \frac{(x-h)^n}{n!} f^n(h)$$

The MacLaurin series is the Taylor series expanded about zero, i.e., zero is substituted for h, or

$$f(x) = f(0) + \sum_{n=1}^{\infty} \frac{(x)^n}{n!} f^n(0)$$

If finding the sine of an angle is the objective, we can substitute $\sin(x)$ for $f(x)$. This causes the equation to greatly simplify. First, $f(0)$ becomes $\sin(0)$, which is equal to zero, and the first term merely drops out. Second, the final factor $f^n(0)$ or n^{th} derivative of $\sin(0)$ is quite easy to calculate.

$$f(x) = \sin(x) \qquad\qquad \sin(0) = 0$$
$$f'(x) = \cos(x) \qquad\qquad \cos(0) = 1$$
$$f''(x) = -\sin(x) \qquad\qquad -\sin(0) = 0$$
$$f'''(x) = -\cos(x) \qquad\qquad -\cos(x) = -1$$

Further derivatives merely repeat the pattern for the first four. This means that the summation resolves to:

$$\sin(x) = \sin(0) + \frac{x}{1!}(\cos(0)) + \frac{x^2}{2!}(-\sin(0)) + \frac{x^3}{3!}(\cos(0)) + \frac{x^4}{4!}(\sin(0))$$

$$+ \frac{x^5}{5!}(\cos(0)) + \frac{x^6}{6!}(-\sin(0)) + \frac{x^7}{7!}(-\cos(0)) + \cdots$$

or after substituting for the sine and cosine functions

$$\sin(x) = x - \frac{x^3}{3!} + \frac{x^5}{5!} - \frac{x^7}{7!} + \cdots$$

The end result of the mathematics is that after the manipulations have been made there is a simple-to-evaluate, or at least simple-to-program, method for calculating the sine function at any angle. The only proviso is that the angle must be in radians rather than the more common units, degrees. Since C++ has no built-in function for calculating factorials, that problem falls to the programmer. It also makes sense to create our own power function. If we assume access to the C++ pow() function, that would imply access to the math library where we could also find the sin() function, making the program unnecessary.

PROBLEM 2.8 *Calculate the value of the sine function for an arbitrary angle.*

Initial Data: **1.** MacLaurin series expansion for the sine function.

2. An angle chosen by the user.

3. Need for a factorial function.

4. Need for a power function.

5. The practiced ability from previous problems to sum a near infinite series to an arbitrary tolerance.

Output: The value of the sine of the angle entered by the user.

With the MacLaurin series expansion doing most of the work the problem solver is left with two questions: How can the factorials in the denominators of the fractions be calculated, and how many fractions in the infinite series have to be generated?

The definition of a factorial answers the first question. The factorial of an integer is that integer multiplied by all positive integers less than that number. For example,

$$7! = 7 * 6 * 5 * 4 * 3 * 2 * 1$$

Of course, the final multiplication by one is unnecessary. The second question depends on how much accuracy we need for the problem that requires the calculation of the sine function. Since there is no larger problem making use of the sine value that is being calculated, the accuracy is arbitrary. For our purposes we can decide that when the next fraction in the series is smaller than one billionth, it is no longer worth continuing the summation.

Pseudocode

1. Begin
2.   Declare variables.
3.   Message to user.
4.   Begin loop for continuously running program.
5.   Get angle from user.
6.   Initialize variables.
7.   Begin calculation loop.
8.   Get numerator i.e., run power function.
9.   Get denominator i.e., run factorial function.

10.   Calculate next fraction in summation.

11.   Generate running sum for the sine value.

12.   Update sign and counter variables.

13.   End calculation loop when fraction is less than one billionth.

14.   Display output.

15.   Calculate sine for another angle ?

16.   If "no", end loop.

17. End

Flowchart

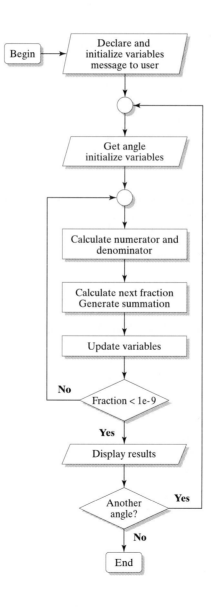

Solution Implemented in C++

```
1    // Problem 2.8
2    #include <iostream.h>
3    #include <conio.h>
4
5    double factorial(int number)
6    {
7        int  x;
8        double y = 1;
9        for (x = number; x > 1; x--)
10       y *= x;
11       return ( y );
12   }
13
14   double power(double in, int count)
15   {
16       int x;
17       double output = in;
18       for (x = 1; x < count; x++)
19           output *= in;
20       return output;
21   }
22
23   int main(void)
24   {
25       double input, output, radians, sign, fraction;
26       int counter;
27       char ch;
28       cout.precision (9);
29       cout << "This program calculates sine values. " << endl << endl;
30       do
31       {
32           cout << "\nEnter the angle in degrees . . . " << flush;
33           cin >> input;
34           radians = input * 3.14159265358979 / 180;    //convert to radians
35           output = 0, sign = 1.0, counter = 1;    //initialize variables
36           do
37           {
38               fraction = power(radians,counter) / factorial(counter);
39               output += sign * fraction;
40               sign *= -1.0;
41               counter += 2;
42               if (fraction < 0)
43                   fraction = -fraction
44           }while (fraction > 1e-9);        //test for < one billionth
45           cout << "The sin of " << input << " degrees is " << output << endl;
47           cout << "\n\nConvert another angle (y/n)?" << flush;
48           cin >> ch;
49       }while (ch != 'n');
50       cout << endl << endl;
51       return(0);
52   }
```

The generation of each new fraction to be added in the summation is greatly simplified if both the numerator and the denominator are created in separate functions and the result returned to line 38 where the term `fraction` is assigned its value.

The `power` function requires information about the angle to be raised to a power and the power to which `radians` will be raised. Inside the `power` function the value of `output` is initialized to the incoming angle value, `in`, which gets its value from `radians`. In order to return the correct value for `output` it is critical that the loop cycle for the correct number of times. For example, to raise a number to the fifth power, five factors of the number must be generated. Since `output` was initialized to `in`, `output` had one factor of `in` before the loop began. This means that the loop should run one less time than `counter`. An alternative would have been to initialize output to one and change the test condition to x less than **or equal** to `counter`.

The `factorial` function consists of a down-counting loop that begins with the value of `counter` from `main()` and multiplies that value by all smaller positive integers. Notice that the test condition stops the loop before multiplication by one. Multiplication by one would not change the final value for `y` and processing time for one cycle of the loop was saved.

Lines 39 and 40 use the `sign` variable to make the sign change that occurs in each subsequent term in the MacLaurin series. Line 40 switches the sign of `sign` and line 39 makes `sign` a factor in each term of the summation.

```
39              output += sign * fraction;

40              sign *= -1.0;
```

Because the sine of zero is zero, all even-numbered terms in the MacLaurin summation evaluate to zero and can be eliminated from the running sum. This is the reason the denominators for the fractions are 1!, 3!, 5!, 7!, and so on. Since `counter` is used as the base of the factorial, `counter` must increment by two in each cycle.

One subtle feature of the factorial function is the return of the double-precision variable. Even though the number passed to the function is an integer and the calculated value of the factorial is also an integer, it is necessary to make the variable holding the value of the factorial a double because of the size of the factorial. Factorials become large quickly and 13! exceeds the value that can be stored in an integer.

One of the nice features of the MacLaurin series is that it correctly calculates values for the sine function in all quadrants.

Output of the C++ Program

```
This program calculates sine values.

Enter the angle in degrees . . . 45
The sin of 45 degrees is 0.707106781


Convert another angle (y/n)?y


Enter the angle in degrees . . . 135
The sin of 135 degrees is 0.707106781
```

Convert another angle (y/n)?y

Enter the angle in degrees . . . 225
The sin of 225 degrees is -0.707106781

Convert another angle (y/n)?y

Enter the angle in degrees . . . -45
The sin of -45 degrees is -0.707106781

Convert another angle (y/n)?n

Solution Implemented in Visual Basic

```
1    Private Sub cmdCalculate_Click()
2        Dim angle As Double, radians As Double
3        Dim fraction As Double, output As Double
4        Dim counter As Integer, sign As Integer
5        counter = 1
6        sign = 1
7        output = 0
8        angle = Val(txtInput.Text)
9        radians = angle * 3.14159265358979 / 180
10       Do
11           fraction = power(radians, counter) / factorial(counter)
12           output = output + sign * fraction
13           sign = sign * -1
14           counter = counter + 2
15           If fraction < 0 Then
16               fraction = -fraction
17           End If
18       Loop While (fraction > 0.000000001)
19       txtOutput.Text = Format(output, ".00000000")
20   End Sub
21
22   Private Sub cmdEnd_Click()
23       Unload frmProblem2_8
24   End Sub
25
26   Private Sub cmdReset_Click()
27       txtInput.Text = ""
28       txtOutput.Text = ""
29       txtInput.SetFocus
30   End Sub
31
32   Private Sub Form_Load()
```

```
33        lblMessage.Caption = "This program calculates the " & _
34            "value of the sine function -- Enter an angle"
35   End Sub
36   Private Sub Form_Activate()
37        txtInput.SetFocus
38   End Sub
39   Private Function power(ByVal number As Double, ByVal count As Integer)
40        Dim x As Integer
41        Dim pow As Double
42        pow = 1
43        For x = 1 To count
44            pow = pow * number
45        Next x
46        power = pow
47   End Function
48   Private Function factorial(ByVal number As Integer)
49        Dim x As Integer
50        Dim y As Double
51        y = 1#
52        For x = number To 1 Step -1
53          y = y * x
54        Next x
55        factorial = y
56   End Function
```

Line 11 generates each term in the MacLaurin series. The code for generating the term is simplified by the use of the power() and factorial() functions. These functions are declared to be functions, rather than procedures, on lines 39 and 48 in order to re-turn values to be used in creating the terms for the series. The summing of the terms is accomplished on line 12.

The alternating of the positive and negative terms is handled by multiplying sign by negative one on each cycle. After each term is added to the running sum, line 13 changes the sign for the next term that is generated. Line 14 adds two to the counter on each cycle ensuring that only odd values are used for the power in the numerator and for the factorial in the denominator.

Output of the Visual Basic Program

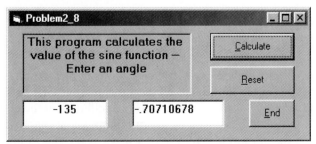

C H A P T E R   3

Zeroing in on Solutions

3.1   STRATEGIC GUESSING

The idea of zeroing in on a solution was introduced in the previous chapter in the Wall and the Superfly problems. Zeroing in on a solution means repeating some operation that will either lead us to the solution or at least bring us close enough to the solution that for all practical purposes can be accepted as correct. In Problem 2.7, the Superfly problem, we never did find out exactly how far Superfly actually flew in the time before his demise. When we added up all the trips he made from the beginning of his flight until the trains were just atomic diameters apart, we found a number that was so close to one mile that we could be confident that one mile was the answer to the problem. There was no proof that the answer is one mile, but there is good reason to be confident that one mile is correct.

The Superfly and the Wall problems allowed us to zero in on a solution by adding to a running sum ever smaller fractional terms. With each additional term the result became more accurate, that is, closer to the true answer. The idea of successively approximating solutions that become accurate to any desired tolerance can be expanded beyond the realm of evaluating an infinite sum. In Problem 3.1 we will use successive approximation to find the value of the square root of a number merely by guessing at the answer.

This is not as arbitrary as it may seem. For strategic guessing to work we must be able to check the quality of each guess so that a new guess can be made that will be even better than the previous guess. By repeatedly refining the guess we expect to be able to guess arbitrarily close to the true answer.

Despite never finding an exact answer there are many problems for which we can find an answer that is as close to correct as we care to be or need to be. In these cases the accuracy of our answer is only limited by how long we choose to work on the problem. With a computer making the calculations quickly, accurately, and tirelessly, this is usually not much of a limit.

We allowed Superfly to continue his trips until the trains were one millionth of an inch apart but one millionth of an inch was chosen arbitrarily. We could have continued the simulation until the trains were only one millionth of the diameter of a proton apart, if such a value has any meaning when talking about macroscopic objects like trains. Even then we still would not have an exact answer and would remain no more or less confident that the total flight distance was one mile.

3.2   CALCULATING SQUARE ROOTS

While there is an arithmetic algorithm for calculating square roots (and cube roots for that matter), the process is tedious and generally unknown. Today, calculating square roots is not a process at all but has been reduced to a button push on a calculator. Since there is nothing instructive about pushing a button, we'll apply the technique of strategic guessing to discovering the square root of a number chosen by the user. The user will be limited to numbers greater than positive one. In Chapter 7 we'll expand on this program to cover all real numbers.

Strategic guessing is applied in the following three steps:

Rule 10   Strategic Guessing Rule

1. Make a reasonable initial guess.
2. Check the accuracy of the guess.
3. Repeatedly refine the guess until the desired accuracy is achieved.

In calculating the square root of a number an initial guess of one half of the number is a reasonable guess. Clearly, the square root cannot be larger than the original number for numbers greater than one. Similarly, the square root cannot be negative. From this halfway value we can create an adjustment value that is one half of the guess. For clarity we'll apply Rule 6 regarding the use of concrete examples. We determine the square root of 200 by following the preceding three steps:

1. Set the initial guess to 100 or half of 200 and make the adjustment to 50 or half of the initial guess.

2. By multiplying the guess times itself we can check the accuracy of the guess. In this case 10,000 is too high so the adjustment is subtracted from the guess to create a new guess of 50. Notice it is important to also create a new adjustment for the next cycle. The new adjustment should be half of the old adjustment or 25. Each new adjustment is dependent on the previous adjustment and after the initial setting is unrelated to the guess.

3. The process is continued as long as necessary. Notice that while the initial guesses are too high a point will be reached when the guess squared is lower than the target number and the adjustment value will have to be added to the old guess to create the new guess. When the absolute value of the difference between the target number and the guess squared is less than the tolerance entered by the user, the problem is finished. Keep in mind the final guess is not the true square root of 200 but it is arbitrarily close to the true answer.

It should be pointed out that the term *true answer* is in this case a bit misleading. The square root for many numbers is an irrational number, that is, one that cannot be displayed as the ratio of two integers. Irrational numbers cannot be written with a finite number of decimals or even as a repeating decimal. While the square root of nine can be written as three, the square root of two can only be accurately written as $\sqrt{2}$. The calculator provided answer of 1.414213562 is only accurate to nine decimal places and does not represent a "true" solution in the sense that it is mathematically exact. In the real world a number more accurate than we can possibly measure is accurate enough.

What constitutes a reasonable initial guess deserves some consideration. By setting the initial guess to half of the user input and the initial adjustment to half of the initial guess, we effectively search all of the numbers from one to the target number for the square root value. This type of searching for a solution is sometimes called a binary tree because it repeatedly divides the search domain by two. In each cycle the range of possible solutions to the problem is reduced by half. This process is similar to the reduction of the distance between the two trains in the Superfly problem except the range is reduced by one half rather than one third. Just as the distance between the trains became small quickly, the range of possible values for the square root also shrinks rapidly.

PROBLEM 3.1   *Find the square root of a number greater than one.*

   Initial Data: A number supplied by the user.

   Output: The square root of the number supplied.

Pseudocode Solution

1. Begin
2.   Declare and initialize variables.
3.   Prompt user for input.
4.   Set guess and adjustment.
5.   Begin loop.
6.   Generate the error value.
7.   Display cycle number, guess, and error.
8.   Make appropriate adjustment to guess.
9.   Make appropriate adjustment to adjust.
10.   End loop if absolute value of error is less than required tolerance.
11. End

Flowchart

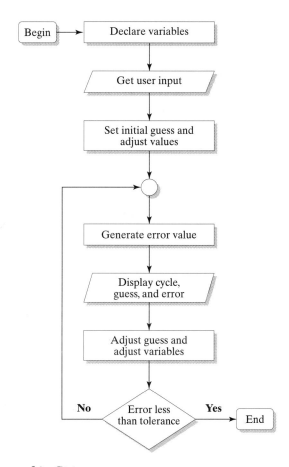

Solution Implemented in C++

```
1    //    Problem3_1.cpp
2    #include <iostream.h>
3    #include <iomanip.h>
4    #include <conio.h>
5    #include <math.h>
6
7    void main(void)
8    {
9        double input, guess, tolerance, adjustment, error;
10       int counter = 1;
11
```

```
12     cout << "This program calculates the square root of any number greater"
13         << "\n\tthan 1 \n\n\t\tEnter a number . . ";
14     cin >> input;
15     cout << "\n\tEnter the tolerance . .   ";
16     cin >> tolerance;                    //  Get user input
17     cout.precision(12);
18     cout << "\n" << endl;
19     cout.setf(ios::fixed|ios::showpoint); //  Set format and precision
20     guess = .5 * input;                  //  Initialize first guess
21     adjustment = .5 * guess;             //     and first adjustment
22     do
23     {
24         error = input - guess * guess;     //  Calculate error using
25         cout << "Guess " << setw(3) << counter << " is " << setw(18)
26             << guess << "  with an error of "
27             << setw(18) << error << endl;  //  Display current cycle number
28                                            //     guess and error
29                                            //     current guess
30         if ( error < 0)
31             guess -= adjustment;
32         else
33             guess += adjustment;           //  Generate new guess based
34                                            //     on the sign of "error"
35         adjustment *= .5;                  //  New adjustment
36         counter++;
37     }while (fabs(error) > tolerance);      //  Continue until absolute
38     getch();                               //     value of error is less
39 }                                          //       than tolerance
```

Line 24 is crucial to understanding the implementation of the algorithm. If the value for error is positive, that means input must be larger than guess squared. This implies that the guess value is not large enough and the adjustment should be added to guess, as implemented on line 33. If the value for error is negative, then input is smaller than guess squared and guess must be made smaller by subtracting the value of adjustment. Regardless of whether the adjustment is added or subtracted the adjustment itself must be made smaller by half, line 35, for the next cycle. As the value of adjustment gets smaller, the value of guess becomes closer and closer to the square root of the input.

Normally there would be no reason to print out all the intermediate guesses and how close their squares are to the target number. The only value of interest would be the final guess that determines the square root to the required accuracy. The final guess would be displayed after the loop had ended or possibly not displayed but used in some further calculation. In this case the purpose was to illustrate the process that led to the answer and, consequently, the display code was placed within the loop. Notice that the guesses became smaller until guess 4, which was 12.5. The adjustment at this point is not shown but would be 6.25. Because 12.5 squared is less than 200, the adjustment was added to the guess, making the fifth guess 18.25. Because 18.25 squared is larger than 200, the adjustment (3.125) was subtracted. This process was continued until the error was less than the user-supplied tolerance of .0000001.

Output of the C++ Program

```
This program calculates the square root of any number greater
        than 1

        Enter a number . .         200
        Enter the tolerance . .    1e-7
```

```
Guess    1 is    100.000000000000  with an error of -9800.000000000000
Guess    2 is     50.000000000000  with an error of -2300.000000000000
Guess    3 is     25.000000000000  with an error of  -425.000000000000
Guess    4 is     12.500000000000  with an error of    43.750000000000
Guess    5 is     18.750000000000  with an error of  -151.562500000000
Guess    6 is     15.625000000000  with an error of   -44.140625000000
Guess    7 is     14.062500000000  with an error of     2.246093750000
Guess    8 is     14.843750000000  with an error of   -20.336914062500
Guess    9 is     14.453125000000  with an error of    -8.892822265625
Guess   10 is     14.257812500000  with an error of    -3.285217285156
Guess   11 is     14.160156250000  with an error of    -0.510025024414
Guess   12 is     14.111328125000  with an error of     0.870418548584
Guess   13 is     14.135742187500  with an error of     0.180792808533
Guess   14 is     14.147949218750  with an error of    -0.164467096329
Guess   15 is     14.141845703125  with an error of     0.008200109005
Guess   16 is     14.144897460938  with an error of    -0.078124180436
Guess   17 is     14.143371582031  with an error of    -0.034959707409
Guess   18 is     14.142608642578  with an error of    -0.013379217125
Guess   19 is     14.142227172852  with an error of    -0.002589408541
Guess   20 is     14.142036437988  with an error of     0.002805386612
Guess   21 is     14.142131805420  with an error of     0.000107998130
Guess   22 is     14.142179489136  with an error of    -0.001240702932
Guess   23 is     14.142155647278  with an error of    -0.000566351832
Guess   24 is     14.142143726349  with an error of    -0.000229176709
Guess   25 is     14.142137765884  with an error of    -0.000060589254
Guess   26 is     14.142134785652  with an error of     0.000023704447
Guess   27 is     14.142136275768  with an error of    -0.000018442401
Guess   28 is     14.142135530710  with an error of     0.000002631024
Guess   29 is     14.142135903239  with an error of    -0.000007905689
Guess   30 is     14.142135716975  with an error of    -0.000002637332
Guess   31 is     14.142135623842  with an error of    -0.000000003154
```

There are two more important features of the program. First, the test for loop termination on line 37 involves a floating-point absolute value function.

```
37        }while (fabs(error) > tolerance);
```

This is necessary to prevent a negative value for the error from terminating the loop. Keep in mind that −5 is less than .00000001. The second item is the meaning of the error variable. Error is not the difference between the guess and the true square root. That would be impossible to calculate because the square root is unknown. If we already knew the square root of the number, there would be no reason for writing the program. Instead the error is the difference between the guess squared and the input number provided by the user.

Solution Implemented in Visual Basic

```
1   Option Explicit
2   Private Sub cmdCalculate_Click()
3      Dim number As Double, guess As Double, error As Double
4      Dim tolerance As Double, adjustment As Double
5      Dim counter As Integer
6      number = txtNumber.Text
7      tolerance = txtTolerance.Text
8      guess = 0.5 * number
9      adjustment = 0.5 * guess
10     counter = 1
11     msgTable.FixedRows = 8
12     msgTable.FixedCols = 1
13     Do
14        error = number - guess * guess
15        msgTable.Row = counter + 1
16        msgTable.Col = 0
17        msgTable.Text = Format(counter, "@@@@")
18        msgTable.Col = 1
19        msgTable.Text = Format(guess, "@@@@@@@@@@@@@@@@@@")
20        msgTable.Col = 2
21        msgTable.Text = Format(error, "@@@@@@@@@@@@@@@@@@")
22        If error < 0 Then
23           guess = guess - adjustment
24        Else
25           guess = guess + adjustment
26        End If
27        adjustment = adjustment * 0.5
28        counter = counter + 1
29     Loop While Abs(error) > tolerance
30  End Sub
31
32  Private Sub cmdEnd_Click()
33     Unload frmProblem3_1
34  End Sub
35
36  Private Sub Form_Load()
37     lblMessage.Caption = "This program generates the square " & _
38        " of any number less than one."
39     msgTable.Rows = 50
40     msgTable.ColWidth(0) = 800
41     msgTable.ColWidth(1) = 2500
42     msgTable.ColWidth(2) = 2500
43     msgTable.Row = 0
44     msgTable.Col = 0
45     msgTable.Text = "Cycle"
46     msgTable.Col = 1
47     msgTable.Text = "Guess"
48     msgTable.Col = 2
49     msgTable.Text = "Error"
50  End Sub
```

As in the C++ program `guess` and `adjustment` receive their initial values outside of the loop, lines 8 and 9. `Counter` is initialized to 1 and used to count the cycles of the do loop and the number of guesses that have been made.

Output of the Visual Basic Program

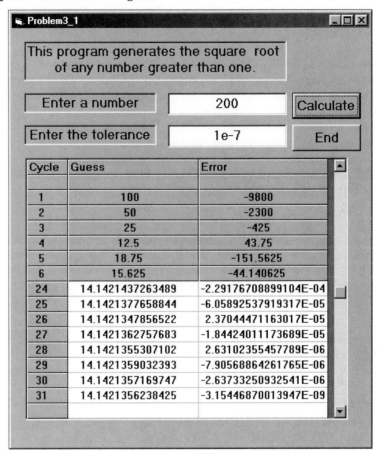

3.3   IMPROVED STRATEGIC GUESSING—NEWTON-RAPHSON METHOD

One fantastic advantage of using computers is the reliable computational power that these devices make available. We can often use a little cleverness and the at-hand computational muscle to derive answers to questions that are mathematically beyond our abilities.

The programs written for the previous section provide square root values to a greater accuracy than we will likely ever need in just over 30 iterations of our guessing algorithm. While the algorithm is effective, it is not terribly efficient. On the other hand, with a computer that makes millions of floating-point operations per second efficiency is often irrelevant. A program that provides an answer in one tenth of a second is just as instantaneous, from a human's point of view, as a program that requires only one millionth of a second.

However, efficiency is not always irrelevant. Some procedures require so many calculations that even high-level computers are taxed by the amount of work to be done. Rotating a model in three-space and weather modeling usually require parallel processing or supercomputers. By bringing enough computer power to bear even 48-bit encryption using the Data Encryption Standard has been broken. While these tasks are beyond the scope of this book, the advantages of adding a more efficient algorithm to computer power can be illustrated by reexamining the square root problem.

Before the era of the computer when calculations were done by hand, cleverness held a higher priority. Performing by hand the series of 31 calculations involved in calculating the square root of 200 that the computer made in a fraction of a second would likely make a mathematician change his profession. Or, in the case of Isaac Newton, at least search for a more efficient method of guessing. No book on problem solving would be complete without some discussion of the Newton-Raphson method.

The **Newton-Raphson method** is a general successive approximation algorithm that guesses at the solutions to problems. This method makes its guesses in a far more efficient manner than the algorithm used in the square root problem and it is applicable to a wider range of problems.

The mathematical expression for the Newton-Raphson Method is:

$$x_{n+1} = x_n - \frac{f(x_n)}{f'(x_n)}$$

The meaning of the equation is that the next guess (x_{n+1}) is equal to the previous guess (x_n) minus the value of the equation evaluated at the previous guess divided by the first derivative evaluated at the previous guess.

The implication is that to use the method we need to express the problem as a mathematical equation. In order to find the square root of a number, it's necessary to find the value of x that satisfies the equation

$$\text{Input} = x^2$$

where input is the user-supplied number and x is the square root. A little algebra is required to change this equation into a form that is ready for the Newton-Raphson method.

$$0 = x^2 - \text{Input} \ \text{ or}$$
$$f(x) = x^2 - \text{Input} \ \text{ and}$$
$$f'(x) = 2x$$

Because input is a constant, the first derivative of $f(x) = x^2$ is merely $2x$. However, the method requires both the equation and its derivative to be evaluated at a point, namely, x_n. In our case that point is the guess for the square root of input. With that in mind the equation

$$x_{n+1} = x_n - \frac{f(x_n)}{f'(x_n)}$$

becomes

$$new\_guess = guess - \frac{f(guess)}{f'(guess)}$$

Substituting the equations for the function notation gives

$$new\_guess = guess - \frac{guess^2 - input}{2 \times guess}$$

A little more algebra produces

$$new\_guess = \frac{2 \times guess^2}{2 \times guess} - \frac{guess^2 - input}{2 \times guess}$$

$$new\_guess = \frac{guess^2 + input}{2 \times guess}$$

$$new\_guess = .5\left(guess + \frac{input}{guess}\right)$$

This final equation can be used in the square root problem in place of adding or subtracting the adjustment.

PROBLEM 3.2   *Find the square root of a positive number using the Newton-Raphson method.*

The pseudocode is identical to the code for the previous problem except that there is no longer any need for step 9. The adjustment, larger or smaller, is embedded in the equation for creating the new guess.

Pseudocode Solution

1. Begin
2. Declare and initialize variables.
3. Prompt user for input.
4. Set guess and adjustment.
5. Begin loop.
6. Generate the error value.
7. Display cycle number, guess, and error.
8. Make appropriate adjustment to guess.
9. Make appropriate adjustment to adjust.
10. End loop if absolute value of error is less than required tolerance.
11. End

Solution Implemented in C++

```
1   //   Problem3_2.cpp
2   #include <iostream.h>
3   #include <iomanip.h>
```

```
4    #include <conio.h>
5    #include <math.h>
6
7    void main(void)
8    {
9        double input, guess, tolerance, error;
10       int counter = 1;
11
12       cout << "This program calculates the square root of any number"
13           << "greater\n\tthan zero \n\n\tEnter a number . . ";
14       cin >> input;
15       cout << "\tEnter the tolerance . .   ";
16       cin >> tolerance;                        //  Get user input
17       cout << setprecision(12) << endl;
18       cout.setf(ios::fixed|ios::showpoint);    //  Set format and precision
19       guess = .5 * input;
20       do
21       {
22           error = input - guess * guess;
23           cout << "Guess " << setw(3) << counter << " is " << setw(18)
24               << guess << "  with an error of "
25               << setw(18) << error << endl;
26           guess = .5 * ( guess + input / guess);//  Newton-Raphson guess
27           counter++;
28       }while (fabs(error) > tolerance);        //  Continue until absolute
29       getch();                                 //      value of error is less
30   }                                            //      than tolerance
```

The only substantive difference between this code and the code written for Problem 3.1 is the substitution of line 26 for the calculations involving the adjustment variable. The effective difference between the two methods is apparent in the output.

Output of the C++ Program

```
This program calculates the square root of any number greater
        than zero

        Enter a number . .      200
        Enter the tolerance . .      1e-7

Guess   1 is    100.000000000000  with an error of -9800.000000000000
Guess   2 is     51.000000000000  with an error of -2401.000000000000
Guess   3 is     27.460784313725  with an error of  -554.094675124952
Guess   4 is     17.371948743796  with an error of  -101.784603157075
Guess   5 is     14.442380948662  with an error of     -8.582367466284
Guess   6 is     14.145256551487  with an error of     -0.088282907397
Guess   7 is     14.142135968023  with an error of     -0.000009738041
Guess   8 is     14.142135623731  with an error of     -0.000000000000
```

Clearly, the Newton-Raphson method collapses to a solution of the required accuracy far more quickly than the binary tree method used in Problem 3.1. There is also a less obvious benefit. Creating the guess using

$$new\_guess = .5\left(guess + \frac{imput}{guess} \right)$$

eliminates a problem in calculating the square root of fractions between zero and one. The problem shows up in the first method because the square root of a number between zero and one is larger, rather than smaller, than the input number. This difficulty will be addressed in Chapter 7 but does not exist using the Newton-Raphson method. Running the Newton-Raphson program to determine the value of the square root of 0.9 yields:

```
This program calculates the square root of any number greater
      than zero


            Enter a number . .     .9
            Enter the tolerance . .     1e-7


Guess   1 is     0.450000000000  with an error of     0.697500000000
Guess   2 is     1.225000000000  with an error of    -0.600625000000
Guess   3 is     0.979846938776  with an error of    -0.060100023428
Guess   4 is     0.949178871627  with an error of    -0.000940530343
Guess   5 is     0.948683427422  with an error of    -0.000000245465
Guess   6 is     0.948683298051  with an error of    -0.000000000000
```

In just six iterations the value of the square root of 0.9 is shown to be 0.948683298051 with all digits accurate.

Solution Implemented in Visual Basic

```
1    Option Explicit
2    Private Sub cmdCalculate_Click()
3        Dim number As Double, guess As Double, error As Double
4        Dim tolerance As Double
5        Dim counter As Integer
6        number = txtNumber.Text
7        tolerance = txtTolerance.Text
8        guess = 0.5 * number
9        counter = 1
10       msgTable.FixedRows = 8
11       msgTable.FixedCols = 1
12       Do
13          error = number - guess * guess
14          msgTable.Row = counter + 1
15          msgTable.Col = 0
16          msgTable.Text = Format(counter, "@@@@")
17          msgTable.Col = 1
18          msgTable.Text = Format(guess, "@@@@@@@@@@@@@@@@@@@")
19          msgTable.Col = 2
```

```
20        msgTable.Text = Format(error, "@@@@@@@@@@@@@@@@@@@@")
21        guess = 0.5 * (guess + number / guess)
22        counter = counter + 1
23    Loop While Abs(error) > tolerance
24  End Sub
25
26  Private Sub cmdEnd_Click()
27    Unload frmProblem3_2
28  End Sub
29
30  Private Sub Form_Load()
31    lblMessage.Caption = "This program generates the square " & _
32        " root of any positive number."
33    msgTable.Rows = 50
34    msgTable.ColWidth(0) = 800
35    msgTable.ColWidth(1) = 2500
36    msgTable.ColWidth(2) = 2500
37    msgTable.Row = 0
38    msgTable.Col = 0
39    msgTable.Text = "Cycle"
40    msgTable.Col = 1
41    msgTable.Text = "Guess"
42    msgTable.Col = 2
43    msgTable.Text = "Error"
44  End Sub
```

Output of the Visual Basic Program

```
Problem3_2                                              _ □ ✕

  ┌─────────────────────────────────────────────────┐
  │ This program generates the square  root         │
  │           of any positive number.               │
  └─────────────────────────────────────────────────┘

  ┌─────────────────┐  ┌───────────────┐  ┌───────────┐
  │ Enter a number  │  │     200       │  │ Calculate │
  └─────────────────┘  └───────────────┘  └───────────┘

  ┌─────────────────┐  ┌───────────────┐  ┌───────────┐
  │ Enter the tolerance │ │   1e-7      │  │    End    │
  └─────────────────┘  └───────────────┘  └───────────┘
```

Cycle	Guess	Error
1	100	-9800
2	51	-2401
3	27.4607843137255	-554.094675124952
4	17.371948743796	-101.784603157075
5	14.4423809486623	-8.58236746628429
6	14.1452565514874	-8.82829073965967E-02
7	14.1421359680227	-9.73804114616506E-06
8	14.142135623731	-1.15268905531707E-13

It would appear that there is a discrepancy in the data on line 8 of the Visual Basic output compared to the final value for the `error` as displayed in the output of the C++ program. In Visual Basic the default display for a double-precision float is to display all 15 significant figures stored in memory if there is a fractional part to the number. In the C++ program the code

```
17      cout << setprecision(12) << endl;
18      cout.setf(ios::fixed|ios::showpoint);
```

instructs the computer to display 12 decimal places. If the instruction `ios::fixed` is deleted, the precision of 12 becomes 12 significant figures instead of 12 decimal places and the C++ program produces data in agreement with the Visual Basic program.

3.4   THE LADDER PROBLEM

The hallmark of a problem that can be solved by strategic guessing is an available value that can be used to test the accuracy of the guess. In the square root problem the number entered by the user represented that value. Each guess was multiplied by itself and subtracted from the input number. The resulting error was then compared to the tolerance.

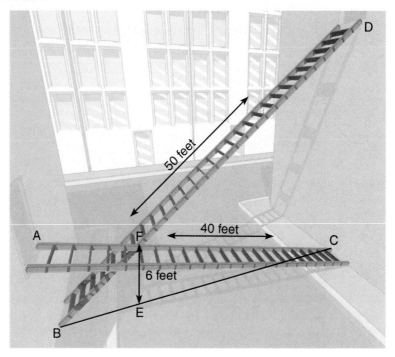

The ladder problem provides a similar opportunity for this type of guessing.

PROBLEM 3.3   *The ladder problem involves two ladders in an alley. The first ladder is 40 feet long and leans against one building with its base against the second building. The second ladder is 50 feet long and leans against the second building with its base against the first. The point where the ladders cross is 6 feet above the ground. How wide is the alley?*

As always the place to begin is with a clear understanding of the problem.

Initial Data: **1.** The two ladders are 50 feet and 40 feet long.

2. The crossing point is 6 feet above the ground.

3. Triangles ABC and FEC are similar triangles.

4. Triangles DCB and FEB are similar triangles.

5. Triangles ABC and DCB have side BC in common.

6. Triangles FEB and FEC have side FE in common.

7. Angles FEB and FEC are right angles.

Output: Determine the width of the alley.

At first glance the volume of information available would appear to make this problem fairly easy to solve by algebraic or trigonometric methods. The problem can be solved using only the Pythagorean Theorem or by using trigonometry functions; however, there is not quite enough information to solve the problem easily. The solution by the Pythagorean Theorem leads to a fourth-order equation, and the trigonometric solution leads to a set of four simultaneous equations that need to be solved.

The alternative is to guess at the solution. Once the width of the alley is known (the guess represents a tentative answer) it is simple to calculate the height of the crossing point. If the calculated crossing point turns out to be too high, the guess for the alley width is too small and must be increased. If the calculated crossing point is too low, then the alley is too wide and must be made narrower. Notice that there is an element of working backward (Rule 4) in this plan. Instead of calculating the alley width, the width is guessed and we work backward to compare a calculated value to a value specified in the problem statement, namely, the crossing point six feet above the ground.

The first step is to determine a reasonable initial guess for the alley width. Obviously the width of the alley cannot be zero or less or there would be no alley. Zero then is an absolute lower limit for the guess. We also know that the alley cannot be wider than 40 feet. This is clear because the 40-foot ladder is leaning. If the alley were wider than 40 feet, the ladder would be lying flat on the ground. If the alley must be between zero and 40 feet, 20 feet represents a reasonable first guess.

Now we have an opportunity to make use of the experience gained in solving the square root problem. By making an adjustment variable that begins at 10 and reduces by half in each cycle we can raise or lower the guess by the adjustment until we have zeroed in on the answer.

The remaining problem is how to calculate the height of the crossing point using the guess value for the alley width. Instead of making the calculations for the general case we'll use 20 feet for the guessed width of the alley in order to work with a concrete example. Later the variable `guess` can be substituted for the 20 feet.

Before starting, the initial data must be updated to reflect our guessed value.

1. The width of the alley is assumed to be 20 feet.

2. Using the value of 20 feet for the alley width, the height of the crossing point for the ladders can be calculated. If the crossing point is less than 6 feet, we will make the alley narrower. If it is greater than 6 feet, we will make the alley wider. We will continue this process until the difference between 6 feet and the calculated crossing point height is less than the tolerance.

3. If the alley is assumed to be 20 feet wide, then the length EC can be expressed as $20 - BE$.

The new objective is to calculate the height of the crossing point given an assumed alley width. While the calculations may not be obvious, they require nothing more than the definitions of cosine and tangent, and the ability to manipulate fractions.

The angles ACB and DBC can be determined by

$$\angle ABC = \cos^{-1}\left(\frac{20}{40}\right)$$

$$\angle DBC = \cos^{-1}\left(\frac{20}{50}\right)$$

The height of the crossing point can be expressed in two ways based on two different triangles:

$$FE = EC\tan(ACB)$$

$$FE = (20 - BE)\tan(ACB)$$

$$FE = BE\tan(DBC)$$

FE is the common side of two triangles. Therefore, it only has one length and expressions for that length must be equal to each other. That is, the preceding second and third equations can be solved as simultaneous equations for the quantity BE.

$$(20 - BE)\tan(ABC) = BE\tan(DBC)$$

$$\frac{20 - BE}{BE} = \frac{\tan(DBC)}{\tan(ACB)}$$

$$\frac{20}{BE} - 1 = \frac{\tan(DBC)}{\tan(ACB)}$$

$$\frac{20}{BE} = \frac{\tan(DBC)}{\tan(ACB)} + 1$$

$$\text{Let alpha} = \frac{\tan(DBC)}{\tan(ACB)}$$

$$\frac{20}{BE} = \text{alpha} + 1$$

$$BE = \frac{20}{\text{alpha} + 1}$$

The use of the temporary variable **alpha** is merely a convenience to avoid the nastiness of a compound fraction. Keep in mind that both **tan(DBC)** and **tan(ACB)** are values based on the assumed alley width of twenty feet. Consequently, **alpha** is also known and the length of BE is calculated from **alpha**. Once we have a value for BE the height FE can be calculated by:

$$FE = BE \times \tan(DBC)$$

The length of FE was the objective. Its length can now be compared to the required height of 6 feet to determine if the alley is wider or narrower than 20 feet. As it turns out, 20 feet is too narrow and the adjustment of 10 feet should be added. The adjustment is then reduced by half to 5 feet and the process of determining FE is repeated for the new alley width. With all of this in mind, we can write the pseudocode for the program.

Pseudocode Solution

1. Begin

2.   Declare and initialize variables.

3.   Prompt user for tolerance.

4.   Set column headings and formatting.

5.   Begin loop.

6.   Determine values for angles and alpha.

7.   Calculate the height of the crossing point.

8.   Calculate the error.

9.   Display results.

10.   Make appropriate adjustment to alley width.

11.   End loop if absolute value of error is less than required tolerance.

12. End

Flowchart

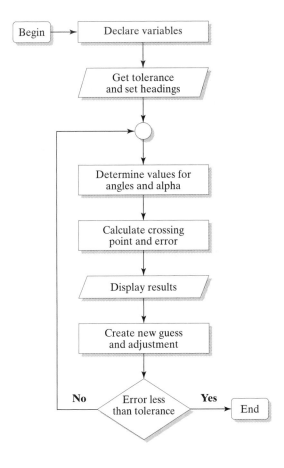

Problems that involve reasonable complexity, as the ladder problem does, make it clear that the thinking must be done before the pseudocode is written or a flowchart drawn. Once the logic for the solution has been determined, the pseudocode or flowchart organizes the logic in preparation for the translation to computer code.

Solution Implemented in C++

```
1    //    The Legendary Ladder Problem
2    //    Problem3.3
3
4    #include <iostream.h>
5    #include <iomanip.h>
6    #include <math.h>
7
8    void main (void)
9    {
10       double angle_ACB, angle_DBC, side_BE, height_FE, alpha;
11       double tolerance, guess = 20.0, error, adjustment = 10;
12       int counter = 1;
13
14       cout << "This program solves the Legendary Ladder problem to an\n "
15           << "\tarbitrary accuracy\n\n"
16           << "\t\tEnter the tolerance . .    ";
17       cin >> tolerance;
18       cout << endl;
19       cout << "Guess" << setw(20) << "Alley Width" << setw(20)
20           << "Crossing Point" << endl << endl;
21       cout.precision(12);
22       cout.setf( ios::fixed|ios::showpoint);
23       do
24       {
25          angle_ACB = acos (guess / 40);
26          angle_DBC = acos (guess / 50);
27          alpha = tan(angle_DBC) / tan(angle_ACB);
28
29          side_BE = guess / (alpha + 1) ;
30          height_FE = side_BE * tan(angle_DBC);
31          error = 6.0 - height_FE;
32
33           cout << setw(5) << counter++ << setw(22) << guess << setw(22)
34              << height_FE << endl;
35          if (error < 0)
36             guess += adjustment;
37          else
38             guess -= adjustment;
39          adjustment /= 2;
40       }while ( fabs ( error) > tolerance);
41       cout << "\n\n";
42    }
```

The logic begins on line 25 with the calculations of the angles opposite the crossing point height, height_FE. Since we are given the hypotenuse and one side of each of two triangles, calculating the included angle would be a reasonable place to start even if we didn't have a definite plan for solving the problem.

Line 29 calculates the value of side_BE based on the results of solving the simultaneous equations on page 108. Once there is a value for side_BE, the calculation of height_FE is a simple trigonometry function and is implemented on line 30. Line 31 calculates the error value. The sign of error determines whether the adjustment will be added to the guess or subtracted, lines 35 through 38. Finally, the magnitude of error determines whether the loop will continue or the current value of guess is sufficiently close to the correct value.

Output of the C++ Program

```
This program solves the Legendary Ladder problem to an
        arbitrary accuracy

            Enter the tolerance . .    1e-7
```

Guess	Alley Width	Crossing Point
1	20.000000000000	19.728028420470
2	30.000000000000	15.924467752259
3	35.000000000000	12.555656142838
4	37.500000000000	9.796307470143
5	38.750000000000	7.550700859767
6	39.375000000000	5.733024577546
7	39.062500000000	6.747969963397
8	39.218750000000	6.275240470423
9	39.296875000000	6.014328255700
10	39.335937500000	5.876462110222
11	39.316406250000	5.946059313573
12	39.306640625000	5.980356037937
13	39.301757812500	5.997382252599
14	39.299316406250	6.005865224297
15	39.300537109375	6.001626237983
16	39.301147460938	5.999504871053
17	39.300842285156	6.000565710848
18	39.300994873047	6.000035330047
19	39.301071166992	5.999770110326
20	39.301033020020	5.999902722630
21	39.301013946533	5.999969026949
22	39.301004409790	6.000002178651
23	39.301009178162	5.999985602838
24	39.301006793976	5.999993890754
25	39.301005601883	5.999998034705
26	39.301005005836	6.000000106678
27	39.301005303860	5.999999070692
28	39.301005154848	5.999999588685
29	39.301005080342	5.999999847682
30	39.301005043089	5.999999977180

The output shows that the initial guess of 20 was considerably less than the required alley width. The successive approximation algorithm causes the guess to grow steadily until the sixth guess, which results in a crossing point that is finally below 6 feet. The next adjustment is subtracted, which again gives a crossing point that is greater than 6 feet.

        7   39.062500000000   6.747969963397

Subsequent guesses vacillate around the correct answer until, by the thirtieth guess, the difference between the crossing point height of the current guess and 6 feet is less than the specified tolerance of one tenth of one millionth of 1 foot.

Solution Implemented in Visual Basic

```
1    Private Sub cmdCalculate_Click()
2        Dim error As Double, tolerance As Double
3        Dim angle_ACB As Double, angle_DBC As Double
4        Dim alpha As Double, side_BE As Double
5        Dim height_FE As Double, guess As Double
6        Dim adjustment As Double
7        Dim counter As Integer
8        counter = 1
9        tolerance = Val(txtInput.Text)
10       guess = 20
11       adjustment = 10
12       Do
13           angle_ACB = acos(guess / 40)
14           angle_DBC = acos(guess / 50)
15           alpha = Tan(angle_DBC) / Tan(angle_ACB)
16           side_BE = guess / (alpha + 1)
17           height_FE = side_BE * Tan(angle_DBC)
18           error = 6# - height_FE
19           msgTable.Row = counter
20           msgTable.Col = Column
21           msgTable.Text = Format(counter, "@@@")
22           msgTable.Col = 1
23           msgTable.Text = Format(guess, "@@@@@@@@@@@@@@@@@@@@@")
24           msgTable.Col = 2
25           msgTable.Text = Format(height_FE, "@@@@@@@@@@@@@@@@@@@@@@")
26           If error < 0 Then
27               guess = guess + adjustment
28           Else
29               guess = guess - adjustment
30           End If
31           adjustment = adjustment / 2
32           counter = counter + 1
33       Loop While Abs(error) > tolerance
34   End Sub
35
36   Private Sub cmdEnd_Click()
37       Unload frmProblem3_3
38   End Sub
```

```
39
40   Private Sub Form_Load()
41       lblMessage.Caption = "This program solves the " & _
42           "legendary ladder problem. Enter the tolerance"
43       frmProblem3_3.Top = (Screen.Height - _
44           frmProblem3_3.Height) / 3
45       frmProblem3_3.Left = (Screen.Width - _
46           frmProblem3_3.Width) / 3
47       msgTable.Cols = 3
48       msgTable.FixedRows = 4
49       msgTable.ColWidth(0) = 600
50       msgTable.ColWidth(1) = 2100
51       msgTable.ColWidth(2) = 2100
52       msgTable.Row = 0
53       msgTable.Col = 0
54       msgTable.Text = "Guess"
55       msgTable.Col = 1
56       msgTable.Text = Format("Alley Width", "@@@@@@@@@@@@@@@@@@@@@@")
57       msgTable.Col = 2
58       msgTable.Text = Format("Cross Point", "@@@@@@@@@@@@@@@@@@@@@@")
59
60   End Sub
61   Private Sub Form_activate()
62       txtInput.SetFocus
63   End Sub
64   Private Function acos(ByVal x As Double)
65       acos = Atn(-x / Sqr(-x * x + 1)) + 2 * Atn(1)
66   End Function
```

Line 12 begins the loop that zeros in on the solution. The logic begins with calculating the angles ACB and DBC using an initial value of 20 for the width of the alley. Alpha is a temporary variable used to simplify the mathematics as developed on page 108. Lines 16 to 18 continue the calculations deriving a value for the error, which is used to determine whether the guessed width of the alley should be increased or decreased.

The only part of the Visual Basic program that might seem a bit odd occurs on line 65. Unlike Visual C++, Visual Basic does not have a built-in arc cosine function. The math library does include functions to calculate sine, cosine, tangent, and arc tangent but the remaining trigonometric functions (arc sine, arc cosine, secant, etc.) must be derived. Fortunately, the help file does contain the formula for the derivation for the arc cosine that is used on line 65. The formula can be cut from the help file and pasted into the function code if one change is made.

The formula in the help file is given as

```
Arccos(X) = Atn(-X / Sqr(-X * X + 1)) + 2 * Atn(1)
```

The change in function name from Arccos to acos is unimportant and was made only to use the same name as the C++ code. Removing the "(X)" from the Arccos is important. Failure to remove this will result in a recursive function (discussed in chapter 8) and cause a stack overflow.

Output of the Visual Basic Program

Guess	Alley Width	Cross Point
1	20	19.7280284204697
2	30	15.9244677522594
3	35	12.5556561428383
15	39.300537109375	6.00162623798274
16	39.3011474609375	5.99950487105281
17	39.3008422851563	6.00056571084831
18	39.3009948730469	6.00003533004693
19	39.3010711669922	5.99977011032568
20	39.3010330200195	5.99990272263004
21	39.3010139465332	5.99996902694939
22	39.30100440979	6.00000217865088
23	39.3010091781616	5.99998560283832
24	39.3010067939758	5.99999389075415
25	39.3010056018829	5.9999980347049
26	39.3010050058365	6.00000010667849
27	39.3010053038597	5.99999907069185
28	39.3010051548481	5.9999995886852
29	39.3010050803423	5.99999984768186
30	39.3010050430894	5.99999997718018

The program window "frmProblem3_3" displays: "This program solves the legendary ladder problem. Enter the tolerance", with input field "1e-7", buttons "Calculate" and "End".

3.5   THE UNSOLVABLE EQUATION

Fifth-order equations, that is, equations of the form

$$0 = Ax^5 + Bx^4 + Cx^3 + Dx^2 + Ex + F$$

were chosen for this section not because they are commonly encountered equations, but because they are fair representatives of equations that can't be solved. At least they can't be solved by algebraic means (hence, they are never taught in algebra classes). The lack of an algebraic method for solving fifth-order equations should be not at all troubling by this point. We know quite well that we can always guess at the correct value for x and, if we are correct, the right-hand side of the equation will evaluate to zero.

Of course, the objective is to guess strategically in the hopes of zeroing in on the solutions to the equation in a reasonable amount of time.

PROBLEM 3.4   *How can you find the solutions to a fifth-order equation?*

The initial data in the problem is minimal, however, a great deal of insight can be gained by keeping in mind the fundamental theorem of algebra and making a graph of the general equation

$$f(x) = Ax^5 + Bx^4 + Cx^3 + Dx^2 + Ex + F$$

According to the fundamental theorem of algebra, an equation must have as many solutions as the order of the equation. There may be two solutions at one point or some of the solutions may be imaginary but a fifth-order equation does have five solutions. Since this is well known to algebra students, we can list it as initial data.

The next step is to draw a picture of an equation that has five solutions, that is, an equation that crosses the *x*-axis five times. The shape of the curve is irrelevant. The important idea is that there are five *x*-axis crossings. Remember we are looking for the values of *x* that make the right-hand side of the equation equal zero; that is, $y = f(x) = 0$.

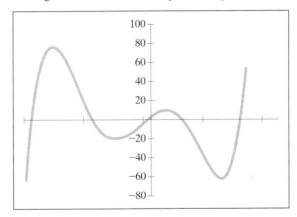

Since there is no known algebraic method for solving a fifth-order equation, we are left to use a guessing successive approximation approach to the problem. We can draw on the experience gained in the previous problems; however, there are a couple of differences in the current problem. In both the square root problem and the ladder problem we made a guess at the midpoint between two limits and then tested the guess. In the square root problem the upper limit was set by the input number itself and the lower limit was one. Halfway in between became the initial guess. In the ladder problem we knew that the width of the alley could not be greater than the length of the shorter ladder and had to be greater than zero. In solving the fifth-order equation not only do we have no clear limits defined in this problem but, compounding the problem, there are potentially five solutions within whatever limits we might set.

The other difference is that once a range is decided on for searching for all five solutions, it is necessary to find limits around each of the five solutions. Within these more narrow limits we can use the technique of zeroing in on a solution by successively dividing the range by half. Finding these limits becomes the first step in the solution.

A close examination of the graph can provide some insight. Remember even a crude drawing is usually beneficial. In this case we have no real scaling for the x-axis but that is unimportant. All we have is a squiggle that crosses the x-axis five times. Still it is apparent that for increasing values of x, something testable happens at the solution points. Around each solution the sign of the y-value, or the value of the function, changes either from negative to positive or positive to negative. If we evaluate the expression on the right side of the equation for some pair of numbers on the x-axis and we find a sign change in the y-values, then there must be a solution in between those numbers.

For example, if we choose to evaluate the equation for all integer values from -100 to $+100$ and between -1 and 0 we find a sign change, then we can use -1 and 0 as the limits for our guessing routine with the first guess at $-\frac{1}{2}$.

Now if we list the initial information for the program we have a bit more to work with.

Initial Data:
   1. The coefficients of the equation are supplied by the user.

   2. The fundamental theorem of algebra tells us that there are potentially five real solutions.

   3. On either side of a value of x that solves the equation the value of the function will change sign.

   4. If we can find consecutive integers values for x that result in a sign change for the function, we can zero in on a solution using the successive approximation technique learned in the previous problems.

Several difficulties are apparent with this approach.

1. A solution or several solutions may fall outside the domain of -100 to $+100$. If we find an insufficient number of solutions we can alter the program to cast a wider net, e.g., $-1,000$ to $+1,000$. In reality we will never have a fifth-order equation or any other potentially unsolvable equation merely thrust upon us. Instead the equation will correspond to some real-world problem and that problem will suggest a reasonable domain where we might go searching for solutions.

2. There may be more than one solution between two integers in which case there would be no sign change and the solutions would be missed. In real-world problems this is not terribly likely but, if it does occur and there is an insufficient number of solutions to the equations, the program can be altered to evaluate the equation for values of x that increase by one tenth instead of one.

3. This solution requires an enormous amount of work. It involves the evaluation of a difficult expression hundreds, more likely thousands, of times. This would be untenable if we were doing the work by hand but all the calculations can be handled by a modern desktop computer in less than a heartbeat.

4. Some of the solutions may be imaginary. The graph may cross the x-axis fewer than five times. In this case widening the search domain and making the resolution smaller will not find all the solutions.

> **Rule 11   The Functions Rule**
> As problems become more complex, it becomes increasingly important to divide the logic into smaller units that solve individual parts of the problem. These units correspond to programming functions.

For our fifth-order equation solving program, there are three tasks that can be used as logical subunits for the solution.

1. Introduce the problem and get the necessary information from the user.
2. Scan the selected domain looking for changes in sign for the function values.
3. If a change in sign is found use the guessing successive approximation routine to zero in on the solution.

Step 1 is trivial and step 3 is a known and practiced operation. Only step 2 is a new operation. But step 2 is little more than a for () loop that begins by evaluating the equation at −100 and −99, checking for a change in sign. If a sign change is found, successive approximation is used between −100 and −99 to zero in on a solution. If there is no sign change, the loop moves on and evaluates the equation for the values −99 and −98. This process continues until the loop reaches the end of the search domain at +100.

The key to the solution for this problem is recognizing that the method for solving the square root and the ladder problems can be applied as part of the solution of a new and more complex problem. Using the technique of zeroing in on a solution between two limits in a simpler problem makes the technique familiar and makes the problem solver more aware of opportunities when the technique might be applied.

Pseudocode Solution:

1. Begin
2. Declare and initialize variables.
3. Prompt user for coefficients to the equation.
4. Call solutions function to scan the domain.
5. Calculate function value for $x = -100$.
6. Begin loop for $x = -99$ to +100.
7. Calculate function value for x.
8. Test—is the function value zero?
9. If so, the x-value is a solution.
10. Store and print solution.
11. Continue to next integer.
12. Test for sign change from the value of the function at $x - 1$ to x.
13. If sign change, call second-pass function.
14. Second-pass function zeros in on solution between the integer and one greater than the integer.

15.   Return solution to solutions function.

16.   Store and print solution.

17.   Shift second value to first value for next cycle.

18.   End loop.

19.   Return to main().

20. End

Flowchart

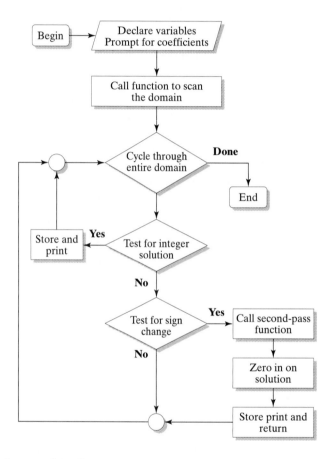

Solution Implemented in C++

```
1    //  Problem3_4  Fifth order equation solver
2    #include <iostream.h>
3    #include <math.h>
4    #include <iomanip.h>
5
6    void solutions(double [], double[]);
7    double second_pass(double, double []);
8    const double TOLERANCE = 1e-7;
9
```

```
10   void main(void)
11   {
12      double answers[10], coef[6];// = {4.8, 21.2, -16.6, -12.6, 2.2, 1};
13      const char input[6] = {'F', 'E', 'D', 'C', 'B', 'A'};
14      int counter;
15      cout.precision(6);
16      cout << "This program finds the solutions to fifth-order equations"
17          << "\n\tof the form Ax^5 + Bx^4 + Cx^3 + Dx^2 + Ex + F = 0"
18          << endl << endl;
19      for (counter = 5; counter >= 0; counter--)
20      {
21         cout << "Enter the value for " << input[counter] << "     " << flush;
22         cin >> coef[counter];
23      }
24      cout << endl;
25      solutions(answers, coef);
26      cout << endl;
27   }
28
29   void solutions(double ans[], double co[])
30   {
31      int count = -100, ans_counter = 0;
32      double value[2];
33      value[0] = co[5] * pow(count,5) + co[4] * pow(count,4) +
34            co[3] * pow(count,3) + co[2] * pow(count,2) +
35            co[1] * count + co[0];
36      for (count = -99; count <= 100; count++)
37      {
38         value[1] = co[5] * pow(count,5) + co[4] * pow(count,4) +
39               co[3] * pow(count,3) + co[2] * pow(count,2) +
40               co[1] * count + co[0];
41
42         if (fabs(value[1]) < TOLERANCE)
43         {
44            ans[ans_counter++] = count;
45            cout << " x = " << setw(5) << count << endl;
46            value[0] = 0;
47            continue;
48         }
49         if (value[0] < 0 && value[1] > 0 || value[0] > 0 && value[1] < 0)
50         {
51            ans[ans_counter] = second_pass(count - 1, co);
52            cout << " x = " << setw(5) << ans[ans_counter++] << endl;
53         }
54         value[0] = value[1];
55      }
56   }
57   double second_pass(double solution, double co[])
58   {
59      double adjustment = .5, solution_plus_adjust, value[2];
60      do
```

```
61    {
62        solution_plus_adjust = solution + adjustment;
63        value[0] = co[5] * pow(solution,5) + co[4] * pow(solution,4) +
64            co[3] * pow(solution,3) + co[2] * pow(solution,2) +
65            co[1] * solution + co[0];
66        value[1] = co[5] * pow(solution_plus_adjust,5) +
67            co[4] * pow(solution_plus_adjust,4) +
68            co[3] * pow(solution_plus_adjust,3) +
69            co[2] * pow(solution_plus_adjust,2) +
70            co[1] * solution_plus_adjust + co[0];
71        if (value[0] < 0 && value[1] > 0 || value[0] > 0 && value[1] < 0)
72            adjustment /= 2;
73        else
74            solution += adjustment;
75    }while(adjustment > TOLERANCE);
76    return solution;
77 }
```

The declaration of the variables and prompting of the user for values for the coefficients is handled on lines 12 through 23. Rather than writing six prompts and six cin statements it is more efficient to set up a loop to successively prompt the user for each coefficient and to store them in the coef array. The commented data on line 12 is a standard troubleshooting technique. When testing the program to ensure that the solutions it derives are correct, it is convenient to bypass the user entry part of the program by commenting out the loop that does the data entry and to hardcode in values for the coefficients that yield known solutions to the equation. In this program comment marks around lines 19 to 23 will eliminate the user input and removing the semicolon and comment marks on line 12

```
12    double answers[10], coef[6];// = {4.8, 21.2, -16.6, -12.6, 2.2, 1};
```

will set the values for coef[6] to the values inside the curly braces.

Lines 33 to 35 calculate the initial value of the function at $x = -100$. Subsequent values for the function are calculated inside the loop as x ranges from -99 to $+100$. Step 8 in the pseudocode calls for a test of the current value of x to check whether $f(x)$ is equal to zero. If $f(x)$ is equal to zero, then x is a solution to the equation. If the integer value of x is a solution to the equation, then there is no need to use successive approximation to zero in on a solution. Line 42 makes this test except there is no test for equality. Instead we test whether the value of the function is quite close to zero. Floating-point numbers (and double-precision, floating-point numbers) should never be tested using the equality operator.

This is because of a rounding operation that is used when computers store floating-point numbers. The details of how floats are stored would create a considerable divergence here. Suffice it to say that computers are unable to exactly store numbers containing fractional parts that cannot be expressed as the sum of powers of two. For example, the number 4.2 is simple to express as a decimal number but computers must save this value in binary, i.e., 100.00110011001100110011. In this number the bits 0011 represent a repeating bit pattern comparable to a repeating decimal. At some point the computer must truncate the decimal, leaving a number that is slightly less than 4.2. For floating point numbers the error shows up in the seventh significant figure. For doubles the values are correct to 15 significant figures.

This error introduced by rounding is generally not a problem. No one wants to, or is able to, measure the length of his or her desk to seven significant figures. Under normal circumstances the only place this rounding creates a problem is in tests for equality. **Never use a test for equality with floating-point numbers.** The test may or may not work.

After testing for an integer value for the equation the next test, line 49, tests for changes in sign between value[0] and value[1]. Notice that a compound conditional is used because the sign change may be from positive to negative or negative to positive. Keep in mind that value[1] is the value of the function at the current value of x and value[0] is the value of the function at $x - 1$. If a sign change is detected, $x - 1$ (actually counter - 1) is sent to the function second_pass to zero in on the solution that must be between $x - 1$ and x.

The second_pass function zeros in on the solution to the equation within the limit set by TOLERANCE. That value is returned to the solutions function for display and storage in the ans array.

The final task for the solutions function is to shift the value of value[1] into value[0]. This prepares the program for the next cycle of testing when the value of count will be incremented and a new value of value[1] will be calculated.

Output of the C++ Program

```
This program finds the solutions to fifth-order equations
          of the form Ax^5 + Bx^4 + Cx^3 + Dx^2 + Ex + F = 0

Enter the value for A     1
Enter the value for B     2.2
Enter the value for C     -12.6
Enter the value for D     -16.6
Enter the value for E     21.2
Enter the value for F     4.8


  X =     -4
  X =     -2
  X =   -0.2
  X =      1
  X =      3
```

These solutions for the equation can be tested by substituting each value into the original equation. Substituting the first value of -4 for x yields

$$0 = x^5 + 2.2x^4 - 12.6x^3 - 16.6x^2 + 21.2x + 4.8$$
$$0 = (-4)^5 + 2.2(-4)^4 - 12.6(-4)^3 - 16.6(-4)^2 + 21.2(-4) + 4.8$$
$$0 = -1024 + 563.2 + 806.4 - 265.6 - 84.8 + 4.8$$
$$0 = 0$$

indicating that -4 produces a true statement and is, therefore, a valid solution. Similarly, the other four values could be verified. In this case there is no need because the original equation was generated by using these five solutions.

$$0 = (x + 4)(x + 2)(x + 0.2)(x - 1)(x - 3)$$

Of course, the solutions are not generally known in advance and each solution would need to be verified.

Solution Implemented in Visual Basic

```
1    Private Const TOLERANCE As Double = 0.0000001
2    Private Sub cmdCalculate_Click()
3        Dim answers(0 To 9) As Double
4        Dim coef(0 To 5) As Double
5        coef(0) = Val(txtInputA.Text)
6        coef(1) = Val(txtInputB.Text)
7        coef(2) = Val(txtInputC.Text)
8        coef(3) = Val(txtInputD.Text)
9        coef(4) = Val(txtInputE.Text)
10       coef(5) = Val(txtInputF.Text)
11       Call solutions(answers(), coef())
12   End Sub
13   Private Sub solutions(ByRef ans() As Double, ByRef co() As Double)
14       Dim count As Integer, ans_counter As Integer
15       Dim value(0 To 1) As Double
16       Dim row_number As Integer, col_number As Integer
17       row_number = 1
18       msgTable.Col = 1
19       count = -100
20       ans_counter = 0
21       value(0) = co(0) * count ^ 5 + co(1) * count ^ 4 + co(2) * count ^ 3 + _
22           co(3) * count ^ 2 + co(4) * count + co(5)
23       For count = -99 To 100
24           value(1) = co(0) * count ^ 5 + co(1) * count ^ 4 + _
25               co(2) * count ^ 3 + co(3) * count ^ 2 + co(4) * count + co(5)
26           If (Abs(value(1)) < TOLERANCE) Then
27               msgTable.Row = row_number
28               ans(ans_counter) = count
29               float_count = count
30               msgTable.Text = Format(FormatNumber(ans(ans_counter), 6), _
31                   "@@@@@@@@@@@@")
32               row_number = row_number + 1
33               ans_counter = ans_counter + 1
34               value(0) = 0
35           Else
36               If value(0) < 0 And value(1) > 0 Or value(0) > 0 _
37                       And value(1) < 0 Then
38                   ans(ans_counter) = second_pass(count - 1, co())
39                   msgTable.Row = row_number
40                   msgTable.Text = Format(FormatNumber(ans(ans_counter), 6), _
41                       "@@@@@@@@@@@@")
42                   row_number = row_number + 1
43                   ans_counter = ans_counter + 1
44               End If
45           End If
46           value(0) = value(1)
```

```
47      Next count
48   End Sub
49   Private Function second_pass(ByVal solution As Double,_
50         ByRef co() As Double)
51      Dim adjustment As Double
52      Dim solution_plus_adjustment As Double
53      Dim value(0 To 1) As Double
54      adjustment = 0.5
55      Do
56         solution_plus_adjustment = solution + adjustment
57         value(0) = co(0) * solution ^ 5 + co(1) * solution ^ 4 + _
58            co(2) * solution ^ 3 + co(3) * solution ^ 2 + _
59            co(4) * solution + co(5)
60         value(1) = co(0) * solution_plus_adjustment ^ 5 + _
61            co(1) * solution_plus_adjustment ^ 4 + _
62            co(2) * solution_plus_adjustment ^ 3 + _
63            co(3) * solution_plus_adjustment ^ 2 + _
64            co(4) * solution_plus_adjustment + co(5)
65         If value(0) < 0 And value(1) > 0 Or value(0) > 0 _
66               And value(1) < 0 Then
67            adjustment = adjustment / 2
68         Else
69            solution = solution + adjustment
70         End If
71      Loop While adjustment > TOLERANCE
72      second_pass = solution
73   End Function
74   Private Sub cmdEnd_Click()
75   Unload frmProblem3_4
76   End Sub
77   Private Sub cmdReset_Click()
78      txtInputA.Text = ""
79      txtInputB.Text = ""
80      txtInputC.Text = ""
81      txtInputD.Text = ""
82      txtInputE.Text = ""
83      txtInputF.Text = ""
84      msgTable.Col = 1
85      msgTable.Row = 1
86      msgTable.Text = ""
87      msgTable.Row = 2
88      msgTable.Text = ""
89      msgTable.Row = 3
90      msgTable.Text = ""
91      msgTable.Row = 4
92      msgTable.Text = ""
93      msgTable.Row = 5
94      msgTable.Text = ""
95      txtInputA.SetFocus
96   End Sub
97   Private Sub Form_Load()
```

```
98      Dim x As Integer
99      frmProblem3_4.Top = (Screen.Height - _
100                                 frmProblem3_4.Height) / 3
101     frmProblem3_4.Left = (Screen.Width - _
102                                 frmProblem3_4.Width) / 3
103     lblMessage.Caption = "This program solves fifth order " & _
104        "equations of the form " & vbCrLf & _
105        "Ax^5 + Bx^4 + Cx^3 + Dx^2 + Ex + F = 0"
106     msgTable.ColWidth(0) = 1000
107     msgTable.ColWidth(1) = 1680
108     msgTable.Row = 0
109     msgTable.Col = 0
110     msgTable.Text = "Variable"
111     msgTable.Col = 1
112     msgTable.Text = "    Value"
113     msgTable.Col = 0
114     For x = 1 To 5
115        msgTable.Row = x
116        msgTable.Text = "    X = "
117     Next x
118 End Sub
119 Private Sub Form_Activate()
120     txtInputA.SetFocus
121 End Sub
```

The structure of the Visual Basic program is the same as the C++ program except for the information display of the input and output. The loop used to gather the coefficients from the user in C++ has been replaced by individual inputs from different text boxes. The output display has been set in table form.

Output of the Visual Basic Program

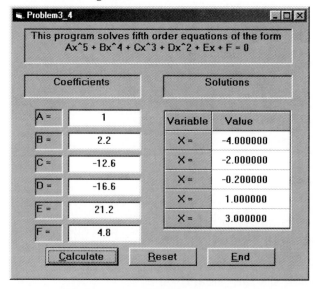

C H A P T E R 4

Brute Force

4.1 NONSTRATEGIC GUESSING

The fifth-order equation solver in Chapter 3 actually combined two problem-solving techniques. Once two integers were known that surrounded a solution, strategic guessing was used to zero in on the solution between these numbers. However, to find those two limits a type of guessing was used that was systematic but not very strategic.

The idea was to test all possible integer values that might enclose a solution to the equation. Actually not all possible values were tested because that would be too big a task for any computer, but enough values were tested through a reasonable range. That range of values could have been made larger or the resolution between samples made smaller but the idea would be the same. The likelihood of finding all pairs of values that surrounded a sign change for the function would be increased, but the microprocessor would have more work to do and the user might have to wait longer for the results.

Some problems have no known logical or mathematical solution and the only recourse is to examine and test all possible potential solutions. In other cases the calculated solution may merely be too difficult for the nonspecialist and the programmer may have no choice but to plow through the problem using the brute force provided by the computer.

> **Rule 12 The Brute Force Rule**
> When all else fails, try examining all possible solutions in a systematic manner through some reasonable range.

4.2 THE LIARS PROBLEM

The option to use brute force to solve a problem is not restricted to those problems with so many solutions that computer power is required. The problem may have a limited number of possibilities to examine. Consider the problem sometimes called the world's shortest logic problem.

PROBLEM 4.1

1. *A says that B lies.*
2. *B says that C lies.*
3. *C says that A and B lie.*

Is anyone telling the truth?

In the fifth-order equation problem we started by examining $x = -100$ and $x = -99$. Because the function produced no sign change for those numbers, we moved on to the next pair, $x = -99$ and $x = -98$. Uninteresting pairs were ignored; pairs that produced a sign change were sent on to the `second_pass` function for further study. That is, we assumed that there was a solution between $x = -100$ and $x = -99$ and tested the value of the function at those points. Since no difference in sign resulted, the assumption that a solution was in the range must have been false.

The same approach can be applied to logical problems. In these problems we assume a logical statement is true and then derive logical conclusions based on that assumption. If we encounter a contradiction, the original assumption must be false.

Rule 13   The Self-Consistency Rule

If a statement is assumed to be true and then leads to a conclusion contrary to some known fact, the original assumption must be false. If a statement is assumed to be false and leads to a conclusion contrary to some known fact, the original assumption must be true. All real-world scenarios must be self-consistent.

Rules 12 (brute force) and 13 (self-consistency) can be used together to solve the liars problem. In this case the number of possibilities to be examined is small.

1. A is telling the truth.
2. B is telling the truth.
3. C is telling the truth.

By examining the problem three times, each time using one of the preceding assumptions, we also will determine if no one is telling the truth or if multiple people are telling the truth. A list of the initial data is unnecessary since the data was itemized in the statement of the problem. For each of the three times we will consider the problem, one of the preceding assumptions will be added to the initial data and provide a starting point for the logic.

Possibility One   A is telling the truth

If A is telling the truth, then B is a liar.   (Statement One)

If B is lying when B claims that C is a liar,
   C must be telling the truth.   (Statement Two)

If C is telling the truth, then A must be a liar.   (Statement Three)

But deciding A is a liar contradicts the initial assumption
    that A is telling the truth.

Therefore, possibility one is not true.

Possibility Two   B is telling the truth

If B is telling the truth, then C is a liar.   (Statement Two)

If C is lying, then A or B or both must be telling the truth.   (Statement Three)

If B is telling the truth (the original assumption),
    then A may be lying or not.   (Statement Three)

If A is lying when A claims B is lying,
    then B must be telling the truth.   (Statement One)

There is no contradiction and the system is self-consistent.

Therefore, B *may be* telling the truth.

Possibility Three   C is telling the truth

If C is telling the truth, then both A and B are liars.   (Statement Three)

If A is lying when A says that B is a liar,
    then B must be telling the truth   (Statement One)

If B is telling the truth when B says that C lies, then C is lying.   (Statement Two)

But, if C is lying, that contradicts the original assumption
    that C is telling the truth.

Therefore, possibility three is not true.

This analysis indicates that B is the only one that can be telling the truth but it raises the question of whether B is *possibly* telling the truth or *necessarily* telling the truth. This can be considered by assuming that B is lying.

If B is lying, then C is telling the truth.   (Statement Two)

If C is telling the truth, then both A and B are lying.   (Statement Three)

If A is lying about B being a liar, then B is telling the truth.   (Statement One)

But B telling the truth contradicts the assumption that B is lying.

Therefore, B cannot be lying.

This indicates that it is *necessarily* true that B and only B is telling the truth. The problem is solved.

Since the problem has been solved, there is little reason to write a computer program to execute the steps that have been carried out by hand. More commonly the number of possibilities is vast and to explore them all requires computer power.

4.3   THE COMEDIANS' HATS

Let's consider one more problem that has a limited number of easily searched possibilities. The problem involves three comedians and five hats.

PROBLEM 4.2   *Late one night after the last performance the master of ceremonies gathers his three comedians and poses a question. The one who can answer the question will get a $1,000 bonus. The first comedian, Al, has 20/20 vision in both eyes. The second comedian, Bob, has perfect vision in one eye but is blind in the other. The third comedian, Carl, is blind in both eyes. The master of ceremonies places one of five hats on each comedian's head. The hats were chosen from a pool of three red hats and two blue hats. There is no way for any comedian to see his own hat or the remaining unused hats. When Al is asked what color his hat is, he looks at Bob and Carl and says, "I don't know." When Bob is asked what color his hat is, he looks at Al and Carl and says, "I don't know." The master of ceremonies assumes that Carl, being blind, cannot possibly know what color his hat is and doesn't even ask. But Carl says, "My hat is _____," and wins the $1,000 bonus. What color was Carl's hat?*

This problem can be approached in the same manner as the liars problem; however, this time the information is embedded in many words and Rule 1 should be invoked. For the sake of clarity we'll list the information of the problem.

Initial Data: **1.** Al could not determine what color his hat was.

2. *After Al said he couldn't determine the color of his hat,* Bob also couldn't determine his hat color.

3. There are a limited number of possible hat combinations that can be made from three red and two blue hats.

4. Carl is blind.

5. Items 1, 2, and 3 were all that Carl needed to determine his hat color.

Item three suggests that brute force might be a reasonable plan of attack for the problem. Again the need for clarity indicates that a list of the hat possibilities is a good place to start.

The sixth column has been added for readers who are familiar with binary numbers. Since there are only two possible colors for the hats, we can ensure that no possibilities have been skipped or duplicated by listing options in binary order. In this case RED is indicated by a zero and BLUE is indicated by a one. Notice that the binary count only goes from zero to six. Seven (111) would imply three blue hats, which cannot occur.

Item one on the list of initial data indicates that Al cannot decide what color his hat is. This means that option four is not possible. If Al saw blue hats on Bob and Carl, he would know his hat had to be red. With both blue hats accounted for, his hat would have to be one of the three red hats. Since option four leads to a contradiction, it cannot describe the true situation.

The same reasoning applies to option six. If Bob saw blue hats on Al and Carl, he would know that is hat had to be red. This contradicts the initial data that Bob could not determine his hat color. Therefore, option six has to be eliminated.

Option	Al	Bob	Carl		Binary
1	RED	RED	RED		000
2	RED	RED	BLUE	NOT POSSIBLE	001
3	RED	BLUE	RED		010
4	RED	BLUE	BLUE	NOT POSSIBLE	011
5	BLUE	RED	RED		100
6	BLUE	RED	BLUE	NOT POSSIBLE	101
7	BLUE	BLUE	RED		110

Option two is a little more complicated. If Bob saw a red hat on Al and a blue hat on Carl, he would know that his hat had to be red. Bob knows this because if his hat were blue, Al would have seen two blue hats (on Bob and Carl) and would have known his hat had to be red. But Al didn't know his hat color, so Bob's hat would have to be red. However, the scenario where Bob knew his hat color didn't occur, so option two is false and must be struck from the list.

Amazingly enough the problem is solved. There is no need to examine the other four options. Each of the remaining options, 1, 3, 5, and 7, indicate a red hat for Carl. There is no need for Carl to be able to see Al's or Bob's hats. In this problem we began with the intention to examine all possible combinations of hats but discovered that we could stop early after options 2, 4, and 6 were eliminated.

4.4   PRIME NUMBERS

Prime number generators have always been a standard part of introductory programming classes. More recently prime numbers have received even more attention because dual-key encryption usually involves large prime numbers. While multiplying two large prime numbers together is easy, reversing the process and finding the prime factors is very difficult. Determining whether a large number is prime or can be factored involves considerable brute force. Even using more sophisticated algorithms such as a quadratic sieve, the job still requires considerable time and computer power.

If the number involved is not quite so large, then determining whether the number is prime, or, if it is not prime, determining its prime factors requires little more than the definition of a prime number and an average personal computer.

PROBLEM 4.3   *Determine whether a number less than four billion is prime and, if not, what are the prime factors.*

There is slightly more information available in the problem than would first appear.

Initial Data: **1.** The user will provide a number that is an integer and is less than four billion.

2. By definition a prime number is only divisible by itself and one.

3. The smallest prime factor any number can have is 2.

4. The largest prime factor any number can have is one half of the input number. For example, the prime factors of 74 are 2 and 37.

Output: An indication that the input number is prime or a list of the prime factors.

The definition of a prime number suggests that a brute force approach will be effective, though not necessarily efficient. To prove a number is prime it will be sufficient to divide the number by all integers from two to up to half of the number. *If any of these divisions produces a remainder of zero, then the number is not prime.* Furthermore, if the remainder is zero, then two factors have been found. This raises the issue of how we can ensure that all the factors are prime factors.

Resolution can be found by remembering Rule 8 and examining a specific case. Consider the number twelve. Three and four are factors of twelve, as are two and six, but the prime factors are two, two, and three. The objective is to get the pair of "two" factors and the "three" factor, but not the "four" or "six" factors.

Keep in mind that while we are not being strategic in our guessing we are being systematic. In this case it means testing the potential factors in order, from two to half of the input number. If two is found to be a factor, then that factor can be removed from further consideration by dividing the input by two. Dividing twelve by the discovered factor of two results in a new target number of six. Because four is not a factor of six, when the four test is made, it will fail and four will not be listed as a prime factor.

The next question is how we can be sure to get both factors of two. The testing routine should be constructed so that if two is *not* found to be a factor we move on and test three as a potential factor. However, if two is a factor, we do not increment the test number and two is used again in the next cycle of testing.

By testing in this fashion twelve will be found to have a factor of two. Then the input will be divided by two, and six will be the new target number. The incrementing of two is canceled and two is tested again. Because six divided by two is again without a remainder, there is a second "two" to be listed among the prime factors: Six divided by two is three. Again the input is divided by two but this time there is a remainder so there is no third "two" among the factors and the test number is incremented to three. The target (now three) divided by three gives a remainder of zero so three is the third prime factor. Dividing the input by three gives a quotient of one, ensuring that no other test divisors will produce a zero remainder.

Pseudocode Solution

1. Begin
2.   Declare variables.
3.   Create continuous loop for checking factors of many numbers.
4.   Message to the user and prompt for input.
5.   Initialize the limit and set the flag indicating no factor has yet been found.
6.   Begin test loop—run from two to the limit.
7.   Test potential factor.
8.   If not equal to zero, continue.
9.   Else
10.   Display the factor.
11.   Set the flag.

12.   Create new input value.

13.   Cancel the factor increment.

14.   End test loop.

15.   If flag has never been set, display prime number message.

16.   Check another integer.

17.   Repeat or end outer loop.

18. End

Flowchart

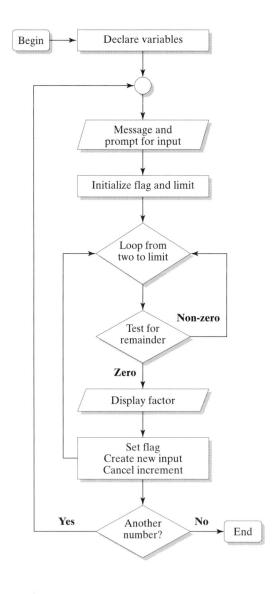

Solution Implemented in C++

```
1    //    Problem 4.3
2    #include <iostream.h>
3    #include <math.h>
4    #include <time.h>
5
6    int main(void)
7    {
8        unsigned input, factor, limit, flag;
9        char again;
10       long start, finish;
11       do
12       {
13          cout << endl << "This program determines prime factors for "
14              << "numbers less than 4 billion\n\n\t"
15              << "Enter an integer . .   " << flush;
16          cin >> input;
17          time(&start);
18          limit = input / 2;
19          flag = 0;
20          cout << "Factors:   " << flush;
21          for (factor = 2; factor <= limit; factor++)
22          {
23             if (input % factor == 0)
24             {
25                cout << factor << "   " << flush;
26                flag = 1;
27                input /= factor;
28                factor--;
29             }
30          }
31          if (flag == 0)
32             cout << "The input is prime." << flush;
33          time(&finish);
34          cout << "\nElapsed time for the calculation is "
35              << finish - start << " seconds. " << endl;
36          cout << "\n\tTest another number?  (y/n)    " << flush;
37          cin >> again;
38       }while (again == 'y' || again == 'Y');
39       return(0);
40   }
```

There are two reasons for limiting the input number to less than four billion. First, four billion is approximately the largest number that can be stored in an unsigned integer. The program could be adapted to use a double-precision float for the input, which would allow integers with up to 15 digits. This would require changing line 19 to use the fmod() function for finding the remainder of a float. Since the number being stored as a double is in fact an integer, the test for equality can be kept.

The second problem is time related. Running the program for an input of 666666691, approximately two thirds of a billion, required 31 seconds of run time on a

450 MHz, Pentium III. Testing a number around four billion requires over three minutes. Testing a number around four trillion would require approximately 1,000 times as long, i.e., more than two days. This illustrates the prime drawback to a brute force solution and the advantage of attacking problems with cleverness instead of force. Still for reasonable numbers brute force can produce the required information in a reasonable time. The speed of the processor can make the user oblivious to the incredible amount of work that is being done. The programmer should be a bit more aware.

The use of the `flag` variable deserves some comment. Flag variables, often given the name `flag`, are used to remember that something of significance has happened. In this program the event to remember is that a divisor has been found that produces a remainder of zero indicating that the number is not prime. Line 31 tests the `flag` variable and, if it has never been set by any of the divisions carried out in the loop, the prime number message is sent to the user. When using flag variables, it is important to reset the flag to its original condition before another number is tested. Line 19 resets the flag and is inside the outer loop.

Output of C++ Program

```
This program determines prime factors for numbers less than 4 billion

        Enter an integer . .    21
Factors:  3  7
Elapsed time for the calculation is 0 seconds.


        Test another number?  (y/n)    y


This program determines prime factors for numbers less than 4 billion

        Enter an integer . .    133333331
Factors:  11287   11813
Elapsed time for the calculation is 6 seconds.


        Test another number?  (y/n)    y


This program determines prime factors for numbers less than 4 billion

        Enter an integer . .    666666689
Factors:  13   51282053
Elapsed time for the calculation is 31 seconds.


        Test another number?  (y/n)    y


This program determines prime factors for numbers less than 4 billion

        Enter an integer . .    666666691
Factors:  The input is prime.
Elapsed time for the calculation is 31 seconds.


        Test another number?  (y/n)    n
```

Solution Implemented in Visual Basic

```
1    Option Explicit
2    Private Sub cmdCalculate_Click()
3       Dim number As Long, factor As Long, result As Long
4       Dim limit As Long, flag As Integer, it As Integer
5       Dim start As Long, finish As Long
6       number = Val(txtInput.Text)
7       limit = number / 2
8       flag = 0
9       start = Timer
10      For factor = 2 To limit
11         result = number Mod factor
12         If result = 0 Then
13            txtOutput.Text = txtOutput.Text & Str(factor) & ", "
14            flag = 1
15            number = number / factor
16            factor = factor - 1
17         End If
18      If (factor Mod 50000000) = 0 Then
19          DoEvents
20          'txtTime.Text = Str(factor)
21      End If
22
23      Next factor
24      If flag = 0 Then
25         txtOutput.Text = "The input number is prime"
26      End If
27      finish = Timer
28      txtTime.Text = "Elapsed time for the calculation is " & _
29         Str(finish - start) & " seconds"
30   End Sub
31   Private Sub cmdEnd_Click()
32      Unload frmProblem4_3
33   End Sub
34   Private Sub cmdReset_Click()
35      txtInput.Text = ""
36      txtOutput.Text = ""
37      txtInput.SetFocus
38   End Sub
39   Private Sub Form_Load()
40      lblMessage.Caption = "This program determines whether " & _
41         "a number is prime and if it is not, generates all " & _
46         "of the prime factors."
47      lblInput.Caption = "Enter an integer"
48      txtOutput.Text = ""
49      frmProblem4_3.Top = (Screen.Height - frmProblem4_3.Height) / 3
50      frmProblem4_3.Left = (Screen.Width - frmProblem4_3.Width) / 3
51   End Sub
52   Private Sub Form_Activate()
53      txtInput.SetFocus
54   End Sub
```

Output of the Visual Basic Program

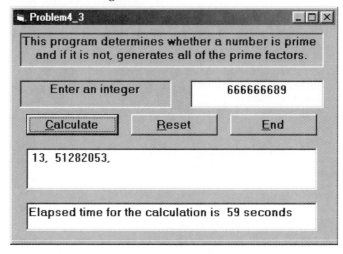

The only item of special interest in the Visual Basic code is the `if` statement on line 18. For technical internal reasons the Visual Basic code can hang if the `DoEvents` command is not periodically executed. `DoEvents` involves considerable overhead and can significantly slow a program so it is only executed once for every 50,000,000 possible factors checked. Line 20 is commented out and is only used for troubleshooting. Removing the comment will show the progress the program is making by creating a display in the `Time` textbox every time a factor evenly divisible by 50,000,000 is checked by the `For` loop.

There are many technical differences between Visual C++ and Visual Basic, which are of little concern to the average problem solver. However, the prime factor generator illustrates two differences that are apparent and significant. Visual Basic allows the quick and simple generation of a program that is nicely formatted in familiar windows and responds to input from a mouse. The same graphical output could be generated in C++ by using the Microsoft Foundation Classes but not nearly so quickly nor so easily.

On the other hand, there is a considerable performance difference between the two languages. Despite the fact that the section of each program that performs the calculations match nearly line for line, the performance advantage using C++ is clear. Searching for all the prime factors for 666,666,689 required 31 seconds for the C++ program compared to 59 seconds for the Visual Basic program. It should be noted that the 59 seconds was the time required for the executable program to find the prime factors of 666,666,689. If the program is run within the Visual Basic environment, it will run as an interpreted program, which is considerably slower (nearly 4.5 minutes).

The choice of programming language is based on using the right tool for the job. If rapid development of a solution with a familiar interface is important, Visual Basic is the preferred tool. If number-crunching power and speed are required and the user is comfortable in a command window, i.e., a DOS-style window with white Courier font on a black background, then the choice should be C++.

4.5   SEARCHING ROUTINES

Computer scientists are pursuing the goal of developing computer algorithms that will understand the *meaning* of text. For now Web and database searches are usually made on the basis of keyword searches. Unfortunately searching for one or more keywords often provides hundreds of hits that are unrelated or only obliquely related to the information sought. If the meaning of the text and the meaning of the query could be understood, the false hits could be eliminated.

Current methods for making computers "understand" clear text involve many levels of analysis including the dictionary meaning of the words, the context in which each word is used based on the words surrounding it, whether the word is the subject, predicate, or object of the sentence, and many other criteria. However, the starting position for these schemes is the division of the text into component words. In other words, the problem of making computers understand text or making computers search for keywords begins with the isolation of individual words in the text. This represents a brute force task for the computer.

PROBLEM 4.4   *Divide a sentence provided by the user into its component words.*

To illustrate our method for isolating words we'll limit the problem to a single sentence with no more than 20 words of no more than 20 characters each. In Chapter 8 we'll eliminate this limitation and expand the solution to the examination of an entire book. For now it is best to apply Rule 7 and limit the problem to a single string entered by the user. Although expanding the program to also recognize numbers would not be difficult, for the sake of clarity, only words will be considered.

Initial Data: **1.** A sentence will be provided by the user.

2. A word begins with a letter.

3. Letters can be identified by checking certain ranges of the ASCII table.

4. A word ends with white space or punctuation.

5 Two punctuation marks do not end a word, namely the apostrophe and the hyphen.

6. The words will need to be stored in a double subscripted array.

Output: Create a list of the words in the sentence.

A human would have no problem recognizing the words in the input sentence and copying each one from the sentence to a holding area in the array. However, the computer doesn't know what a word is, at least until it is taught, and recognizes only a stream of characters. So the real objective is to make each word a recognizable unit to the program, that is, a continuous sequence of valid letters or characters surrounded by nonvalid characters. Fortunately, this is not difficult and all that is required is to teach the program to do exactly what a human does to recognize words.

A word is a unit that begins with a letter, either uppercase or lowercase, and continues until a non-letter is found. Actually there are a couple of exceptions to this rule. Valid words may have apostrophes or hyphens. Since there is little choice but to examine each character in the input sentence and make decisions about words, a brute force approach is called for.

The first step is to set up a double-subscripted array to store the words that are found in the input sentence. Then the user is prompted for the sentence, which is stored in its own array. The logic begins with an examination of the first character in the input array. If it is a valid letter, it is placed in the first position of the first word array, otherwise we move on to the second letter. Once a letter is found, we continue to make the transfer until an invalid character is found. The scheme is then repeated until the end of the sentence is found.

Pseudocode

1. Begin
2.   Declare and initialize variables.
3.   Message to user.
4.   Get sentence.
5.   Begin examination of the characters in the sentence.
6.   If the character is a valid letter.
7.   Make a copy of the character in the proper place in the words array.
8.   Increment the letter counter.
9.   Set the word_flag.
10.   Else If the character is an apostrophe or a hyphen and the next character is a letter.
11.   Copy the character.
12.   Increment the letter counter.
13.   If the character is neither a letter nor apostrophe or hyphen and the word flag is set.
14.   Terminate the current word with a NULL.
15.   Increment the word counter.
16.   Reset the letter counter to zero.
17.   Reset the word flag.
18.   Increment the sentence counter.
19.   End the loop when the NULL is found terminating the sentence.
20.   Output a list of words.
21. End

Flowchart

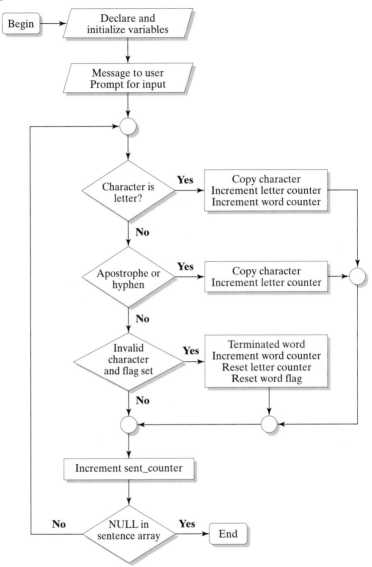

Solution Implemented in C++

```
1    //  Problem 4.4
2    #include <iostream.h>
3
4    int main(void)
5    {
6        char sentence[401], words[20][21];
```

```
7     int sent_counter = 0, word_counter = 0, letter_counter = 0;
8     int word_flag = 0, output;
9     cout << "Enter a sentence . .    " << endl;
10    cin.getline(sentence,401,'\n');
11    cout << endl;
12    do
13    {
14       if (sentence[sent_counter] >= 'A' && sentence[sent_counter] <= 'Z'
15             ||    sentence[sent_counter] >= 'a'
16          && sentence[sent_counter] <= 'z')
17       {
18          words[word_counter][letter_counter++] = sentence[sent_counter];
19          word_flag = 1;
20       }
21       else if ((sentence[sent_counter] == 39
22             || sentence[sent_counter] == '-')
23             && sentence[sent_counter + 1] >= 'a'
24             && sentence[sent_counter + 1] <= 'z')
25          words[word_counter][letter_counter++] = sentence[sent_counter];
26       else if (word_flag == 1)
27       {
28          words[word_counter][letter_counter] = 0;
29          word_counter++, letter_counter = 0;
30          word_flag = 0;
31       }
32       sent_counter++;
33    }while(sentence[sent_counter] != 0);
34    if (word_flag == 1)
35    {
36       words[word_counter][letter_counter] = 0;
37       word_counter++, letter_counter = 0;
38    }
39    for (output = 0; output < word_counter; output++)
40       cout << "word[" << output << "] = " << words[output] << endl;
41    return(0);
42 }
```

Lines 39 and 40 list the words that were found in the text. In reality this list would generally not be the end point of the program. If some position indicator were stored with each word, a keyword could be compared to the list with the purpose of determining whether the keyword was in the text and where it would be found. In other words, isolating individual words might be the first step in creating an indexing program. A spell checker could be created by comparing each word in the list with the words in a dictionary file.

There are two nonobvious features in this program. The first is the use of the word_flag variable. The use of the word *flag* in the name indicates that the variable is probably used to keep track of some event. When word_flag is set, a word has been started. When some punctuation or white space is encountered and the word_flag is set, then the word should be terminated and the word_counter is incremented and letter_counter is reset to zero so the next set of proper characters is placed in the correct array starting at the beginning.

The second nonobvious feature is the `if` statement on lines 34 to 38. This code terminates the last word in the list with a NULL and properly increments the counter if the user fails to end the sentence with a punctuation mark.

Output of C++ Program

```
Enter a sentence . .
"123 isn't a number of which I approve!" said Erica semi-emphatically.

word[0] = isn't
word[1] = a
word[2] = number
word[3] = of
word[4] = which
word[5] = I
word[6] = approve
word[7] = said
word[8] = Erica
word[9] = semi-emphatically
```

When the analysis begins, the first five characters fail to begin a word. Only when the "i" in `isn't` is found does the program begin to copy letters into `words[0]`. Notice that the apostrophe in `isn't` and the hyphen in `semi-emphatically` do not terminate the words but the exclamation point after `approve` does.

Solution Implemented in Visual Basic

```
1    Option Explicit
2    Private Sub cmdExit_Click()
3      Unload Me
4    End Sub
5    Private Sub cmdFind_Click()
6        Dim Sentence  As String
7        Dim Words(0 To 19) As String
8        Dim Letter As String
9        Dim NextLetter As String
10       Dim WordCtr As Integer
11       Dim SentenceCtr As Integer
12       Dim Index As Integer
13       Dim WordFlag As Boolean
14       WordCtr = 0
15       SentenceCtr = 1
16       WordFlag = False
17       Sentence = txtInput.Text
18       Do While SentenceCtr <= Len(Sentence)
19           Letter = Mid(Sentence, SentenceCtr, 1)
20           NextLetter = Mid(Sentence, SentenceCtr + 1, 1)
21           If Letter >= "A" And Letter <= "Z" _
22               Or Letter >= "a" And Letter <= "z" Then
23                 Words(WordCtr) = Words(WordCtr) & Letter
24                 WordFlag = True
25           ElseIf (Letter = "-" Or Letter = "'") _
26                   And (NextLetter >= "a" And NextLetter <= "z") Then
```

```
27              Words(WordCtr) = Words(WordCtr) & Letter
28          ElseIf WordFlag = True Then
29              WordCtr = WordCtr + 1
30              WordFlag = False
31          End If
32          SentenceCtr = SentenceCtr + 1
33      Loop
34      If Words(WordCtr) = "" Then
35          WordCtr = WordCtr - 1
36      End If
37      Call lstOutput.Clear
38      For Index = 0 To WordCtr
39          lstOutput.AddItem ("word[" & Format(Index) & "] = " & _
40          Words(Index))
41      Next Index
42  End Sub
43  Private Sub cmdReset_Click()
44      txtInput.Text = ""
45      Call lstOutput.Clear
46  End Sub
47  Private Sub Form_Activate()
48      txtInput.SetFocus
49  End Sub
```

Output of the Visual Basic Program

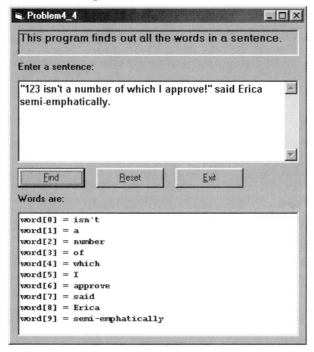

The algorithm used in the basic program is nearly identical to one used in the C++ program. However, it is more convenient in Visual Basic to use variables of the data type `string` to store the words constructed from the user input. Line 7 declares the array of 20 `string` variables. The C++ program could have used a similar string object but C-style strings constructed in character arrays are more commonly used in introductory classes with string objects introduced later. To transfer the individual characters from the input string to the proper members of the string array, the `Mid()` function was used for the extraction of the characters (line 19) and concatenation used to build each new word (line 27).

The idea of searching text for individual words leads to other types of searches that make good use of the speed and perseverance of a computer.

Before the age of digital encryption the frequency for the occurrence of letters was the basis for breaking letter substitution ciphers. Some board games place point value on letters based on this same frequency of occurrence. The idea of letter frequency in a language raises the question posed in Problem 4.5.

PROBLEM 4.5   *What are the most commonly used letters in the English language?*

Of course, to truly answer this question we would need to brute force our way through a vast amount of text written in English. This would not be difficult for the computer, but it would be rather tedious for the human who had to enter the text. One way around this difficulty would be to find a rather large text file on the Internet and have the program open the file and count the occurrence of each letter. A Steven King novel might be representative of current American writing. The Constitution of the United States might also serve, although the writing is in an older, more formal style. It might seem that examining a dictionary would be a means to find an absolute answer to the question. However, in English words like *the*, *a*, and *to* are used far more frequently than *cozen*, which increases the frequency of certain letters. To get a reasonable answer we will merely have the user enter a large amount of text, perhaps up to 4,000 characters.

Initial Data:	**1.**	A large amount of text to be examined will be supplied by the user.
	2.	Each letter in the input string can be used to increment an appropriate counter.
	3.	The frequency can be found by dividing the number of times an individual letter appears by the total number of letters.
Output:		Find how often each letter appears in the text as an absolute count and a percentage of the total number of letters.

Luckily, the problem poses a secondary problem for the programmer. After studying Problem 4.4, scanning the input string presents no problem and testing against every possible letter (counting uppercase and lowercase there are 52 letters) can be easily done. However, writing the code to make 52 individual tests for 52 possible characters and manually tracking 26 counters represent more typing tedium than most programmers would enjoy. Brute force is for computers, not programmers. So the more interesting problem is how to conveniently program all these tests.

First, we need a more convenient way to move through the input string than incrementing a counter for the array that stores the input. C++ allows the use of pointer variables that store address locations. Since the input string is stored in continuous memory, we can set a pointer to the beginning of that memory area and merely move the pointer from one character to the next. This means that every character examined is referred to in the same way, that is, the character that the pointer points to. If ptr is declared as a pointer and the pointer is set to the beginning of the input[4000] array, lines 8 and 16 in the following program, then ptr starts by pointing to input[0]. At the end of the first loop cycle the pointer is incremented, ptr++, and then ptr points to input[1]. In this way one and the same variable, *ptr, is used to indicate each character in the input array.

It's clear that there is a need for 26 variables to store the number of times each character appears in the text. Rather than defining these as a_counter, b_counter, or c_counter an array of counters such as letters[26] will be more convenient. This will allow each letter found in the text to choose its own counter. The trick here is to list as initial data the fact that computers do not store letters. Computers only store 1s and 0s. To store a representation of a letter the computer really stores a binary number that is equivalent to the ASCII value of the letter.

Lowercase letters range from $a = 97$ to $z = 122$. If the pointer, *ptr, is pointing to an a, the letters[0] counter can be chosen to be incremented by

```
20    letters[*ptr - 97]++
```

Remember if *ptr is pointing to the letter a, the real value of *ptr is 97, the ASCII value for a. By subtracting 97 from *ptr the index for letters becomes zero, i.e., letters[0]. The "++" operator following the index causes letters[0] to increment by one. Similarly, if *ptr points to a b, then 97 is subtracted from the ASCII value for b or 98, causing letters[1] to be incremented.

The end result of this method is that we can make one test to determine if the current character is in the range from a to z (ASCII 97 to 122) and, if it is, then the letter itself will choose the correct counter to increment. The same operation needs to be performed for the uppercase letters. Since the uppercase letters begin with $A = 65$, the only change to line 20 is to subtract 65 instead of 97, that is,

```
22    letters[*ptr - 65]++
```

Now that the problem within the problem is solved, the pseudocode can be written.

Pseudocode

1. Begin
2.   Declare and initialize variables.
3.   Message to user and prompt for input.
4.   Begin testing loop.
5.   Test for lowercase letters.

6.   If found, increment letter and total letter counters.

7.   Test for uppercase letters.

8.   If found, increment letter and total letter counters.

9.   Move pointer to next letter.

10.   End loop if pointer points to NULL.

11.   Display results.

12. End

Flowchart

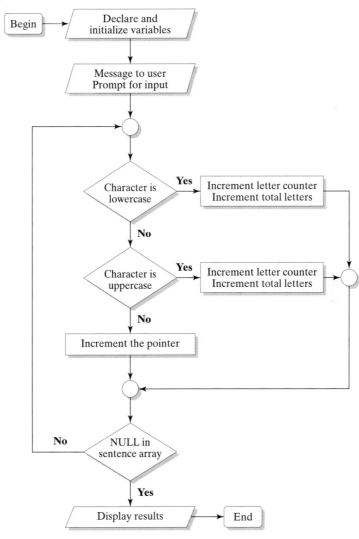

Solution Implemented in C++

```
1    // Problem 4.5
2    #include <stdio.h>
3    #include <conio.h>
4    #include <iomanip.h>
5
6    void main(void)
7    {
8       char *ptr, input[4000];
9       int letters[26] = {0}, counter, total_letters = 0;
10      cout << "This program will calculate the frequency of "
11          << "\n\tthe letters 'a' through 'z' in sample text."
12          << "\n\nEnter the text ... Hit <Esc> to stop entering\n\n" << endl;
13      cin.getline(input,4000,27);
14      cout.precision(2);
15      cout.setf(ios::fixed|ios::showpoint);
16      ptr = input;
17      do
18      {
19         if (*ptr >= 'a' && *ptr <= 'z')
20            letters[*ptr - 97]++, total_letters++;
21         if (*ptr >= 'A' && *ptr <= 'Z')
22            letters[*ptr - 65]++, total_letters++;
23         ptr++;
24      }while(*ptr != 0);
25      cout << endl;
26      for (counter = 0; counter < 13; counter++)
27      {
28         cout << setw(2) << static_cast<char>(counter + 97) << " -> "
29             << setw(4) << letters[counter] << " -> " << setw(7)
30             << letters[counter] * 100.0 / total_letters << "%            "
31             << setw(2) << static_cast<char>(counter + 110) << " -> "
32             << setw(4) << letters[counter + 13] << " -> " << setw(7)
33             << letters[counter + 13] * 100.0 / total_letters << "%"
34             << endl;
35      }
36   }
```

Line 8 declares the input array to be large enough for 4,000 characters, which is large enough for a proof-of-concept even if it is too small for an accurate answer to the question. The pointer variable is initialized to the address of input on line 16. Notice that ptr can be assigned the value of input because input itself is a pointer. The name of any array stores an address that points to the beginning of the array. However, the name of an array is a pointer constant and can never change. The use of input++ would produce a compiler error. Ptr can move through the array because it is a pointer variable; input may never point anywhere except to the beginning of the array.

The use of ptr isn't strictly necessary but it is a great convenience. If the pointer were not used, line 20 would become

```
20   letters[index[counter]- 97]++
```

where `counter` is used to indicate each of the letters of the `input` string. Nesting array indexes tend to cause confusion.

The output display deserves a little explanation. Microsoft's C++ compiler no longer recognizes commands to place text in a specified location in a command window. In earlier versions one column of information could be sent to the screen and then a second column constructed to the right of the first. To simulate the effect of two columns the output display loop constructs 13 lines of output. Each line displays the information for one letter and then, to the right, displays the information for the letter 13 places farther into the alphabet. Consequently, *a* and *n* are on the same line as are *b* and *o*.

Output of the C++ Program

```
This program will calculate the frequency of
   the letters 'a' to 'z' in sample text

Enter the text ...  Hit <Esc> to stop entering

In the year 1878 I took my degree of Doctor of Medicine of the University of
London, and proceeded to Netley to go through the course prescribed for
surgeons in the army. Having completed my studies there, I was duly attached
to the Fifth Northumberland Fusiliers as assistant surgeon. The regiment was
stationed in India at the time, and before I could join it, the second Afghan
war had broken out. On landing at Bombay, I learned that my corps had
advanced through the passes, and was already deep in the enemy's country. I
followed, however, with many other officers who were in the same situation as
myself, and succeeded in reaching Candahar in safety, where I found my
regiment, and at once entered upon my new duties.


a ->    45 ->     7.80%              n ->    47 ->    8.15%
b ->     6 ->     1.04%              o ->    44 ->    7.63%
c ->    18 ->     3.12%              p ->     7 ->    1.21%
d ->    36 ->     6.24%              q ->     0 ->    0.00%
e ->    77 ->    13.34%              r ->    35 ->    6.07%
f ->    16 ->     2.77%              s ->    32 ->    5.55%
g ->    12 ->     2.08%              t ->    49 ->    8.49%
h ->    31 ->     5.37%              u ->    18 ->    3.12%
i ->    39 ->     6.76%              v ->     4 ->    0.69%
j ->     1 ->     0.17%              w ->    11 ->    1.91%
k ->     2 ->     0.35%              x ->     0 ->    0.00%
l ->    13 ->     2.25%              y ->    17 ->    2.95%
m ->    17 ->     2.95%              z ->     0 ->    0.00%
```

The text chosen is the opening paragraph of *A Study in Scarlet* by Sir Arthur Conan Doyle. While a single paragraph is not strictly representative of all English text, it does give a fair solution to the question posed in Problem 4.5. The reader who requires a more definitive answer is welcome to type several pages into the program or to jump ahead to Chapter 7 where the entire text of *A Tale of Two Cities* is examined. Regardless of the text chosen *e* and *t* are invariably found to be the most common letters.

Solution Implemented in Visual Basic

```
1    Option Explicit
2    Private Sub cmdCount_Click()
3       Dim InputStr As String
4       Dim Letter(0 To 25) As Integer
5       Dim TotalLetters As Integer
6       Dim ptr As String
7       Dim Ctr As Integer
8       Dim AsciiVal As Byte
9       Dim OutputStr As String
10      Dim Str As String
11      Ctr = 1
12      TotalLetters = 0
13      InputStr = txtInput.Text
14
15      Do While Ctr <= Len(InputStr)
16         ptr = Mid(InputStr, Ctr, 1)
17         AsciiVal = Asc(ptr)
18         If ptr >= "a" And ptr <= "z" Then
19            Letter(AsciiVal - 97) = Letter(AsciiVal - 97) + 1
20            TotalLetters = TotalLetters + 1
21         ElseIf ptr >= "A" And ptr <= "Z" Then
22            Letter(AsciiVal - 65) = Letter(AsciiVal - 65) + 1
23            TotalLetters = TotalLetters + 1
24         End If
25         Ctr = Ctr + 1
26      Loop
27
28      lstOutput.Clear
29      If TotalLetters > 0 Then
30         For Ctr = 0 To 12
31            Str = Space(2)
32            RSet Str = Format(Letter(Ctr))
33            OutputStr = Chr(Ctr + 97) & " -> " & Str & " -> "
34            Str = Space(6)
35            RSet Str = Format((Letter(Ctr) / TotalLetters), "0.00%")
36            OutputStr = OutputStr & Str
37            Str = Space(2)
38            RSet Str = Format(Letter(Ctr + 13))
39            OutputStr = OutputStr & vbTab & vbTab & Chr(Ctr + 110) & _
40               " -> " & Str & " -> "
41            Str = Space(6)
42            RSet Str = Format((Letter(Ctr + 13) / TotalLetters), "0.00%")
43            OutputStr = OutputStr & Str
44            lstOutput.AddItem (OutputStr)
45         Next Ctr
46      End If
47   End Sub
48   Private Sub cmdExit_Click()
49      Unload Me
50   End Sub
```

```
51  Private Sub cmdReset_Click()
52     txtInput.Text = ""
53     Call lstOutput.Clear
54     txtInput.SetFocus
55  End Sub
56  Private Sub Form_Activate()
57     txtInput.SetFocus
58  End Sub
```

As in the C++ program an array of integers was declared (line 4) to store the count for the number of times each letter was found in the text. Line 15 begins the loop that scans the input string, extracting one letter per cycle and incrementing the proper counter. The counter to be incremented was chosen by generating the ASCII value for each letter with the Asc() function on line 17 and the incrementing was performed on either line 19 or 22 depending on whether the letter was lowercase or uppercase.

Because Visual Basic does not use pointers, the integer variable Ctr was used as an indexing variable to step through the input string. Each character was stored temporarily in the one character string called ptr by extracting the characters from the input string with the Mid() function. Unlike the C++ program, comparisons were made to the strings *a* through *z* (line 18) or *A* through *Z* (line 21).

Output of the Visual Basic Program

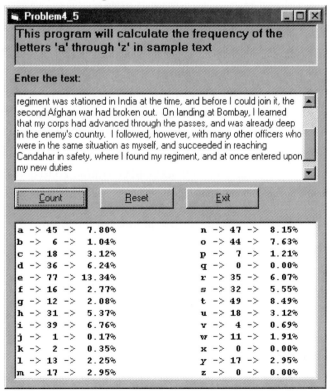

4.6   SORTING ROUTINES

Sorting data, like searching data, falls under the heading of data processing. Automatic data processing is a field that was arguably invented by Herman Hollerith, an agent for the Census Bureau. The 1880 census took one year to collect the information about the U.S. population and nine years to make sense of the data. Hollerith invented a process for mechanizing this brute force task. By encoding the census information on punch cards and feeding the cards through his invention that had wire fingers that would close an electrical circuit when a finger fell through a hole, he could count people in an age group or a profession.

His device became the initial product for his Tabulating Machine Company. In 1911 he merged with three other companies to become the Computing-Tabulating-Recording Company, which later changed its name to International Business Machines (IBM). For the past century sorting data has been a labor-intensive, brute force task that was well suited for the developing computer industry.

In the era when the cost of a computer was listed in millions of dollars only universities and the military could afford to merely have the computer make calculations. For computers to be cost-effective for business the computer had to do something that could result in a return on investment. That profitable task was storing and manipulating data. Consequently, sorting routines have always been included in programming classes, which raises the question in Problem 4.6.

PROBLEM 4.6   *How can a list of 20 numbers be sorted?*

The answer to the question involves the importance of clarity in the objective. The human answer to the question is to "put the biggest (or the smallest) number first, the second biggest number second, and so on." This is a starting point but it relies on the human ability to recognize the biggest number. For a computer to recognize the biggest number in a set of numbers, every number must be compared to each of the other numbers. The biggest number is the number found to be the larger in every comparison.

Initial Data:	**1.** A list of 20 numbers supplied by the user to be sorted.
	2. Two numbers can be compared to determine which is bigger.
	3. If a number is tested against each of the other numbers in a group of numbers and in every case is found to be the larger, it is the biggest number in the group.
Output:	The biggest number is to be listed first, then the second biggest, and so on.

While this is helpful, the initial data does not in itself suggest a plan of attack. Consider a backward approach (Rule 4) and change the question. Instead of asking which number is biggest, ask if the first number is the biggest. This is readily testable. Answering this question is easier if we have a concrete example (Rule 8). Consider the following set of numbers.

4 3 8 6 9

To determine whether four is the biggest number and should remain in the first position it has to be tested against each of the other numbers. The test against three shows four is bigger. The test against eight shows that four is smaller than eight. At this point it is reasonable to switch the positions of four and eight. *Among the first three numbers*, eight is the biggest and should be in the first position.

$$8\ 3\ 4\ 6\ 9$$

Continuing the testing of the first number against the others, we have eight compared to six. Because eight is larger, there is no need for any change. When eight is compared to nine, nine is found to be larger and should be in the first position so the numbers are switched.

$$9\ 3\ 4\ 6\ 8$$

Since the first number in the series has been compared to all others or to the largest in a group of numbers, nine is known to be the biggest number. Notice we know nothing about the other numbers except that none of them is larger than nine. However, we can shift our focus from the first number to the second and repeat the process. In this round all tests will result in switches.

$$9\ 4\ 3\ 6\ 8$$
$$9\ 6\ 3\ 4\ 8$$
$$9\ 8\ 3\ 4\ 6$$

At the conclusion of this cycle of testing the biggest and second biggest number are in their proper positions.

Now we have a repeatable, brute force plan for sorting an arbitrary list of numbers and we are ready to write the pseudocode.

Pseudocode

1. Begin
2.   Declare and initialize variables.
3.   Begin data entry loop for 20 grades.
4.   Prompt for number.
5.   Get grade.
6.   End data entry.
7.   Begin outer loop cycling the target number.
8.   Begin inner loop cycling through the test numbers.
9.   If target number is smaller than test number, switch.
10.   End test loop.
11.   End target loop.
12.   Display 20 numbers.
13. End

Flowchart

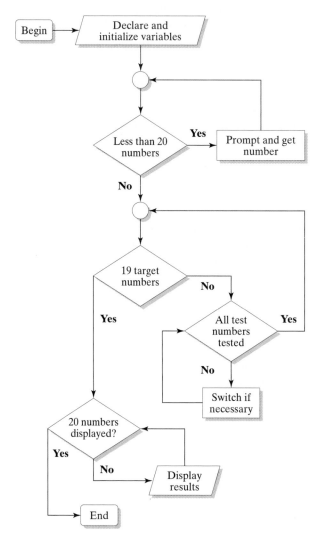

Solution Implemented in C++

```
1    // Problem 4.5
2    #include <iostream.h>
3    #include <iomanip.h>
4
5    int main(void)
6    {
7       int numbers[20], target, test, temp;
8       char ord[20][13] = {"first", "second", "third", "fourth", "fifth",
9       "sixth", "seventh", "eighth", "ninth", "tenth", "eleventh", "twelfth",
10         "thirteenth", "fourteenth", "fifteenth", "sixteenth",
```

```
11           "seventeenth", "eighteenth", "nineteenth", "twentieth"};
12           cout.setf(ios::left);
13       for (target = 0; target < 20; target++)
14       {
15           cout << "Enter the " << setw(11) <<ord[target] << " number . . "
16              << flush;
17           cin >> numbers[target];
18       }
19       for (target = 0; target < 19; target++)
20          for (test = target + 1; test < 20; test++)
21             if (numbers[target] < numbers[test])
22             {
23                 temp = numbers[target];
24                 numbers[target] = numbers[test];
25                 numbers[test] = temp;
26             }
27       for (target = 0; target < 20; target++)
28          cout << " The " << setw(11) << ord[target] << " grade is "
29             << numbers[target] << endl;
30       return(0);
31   }
```

The ordinal numbers, ord[20][13], are not necessary to the logic of the program but do make the input prompts and the output display more readable.

The logic of the nested loops has already been described but the switching routine itself, beginning with the if() statement on line 21, deserves some explanation. The value of numbers[target] has to be stored in a temporary site (namely, the variable temp) before the code

```
24                numbers[target] = numbers[test];
```

is executed. If a temporary copy is not made, the valued stored in numbers[target] will be overwritten, erasing the value that should later be placed in numbers[test].

Having derived an algorithm that will order the largest number first, the next logical question is how the program might be altered to reverse the numbers to produce a list with the smallest number first. The answer is in the test condition on line 21.

```
21                if (numbers[target] < numbers[test])
```

Line 21 tests whether the first number, numbers[target], is smaller than the number it is being tested against, numbers[test]. If the test returns a true, the numbers are switched placing the larger of the two first. If the less than operator is replaced by greater than, the smaller number will be placed first if it's not there already. It should also be noticed that in case of a tie in the test, no switch is made. The switch could be made but the result of the switch would be unnoticeable if the numbers were the same.

While the execution of this program is virtually instantaneous, the number of operations involved should not be overlooked. If the list of numbers is large, the amount of work for the microprocessor grows considerably. A more efficient algorithm might be advisable for the sorting of all the subscribers to a popular magazine by zip code. Sorting the census records by household income is another example where the select sort might not be the best approach.

Output of the C++ Program

```
Enter the first       number . .  44
Enter the second      number . .  56
Enter the third       number . .  67
Enter the fourth      number . .  34
Enter the fifth       number . .  -9
Enter the sixth       number . .  0
Enter the seventh     number . .  -45
Enter the eighth      number . .  3
Enter the ninth       number . .  282
Enter the tenth       number . .  63
Enter the eleventh    number . .  12
Enter the twelfth     number . .  -34
Enter the thirteenth  number . .  33
Enter the fourteenth  number . .  90
Enter the fifteenth   number . .  93
Enter the sixteenth   number . .  23
Enter the seventeenth number . .  293
Enter the eighteenth  number . .  23
Enter the nineteenth  number . .  132
Enter the twentieth   number . .  234

   The first       grade is 293
   The second      grade is 282
   The third       grade is 234
   The fourth      grade is 132
   The fifth       grade is 93
   The sixth       grade is 90
   The seventh     grade is 67
   The eighth      grade is 63
   The ninth       grade is 56
   The tenth       grade is 44
   The eleventh    grade is 34
   The twelfth     grade is 33
   The thirteenth  grade is 23
   The fourteenth  grade is 23
   The fifteenth   grade is 12
   The sixteenth   grade is 3
   The seventeenth grade is 0
   The eighteenth  grade is -9
   The nineteenth  grade is -34
   The twentieth   grade is -45
```

Solution Implemented in Visual Basic

```
1    Option Explicit
2    Private Numbers(0 To 19) As Integer
3    Private Ctr As Integer
4    Private Order(0 To 19) As String
5
6    Private Sub cmdAdd_Click()
7        Dim Str As String
8        Dim Num As Integer
9        If IsNumeric(txtInput.Text) = False Then
10           Call MsgBox("Invalid input", vbInformation + vbOKOnly)
11           Exit Sub
12       End If
13       Num = CInt(txtInput.Text)
14       Numbers(Ctr) = Num
15       Str = "The " & Order(Ctr) & vbTab & "number " & ": " & _
16           Format(Num)
17       lstOutput.AddItem (Str)
18       Ctr = Ctr + 1
19       If Ctr >= 20 Then
20           cmdAdd.Enabled = False
21           cmdSort.Enabled = True
22           Exit Sub
23       End If
24       lblNumber.Caption = Format(Ctr + 1)
25       txtInput.Text = ""
26       Call txtInput.SetFocus
27   End Sub
28   Private Sub cmdExit_Click()
29       Unload Me
30   End Sub
31   Private Sub cmdSort_Click()
32       Dim target As Integer
33       Dim test As Integer
34       Dim temp As Integer
35       Dim Str As String
36       For target = 0 To 18
37           For test = target + 1 To 19
38               If Numbers(target) < Numbers(test) Then
39                   temp = Numbers(target)
40                   Numbers(target) = Numbers(test)
41                   Numbers(test) = temp
42               End If
43           Next test
44       Next target
45       lstOutput.Clear
46       For target = 0 To 19
47           Str = "The " & Order(target) & vbTab & "number is : " & _
48               Numbers(target)
```

```
49            lstOutput.AddItem (Str)
50        Next target
51   End Sub
52   Private Sub Form_Load()
53        Dim index As Integer
54        Ctr = 0
55        cmdSort.Enabled = False
56        Order(0) = "first"
57        Order(1) = "second"
58        Order(2) = "third"
59        Order(3) = "fourth"
60        Order(4) = "fifth"
61        Order(5) = "sixth"
62        Order(6) = "seventh"
63        Order(7) = "eighth"
64        Order(8) = "ninth"
65        Order(9) = "tenth"
66        Order(10) = "eleventh"
67        Order(11) = "twelfth"
68        Order(12) = "thirteenth"
69        Order(13) = "fourteenth"
70        Order(14) = "fifteenth"
71        Order(15) = "sixteenth"
72        Order(16) = "seventeenth"
73        Order(17) = "eighteenth"
74        Order(18) = "nineteenth"
75        Order(19) = "twentieth"
76   End Sub
```

The sorting algorithm in the Visual Basic program is identical to the one used in the C++ program and is found between lines 36 and 44. Most of the differences between the two programs involve the formatting required for the control buttons and the text boxes. However, there is one element that was added to the Visual Basic program that deserves some comment. For the programs up to this point no effort was made to ensure that the user entered a proper value. The assumption was made that when the user was prompted for an integer value, the user would not enter "dog." In fact this assumption is rather rash and it is often prudent to add error checking to the program. Line 9 tests the user input to determine if it is a numeric value and, if it is not, the subroutine is restarted without attempting to add the improper value to the list of numbers to be sorted.

Output of the Visual Basic Program

Before the sort:

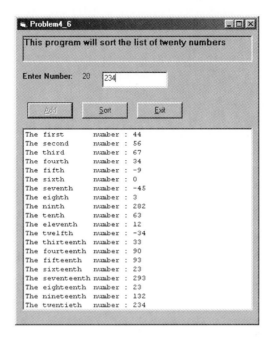

Output of the Visual Basic Program

After the sort:

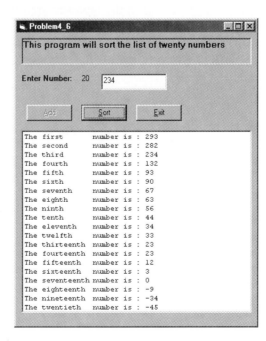

A second and usually more efficient approach to sorting is the bubble sort. Depending on the data, a bubble sort can accomplish a sorting with fewer tests of the data than the previous select sort routine. To create a little variation in Problem 4.6 the student's name will be associated with the number in Problem 4.7.

PROBLEM 4.7   *Sort a list of 20 students by their grades using a bubble sort routine.*

This problem poses two challenges. The first is to develop another sorting routine, apparently called a bubble sort, and second to devise a way to tie students' names to the grades so that, when the grades are sorted, the names are carried along with the grades as the sorting is performed. The first issue is a logic problem; the second is a programming problem.

Consider again the numbers used to develop the select sort in solving Problem 4.6. Instead of selecting the largest and moving it to the beginning of the list, we could compare every pair of adjacent numbers and switch the numbers if necessary. Examining the results of comparing the first to the second, the second to the third, the third to the fourth, and so on through the lists, we find:

$$4\ 3\ 8\ 6\ 9$$
$$4\ 8\ 3\ 6\ 9$$
$$4\ 8\ 6\ 3\ 9$$
$$4\ 8\ 6\ 9\ 3$$

When 3 is compared to 8, the numbers are switched, putting 3 in the third position. The next test compares 3 to 6 and again the numbers are switched and 3 is moved to the fourth position. The final test of 3 and 9 switches 3 to the last position. While 3 moved steadily toward the end, the larger numbers moved up (or bubbled up) one position. The 8 and the 9 haven't reached their final positions, but they are moving in the right direction.

Repeating the operation, starting again with the first pair of numbers, we have

$$4\ 8\ 6\ 9\ 3$$
$$8\ 4\ 6\ 9\ 3$$
$$8\ 6\ 4\ 9\ 3$$
$$8\ 6\ 4\ 9\ 3$$

At this stage 4 and 3 have reached their final position and the larger numbers have again bubbled toward the front of the list.

At this point the obvious question is how many times does this operation have to be repeated before all the numbers are in their correct position? In this case four cycles are required to allow the 9 to reach the beginning of the list, but will the number of grades minus one always be required? If the numbers **8 6 9 4 3** had been the starting sequence, only two rounds of testing would have brought the numbers into their final position of **9 8 6 4 3**.

The fact that further rounds of testing would result in no changes provides the clue as to when to stop the loop. If a flag variable is set to zero at the beginning of each round of testing and any switching of numbers causes the flag to change to one, then a `while` loop can be set up to test the flag. If a round of testing is completed and no switching was needed, the flag would remain at zero, indicating the sorting is complete and the loop should end.

Initial Data: **1.** A list of 20 students and their grades will be hard coded into the program for convenience.

2. Two numbers can be compared to determine which is larger.

3. If a student's grade is tested against the student's grade immediately following in the list and found to be smaller, the students should be switched so the student with the larger grade comes before the student with the smaller.

4. If the process of comparing every grade to the following grade is repeated for each pair of grades, and the procedure is continued until no change is made for the entire cycle, the sorting is complete.

Output: **1.** The highest grade is to be listed first, then the second highest, and so on.

2. The student's name should be kept with each grade.

The second output requirement has not yet been considered. However, programming languages allow for dissimilar types of data to be grouped, in this case, an integer and a string. When the grades are tested and a switch is required, instead of merely switching the grades, *the variables containing the combined integer-string data can be switched.*

Pseudocode

1. Begin

2.   Declare and initialize variables.

3.   Begin outer loop cycling the target number.

4.   Set the flag to zero.

5.   Begin inner loop cycling through the test numbers.

6.   If target number is smaller than target number plus one, switch the structure variables.

7.   End inner loop.

8.   Increment counter; decrement stop.

9. End outer loop.
10. Display 20 grades. Two columns would be nice.
11. End

Most of the pseudocode has already been explained. Step 8 has a couple of new ideas. The counter variable is not really part of the logic of the program but has been included to count the number of cycles of the outer loop. The purpose of using a bubble sort is to minimize the amount of work the program has to perform and presumably create a faster running program. In the select sort program the outer loop ran 19 times, one less than the number of grades to be sorted. Hopefully the bubble sort will finish the task in fewer cycles than the select sort and prove to be more efficient. Displaying the value of the counter will show the improvement.

The purpose of the stop variable will be explained after the C++ code has been presented.

Flowchart

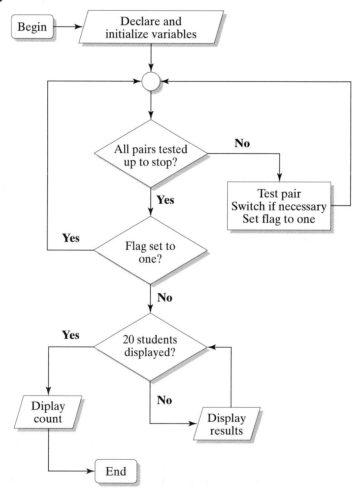

Solution Implemented in C++

```
1   // Problem 4.7          Bubble Sort
2   #include <iostream.h>
3   #include <iomanip.h>
4
5   struct data
6   {
7      char name[30];
8      int grade;
9   };
10
11  int main(void)
12  {
13     data students[20] = {{"Able, John",68},{"Baker, Terry",78},
14        {"Chesterton, Tom",93},{"Dallas, Donald",86},
15        {"Everet, Jan",64},{"Frederick, Al",71},{"Gregory, Paul",61},
16        {"Huston, Halley",96},{"Isaacs, Ian",88},{"Johnson, Jon",74},
17        {"Keys, Arron",89},{"Laws, Lewis",84},{"Laws, Louise",85},
18        {"Moore, Mic",91},{"Norris, Charley",69},{"Ovis, Rad",80},
19        {"Pastor, Reg",75},{"Quince, Zed",76},{"Rantor, Ralph",78},
20        {"Smith, John",74}};
21     data temp;
22     int target, output, flag, stop = 19, counter = 0;
23     do
24     {
25        flag = 0;
26        for (target = 0; target < stop; target++)
27           if (students[target].grade < students[target + 1].grade)
28           {
29              temp = students[target];
30              students[target] = students[target + 1];
31              students[target + 1] = temp;
32              flag = 1;
33           }
34        stop--, counter++;
35     }while (flag == 1);
36     for (output = 0; output < 10; output++)
37        cout << setw(2) << output + 1 << setw(20) << students[output].name
38           << setw(4) << students[output].grade
39           << setw(10) << output + 11 << setw(20)
40           << students[output + 10].name
41           << setw(4) << students[output + 10].grade << endl;
42     cout << endl << "The sorting required " << counter << " cycles."
43        << endl << endl;
44     return(0);
45  }
```

Of course, a real program used to sort values would not have the data included in the program. The data would instead either be entered by the user as in the previous problem or be read from a data file. However, when developing the programs it is often useful to bypass the data entry and focus on the data manipulation. When the program is tested and found to be performing properly, the data entry routine from the user or from a file can be added. To create a point of reference, the original list of student names is arranged in alphabetical order.

Two elements combine to give the bubble sort greater efficiency than the select sort. The first is the use of the `flag` variable to stop the sorting process, possibly before the maximum number of tests are made. The second is the `stop` variable. To compare the efficiency of the two routines we need to reexamine each program more closely.

In the select sort a list of 20 numbers always requires that the same number of tests be made. The outer loop will always run 19 times. The number of times the inner loop runs is variable beginning at 19 times for the first loop and decreasing by one each cycle. The total number of cycles is given by

$$Total\_cycles = 19 + 18 + 17 + \ldots + 1$$
$$Total\_cycles = 190$$

The bubble sort is potentially less efficient. At its worst the outer loop would run 19 times and the inner loop would make 19 tests giving

$$Total\_cycles = 19 \times 19$$
$$Total\_cycles = 361$$

However, after the first cycle of the outer loop, the smallest number will be at the end of the list, meaning that the next cycle will not have to make the final test. Cycle two of the outer loop only requires 18 tests. Similarly, after the second cycle, the second smallest number will be in the second to last position, so cycle three will only require 17 tests. The `stop` variable used in the test condition for the inner loop controls the number of tests made.

```
26          for (target = 0; target < stop; target++)
```

For each cycle of the outer loop the value of `stop` is reduced by one on line 34. By reducing the number of tests in succeeding cycles the total number of tests is reduced to 19 on the first cycle, 18 on the second, 17 on the third, and so on, or

$$Total\_cycles = 19 + 18 + 17 + \ldots + 1$$
$$Total\_cycles = 190$$

the same number as the select sort. With the use of the `stop` variable, the bubble sort at its worst, requires the same number of tests as the select sort. Using the `flag` variable to potentially end the sorting before all the cycles have run gives the bubble sort its advantage. The only time that the bubble sort will run the maximum number of cycles is when the largest number is last in the list.

Output of the C++ Program

1	Huston, Halley	96	11	Rantor, Ralph	78
2	Chesterton, Tom	93	12	Quince, Zed	76
3	Moore, Mic	91	13	Pastor, Reg	75
4	Keys, Arron	89	14	Johnson, Jon	74
5	Isaacs, Ian	88	15	Smith, John	74
6	Dallas, Donald	86	16	Frederick, Al	71
7	Laws, Louise	85	17	Norris, Charley	69
8	Laws, Lewis	84	18	Able, John	68
9	Ovis, Rad	80	19	Everet, Jan	64
10	Baker, Terry	78	20	Gregory, Paul	61

```
The sorting required 12 cycles.
```

The key to making the students' names follow the grades as they are sorted is in the test condition.

```
27              if (students[target].grade < students[target + 1].grade)
28              {
29                  temp = students[target];
30                  students[target] = students[target + 1];
31                  students[target + 1] = temp;
32                  flag = 1;
33              }
```

Notice that the grades are the items being tested on line 27 but the switching routine moves the students, the variable containing names and grades, to their proper place in the sorted list. Line 32 contains the flag variable that was not present in the select sort algorithm.

Solution Implemented in Visual Basic

```
1   Option Explicit
2   Private Type udtStudentData
3       Name As String
4       Grade As Integer
5   End Type
6   Private Students(0 To 19) As udtStudentData
7
8   Private Sub cmdExit_Click()
9       Unload Me
10  End Sub
11
12  Private Sub cmdSort_Click()
13      Dim Target, Output, Flag, StopPoint, Counter As Integer
14      Dim Temp As udtStudentData
15      Dim Str1 As String
16      Dim Str2 As String
17      Dim NumStr As String
18      Flag = 1
19      StopPoint = 18
20
```

```
21      Do While Flag = 1
22          Flag = 0
23          For Target = 0 To StopPoint
24              If Students(Target).Grade < Students(Target + 1).Grade Then
25                  Temp = Students(Target)
26                  Students(Target) = Students(Target + 1)
27                  Students(Target + 1) = Temp
28                  Flag = 1
29              End If
30          Next Target
31          StopPoint = StopPoint - 1
32          Counter = Counter + 1
33      Loop
34
35      For Output = 0 To 9
36          Str1 = Space(20)
37          NumStr = Space(2)
38          RSet Str1 = Students(Output).Name
39          RSet NumStr = Format(Output + 1)
40          Str1 = NumStr & Str1 & " " & _
41              Format(Students(Output).Grade)
42          Str2 = Space(20)
43          RSet Str2 = Students(Output + 10).Name
44          Str2 = Format(Output + 11) & Str2 & " " & _
45              Format(Students(Output + 10).Grade)
46          lstOutput.AddItem (Str1 & vbTab & Str2)
47      Next Output
48  End Sub
49
50  Private Sub Form_Load()
51      Call UpdateStudent("Able, John", 68, 0)
52      Call UpdateStudent("Baker, Terry", 78, 1)
53      Call UpdateStudent("Chesterton, Tom", 93, 2)
54      Call UpdateStudent("Dallas, Donald", 86, 3)
55      Call UpdateStudent("Everet, Jan", 64, 4)
56      Call UpdateStudent("Frederick, Al", 71, 5)
57      Call UpdateStudent("Gregory, Faul", 61, 6)
58      Call UpdateStudent("Huston, Halley", 96, 7)
59      Call UpdateStudent("Isaacs, Ian", 88, 8)
60      Call UpdateStudent("Johnson, Jon", 74, 9)
61      Call UpdateStudent("Keys, Arron", 89, 10)
62      Call UpdateStudent("Laws, Lewis", 84, 11)
63      Call UpdateStudent("Laws, Louise", 85, 12)
64      Call UpdateStudent("Moore, Mic", 91, 13)
65      Call UpdateStudent("Norris, Charley", 69, 14)
66      Call UpdateStudent("Ovis, Rad", 78, 15)
67      Call UpdateStudent("Pastor, Reg", 75, 16)
68      Call UpdateStudent("Quince, Zed", 76, 17)
69      Call UpdateStudent("Rantor, Ralph", 78, 18)
70      Call UpdateStudent("Smith, John", 74, 19)
71  End Sub
72
73  Public Sub UpdateStudent(ByVal Name As String, _
```

```
74                              ByVal Grade As Integer, _
75                              ByVal Index As Integer)
76        Students(Index).Name = Name
77        Students(Index).Grade = Grade
78   End Sub
```

As in the C++ program, the Visual Basic program begins with the definition of the new data type that will store the necessary data, that is, a string and an integer.

The Do While loop beginning on line 21 performs the bubble sort. Line 24 tests the data based on the grade stored in Students data and switches the Students data if necessary. The Flag variable is again used to terminate the loop if no switch is made during a whole cycle, indicating that the data is in the correct order. StopPoint controls the terminating point for the inner loop and eliminates the testing of data that is known to already be in the correct position.

Output of the Visual Basic Program

Searching routines of Section 4.5 and the sorting routines developed in the last two problems are often combined to create an index.

4.7   COMBINING SEARCHING AND SORTING

Each problem solved represents a building block that can be used in more complex problems. As this repertoire of experience grows, larger and more complex problems come to be within the scope of the problemsolver's ability. Problem 4.8 combines searching and sorting.

PROBLEM 4.8   *Create an index for text entered by the user.*

Typically an index is created for a large amount of text, this book, for example. However, as a proof-of-concept exercise, we can use a smaller amount of text, isolate each word, note its position in the text, and alphabetize the list. To make a real index the program would be altered to accept an unlimited amount of text, most likely from a file, and track page numbers instead of word positions. This is not terribly difficult but requires the program to access memory dynamically in order to handle the potentially large volume of information contained in the text which is unknown until run time. These more expansive topics will be addressed in Chapters 7 and 8.

Because of the experience gained in the previous sections, the initial data available for solving Problem 4.8 is surprisingly large.

Initial Data: **1.** The user will supply some text.

2. Separating the text into component words is a known and practiced operation. (Problem 4.4)

3. Tying the word position (an integer) to a word (a string) is the same as tying a grade (an integer) to a student (a string). (Problem 4.7)

4. Strings can be sorted the same way that integers are sorted because letters are stored in memory as ASCII values, that is, as integers.

5. If two strings are compared that begin with the same letter, the tie can be broken by comparing the second letters. If there is still a tie, subsequent letters can be compared.

6. Luckily, C++ has a string compare function that will make the necessary tests for ordering the strings automatically.

Output: List the words alphabetically with their position numbers.

Not only is there a surprisingly large amount of information for attacking the problem, but also there is surprisingly little to do that hasn't been done in previous programs. The data structure will contain one string and one integer, just as in Problem 4.7. The sentence will be broken into component words, just as in Problem 4.4, except that the words will be stored in an array of structures instead of an array of words. A bubble sort will be used for the sorting routine. And the display loop will show one word and its position on each output line in a two-column format.

As problems become more complex, it becomes increasingly important to keep in mind the functions rule (Rule 11). This is especially true when the functions are little more than problems already solved, that is, programs already written. With this in mind the pseudocode should be written twice: once in broad strokes, ignoring the details, and a second time with more of the details included.

Pseudocode—First Pass

1. Begin

2. Get text from the user.

3. Break the text into words storing the words and their positions in an array of data structures.

4. Sort the array alphabetically using a bubble sort.

5. Display the words and their original positions in the text.

6. End

Pseudocode—Second Pass

1. Begin

2. Declare data structure, declare and initialize variables.

3. Prompt user for text.

4. Get text.

5. Begin loop that finds words and stores them.

6.   If character is letter.

7.   Copy letter to word in data array.

8.   Set the word-started flag.

9.   If character is hyphen or apostrophe and next character is letter.

10.   Copy character to current words.

11.   If character is not a letter or hyphen or apostrophe and a word has been started.

12.   Set position value for the word.

13.   Terminate the word with a NULL.

14.   Increment word_counter.

15.   Reset letter_counter and word_flag.

16.   Increment sentence_counter.

17. End loop when the NULL is found.

18. Begin the bubble sort loop.

19.   Reset the flag to zero.

20.   Begin the scanning loop.

21.   If words are out of order.

22.   Switch the data variables containing the words.

23.   Decrement the terminal count.

24.   End the loop when the stop point is reached.

25. End sorting loop when no switch is made in a cycle.

26. Begin display loop.

27.   Create two-column display.

28. End loop when all data is displayed.

29. End

Flowchart

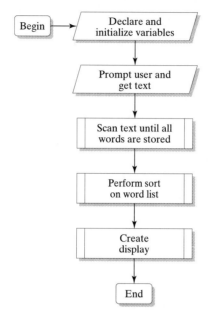

As programs become large and complex, flowcharts become unwieldy. They require either rather large pieces of paper or the use of many sheets where each function is described in detail. Either way, the clarity that makes flowcharts useful begins to fade. The foregoing flowchart corresponds to the initial pseudocode. The three-section rectangles indicate a function or a large section of code whose details have been ignored or drawn in another flowchart.

Solution Implemented in C++

```
1    //  Problem 4.8
2    #include <iostream.h>
3    #include <iomanip.h>
4    #include <string.h>
5
6    struct item
7    {
8        char word[21];
9        int position;
10   };
11
12   int main(void)
13   {
14       char sentence[1000];
15       item words[50], temp;
16       int sent_counter = 0, word_counter = 0, letter_counter = 0;
17       int flag, target, stop, half, word_flag = 0;
18       cout << "Enter a sentence . . (End with <Esc>) " << endl;
19       cin.getline(sentence,999,27);
20       cout << endl;
```

```
21    do
22    {
23       if (sentence[sent_counter] >= 'A' && sentence[sent_counter] <= 'Z'
24             || sentence[sent_counter] >= 'a'
25             && sentence[sent_counter] <= 'z')
26       {
27          words[word_counter].word[letter_counter++]
28             = sentence[sent_counter];
29          word_flag = 1;
30       }
31       else if ((sentence[sent_counter] == 39
32             || sentence[sent_counter] == '-')
33             && sentence[sent_counter + 1] >= 'a'
34             && sentence[sent_counter + 1] <= 'z')
35          words[word_counter].word[letter_counter++]
36             = sentence[sent_counter];
37       else if (word_flag == 1)
38       {
39          words[word_counter].position = word_counter + 1;
40          words[word_counter].word[letter_counter] = 0;
41          word_counter++, letter_counter = 0;
42          word_flag = 0;
43       }
44       sent_counter++;
45    }while(sentence[sent_counter] != 0);
46    if (word_flag == 1)
47    {
48       words[word_counter].position = word_counter + 1;
49       words[word_counter].word[letter_counter] = 0;
50       word_counter++;
51    }
52    stop = word_counter - 1;
53    do
54    {
55       flag = 0;
56       for (target = 0; target < stop; target++)
57          if (strcmpi(words[target].word,words[target + 1].word) > 0)
58          {
59             temp = words[target];
60             words[target] = words[target + 1];
61             words[target + 1] = temp;
62             flag = 1;
63          }
64       stop--;
65    }while(flag == 1);
66    half = static_cast<int>(.5 * (word_counter + 1));
67    cout << setw(20) << "Word" << setw(10) << "Position"
68       << setw(16) << "Word" << setw(10) <<endl << endl;
69    for (target = 0; target < half; target++)
70    {
71       cout << setw(20) << words[target].word << setw(10)
72          << words[target].position;
```

```
73          if (target + half < word_counter)
74              cout << setw(20) << words[target + half].word
75                  << setw(10) << words[target + half].position << endl;
76      }
77      cout << endl;
78      return(0);
79  }
```

A great deal of the code in the solution to Problem 4.8 has been used before. The bubble sort using structure variable was lifted from the code for Problem 4.7. The routine for separating the text into its component words is a copy from Problem 4.4. However, there is a new twist in the loop for the output display.

The preceding code is not quite the code used for a two-column display in the bubble sort program. That code was simpler to write because there was a known number of data elements to display. In the code for Problem 4.8 the number of words might be even or odd. This complicates determining the number of rows for the display and, if the number of output variables is odd, it requires that the second cout in the loop be suppressed for the last cycle. If it is not suppressed the program will attempt to display a string without a terminating NULL causing unfortunate results.

The correct handling of the display constitutes another problem within the problem. As so often is the case, this problem can be solved by being clear about what needs to be accomplished, using a concrete example, and applying a little backward thinking.

The word_counter variable holds the key information for generating the correct number of rows. If there are six words in the text, three rows of information should be displayed. If there are five words, there should still be three rows but the second display in the third row must be suppressed. Getting the correct number of rows requires the use of the half variable in the test condition on line 68. In order for half to have the value of three for both a word_count of five or six, half is generated by the mathematics of line 66.

```
66      half = static_cast<int>(.5 * (word_counter + 1));
```

If word_counter is five, adding one makes six and one half of six is three. If word_counter is six, adding one makes seven. One half of seven is 3.5 but the decimal is lost when the value is converted to an integer. Again half is assigned the value of three. Clearly this scheme will work for all odd/even pairs.

The suppression of the extra output is controlled by the if statement on line 72.

Output of the C++ Program

```
Enter a sentence . . (End with <Esc>)
The Darkness whispers in timeless patience
The Mind rewinds in idle turning
The Day replays in endless cycles
The Images that should have been.
```

Word	Position		Word	Position
been	24		patience	6
cycles	18		replays	15
Darkness	2		rewinds	9
Day	14		should	22

endless	17	that	21
have	23	The	1
idle	11	The	7
Images	20	The	13
in	4	The	19
in	10	timeless	5
in	16	turning	12
Mind	8	whispers	3

The verse is from *FourAM*, a poem describing a sleepless night, possibly written by a programmer. It provides several capitalized words that need to be sorted as though they began with lowercase letters. Keep in mind that uppercase letters occupy the range of ASCII values from $A = 65$ to $Z = 90$ while lowercase letters are $a = 97$ to $z = 122$. An ordinary sort would place *Zebra* ahead of *aardvark*. Fortunately, C++ provides the case-independent string compare function, strcmpi(), used on line 57.

Solution Implemented in Visual Basic

```
1    Option Explicit
2    Private Type udtItem
3        word As String
4        position As Integer
5    End Type
6
7    Private Sub cmdExit_Click()
8        Unload Me
9    End Sub
10
11   Private Sub cmdFind_Click()
12       Dim sentence As String
13       Dim words(0 To 49) As udtItem
14       Dim sent_counter, word_counter, target, count, _
15           flag, targe, stop_point, half, word_flag As Integer
16       Dim letter As String
17       Dim next_letter
18       Dim temp As udtItem
19       Dim str, str1, str2 As String
20
21       sent_counter = 1
22       word_counter = 0
23       word_flag = 0
24
25       sentence = txtInput.Text
26
27       Do While sent_counter <= Len(sentence)
28           letter = Mid(sentence, sent_counter, 1)
29           next_letter = Mid(sentence, sent_counter + 1, 1)
30           If letter >= "A" And letter <= "Z" Or _
31               letter >= "a" And letter <= "z" Then
32               words(word_counter).word = words(word_counter).word & _
33                   letter
34               word_flag = 1
```

```
35         ElseIf letter = "-" Or letter = "'" And _
36             next_letter >= "a" And next_letter <= "z" Then
37           words(word_counter).word = words(word_counter).word & _
38             letter
39         ElseIf word_flag = 1 Then
40           words(word_counter).position = word_counter + 1
41           word_counter = word_counter + 1
42           word_flag = 0
43         End If
44         sent_counter = sent_counter + 1
45       Loop
46       If word_flag = 1 Then
47         words(word_counter).position = word_counter + 1
48         word_counter = word_counter + 1
49       End If
50       stop_point = word_counter - 1
51       flag = 1
52
53       Do While flag = 1
54         flag = 0
55         For target = 0 To stop_point - 1
56           If StrComp(words(target).word, words(target + 1).word, _
57               vbTextCompare) > 0 Then
58             temp = words(target)
59             words(target) = words(target + 1)
60             words(target + 1) = temp
61             flag = 1
62           End If
63         Next target
64         stop_point = stop_point - 1
65       Loop
66
67       Call lstOutput.Clear
68       half = Int((word_counter + 1) / 2)
69       str1 = Space(13)
70       LSet str1 = "Word"
71       str2 = Space(10)
72       RSet str2 = "Position"
73       lstOutput.AddItem (str1 & str2 & "          " & str1 & str2)
74
75       For target = 0 To half - 1
76         str1 = Space(13)
77         LSet str1 = words(target).word
78         str2 = Space(10)
79         RSet str2 = words(target).position
80         str = str1 & str2
81         If target + half < word_counter Then
82           str1 = Space(13)
83           LSet str1 = words(target + half).word
84           str2 = Space(10)
85           RSet str2 = words(target + half).position
86           str = str & "          " & str1 & str2
```

```
87          End If
88          lstOutput.AddItem (str)
89      Next target
90  End Sub
91
92  Private Sub cmdReset_Click()
93      lstOutput.Clear
94      txtInput.Text = ""
95  End Sub
96
97  Private Sub Form_Activate()
98      txtInput.SetFocus
99  End Sub
```

The case-independent sorting is handled by the StrComp() function used on line 56. Visual Basic does not have a special function to ignore case while sorting as C++ does. Instead a third optional argument, vbTextCompare, is given to StrComp() to generate sort without reference to case.

The routine for suppressing the last output in the second column is only slightly different in the Visual Basic program. In the C++ version an if() statement only allows the output of a final word in the second column if there is an even number of words. The Visual Basic program does not add str1 and str2 to str (line 86) unless there is an even number of words (line 81).

Output of the Visual Basic Program

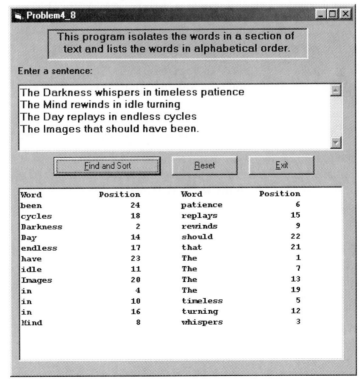

Problem4_8

This program isolates the words in a section of text and lists the words in alphabetical order.

Enter a sentence:

The Darkness whispers in timeless patience
The Mind rewinds in idle turning
The Day replays in endless cycles
The Images that should have been.

| Find and Sort | Reset | Exit |

Word	Position	Word	Position
been	24	patience	6
cycles	18	replays	15
Darkness	2	rewinds	9
Day	14	should	22
endless	17	that	21
have	23	The	1
idle	11	The	7
Images	20	The	13
in	4	The	19
in	10	timeless	5
in	16	turning	12
Mind	8	whispers	3

C H A P T E R   5

Look-Up Tables

5.1   THE LOOK-UP TABLE

One of the most common tasks computers are asked to perform involves the search of a database. Active server pages create Web pages on-the-fly based on the information stored in a database. Database managers search databases for our personal, financial, or medical records. Extranets allow computer programs of one company to interact with the databases of other companies. These activities can be considered an expansion of the computer's ability to search. The idea is to search for information and do something useful based on the results of the search. Writing the software for a database manager or for the creation of active server pages is far beyond the scope of this text but the concept can be explored in a scaled-down fashion. If the amount of data is not great and the data rarely changes, the information becomes a look-up table and can be embedded in the program.

Often the information is stored in an array of data structures. Finding one element in the data record provides access to related information. Problem 4.7 used this type of table for storing the students' names and grades. However, the "table" can be as simple as an array in a translation table for encrypting text.

PROBLEM 5.1   *Encode and decode a message with an unbreakable code.*

When the term *unbreakable* is used to modify *code*, it looses the absolute quality that is generally associated with the word. Whether a code is unbreakable or not depends on who is doing the breaking, the time allotted for the breaking, and the amount of computer power that is brought to bear.

Codes run the gamut from simple letter substitution ciphers found in the Sunday paper that can be broken by virtually anyone with a spare hour, to the 56-bit Data Encryption Standard, which, by 1998, could be broken in less than three days by a specially built computer costing $250,000. As an exercise in problem-solving logic we'll define *unbreakable* to mean quite difficult to break.

A letter substitution cipher is made by creating a table that substitutes one letter for another. For example, *f* might be substituted for *a*, *z* might be substituted for *b*, and so on. Reversing the process will decode an encoded message.

Breaking the code involves discovering the encryption table by examining the message to be decoded. Because we have already written a program to solve Problem 4.5, we know which letters occur most frequently in ordinary text. (There is no substitute for experience.) The letter that appears most often in a message encoded by a letter substitution encryption most likely represents an *e*. The second most frequent letter probably represents a *t*.

A letter substitution code could be made far more difficult to break if, after encoding one letter, the code table were changed. The first time an *a* appeared in the message it might be encoded by a *q* and the next time encoded by a *g*. Since the code is constantly changing, the word *house* might be encoded by *eeeee*. Decoding *eeeee* would be quite difficult. There would be no clue except that the word had five letters.

But the space that divides words is merely an ASCII value and could also be encoded with a different character each time. That means "I think I saw a tiger" might encode as *abcdefghijklmnopqrstu*. Even though the letter *i* appears four times in the message, each time it occurs it is encoded with a different letter. Each time a space occurs in the original message it is encrypted by a different letter. It would seem that we have a plan for a pretty good if not "unbreakable" code.

Initial Data: **1.** Text from the user will be encoded.

2. There must be a way to decode the message. (If the information cannot be retrieved, the code is of little value.)

3. In reality the encrypted message would be written to disk but in this proof-of-concept program the encrypted message will be immediately decoded.

4. Coded letters will be taken from a look-up table.

5. The code will be changed after each letter.

6. The look-up table will contain all the characters we choose to encode.

Output: **1.** The encoded message.

2. The original message retrieved from the encoded message.

Yet to be decided is what should be in the look-up table and how that table should be used. The table could be the entire ASCII table or it could be a subset of characters that we decide will be useful. The choice is rather arbitrary and for our purposes we'll limit the characters to lowercase letters, numbers, space, period, comma, question mark, and the new line character. Uppercase letters could be included but, for no purpose other than showing it can be done, we'll map the uppercase letters to the lowercase letters before encoding. Of course, this means we will be unable to retrieve the uppercase letters in their uppercase form in the decoding process but this will not affect the readability of the text. The look-up table can be stored in a character array. Since the table will never be changed, it should be declared to be a constant.

```
5    const char TABLE[42] = "abcdefghijklmnopqrstuvwxyz .,1234567890?\n";
```

One way to use the look-up table would be find the letter to be encoded in the table, move a set number of spaces to the right, and use the letter at that position in the encoded message. If we move five places to the right, *a* becomes *f*; *b* becomes *g*; and so on. The resulting coded message would be very easy to break. But if we allow the random number generator to choose how far we move to the right and we choose a new random number for each letter in the text to be encoded, the resulting message is based on a randomly chosen sequence of numbers.

To decode the message the same sequence of random numbers must be reproduced and the encoding process reversed by moving to the left in the table. Fortunately, the random number generators built into programming languages are pseudorandom number generators that will reproduce the same sequence each time they are given the same seed number. The seed number then becomes the key for the code.

This creates the problem of determining what to do if moving to the right takes us off the table. The most reasonable solution is to circle around the table and reenter it at the left continuing to move to the right. For example, if the character to be encoded is the question mark and the random number generator provides a six, the replacement character is the *e*. With this in mind the pseudocode can be written.

Pseudocode

1. Begin

2.   Declare and initialize variables.

3.   Begin major loop for continuous running.

4.   Call the start function.

5.   Prompt the user for encoding or decoding.

6.   Get the encode/decode value.

7.   If encoding.

8.   Prompt for text.

9.   Get the text.

10.   Return text and encode/decode value.

11.   If encoding, call encode function.

12.   Get the key.

13.   Seed the random number generator with key.

14.   Loop—scan the text until the NULL.

15.   If the letter is uppercase map to lowercase.

16.   Loop—scan the table for the text character.

17.   When found, add a random number to the index of the table array.

18.   Overwrite the text character with new character.

19.   Increment input index.

20.   Repeat loop.

21.   Return to main.

22.   Else if decoding, call decode function.

23.   Get the key.

24.   Seed the random number generator with key.

25.   Loop—scan the message until the NULL.

26.   Loop—scan the table for the message character.

27.   When found, subtract random number from the index of the table array.

28.   Overwrite the text character with the new character.

29.   Increment input index.

30.   Repeat loop.

31.   Return to main.

32.   Prompt to continue.

33. End

Flowchart

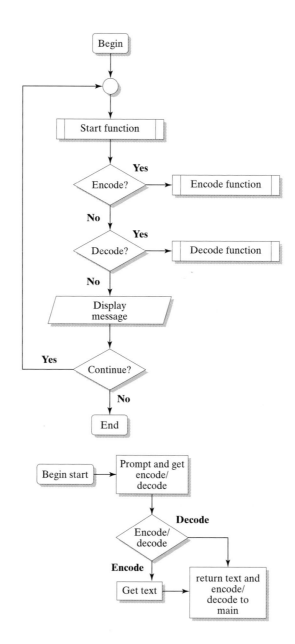

Flowchart (Cont.)

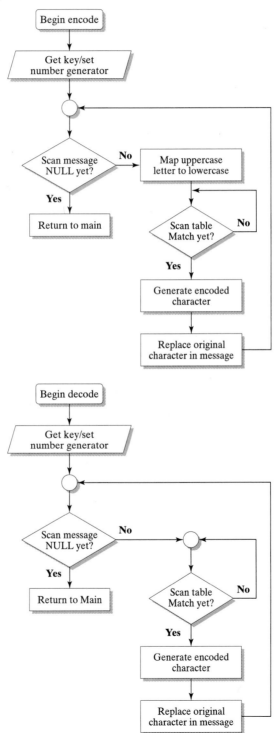

Solution Implemented in C++

```
1    //    Problem 5.1
2    #include <iostream.h>
3    #include <stdlib.h>
4    #include <stdio.h>
5    #include <string.h>
6    const char TABLE[42] = "abcdefghijklmnopqrstuvwxyz .,1234567890?\n";
7
8    int start (char input[400])
9    {
10       int code;
11       char temp[3] = "",waste;
12       do
13       {
14          cout << "This program encodes or decodes a message\n" << endl;
15          cout << "\tEncode  --  1\n\tDecode  --  2    " << flush;
16          cin.getline(temp, 3, '\n');
17          code = atoi(temp);
18       }while (code != 1 && code != 2);
19       if( code == 1)
20       {
21          cout << "\n\tEnter the message to be encoded (End with <Esc>)"
22             << endl;
23          fflush(stdin);
24          cin.getline(input,400, 27);
25          cin.get(waste);
26       }
27       return code;
28   }
29
30   void encode(char input[])
31   {
32       int message_index = 0, table_index, key;
33       char key_string[10] = "";
34       cout << "\nEnter the key    " << flush;
35       fflush(stdin);
36       cin.getline(key_string,10, '\n');
37       key = atoi(key_string);
38       srand(key);
39       while(input[message_index] != NULL)
40       {
41          if (input[message_index] > 64 && input[message_index] < 93)
42             input[message_index] += 32;
43          table_index = 0;
44          do
45          {
46             if (input[message_index] == TABLE[table_index])
47                break;
48             table_index++;
```

```
49          }while (table_index < 42);
50          table_index = (table_index + (rand() % 41 + 1)) % 41;
51          input[message_index] = TABLE[table_index];
52          message_index++;
53      }
54  }
55  void decode(char input[])
56  {
57      int message_index = 0, table_index, key;
58      char key_string[10] = "";
59      cout << "Enter the key   " << flush;
60      cin.getline(key_string,10, '\n');
61      key = atoi(key_string);
62      srand(key);
63      while(input[message_index] != NULL)
64      {
65          table_index = 0;
66          do
67          {
68              if (input[message_index] == TABLE[table_index])
69                  break;
70              table_index++;
71          }while (table_index < 42);
72          table_index = ((table_index - (rand() % 41 + 1)) + 41) % 41;
73          input[message_index] = TABLE[table_index];
74          message_index++;
75      }
76  }
77  int main(void)
78  {
79      char message[400] = "", again[3] = "";
80      int encode_decode;
81      do
82      {
83          encode_decode = start(message);
84          if (encode_decode == 1)
85              encode(message);
86          else
87              decode(message);
88          cout << endl << message << endl;
89          cout << "Continue (y/n)     " << flush;
90          cin.getline(again,3,'\n');
91      }while(again[0] == 'y' || again[0] == 'Y');
92      return 0;
93  }
```

Global variables should, in general, be avoided. Functions that do not need access to a variable should not have access to the variable. Global variables open the possibility that, through a programming error, a function that should not have access to the variable will manage to alter its value. The table is made global in this program because it is needed by both the encode() and decode() functions and it has been declared to be constant, making it unchangeable. As a matter of convention, constants are declared in all uppercase letters.

The flow of the program follows the logic outlined in the pseudocode and the flow-chart. The main() function organizes the program and the three distinct operations, the menu presentation, the encoding, and the decoding, are each handled by a function.

The first item deserving special notice is line 18, the test condition for the do/while loop in the start() function.

```
18    }while (code != 1 && code != 2);
```

By placing the user input for the choice to encode or decode in a loop, error check-ing is provided. If the user enters anything except a one or a two, the loop will repeat again prompting for a proper input. Those familiar with de Morgan's theorem (or have a very logical mind) will recognize that repeating the loop if the user input is *not* one *and not* two, is the same as *not* repeating if the user input is a one *or* a two, that is, $!A \cdot !B = !(A + B)$.

Lines 36 and 37 obtain the key for the code from the user. This key is entered as a string and converted to an integer by the atoi() function. The integer value stored in key is used as the seed number for the random number generator.

Line 41 handles the mapping of uppercase letters into the corresponding lowercase letter. There is a function defined in the stdlib.h header file that will perform this op-eration; however, since it only requires the addition of 32 to the ASCII value of the char-acter, the program will run faster if the operation is coded rather than making a function call.

The encoding is handled on line 50.

```
50        table_index = (table_index + (rand() % 41 + 1)) % 41;
```

The operation of moving to the right in the table is really a matter of increasing the index, table_index, of the message character. This is accomplished in several steps.

1. A number between zero and 32,767 (hex 7FFF) inclusive is generated by the pseudorandom number generator.
2. The random number is converted to the range of zero to 40 by the modulus operator.
3. One is added to the number to convert the range to one to 41.
4. The last % 41 operation provides the wraparound feature in case the table_index should go out of range.

After a value for table_index has been calculated, line 51 overwrites the char-acter in the original message with the value chosen from the look-up table by the new table_index.

The decoding function is nearly identical to the encoding function except for two items. First, there is no need for the uppercase to lowercases mapping, since there is no possibility that the encoded message will have an uppercase letter. Second, the decoding operation requires moving through the look-up table to the left rather than to the right.

Keep in mind that reseeding the pseudorandom number generator with the same seed used in the encoding function produces the same sequence of random numbers that was used for encoding. By subtracting the number instead of adding, the move to the right becomes a move to the left and recovers the character in the original text. However, the move to the left of line 72 is slightly more complex than the encoding process.

```
72              table_index = ((table_index - (rand() % 41 + 1)) + 41) % 41;
```

After the random number in the range of 1 to 41 is generated, 41 is added to prevent the `table_index` from becoming a negative number after the subtraction. That is, the + 41 prevents going out of range to the left and the % 41 prevents going out of range to the right.

Output of the C++ Program

```
This program encodes or decodes a message

        Encode  --  1
        Decode  --  2    1


        Enter the message to be encoded (End with <Esc>)
The Darkness whispers in timeless patience
The Mind rewinds in idle turning
The Day replays in endless cycles
The Images that should have been

Enter the key    32

10hl cs5y4jbe

bi7gn.atj5dvvtnre?fvrf9jefd3tanv4rrts?qwagle gntu6d
tobb?fk
06mhkb
 f6ff6
pirtd6qw7ua1,.ttvi9qaoyg 4no1bga5d9kz?9rh2,19vb76 8p
Continue (y/n)    y
This program encodes or decodes a message

        Encode  --  1
        Decode  --  2    2
Enter the key    32

the darkness whispers in timeless patience
the mind rewinds in idle turning
the day replays in endless cycles
the images that should have been
```

In the output of the program there are three *t*'s in the first line of the poem that have been encoded by *b*, *f*, and *s*, respectively. In the decoding process these letters are all correctly translated back into *t*'s. By encoding the spaces between the words the length of each word is disguised and encoding the new line character leaves no clue to the length of each line or even the number of lines in the original message.

The final question is just how unbreakable is this code, assuming the code breaker has nothing more than the encoded text? Since the only pattern involved in the encoding process is the pattern of pseudorandom numbers generated, there is little in the encoded text to suggest a starting point for breaking the code. That leaves brute force methods that will try every possible key. Of course, that would mean the code breaker must know that it was the Visual C++ random number generator that was used to make the code and the code breaker must know the table of letters that was used. Given this information a program could be written to try every one of the 32,767 possible keys. Not a great task for a computer. However, there is no reason for using such an ordered table. If the letters in the table were randomized, the code-breaking routine would need to use every possible key for every possible table. This is complicated further because the code breaker would not know how many letters were in the table.

If the characters in the table were scrambled before the encoding took place, then the brute force breaking would have to guess the key and the characters in the table and their order. Knowing neither the key nor the table would make the brute force decoding a sizable task assuming the code breaker knew that the Visual C++ pseudorandom number generator was used.

Solution Implemented in Visual Basic

```
1    Option Explicit
2    Private Table(0 To 41) As Byte
3
4    Private Sub cmdExit_Click()
5        Unload Me
6    End Sub
7
8    Private Sub cmdGo_Click()
9        Static Message As String
10       Dim Num, Count As Integer
11       If optEncode.Value = True Then
12           Message = txtInput.Text
13           Call encode(Message)
14       Else
15           Call decode(Message)
16       End If
17       txtOutput.Text = ""
18       For Count = 1 To Len(Message)
19           If Mid(Message, Count, 1) = Chr(13) Then
20               Count = Count + 1
21               txtOutput.Text = txtOutput.Text & vbCrLf
22           Else
23               txtOutput.Text = txtOutput.Text & _
24                   Mid(Message, Count, 1)
25           End If
26       Next
27   End Sub
28
29   Private Sub cmdReset_Click()
```

```
30      txtInput.Text = ""
31      txtOutput.Text = ""
32      txtKey.Text = ""
33      txtInput.Enabled = True
34  End Sub
35
36  Private Sub Form_Load()
37      Dim Index As Long
38
39      For Index = 0 To 25      ' Build the Look-Up Table
40          Table(Index) = Index + 97
41      Next Index
42
43      For Index = 26 To 35
44          Table(Index) = Index + 49 - 26
45      Next Index
46
47      Table(36) = Asc("?")
48      Table(37) = Asc(".")
49      Table(38) = Asc(",")
50      Table(39) = Asc(" ")
51      Table(40) = 13 'the return char
52      Table(41) = 0  'the null
53      optEncode.Value = True
54  End Sub
55
56  Private Sub optDecode_Click()
57      txtInput.Enabled = False
58  End Sub
59
60  Private Sub optEncode_Click()
61      txtInput.Enabled = True
62  End Sub
63
64  Public Sub encode(ByRef Msg As String)
65      Dim Key As Single
66      Dim msg_index As Integer
67      Dim letter As String
68      Dim asc_val As Long
69      Dim table_index As Integer
70      Dim temp As Integer
71
72      If IsNumeric(txtKey.Text) = False Then
73          Call MsgBox("Enter a valide key", vbOKOnly + vbInformation)
74          Exit Sub
75      End If
76
77      Key = CSng(txtKey.Text)
78      msg_index = 1
79      Rnd (-1)
80      Randomize (Key)
81      Do While msg_index <= Len(Msg)
82          letter = Mid(Msg, msg_index, 1)
```

```
83          asc_val = Asc(letter)
84          If asc_val > 64 And asc_val < 93 Then
85              asc_val = asc_val + 32
86              Mid(Msg, msg_index, 1) = Chr(asc_val)
87          End If
88          table_index = 0
89          Do While table_index < 40
90              If asc_val = Table(table_index) Then
91                  Exit Do
92              End If
93              table_index = table_index + 1
94          Loop
95          temp = 41 * Rnd()
96          table_index = (table_index + (temp Mod 41) + 1) Mod 41
97          Mid(Msg, msg_index, 1) = Chr(Table(table_index))
98          msg_index = msg_index + 1
99      Loop
100 End Sub
101
102 Public Sub decode(ByRef Msg As String)
103     Dim Key As Single
104     Dim msg_index As Integer
105     Dim letter As String
106     Dim asc_val As Long
107     Dim table_index As Integer
108     Dim temp As Integer
109
110     If IsNumeric(txtKey.Text) = False Then
111         Call MsgBox("Enter a valide key", vbOKOnly + vbInformation)
112         Exit Sub
113     End If
114     Key = CSng(txtKey.Text)
115     Rnd (-1)
116     Randomize (Key)
117     msg_index = 1
118     Do While msg_index <= Len(Msg)
119         table_index = 0
120         Do While table_index < 40
121             asc_val = Asc(Mid(Msg, msg_index, 1))
122             If asc_val = Table(table_index) Then
123                 Exit Do
124             End If
125             table_index = table_index + 1
126         Loop
127         temp = 41 * Rnd()
128         table_index = ((table_index - ((temp Mod 41) + 1)) + 41) Mod 41
129         Mid(Msg, msg_index, 1) = Chr(Table(table_index))
130         msg_index = msg_index + 1
131     Loop
132 End Sub
```

The look-up table for the encoding process is not so compactly made in Visual Basic as it is in C++. Line 2 declares the byte array called Table that will store the look-up table but the table is not initialized until lines 39 through 52. The two option buttons, `optEncode` and `optDecode`, take the place of the menu display used in the C++ program. When the Go button is clicked, the value of `optEncode` is tested on line 11 to determine whether the encoding or decoding process should be called. Notice that when the Decode button is clicked it disables the `txtInput` text box preventing the input text from being altered until the Reset button is clicked to change the value of `txtInput.Enable` back to `True`.

The random number generator in Visual Basic is considerably different from the random number generator in C++ on several counts. First, the range of random numbers is different. C++ generates pseudorandom integers from 0 to 32,767. Visual Basic generates single-precision fractions greater than or equal to zero but less than one. Lines 95 and 127 convert these fractions into useful integers from zero to 40. The second difference is the use of `Randomize` with the key number to seed the pseudorandom number generator as opposed to the `srand()` function in C++. However, the most subtle difference is the manner in which the generator is reseeded to produce the same sequence for decoding that it used for encoding. This is accomplished by the use of `Rnd` with a negative number for an argument, lines 79 and 115.

The method for moving through the input message, comparing each character of the message to the look-up table, and moving a random number of characters to the right or left is the same in both programs. Lines 96 and 128 generate the new index for the encoded or decoded character. Lines 97 and 129 place the chosen character in the message string.

The Output of the Visual Basic Program—After Encoding

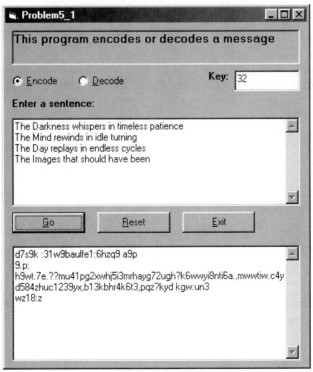

Notice that not only are the sizes of the words disguised but the length of the lines is also indeterminable in the encoded message.

The Output of the Visual Basic Program—After Decoding the Encrypted Message

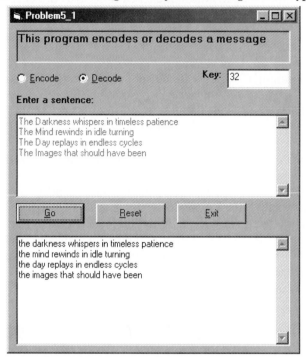

5.2 THE UNDERSTOOD LOOK-UP TABLE

In the encryption problem the look-up table was created to contain whatever characters were considered necessary for the text to be encrypted. In other cases the table may be already known. For example, the addition and multiplication tables are known to everyone and, if relevant, can be considered initial data in a problem.

Consider the task of doing large-scale arithmetic operations. Unsigned long integer variables are capable of storing numbers just a bit larger than four billion. Double-precision variables can store numbers containing 15 significant digits. But if the arithmetic involves larger numbers containing 20, 50, or 100 digits, there is a storage problem for the numbers to be added or multiplied and for the results of the operation.

PROBLEM 5.2 *How can 50-digit positive integers be added together?*

This problem is deceptively simple to solve. The key is to be clear about what exactly is the problem. Clearly, the issue is not the addition of large numbers. Everyone past the age of nine has arithmetic skills sufficient for adding multidigit integers. The real question is how this well-known algorithm can be taught to the computer so that this tedious task no longer troubles humans. Even though they are not specifically listed in the computer code, there are actually two tables involved in this problem. The first is the addition table for single-digit numbers. The second is the ASCII table that is used to convert character digits into integers.

Of course, the place to start is the same place we always start, that is, by being clear about the information we have to work with.

Initial Data:
1. Two integers of up to 50 digits each will be supplied by the user.

2. The integers cannot be stored as integers or as floating-point numbers and can only be stored as strings of characters. In this case the characters will be the digits zero through nine.

3. The algorithm for addition is well known.

4. The characters of the strings representing the digits to be added are really ASCII values of those characters. Specifically, the characters zero through nine are the ASCII values 48 through 57.

5. The **integers** zero through nine can be derived from the **characters** zero through nine by subtracting 48 from the character (actually the ASCII value of the character). Addition can be performed with these integer values.

6. Once a sum digit is determined, it can be converted to a character for storage in the answer string by adding 48.

7. Addition of multidigit numbers may involve carrying a one from one column to the next.

Output:
The output of the program should be a string containing characters that represent a large integer that is the sum of two other similarly large integers.

As mentioned earlier the real problem is not performing addition but how the computer can be taught to perform addition given the fact that the numbers to be added must be stored as strings. Fortunately the initial data is considerable. Making use of this information is made clearer by the use of a concrete example (Rule 8). Consider:

Normal Order	Reversed
2567	7652
+ 812	218
3379	9733

The first difficulty that becomes immediately apparent from the example is that strings store information left to right but addition is performed right to left. The first column to be added in the example addition problem above involves the seven and the two, or the fourth character in the top string and the third character in the bottom string. Because the numbers may have significantly different numbers of digits, keeping track of which element of one array is to be added to the which element of the other array can produce some confusion. However, if the digits in each number are reversed, the addition is performed from left to right, as in the reversed addition problem. This implies that the zero element of the top number is added to the zero element of the bottom number and the sum is recorded in the zero position of the array holding the answer. The addition can then proceed until all columns have been added and then the result reversed to produce the correct answer. This reversing of the strings is a simple process that can be relegated to a function and can save a great deal of effort in tracking array subscripts.

Once the correct elements to be added have been identified and lined up starting on the left, the next step is to perform the addition. This entails using the ASCII table to look up the numeric value for the characters. The ASCII table indicates that the numeric characters zero through nine are stored in memory as the numbers 48 through 57. This implies that subtracting 48 from a digit stored as a character will reduce its value to the number represented by the digit. For example, the character 7 (the least significant digit in the top number of the example) is stored in the computer's memory as 55. Subtracting 48 reduces the value to 7, a number which can be used in the stated addition problem. Similarly, the least significant digit of the lower number can be extracted as 2.

Adding the two numbers produces a sum of nine but this value must be stored in the answer array as a character representing nine. Adding 48 to 9 gives 57 or the ASCII value for the character 9.

This process would be adequate if it were not for the possibility of a column generating a sum greater than nine. Should this happen a carry is generated that must be stored and added to the next column. In addition the sum must be reduced by 10 so that a single digit is stored in the current column. In the addition example a carry is generated in the third column when eight is added to five. The result is 13. The three is stored in the current position in the answer array and the carry is added to the next column.

In the fourth column the top number shows a two but there is no digit in the lower number. Of course, there is no such thing as nothing in computer memory. In this case it is necessary to fill all unused array elements with the NULL character so that the addition process is signaled to use the additive identity.

With all this in mind it is time to write the pseudocode.

Pseudocode

1. Begin
2. Declare and initialize three arrays of appropriate SIZE.
3. Prompt user for two numbers to be added.
4. Call the bigAddition routine.

5.   Reverse the order of the digits in the two large integers.

6.   Find which integers have the largest number of digits and use that length as the terminator in the addition loop.

7.   Begin the loop—run for as many cycles as the number of digits in the bigger number.

8.   Convert the digit pointed to by the counter in the first number to its numeric value or zero if number of digits is exceeded.

9.   Convert the digit pointed to by the counter in the second number to its numeric value or zero if the number of digits is exceeded.

10.   Add the values and the carry.

11.   Convert the least significant digit in the sum to a character and store it in the answer array.

12.   Create the carry for the next column.

13.   End loop.

14.   If the carry was set to one when the loop ended, place one in the next position of the answer array.

15.   Reverse all three arrays.

16.   Return to main.

17.   Call the display function.

18.   Calculate the number of spaces to place before first integer so least significant digit is 70 spaces from left of window and display spaces.

19.   Display the first array.

20.   Calculate the number of spaces to place before the plus sign, a space, and the second integer so the least significant digit is 70 spaces from the left of the window and display spaces.

21.   Display the plus, the spaces, and the second array.

22.   Calculate the number of space to place before the first integer so the least significant digit is 70 spaces from the left of the window and display the spaces.

23.   Display the answer array.

24.   Return to main.

25.   End

Flowchart

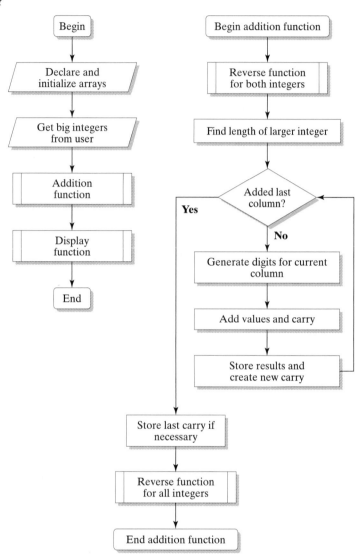

Flowchart (Cont.)

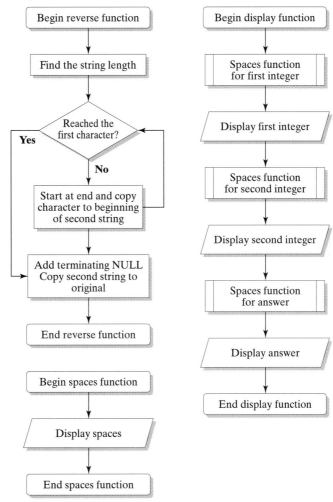

Solution Implemented in C++

```
1    //  Problem5.2
2    #include <iostream.h>
3    #include <stdio.h>
4    #include <string.h>
5    #include <iomanip.h>
6    #define SIZE 52
7
8    void reverse(char input[SIZE])
9    {
10       int x = 0, y = 0, z;
```

```
11      char output[SIZE];
12      x = strlen(input);
13      z = x;
14      for ( y = 0; y < z; y++, x--)
15          output[y] = input[x - 1];
16      output[y] = 0;
17      strcpy(input, output);
18  }
19  void spaces(int s)
20  {
21      int counter;
22      for (counter = 0; counter < s; counter++)
23          cout << " ";
24  }
25  void bigAddition(char a[], char b[], char c[])
26  {
27      int flag_a = 0, flag_b = 0, counter, end, length_a, length_b;
28      int digit_a, digit_b, digit_c, carry = 0;
29      reverse(a);
30      reverse(b);
31      length_a = strlen(a);
32      length_b = strlen(b);
33      length_a > length_b ? end = length_a : end = length_b;
34      for (counter = 0; counter < end; counter++)
35      {
36          *(a + counter) == 0 ? digit_a = 0 :digit_a = (int)(*(a + counter) -
37              48);
38          *(b + counter) == 0 ? digit_b = 0 :digit_b = (int)(*(b + counter) -
39              48);
40          digit_c =  digit_a + digit_b + carry;
41          *(c + counter) = (char)(digit_c % 10 + 48);
42          carry = digit_c / 10;
43      }
44      carry == 0 ? *(c + counter) = 0 : *(c + counter) = 49;
45      reverse(c);
46      reverse(a);
47      reverse(b);
48  }
49  void displayAddition(char a[], char b[], char c[])
50  {
51      int space_a, space_b, space_c;
52      space_a = 70 - strlen(a);
53      cout << endl;
54      spaces(space_a);
55      cout << a << endl;
56      space_b = 70 - strlen(b);
57      spaces(space_b - 2);
58      cout << "+ " << b << endl;
59      space_c = 70 - strlen(c);
60      spaces(space_c);
```

```
61      cout << c << endl;
62  }
63
64  void main(void)
65  {
66      char first[SIZE] = {0}, second[SIZE] = {0}, answer[SIZE + 1] = {0};
67      cout << "This program adds two integers of up to 50 digits"
68          << endl << endl << "Enter the first integer" << endl
69          << "                                           |-- limit"
70          << endl;
71      cin.getline(first, SIZE, '\n');
72      cout << endl << "Enter the second integer" << endl;
73      cin.getline(second, SIZE, '\n');
74      bigAddition(first, second, answer);
75      displayAddition(first, second, answer);
76      cout << endl;
77  }
```

The preceding program has been written as the solution to the problem asking how 50-digit positive integers can be added. In answering such a question it is reasonable to consider that there might later be a need to add still larger numbers, 100 digits or 300 digits. Adaptability can be built into the program by the use of a constant for all references to the size of the integers. In this case the constant SIZE was initially defined to be 52. Changing this one value to some larger number makes all necessary changes to the program. Note: The arrays were declared to have 52 elements rather than the expected 51 (50 digits plus the NULL) to accommodate the manner in which the getline() function handles the delimiter.

The solution to the addition problem is an excellent example of the advantages of dividing the program into functions. The main function handles the user input and then merely states that the numbers should be added and then displayed. The purpose of the main function is perfectly clear without any muddling details.

The heart of the logic is contained in the bigAddition() function. However, before the addition process is begun, the strings to be added must be reversed. When the addition is complete, the numbers added and the sum must all be reversed. The reverse() function not only provides clarity but considerable convenience in that the reversing code would have to be written five times (once for each time the reverse() function was called) rather than once if the function had not been used. By merely stating that the strings should be reversed, the focus of the bigAddition() function remains on the addition.

The displayAddition() function is not at all necessary for the logic of the program; however, addition problems are far easier to read and check if the numbers are right justified. The right justification is simplified by having the function displayAddition() calculate the correct number of spaces to be printed before each integer. The spaces() function actually displays the number of spaces determined by displayAddition(). The displayAddition() and the spaces() functions are not necessary for the correct functioning of the program and were included for the reader's edification and the author's amusement. The functions could be eliminated and C++ formatting features used instead but that adaptation to the program is left for the reader.

Output of the C++ Program

This program adds two integers of up to 50 digits

Enter the first integer
```
                                                       |-- limit
1234567891234567891234567891234567891234567 89
```

Enter the second integer
```
99999999999999999999999999999999999999999999999999
```

```
                  1234567891234567891234567891234567891234 56789
              +   9999999999999999999999999999999999999999999999999 9
                  100000012345678912345678912345678912345678 9123456788
```

Solution Implemented in Visual Basic

```
1    Option Explicit
2
3    Private Sub cmdAdd_Click()
4        Dim First, Second, Answer As String
5
6        First = txtFirst.Text
7        Second = txtSecond.Text
8
9        Answer = bigAddition(First, Second, Answer)
10       Call displayAddition(First, Second, Answer)
11
12   End Sub
13
14   Public Function bigAddition(ByVal a As String, _
15                               ByVal b As String, _
16                               ByVal c As String) As String
17
18       Dim flag_a, flag_b, counter, end_point, length_a, _
19           length_b As Integer
20       Dim digit_a, digit_b, digit_c, carry As Integer
21       Dim result As String
22       flag_a = flag_b = carry = 0
23       Call reverse(a)
24       Call reverse(b)
25       length_a = Len(a)
26       length_b = Len(b)
27       If length_a > length_b Then
28           end_point = length_a
29       Else
30           end_point = length_b
31       End If
32
33       For counter = 1 To end_point
34           If counter > length_a Then
35               digit_a = 0
```

```
36            Else
37                digit_a = CInt(Mid(a, counter, 1))
38            End If
39            If counter > length_b Then
40                digit_b = 0
41            Else
42                digit_b = CInt(Mid(b, counter, 1))
43            End If
44            digit_c = digit_a + digit_b + carry
45            c = c & Format((digit_c Mod 10))
46            carry = getCarry(digit_c) 'to avoid round up
47        Next counter
48        If carry > 0 Then
49            c = c & Format(carry)
50        End If
51        Call reverse(c)
52        bigAddition = c
53   End Function
54
55   Public Sub displayAddition(ByVal a As String, _
56            ByVal b As String, ByVal c As String)
57        Dim str As String
58        Call lstOutput.Clear
59        str = Space(64)
60        RSet str = a
61        lstOutput.AddItem (str)
62        str = Space(64)
63        RSet str = "+ " & b
64        lstOutput.AddItem (str)
65        str = Space(64)
66        RSet str = c
67        lstOutput.AddItem (str)
68   End Sub
69
70   Public Sub reverse(ByRef str As String)
71        Dim output As String
72        Dim x, y, z As Integer
73        Dim temp As String
74        x = Len(str)
75        z = x
76        For y = 1 To z
77            output = output & Mid(str, x, 1)
78            x = x - 1
79        Next y
80
81        str = output
82   End Sub
83
84   Public Function getCarry(ByVal num As Integer) As Integer
85        Dim str As String
86        str = Format(num / 10)
87        If (InStr(str, ".") - 1) > 0 Then
```

```
88              str = Left(str, (InStr(str, ".") - 1))
89        End If
90        getCarry = CInt(str)
91   End Function
92
93   Private Sub cmdExit_Click()
94        Unload Me
95   End Sub
96
97   Private Sub cmdReset_Click()
98        txtFirst.Text = ""
99        txtSecond.Text = ""
100       Call lstOutput.Clear
101  End Sub
```

The simplicity of the main() function in the C++ program is captured in cmdAdd() action coded between lines 3 and 12. The numbers to be added are accepted from the user on lines 6 and 7, and the addition of the numbers and their display are indicated by two function calls.

The bigAddition() function begins by reversing the strings so the addition can be performed from left to right as the digits are taken in normal order from the strings holding the input integers. The for loop beginning on line 33 extracts the value from each numeric character of the string and performs the addition. If one string is shorter than the other, the if statements provide zero for the addition (lines 35 and 40). The value of the carry is generated on line 46 by the getCarry() function and used in the addition of the following cycle on line 44.

Output of the Visual Basic Program

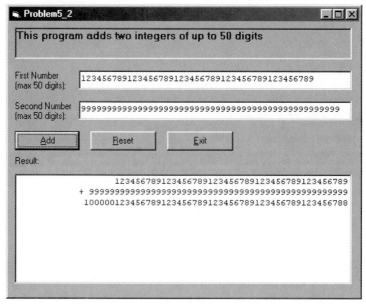

5.3   THE UNSOLVABLE PROBLEM

Just as some equations have no algebraic solution, some problems have no known method for mathematically determining a solution. The traveling salesman problem falls into this category.

PROBLEM 5.3   *A traveling salesman intends to visit five cities. In order to minimize time and expense, he needs to know the shortest path that connects all the cities. Determine the shortest path for five randomly chosen cities.*

While the problem has been stated in its traditional, somewhat trivial, setting, minimum distance solutions have important applications when more practical minimum distances are required. Finding the most cost-effective method for connecting cities with fiber optic cables or determining the most efficient use of a fleet of airplanes, are more practical examples of minimum distance problems. Unfortunately, there is no mathematical algorithm for determining minimal distances. (However, there is a proof that a path with a distance less than 2 percent greater than the true minimal distance can be found mathematically.) The only known method for finding the absolute minimal distance is to examine every possible path and then to choose the path with the shortest total distance. In short, this is a problem that can only be solved using brute force.

The table of data in this problem will be generated by the user. The information entered for each city will be used to build a table of information about the intercity distance for each pair of cities. After the table is built, these distances will be used to determine the total distance for every path connecting all of the cities.

The general problem involves an unknown number of cities and will be investigated in Chapter 8, but here the problem has been limited to five cities with the hope that the limited solution will provide insight into a more general solution. There are a few other limitations that need to be placed on the problem.

1. The cities should be considered point positions on a map. Rather than thinking of a city as a wide area covering many square miles, the term *city* will refer to the city center and distances will be measured from that point.

2. We need a method to locate the cities relative to each other in two-dimensional space. The normal system of latitude and longitude will serve this purpose.

3. The real world is a sphere and distances between cities are really measured on the surface of the sphere along a great circle routes. Minimum distances on a sphere are called great circle routes. Since this would add considerable complexity to the problem, the world will be considered to be a flat projection of the globe and the cities will be chosen so the error introduced will be minimal.

4. One degree of distance, either latitude or longitude, will be considered to be 69 miles. Of course, distance described by one degree of longitude is dependent on the latitude but 69 miles is a fair average in the United States.

In reality the distances between the cities would not be a straight line but would be the road mileage that the salesman would have to drive or the most direct path that the communications company would have access to for laying cable.

Drawing a picture of the situation (Rule 3) provides a few more important pieces of information.

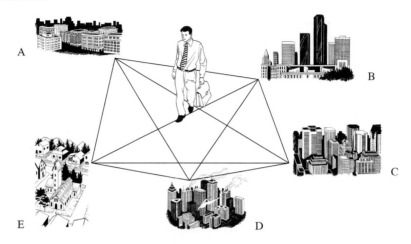

The drawing shows that the starting point of the path is irrelevant. The path *ACEBD* is the same path as *BDACE*. That is, both paths have the same total distance. Stated another way, each path has five possible starting points.

The number of possible paths now becomes apparent. If *A* is the starting point then there are four possible choices for the second city, that is, *B*, *C*, *D*, and *E*. After a second city is chosen, there are three remaining cities to be visited. After the salesman reaches the third city, two remain. From the fourth city there is no longer any choice because only one city remains. From the fifth city the salesman must return to his starting point. This implies that the total number of paths to be investigated is given by:

$$\text{Paths} = (\text{Cities} - 1)!$$
$$\text{Paths} = (5 - 1)!$$
$$\text{Paths} = 4 \times 3 \times 2 \times 1 = 24$$

Twenty-four paths of five calculated distances per path and the comparison of one path to the other is more than a human would ordinarily enjoy, but it is completed almost instantaneously by a personal computer. On the other hand, if 10 cities are considered, the number of paths increases to:

$$\text{Paths} = (10 - 1)!$$
$$\text{Paths} = 9 \times 8 \times 7 \times 6 \times 5 \times 4 \times 3 \times 2 \times 1 = 362{,}880$$

Not an insurmountable task for a PC but no longer instantaneous. Increase the number of cities to 20 and

$$\text{Paths} = (20 - 1)!$$
$$\text{Paths} = 19! \approx 1.216 \times 10^{17}$$

brute force begins to show its limitations.

Initial Data: **1.** The salesman must start at one city, travel to the other four, and return to the starting city.

2. The cities will be located by latitude and longitude.

3. One degree latitude or longitude is assumed to be 69 miles.

4. The distance from one city to another can be calculated using the Pythagorean Theorem because the world is assumed to be relatively flat for the small area enclosed by the five cities.

5. The distance from one city to all others can be stored in a structure variable containing the destination city and the distance to that city.

Output: Determine the distance for every possible path that connects the cities and choose the shortest path.

Despite the mathematical difficulty in this problem, the solution by brute force is quite straightforward. Consider the steps required to reach the final output and the difficulty in performing each step.

1. Get the five cities and their latitudes and longitudes. A simple loop prompting the user for information will handle this task.

2. Find a way to organize the data. Handling the data in a neat, organized, and clear manner is key to solving the problem. This is slightly complex consisting of arrays of nested data structures, but the task is not unmanageable if we are clear about the data storage requirements. Consider:

a. There should be an array of cities.

b. Each city (each element of the array) is a data structure (`struct location`) storing its name, latitude and longitude, and distances to all other cities.

c. Storing the distances to all other cities requires another array of data structures (one element for each city) containing the name of the city and the distance to that city (`struct data`).

d. Specifically

```
struct data
{
    char name[40];
    double distance;
};
struct location
{
    char name[40];
    double latitude, longitude;
    data dis_to_cities[5];
};
```

While these nested structures may not be obvious, they are the result of the requirements of the problem and represent a compact and clear way of storing all the required data.

3. Calculate the distance from each city, to every other city, storing the data in the dis_to_cities data structure. This is a logical unit and should be performed by a function. The notation for the nested structures can be confusing but the calculations can be conveniently carried out by nested loops with the outer loop controlling the starting point and the inner loop cycling through each possible destination. In a real minimum distance problem this step would be unnecessary. The distance for the salesman would be measured in highway miles or, if optical cable were being laid, the exact mileage would be determined by the communications company's right-of-way. Here the distance will be calculated "as a crow flies" from city to city using the Pythagorean Theorem.

4. Devise a method for systematically determining all possible paths. There are clever ways to attack this problem but with brute force we can find every path without repeating a path or doubling back to a previous city by using a set of nested loops.

5. Calculate the distance for each path. This is the addition of the distances from city to city as each path is determined.

6. Find the shortest path. This is a simple matter of saving the first path examined as the shortest and replacing the current shortest path with any path found to be shorter. The length of each new path that is calculated is compared to the length of the shortest path discovered up to that point and, if the new length is shorter, it replaces the old champion.

7. Display the results. In the end the shortest path is saved in the array that stores the indexes of the cities in the order that was determined to be shortest (int path[5]). To display the route, the cities corresponding to the indexes are presented to the user.

The preceding seven steps represent the general plan. The next move is to write the pseudocode.

Pseudocode

1. Begin
2.   Declare and initialize variables.
3.   Get the data from the user for the five cities.
4.   Call function to calculate distances.
5.   Start outer loop to cycle through each of the five cities as a starting point.
6.   Start inner loop to cycle through each of the cities as a destination.
7.   Use Pythagorean Theorem to calculate the diagonal distance from city to city.
8.   Copy the name of the destination city into the data structure storing the distance.
9.   End inner loop.
10.   End outer loop.
11.   Return from calculation function.
12.   Call display function for each of the five cities.

13.	Start loop to display the distance from each city to every other city.
14.	If the starting city and the destination do not have the same name.
15.	Display the destination city and the distance.
16.	End loop.
17.	Return from function.
18.	Arbitrarily assume a starting city (city[0]).
19.	Begin a loop that begins a path from the starting city to every other city.
20.	Begin a nested loop that continues the path from every second city to every possible third city except for the path back to the first city.
21.	Begin a nested loop that continues the path from every third city to every possible fourth city except for the paths back to the first and second cities.
22.	Begin a nested loop that continues the path from every fourth city to every possible fifth city except for the paths back to the first, second, or third city.
23.	Since only one city is left, the entire path is known as described by the counters for the nested loops.
24.	Sum the distance along the path.
25.	If the sum is smaller than the current shortest path.
26.	Save the new shortest distance.
27.	Save the new shortest path.
28.	End loop.
29.	End loop.
30.	End loop.
31.	End loop.
32.	End

Flowchart

Having examined the pseudocode for the traveling salesman problem, it is not hard to imagine that the nested loops would cause the flowchart to be an amazing mess. Since the flowchart would offer no clarity, it has no purpose and is omitted.

Solution Implemented in C++

```
1    // Problem5.3
2    #include <iostream.h>
3    #include <math.h>
4    #include <iomanip.h>
5    #include <string.h>
6    #define MAX_CITIES 5
7
8    struct data
9    {
10       char name [40];
```

```
11      double distance;
12    };
13    struct location
14    {
15      char name[40];
16      double latitude, longitude;
17      data dis_to_cities[5];
18    };
19
20    location set_data (void)
21    {
22      location c;
23      cout << "Enter the city name . .  " << flush;
24      cin >> c.name;
25      cout << "   Enter the latitude     " << flush;
26      cin >> c.latitude;
27      cout << "   Enter the longitude    " << flush;
28      cin >> c.longitude;
29      return c;
30    }
31    void calculate_distances(location c[MAX_CITIES])
32    {
33      int start, destination;
34      for (start = 0; start < MAX_CITIES; start++)
35        for (destination = 0; destination < MAX_CITIES; destination++)
36        {
37          c[start].dis_to_cities[destination].distance =
38            sqrt(pow(c[start].latitude - c[destination].latitude, 2) +
39            pow(c[start].longitude - c[destination].longitude, 2))
40            * 69;
41          strcpy(c[start].dis_to_cities[destination].name,
42            c[destination].name );
43        }
44    }
45
46    void display (location a)
47    {
48      int x;
48      cout << "The distance from " << a.name << " to:" << endl;
49      for (x = 0; x < MAX_CITIES; x++)
50        if (strcmp(a.name, a.dis_to_citiesx.name) != 0)
51          cout << setw(30) << a.dis_to_citiesx.name << " is "
52            << setw(5) << a.dis_to_citiesx.distance << " miles "
53            << endl;
54    }
55
56    void main(void)
57    {
58      location cities[5];// = {{"Cincinnati", 39, 85},{"Atlanta", 34, 83},
```

```
59        //{"Minneapolis", 45, 93},{"Wichita", 38, 97},{"Springfield", 40, 90}};
60        int path[5], x, y, z, w;
61        double total_distance, winner = 1e7;
62        cout.setf(ios::fixed|ios::showpoint);
63        cout.precision (2);
64        for (x = 0; x < MAX_CITIES; x++)
65           citiesx = set_data ();
66        calculate_distances (cities);
67        for (x = 0; x < MAX_CITIES; x++)
68           display (citiesx);
69        for (x = 1; x < MAX_CITIES; x++)
70          for (y = 1; y < MAX_CITIES; y++)
71          {
72             if (x == y) continue;
73             for (z = 1; z < MAX_CITIES; z++)
74             {
75                if ( z == x || z == y) continue;
76                total_distance = 0;
77                for (w = 1; w < MAX_CITIES; w++)
78                {
79                   if (w == x || w == y || w == z) continue;
80                   total_distance = cities[0].dis_to_citiesx.distance +
81                      citiesx.dis_to_cities[y].distance +
82                      cities[y].dis_to_cities[z].distance +
83                      cities[z].dis_to_cities[w].distance +
84                      cities[w].dis_to_cities[0].distance ;
85                   if (total_distance < winner)
86                   {
87                      winner = total_distance;
88                      path[0] = 0, path[1] = x, path[2] = y, path[3] = z,
89                         path [4] = w;
90                   }
91                }
92             }
93          }
94        cout << "\nThe shortest path is:\n\t" <<  cities[path[0]].name;
95        cout << " to " << cities[path[1]].name;
96        cout << "\n\tto " << cities[path[2]].name;
97        cout << " to " << cities[path[3]].name;
98        cout << "\n\tto " << cities[path[4]].name;
99        cout << " and back to " << cities[path[0]].name;
100       cout << endl;
101       cout << "\nThe total distance is "<< winner << "miles." << endl;
102 }
```

The scope of this program has been limited in several ways. Only five cities were considered rather than seeking the more general solution for any number of cities. The other limitations are less serious. Since as-the-crow-flies traveling is usually not practical and real distances either by road or right-of-way would be known as part of the problem, the reliance on latitude and longitude and the rash approximation of 69 miles per degree fade in importance.

However, one more type of limiting was added to the solution to this problem that is more a matter of implementation than logic. The function `display(cities[x])` on line 68

```
67        for (x = 0; x < MAX_CITIES; x++)
68            display (cities [x]);
```

has been used to check the initial operations of the program. Satisfactory output at this point does not solve the problem but does indicate that the user input has been correctly stored and the distances from city to city have been correctly calculated. In the following program output, it is easy to see that the distance from Cincinnati to Atlanta is the same as the distance from Atlanta to Cincinnati, as it must be. This can be considered a partial solution or at least a solution to necessary steps in the solving of the problem.

By displaying the results of the initial operations we either gain confidence that the plan of attack is moving in the right direction or have an indication that an early problem has developed that must be rectified before proceeding. In short, there are not only advantages in limiting the problem but also advantages in limiting the solution. After running the partially finished program and finding that the data stored for the city distances is correct, we can implement the rest of the pseudocode with confidence.

Output of the C++ Program

```
Enter the city name . .    Cincinnati
    Enter the latitude     39
    Enter the longitude    85
Enter the city name . .    Atlanta
    Enter the latitude     34
    Enter the longitude    83
Enter the city name . .    Minneapolis
    Enter the latitude     45
    Enter the longitude    93
Enter the city name . .    Wichita
    Enter the latitude     38
    Enter the longitude    97
Enter the city name . .    Springfield
    Enter the latitude     40
    Enter the longitude    90


The distance from Cincinnati to:
                    Atlanta is 371.58 miles
                Minneapolis is 690.00 miles
                    Wichita is 830.87 miles
                Springfield is 351.83 miles
The distance from Atlanta to:
                  Cincinnati is  371.58 miles
                 Minneapolis is 1025.76 miles
                     Wichita is 1004.66 miles
                 Springfield is 636.15 miles
```

```
The distance from Minneapolis to:
                    Cincinnati is   690.00 miles
                       Atlanta is  1025.76 miles
                       Wichita is   556.30 miles
                    Springfield is  402.34 miles
The distance from Wichita to:
                    Cincinnati is   830.87 miles
                       Atlanta is  1004.66 miles
                    Minneapolis is  556.30 miles
                    Springfield is  502.33 miles
The distance from Springfield to:
                    Cincinnati is   351.83 miles
                       Atlanta is   636.15 miles
                    Minneapolis is  402.34 miles
                       Wichita is   502.33 miles


The shortest path is:
        Cincinnati to Atlanta
        to Wichita to Minneapolis
        to Springfield and back to Cincinnati


The total distance is 2686.70
```

In considering the rapid increase in the number of possible paths as the number of cities increases, we have already noted that the brute force method of attacking the problem can become impractical when an excessive number of trials is required. Still the capability of a modern personal computer to handle millions or even hundreds of millions of trials in a relatively short period of time makes many brute force solutions viable. The next chapter examines a special and particularly useful subset of brute force solvable problems.

Solution Implemented in Visual Basic

```
1    Option Explicit
2
3    Private Const MAX_CITIES As Integer = 5
4
5    Private Type udtData
6      name As String
7      distance As Double
8    End Type
9
10   Private Type udtLocation
11     name As String
12     latitude As Double
13     longitude As Double
14     dis_to_cities(0 To 4) As udtData
15   End Type
16   Private cityNumber As Integer
17   Private cities(0 To 4) As udtLocation
18
19   Private Sub cmdCompute_Click()
20     Dim path(0 To 4) As Integer
```

```
21    Dim x, y, z, w As Integer
22    Dim total_distance, winner As Double
23
24    winner = pow(10, 7)
25     '  Call populateCities(cities(0), "Cincinnati", 39, 85)
26     '  Call populateCities(cities(1), "Atlanta", 34, 83)
27     '  Call populateCities(cities(2), "Minneapolis", 45, 93)
28     '  Call populateCities(cities(3), "Wichita", 38, 97)
29     '  Call populateCities(cities(4), "Springfield", 40, 90)
30
31    Call calculate_distances
32
33    For x = 0 To MAX_CITIES - 1
34      Call display(cities(x))
35    Next x
36
37    For x = 1 To MAX_CITIES - 1
38      For y = 1 To MAX_CITIES - 1
38        If x = y Then
39        Else
40          For z = 1 To MAX_CITIES - 1
41            If z = x Or z = y Then
42            Else
43              total_distance = 0
44              For w = 1 To MAX_CITIES - 1
45                If w = x Or w = y Or w = z Then
46                Else
47                  total_distance = cities(0).dis_to_cities(x).distance + _
48                                   cities(x).dis_to_cities(y).distance + _
49                                   cities(y).dis_to_cities(z).distance + _
50                                   cities(z).dis_to_cities(w).distance + _
51                                   cities(w).dis_to_cities(0).distance
52                If total_distance < winner Then
53                  winner = total_distance
54                  path(0) = 0
55                  path(1) = x
56                  path(2) = y
57                  path(3) = z
58                  path(4) = w
59                End If
60              End If
61            Next w
62          End If
63        Next z
64      End If
65      Next y
66    Next x
67    lstOutput.AddItem ("")
68    lstOutput.AddItem ("The shortest path is:")
69    lstOutput.AddItem (vbTab & cities(path(0)).name & " to " & _
```

```
70            cities(path(1)).name)
71    lstOutput.AddItem (vbTab & "to " & cities(path(2)).name & " to " & _
72            cities(path(3)).name)
73    lstOutput.AddItem (vbTab & "to " & cities(path(4)).name & _
74            " and back to " & cities(path(0)).name)
75    lstOutput.AddItem ("The total distance is " & _
76            Format(CStr(winner), "#.##"))
77  End Sub
78
79  Private Sub populateCities(ByRef city As udtLocation, _
80                             ByVal name As String, _
81                             ByVal lat As Double, _
82                             ByVal lon As Double)
83    city.name = name
84    city.latitude = lat
85      city.longitude = lon
86  End Sub
87
88  Public Sub calculate_distances()
89    Dim start, destination As Integer
90
91    For start = 0 To MAX_CITIES - 1
92      For destination = 0 To MAX_CITIES - 1
93        cities(start).dis_to_cities(destination).distance = _
94          Sqr(pow((cities(start).latitude - _
95          cities(destination).latitude), 2) + _
96          pow((cities(start).longitude - _
97          cities(destination).longitude), 2)) * 69
98        cities(start).dis_to_cities(destination).name = _
99          cities(destination).name
100     Next destination
101   Next start
102 End Sub
103
104 Private Function pow(ByVal base As Double, ByVal power As Integer) As Double
105   Dim i As Integer
106   Dim result As Double
107
108   result = 1
109   For i = 0 To power - 1
110     result = result * base
111   Next i
112
113   pow = result
114 End Function
115
116 Private Sub display(ByRef a As udtLocation)
117   Dim Str As String
118   Dim x As Integer
119   lstOutput.AddItem ("The distance from " & a.name & " to:")
```

```
120
121   For x = 0 To MAX_CITIES - 1
122     If a.dis_to_cities(x).name <> a.name Then
123       Str = Space(30)
124       RSet Str = a.dis_to_cities(x).name
125       Str = Str & " is " & _
126         Format(Round(a.dis_to_cities(x).distance, 2)) & " miles"
127       lstOutput.AddItem (Str)
128     End If
129   Next x
130 End Sub
131
132 Private Sub cmdEnter_Click()
133   If cityNumber < 5 Then
134     cities(cityNumber).name = txtName.Text
135     cities(cityNumber).latitude = CDbl(txtLatitude.Text)
136     cities(cityNumber).longitude = CDbl(txtLongitude.Text)
137     cityNumber = cityNumber + 1
138     If cityNumber <> 5 Then
139       lblCityCount.Caption = CStr(cityNumber) & _ " city(ies) entered"
140     End If
141     txtName.Text = ""
142     txtLatitude.Text = ""
143     txtLongitude.Text = ""
144     txtName.SetFocus
145   End If
146   If cityNumber = 5 Then
147     lblCityCount.Caption = "All cities entered" & vbCrLf & "Click Compute"
148   End If
149 End Sub
150
151 Private Sub cmdExit_Click()
152   Unload Me
153 End Sub
154
155 Private Sub cmdReset_Click()
156   cityNumber = 0
157   lblCityCount.Caption = CStr(cityNumber) & " city(ies) entered"
158   txtName.Text = ""
159   txtLatitude.Text = ""
160   txtLongitude.Text = ""
161   txtName.SetFocus
162   lstOutput.Clear
163 End Sub
164
165 Private Sub Form_Load()
166   Label2.Caption = "This program calculates the shortest " & _
167       "path connecting five cities."
168   cityNumber = 0
169   lblCityCount.Caption = CStr(cityNumber) & " city(ies) entered"
170   End Sub
```

Output of the Visual Basic Program—Prior to computing the shortest path

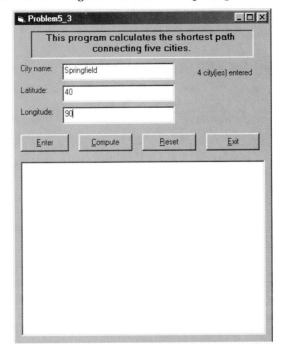

Output of the Visual Basic Program—After computing the shortest path

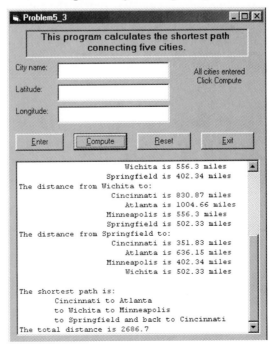

CHAPTER 6

Simulations

6.1 PROBABILITIES

Probabilities represent one of the more difficult branches of mathematics, not because the calculations themselves are so difficult but because this area can be quite counter-intuitive. If a coin is tossed ten times and each time lands heads-up, it would seem that the odds would greatly favor the next toss showing a tails. However, the coin has no memory of those previous ten trials and the odds of seeing a tails on the eleventh toss is still 50-50. There is a considerable difference between the odds of flipping a coin 11 times and seeing a heads every time compared to the odds of seeing a heads on the eleventh flip after a series of ten heads in a row.

Fortunately, the mathematics and the struggle with intuition can be avoided by using a brute force approach and the power of the computer. Actually the computer is not strictly necessary. If a coin were physically flipped ten million times and a count were kept recording how many flips out of the ten million resulted in a heads, a respectable number for the odds could be easily computed. The difficulty is in the time and tedium involved. This is where the computer comes in. By using a random number generator ten million flips of a coin can be accomplished in less than one second.

6.2 CALCULATING THE ODDS

In approaching the topic of probabilities a coin flip is a good place to start because over a large number of flips intuition and reality nicely coincide. However, there are limitations to the accuracy of any simulation and these will be explored in each of the following problems.

PROBLEM 6.1 *What are the odds of a coin landing heads-up in a fair flip?*

While it is commonly known and intuitively obvious that a coin is equally likely to land heads-up or tails-up, it would not be a terrible surprise to experience a coin landing heads-up two, three, or four times in a row. This suggests that to average out these anomalies it would be best to use a large number of trials and the more trials used the more closely the results would approximate a theoretical value. How many trials, or in this case flips, are required? There is no set answer except that the number should be as large as reasonably possible. What is reasonably possible? This depends on how long the user is willing to wait while the computer computes.

Detecting heads or tails is comparable to determining whether a number is even or odd, which is a simple and fast operation for a microprocessor. The entire simulation of a coin flip is

1. Generate a random number.
2. Test whether the number is even.
3. If it is even, increment the heads counter.

This sequence can be run ten million times by a computer in about one second. Ten million times is enough to provide reasonable accuracy and one second is not too long to wait.

Rule 14   The Probability Rule
When probabilities or odds need to be calculated, brute force can usually be applied by simulating the scenario and counting how many times the event of interest occurs.

In solving the coin flip problem, the scenario is the flip of the coin. Since there are only two possible states, heads and tails, and they are equally likely, the scenario requires a simulation with two equally likely outcomes that occur randomly. For the simulation a random number generator will provide the randomness and testing whether the number is even or odd represents the two equally likely outcomes.

Before writing the pseudocode for the problem a few remarks should be made about the random number generator. First, the random number generator is really a pseudorandom number generator. Because the numbers are generated by a mathematical algorithm, the sequence of numbers generated cannot be truly random. However, the algorithms built into C++ and Visual Basic are very good and for all but the most mathematically pure applications can be considered random. Typically the term *pseudorandom number generator* is used for the sake of accuracy.

Second, the pseudorandom number generator will generate the same sequence of numbers every time the program is run. To avoid this limitation on randomness, C++ allows the programmer to seed the generator with a seed number. Unfortunately, this is not a complete solution. If the seed number is hard-coded into the program, the same sequence of random numbers, based on that seed number, will be used every time the program is run. What is required is a method for generating a different seed number at runtime each time the program is started. Such a number is readily available based on the system clock.

Windows-based computers keep track of time by counting the number of seconds that have elapsed since midnight, January 1, 1970. Since this number of seconds will be different every time the program is run (assuming the user cannot run the program twice in less than one second), the seed number for the pseudorandom number generator will be different every time the program is run and a different sequence of numbers generated.

Initial Data: **1.** There are only two possible outcomes to a coin flip.

2. A fair coin is equally likely to land heads or tails.

3. Random chance can produce a series of heads or a series of tails but in the long run these should balance out.

4. There is a pseudorandom number generator built into C++.

Outcome: Determine how many times, out of a large number of flips, the coin will land heads-up.

Pseudocode

1. Begin

2. Declare and initialize variables.

3. Seed the random number generator.

4. Message to user.

5. Begin loop for 10 million cycles.

6. Get random number.

7. Test for even number.

8. If even, increment heads_counter.

9. End loop.

10. Display results.

11. End

Flowchart

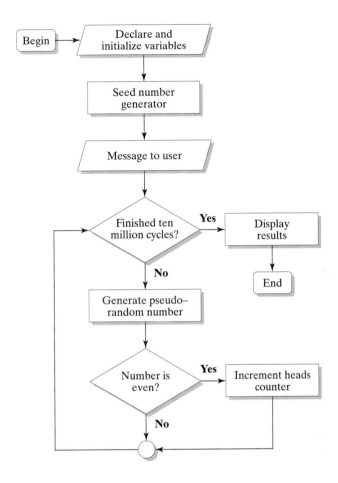

Solution Implemented in C++

```
1    // Problem 6.1
2    #include <stdlib.h>
3    #include <iostream.h>
4    #include <time.h>
5
6    int main(void)
7    {
8        int coin, heads_counter = 0, counter;
9        srand((unsigned) time(NULL));
10       cout << "This program calculates the odds of a coin landing heads-up"
11           << " in a fair flip."
12           << endl << endl;
13       for (counter = 0; counter < 1e7; counter++)
14       {
```

```
15          coin = rand();
16          if (coin % 2 == 0)
17              heads_counter++;
18      }
19      cout << "In one million flips the coin landed heads-up\n\t"
20          << heads_counter << " times or " << heads_counter / 1e5
21          << "% of the time" << endl;
22      return(0);
23  }
```

The code itself is quite straightforward but a few lines deserve some comment. Line 9 uses the `srand()` function to seed the random number generator. The `time()` function with the `NULL` argument returns the number of seconds that have elapsed since midnight, January 1, 1970, and is used as the argument to the `srand()` seeding function. The less obvious element is the `(unsigned)` type cast operator. The `time()` function returns a long integer but the `srand()` function expects an unsigned integer.

Line 13 uses `1e7` in the test condition. This expression is exponential notation for ten million; however, its use is preferred because the meaning is clearer than writing 10000000. Similarly, the use of 1e5 on line 20 is clearer than 100000. One hundred thousand is used in the denominator instead of ten million to convert the fraction from a decimal to a percent. Notice that the result of the division of `heads_counter / 1e5` produces a percent expressed to four decimal places. The problem of integer division is avoided because numbers expressed in exponential notation are considered to be double-precision, floating-point numbers.

The pseudorandom number generator called by the `rand()` function on line 15 has a range of 0 to 32.767 in C++ (or 0 to 7FFF in hexadecimal). In this range there are 16,384 even numbers and 16,384 odd numbers. If the pseudorandom number generator does a good job of picking numbers randomly from the 0 to 32,767 range, then there should be an equal number of even and odd numbers generated in the long run, that is, over an infinite number of random numbers generated. In this program we have approximated an infinite number of random numbers by using ten million.

Line 15 provides the test for equality. If the remainder of division by two is zero, the dividend must have been even and the `heads_counter` should be incremented.

Output of the C++ Program

```
This program calculates the odds of a coin landing heads-up in a fair flip.
In one million flips the coin landed heads-up
        4999857 times or 49.9986% of the time
```

There are three important items to keep in mind regarding this simulation.

1. Because of the random nature of the events of interest, the result of the simulation will not match the theoretical value unless an infinite number of trials are made. This typically does not affect the usefulness of the simulation.

2. The greater the number of trials, the closer the result will be to the theoretical answer. It is a worthwhile exercise for the reader to reproduce the coin flip program to run for one billion or ten billion trials. The results will be significantly closer to the theoretical 50 percent. Caution: If the number of trials is increased beyond approximately 4.3 billion, the counter for the loop can no longer be declared as an integer or even as an unsigned integer.

3. **This particular simulation is invalid.** It contains an error in logic that should be avoided. The program was used first because it illustrates in a simple fashion the process of determining probabilities based on simulating events and, second, because it illustrates one of the problems that can arise when using simulations.

The error in this problem is in assuming the answer before working the problem. The solution was based on the fact that half of all integers are even and this would simulate a coin flip because half of all coin flips are heads. **But determining the odds on a coin landing heads-up was the objective of the problem and cannot be assumed *a priori*, or at the beginning.** The program really shows that the random number generator is quite good at providing an even number one half of the time.

This leads to the larger question of the validity of any simulation. Does the simulation actually reflect what happens when a coin is flipped, dice are rolled, air is blown over an airplane wing, current travels through a transistor, or the weather is predicted? The logical error in the coin flip problem made the solution invalid. More commonly simplifications in simulating events introduce errors that make the results less accurate.

Solution Implemented in Visual Basic

```
1    Option Explicit
2    Private Sub cmdCalc_Click()
3        Dim coin As Integer
4        Dim counter As Single
5        Dim heads_counter As Single
6
7        lblAnswer.Caption = ""
8        Randomize
9        lblMessage.Caption = "Please be patient," & vbCrLf & _
10           "I'm working as fast as I can."
11       DoEvents
12       For counter = 0 To 10000000
13           coin = Int(32767 * Rnd)
14           If coin Mod 2 = 0 Then
15               heads_counter = heads_counter + 1
16           End If
17       Next counter
18
19    lblAnswer.Caption = "In 10,000,000 flips the coin " & _
20        "lands heads-up " & heads_counter & " times or " & _
```

```
21       vbCrLf & (heads_counter / counter) * 100 & _
22       "% of the time"
23  End Sub
24
25  Private Sub Form_Load()
26    lblTitle.Caption = "This program calculates the " & _
27        "odds of a coin landing heads-up in a fair flip."
28  End Sub
```

Output of the Visual Basic Program

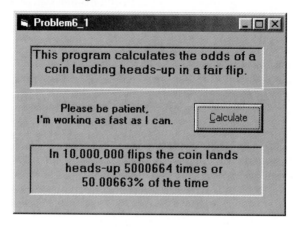

The next problem, based on winning a game of craps on the first roll, makes the assumption that any of the six numbers on a die is equally likely to roll to the top position. However, the objective is not to determine the odds of a six or any other number appearing on the die but, given the odds are one in six for a given number to roll to the top when the die stops, what are the odds of winning the game?

PROBLEM 6.2   *What are the odds of winning a game of craps on the first roll?*

This problem represents a limited version of the general question, "What are the odds of winning a game of craps?" The more general question will be explored in Chapter 7. As always the place to begin is with the initial data.

Initial Data: **1.** Rolling a 7 or an 11 on the first roll will win the game.

2. Rolling any other number will lose or delay the outcome of the game.

3. The number rolled is the sum of the numbers shown on two dice.

4. Some numbers occur more often than others. For example, a 3 can be rolled if 1-2 or 2-1 show on the dice. There are two ways to roll a 3. A 7 is rolled if the dice show 1-6, 6-1, 2-5, 5-2, 3-4, or 4-3. There are six ways to roll a 7.

5. The odds of winning can be determined by rolling the dice 100 million times and counting the number of times a 7 or an 11 appears on the dice.

Outcome: How often will one of the winning numbers show on the dice?

The initial problem is how to simulate the rolling of two dice. After the dice are simulated, the solution is rather similar to that of the coin flip problem. Simulating the dice requires creating two variables representing the dice. Each variable should be given a random number in the range of 1 to 6, inclusive. This brings to mind the encryption problem (Problem 5.1) in which a number in the range of 1 to 41 was needed. To generate a number from 1 to 6 the expression `rand() % 6 + 1` will do the job. Almost.

The use of the modulus operator is the standard method taught in programming classes and used in most programming textbooks for limiting the range of random numbers. However, there is a small problem. Six does not divide evenly into the 32,768 possible numbers generated. If each number from 0 to 32,767 is divided by 6, remainders of 0 and 1 will occur 5,462 times but the remainders 2, 3, 4, and 5 will occur only 5,461 times. The implication is that the random numbers are no longer random but have a slight bias in favor of generating 0s and 1s.

There are two ways to look at this problem. The bias can be considered to be one extra 0 and 1 in every 32,768 trials, or .003%. On the other hand, over the course of generating one billion numbers the absolute bias becomes more striking. The following table is the output of a program that generates one billion random numbers from 0 to 5 and counts how many times each number occurs.

```
0s = 166689530    3s = 166654437
1s = 166692682    4s = 166647246
2s = 166663218    5s = 166652888
```

In these results 0s and 1s appear, on the average, 36,659 more times in one billion trials than the numbers 2 through 5. The theoretical bias indicates 30,518 extra 1s and 0s per one billion trials. The bias is only around .003% even though the absolute numbers are quite large. The question is whether an error of .003% is enough to invalidate the simulation. In most cases, it is not but the question remains whether the bias can be eliminated. The answer is that it can be eliminated and the issue is discussed fully in Chapter 7, Section 4.

Pseudocode

1. Begin
2. Declare and initialize variables.
3. Seed the pseudorandom number generator from the system clock.
4. Message to user.
5. Start the timer.
6. Begin loop for 100 million rolls.
7. Get random number for first die.

  8.   Get random number for second die.

  9.   Total the dice.

10.   Test for 7 or 11.

11.   If true, increment wins counter.

12. End loop.

13. End timer.

14. Display results.

15. End

Flowchart

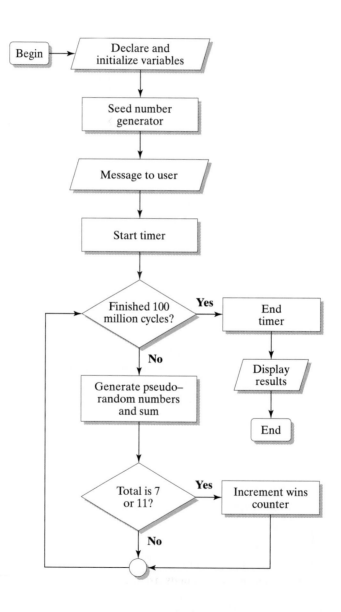

Solution Implemented in C++

```cpp
1    // Problem 6.2
2    #include <iostream.h>
3    #include <time.h>
4    #include <stdlib.h>
5    #include <iomanip.h>
6
7    int main(void)
8    {
9        long counter, wins = 0, first_die, second_die, total;
10       long start, end;
11       cout.setf(ios::fixed|ios::showpoint);
12       cout.precision (2);
13       srand((unsigned)time(NULL));
14       cout << "This program calculates the odds of winning a game of craps"
15           << "\n\ton the first roll.\n" << endl;
16       time(&start);
17       for (counter = 0; counter < 1e8; counter++)
18       {
19           first_die = rand() % 6 + 1;
20           second_die = rand() % 6 + 1;
21           total = first_die + second_die;
22           if( total == 7 || total == 11)
23               wins++;
24       }
25       time(&end);
26       cout << "\nA first roll win occurred " << wins
27           << " times out of 100,000,000"
28           << "\n\t or " << wins / 1000000.0 << " % of the time."
29           << endl << endl
30           << "The program required " << (int)difftime(end, start)
31           << " seconds to complete." << endl;
32       return(0);
33   }
```

An unnecessary but rather useful feature has been added to this program. The time() function on line 16 and on line 25 stores the current time from the system clock. As mentioned earlier, this is the number of seconds since midnight, January 1, 1970 (on Windows-based computers). Recording the time at the start and end of the simulation allows the elapsed time to be calculated by the difftime() function and the number of seconds required for the program to be displayed. This value has little to do with the logic of the simulation but it does provide some insight as to whether it is practical to raise the number of trials. Notice that the time() takes as an argument the address of the long variable that will store the current time.

Output of the C++ Program

```
This program calculates the odds of winning a game of craps
        on the first roll.

A first roll win occurred 22215074 times out of 100,000,000
        or 22.22 % of the time.

The program required 24 seconds to complete.
```

As in the case of the coin flip problem, there was an assumption that each face on a die is equally likely to be face up when it stops rolling or that the odds of any one of the six numbers appearing is one in six. If this assumption is true, then simulating the die with a random number generator that produces the numbers from 1 to 6 makes sense. Unlike the coin flip problem, determining the odds of rolling a specific number is not the objective of the program. The objective in this case is to determine the odds of winning a game of craps on the first roll. If it should be found that the assumption of a one-in-six chance for rolling a specific number is not true, then the simulation is also false. Fortunately, these dice are not loaded.

The real test of any simulation program is whether it produces results that correspond to reality. Comparing the results of this program to the results of playing a very large number of games of craps is somewhat impractical. Fortunately, the theoretical results for rolling a 7 or 11 are easy to calculate. There are 36 possible combinations that can be made by two dice.

	1	2	3	4	5	6
1	1-1	1-2	1-3	1-4	1-5	1-6
2	2-1	2-2	2-3	2-4	2-5	2-6
3	3-1	3-2	3-3	3-4	3-5	3-6
4	4-1	4-2	4-3	4-4	4-5	4-6
5	5-1	5-2	5-3	5-4	5-5	5-6
6	6-1	6-2	6-3	6-4	6-5	6-6

Of those 36 possibilities, six combinations result in a sum of seven (light gray) and two sum to 11 (darker gray). Therefore, the game is won eight times out of 36 equally likely possibilities. Eight divided by 36 yields 22.22% or the number indicated by the simulation.

Notice that the 22.22% is really a repeating decimal. This means that the simulation should have produced a result of 22,222,222 wins out of 100,000,000 games. Two factors account for the discrepancy. First, to get the exact theoretical answer the simulation would need a perfect random number generator and would have to run for an infinite number of games. An infinite number of games is impractical and the random number generator is not perfect. As already mentioned, the generation of better random numbers will be covered in Chapter 7. The real question is how much accuracy is enough. When the question involves the odds of winning at craps on the first roll, four-digit accuracy is probably more than enough.

Solution Implemented in Visual Basic

```
1   Option Explicit
2
3   Private Sub cmdCalc_Click()
4       Dim counter As Long
5       Dim wins As Long
6       Dim first_die As Long
```

```
7       Dim second_die As Long
8       Dim total As Long
9       Dim start As Long
10      Dim finish As Long
11      Dim Message As String
12      Message = "              Working   "
13      Randomize
14      start = Timer
15      lblTime.Caption = Message
16      For counter = 0 To 10000000
17          If counter Mod 500000 = 0 Then
18              Message = Message & Chr(1)
19              lblTime = Message
20              DoEvents
21          End If
22          first_die = Int(6 * Rnd + 1)
23          second_die = Int(6 * Rnd + 1)
24          total = first_die + second_die
25          If total = 7 Or total = 11 Then
26              wins = wins + 1
27          End If
28      Next counter
29      finish = Timer
30
31      lblAnswer.Caption = "A first roll win occurred " & wins & _
32          " times out of 10,000,000" & _
33          " or " & (wins / 10000000) * 100 & "% of the time."
34      lblTime.Caption = "The program required " & finish - start & _
35          " seconds to complete."
36  End Sub
37
38  Private Sub cmdExit_Click()
39      Unload Me
40  End Sub
41
42  Private Sub Form_Load()
43      lblTitle.Caption = "This program calculates the odds of winning " & _
44          "a game of craps on the first roll."
45  End Sub
```

Because Visual Basic runs more slowly than C++, especially when run in the programming environment, the number of games played was reduced (line 15) to 10,000,000 games. Despite the reduced number of trials, Visual Basic provides an answer that is only 78 wins greater than the expected number. This is due to the noninteger return values from the Rnd() function. It also illustrates the need to improve the random number generation of the C++ program.

In the Visual Basic solution to Problem 6.1 a message asking for patience was displayed while the program ran the simulation. This is thoughtful but a static message can leave the user wondering if the program has frozen the computer and whether it is time for the three-finger salute i.e., <Ctrl><Alt><Delete>. A better idea is to create a dynamic scene that regularly changes, indicating that the program is still making progress. This secondary problem is easily solved on lines 17 through 21. The if statement traps every 500,000th game, adds a bar to the "Working" message, and sends Message to the lblTime label box. The user of the program sees another bar appear approximately every one second and knows the program is still running. To make this routine work properly the DoEvents command must be included in the body of the if statement.

Output of the Visual Basic Program—In Progress

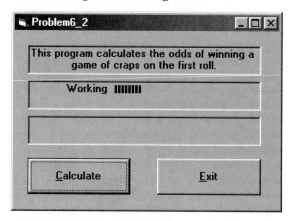

When the program is finished, the "Working" message is replaced by the number of seconds required to complete the simulation.

Output of the Visual Basic Program—Completed

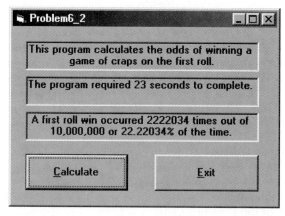

Simulations become more useful as the problems become more complex and calculated solutions are more difficult to determine. Consider the odds of landing on a certain square of a board game.

PROBLEM 6.3   *What are the odds of landing on Indiana Avenue in a game of Monopoly within the first four turns?*

If all factors are considered, this problem is rather difficult to calculate and even a bit awkward to simulate. It makes sense to invoke the rule advising the limiting of the problem (Rule 7). In the game of Monopoly there are several rules that make landing on Indiana Avenue a more interesting event than just a sequence of rolls that totals 23 (the distance from the starting square to Indiana Avenue).

The first difficulty is the extra roll involved if a player rolls doubles. This implies that it is possible to land on Indiana Avenue on the player's first turn by rolling double fours, double fours, and a seven for a total of 23. Further complicating the issue is the rule that three doubles in a row send the player to jail.

Other compounding features are the Go To Jail square (position 30) and the Chance and Community Chest squares where a player chooses a card from a deck that might send him to a new position on the board. For the purposes of this problem the Go To Jail, Chance, and Community Chest squares will be ignored but the rules involving doubles more significantly affect the probability of landing on the target position and will be included.

Initial Data: **1.** Advancing around the board is accomplished by rolling two dice and moving the number of squares indicated.

2. Up to two doubles are permitted per turn with each double earning another roll.

3. Indiana Avenue is square 23 out of 40 squares.

4. It is possible to circle the board up to two times and still land on Indiana Avenue if many large doubles are rolled. Consider successive turns of 12, 12, and 11. After rolling double sixes twice and then rolling 11 for four turns in a row, it is possible to travel 140 squares. It's a tad unlikely but it could happen. This makes Indiana Avenue square 23, square 63 (23 + 40), and square 103 (23 + 40 + 40). It is also square 143 but that distance is not possible in four turns.

5. If the first four rolls of the game are simulated 100 million times and a count is kept recording how many times the player landed on Indiana Avenue, the probability is the hits divided by 100 million multiplied by 100 percent.

Output: Calculate the odds of landing on Indiana Avenue in the first four turns of a game of Monopoly.

It should be mentioned that Monopoly was chosen as a common game but any board game or, in fact, any game that had a random element would present a similar scenario. The details of the play would change but the construction of the simulation would be very similar.

Although the problem appears to have considerable complexity, it simplifies greatly if the problem solver is clear about what operations must be performed and in what order.

1. The simulation should run for 100 million cycles. This suggests a for() loop that runs 100 million times.

2. In each of those cycles the player gets four turns. This suggests another for() loop that runs four times nested within the first loop.

3. Each of those turns will consist of one, two, or three rolls depending on whether the dice match on the first roll, or the first and second roll. Since the number of rolls in each turn is unknown, this suggests a do/while loop nested within the second for() loop.

These three steps will serve as an initial, very rough, but useful pseudocode. Once the structure of the program is determined, the details can be added.

For each new game (for each cycle of the outermost loop) the play must return to the start position and the hit_flag is reset to zero. The hit_flag indicates that the player has landed on Indiana Avenue and the game can be ended regardless of whether four turns have been taken or not. If the hit_flag were eliminated and the program were to continue for the full four turns, some false hits would be recorded and the program would run more slowly. The false hit would result from the cases in which the player landed on Indiana Avenue twice by landing on square 23 and later on square 63 on the next cycle around the board. The slower performance results from the extra unnecessary rolls that the simulation must make. Actually the extra work has to be balanced against the extra testing and resetting of the hit_flag that the program must do. In fact, over the course of 100 million trials, the use of the hit_flag saves about three seconds on a 450 MHz Pentium III computer. For those with a computer science degree the three seconds savings can be determined by examining the assembler code, counting the clock cycles for the extra rolls, and comparing that number to the extra clock cycles for the extra flag checking. Those more grounded in reality generally prefer to put a timer in the program and run it with and without the flag.

For each cycle of the second loop the doubles_flag must be reset to zero. This flag controls whether the turn will have only one roll or have a second and possibly a third roll. The innermost loop controls everything that happens on a roll. First, random numbers are generated representing the dice. The numbers are examined to determine if there should be another roll on that turn. If doubles do occur, then the `doubles_flag` is incremented to continue the loop, that is, provide another roll in the same turn. Notice the inner loop should end if no doubles are rolled or if a third doubles is rolled. The loop only continues if doubles are rolled once or twice. This implies that the `doubles_flag` should be used in the `do/while` test condition.

After the `doubles_flag` has been set appropriately, the number rolled (generated randomly) is added to the current position of the player, either the start square or the position from the previous cycle. If the player lands on Indiana Avenue, the event counter increments, and the game ends. The `hit_flag` is used because the `break` statement only breaks the current loop. In this case the rolls loop and the turns loop must be ended so the next cycle of the games loop can begin.

Pseudocode

  1. Begin
  2.   Declare and initialize variables.
  3.   Message to user.
  4.   Start timer.
  5.   Begin loop for 100 million games.
  6.   Set position and hit_flag variables to zero.
  7.   Begin loop for four turns in each game.
  8.   Set doubles_flag to zero.
  9.   Begin the do/while loop for one, two, or three rolls.
 10.   Roll the dice using pseudorandom number generator.
 11.   If the two dice match
 12.   Increment the doubles_flag.
 13.   Otherwise reset the doubles_flag to zero.
 14.   If the doubles_flag reaches three
 15.   Break out of the do/while loop and the turns loop.
 16.   (more than two doubles send the player to jail).
 17.   Advance the number of squares indicated by the dice.
 18.   If you land on Indiana Avenue
 19.   Increment the Indiana Avenue counter.
 20.   Set the hit flag.
 21.   Break out of the do/while loop and the turns loop.
 22.   End the do/while after one roll unless there has been a doubles.
 23.   End the turns loop.
 24.   End the 100 million trials loop.
 25.   Record end time.
 26.   Display answer.
 27. End

Flowchart

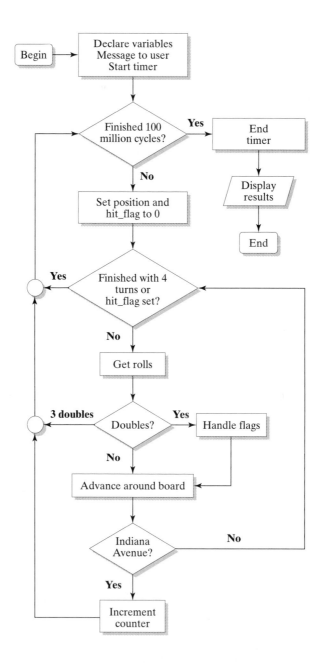

The timer was added to track the time required for the simulation. Experiment-ing showed that one million games required a little over one second. Ten million cycles took about 12 seconds. One hundred million cycles required a little over two minutes but produced a consistent percentage of slightly more than 14.0%.

Solution Implemented in C++

```cpp
1    // Problem 6.3
2    #include <iostream.h>
3    #include <stdlib.h>
4    #include <time.h>
5    #include <iomanip.h>
6    #include <conio.h>
7
8    void main(void)
9    {
10       int position, games, Indiana, turn, first, second, doubles_flag;
11       int hit_flag;
12       long start, end;
13       srand((unsigned) time(NULL));
14       cout << "This program determines the odds of landing on Indiana in "
15           << "\n\tthe first four turns of a Monopoly game.\n" << endl;
16       time(&start);
17       for (games = 1; games <= 1e8; games++)
18       {
19          position = 0; hit_flag = 0;
20          for (turn = 1; turn <= 4; turn++)
21          {
22             doubles_flag = 0;
23             do
24             {
25                first = rand() % 6 + 1;
26                second = rand() % 6 + 1;
27                if (first == second)
28                   doubles_flag++;
29                else
30                   doubles_flag = 0;
31                if (doubles_flag == 3)
32                {
33                   hit_flag = 1;
34                   break;
35                }
36                position += first + second;
37                if (position == 23 || position == 63 || position == 103)
38                {
39                   Indiana++;
40                   hit_flag = 1;
41                   break;
42                }
43             }while(doubles_flag == 1|| doubles_flag == 2);
44             if (hit_flag == 1)
45                break;
46          }
47       }
48       time(&end);
49       cout << "\nThe chance of landing on Indiana is "
50           << Indiana * 100 / 1e8 << "%\n" << endl
51           << "\tRunning time -- " << end - start << " seconds" << endl;
52    }
```

As mentioned earlier, the key to the logic of the program is the nested loops. Line 17 controls the number of games simulated; line 20 counts the four turns; and line 23 manages the rolls, at least one but no more than three per turn. The rest of the logic involves when to increment the Indiana counter and when to break out of loops prematurely. The use of the hit_flag has been given two duties. The apparent use is to break out of both inner loops and to begin the next simulated game. It is also used to produce the same effect on line 33 to break out of both inner loops if the player is sent to jail for rolling doubles three times.

This raises the moderately interesting question of how many times, in the course of the first four rolls of 100 million games, will a player roll doubles three times in a row. The answer is surprisingly high and its determination is left as an exercise for the reader. One of the advantages to using simulations is that once the program is written, simple alterations can produce considerable extra information. In this case we can determine the number of times doubles are rolled three times in a row by merely adding a new counter variable, adding a single line of code to increment the counter after line 32, and displaying the answer.

Output of the C++ Program

```
This program determines the odds of landing on Indiana in

        the first four turns of a Monopoly game.

The chance of landing on Indiana is 14.0013%

        Running time -- 125 seconds
```

Solution Implemented in Visual Basic

```
1    Option Explicit
2
3    Private Sub cmdCalc_Click()
4        Dim position, games, Indiana As Long
5        Dim turn, first, second As Long
6        Dim doubles_flag, hit_flag, start As Long
7        Dim finish As Long
8        Dim Message As String
9        Message = "    Working    "
10       Randomize
11       start = Timer
12
13       For games = 0 To 10000000
14           If games Mod 250000 = 0 Then
15               Message = Message & Chr(1)
16               lblTime.Caption = Message
17               DoEvents
18           End If
19           position = 0
20           hit_flag = 0
21           For turn = 1 To 4
22               doubles_flag = 0
23               Do
24                   first = Int(6 * Rnd + 1)
25                   second = Int(6 * Rnd + 1)
```

```
26                      If first = second Then
27                          doubles_flag = doubles_flag + 1
28                      Else
29                          doubles_flag = 0
30                      End If
31                      If doubles_flag = 3 Then
32                          hit_flag = 1
33                          Exit Do
34                      End If
35                      position = position + first + second
36                      If position = 23 Or position = 63 Or position = 103 Then
37                          Indiana = Indiana + 1
38                          hit_flag = 1
39                              Exit Do
40                      End If
41                 Loop While doubles_flag = 1 Or doubles_flag = 2
42             If hit_flag = 1 Then
43                     Exit For
44             End If
45         Next turn
46     Next games
47     finish = Timer
48     lblAnswer.Caption = "The probability of landing on Indiana " & _
49         "is " & Format(Indiana / games * 100, "##.##") & "%"
50     lblTime.Caption = "            Running time -- " & _
51         finish - start & " seconds."
52 End Sub
53
54 Private Sub cmdExit_Click()
55     Unload Me
56 End Sub
57
58 Private Sub Form_Load()
59     lblTitle.Caption = "This program determines the probability of " & _
60         vbCrLf & "landing on Indiana in the first four turns " & _
61         vbCrLf & "of a Monopoly game."
62 End Sub
```

There is a considerable difference in run speed between the Visual Basic program and the C++ program. The C++ program ran faster despite simulating 100 million games compared to the 10 million used in the Visual Basic program. Maintaining the Windows interface and the DoEvents command are time-consuming features that are the trade-off for choosing Visual Basic with its familiar interface over the command window of the C++ interface. The run time for the Visual Basic program can be reduced by creating an executable file using Make Program6_3.exe option from the File pull-down menu.

Two runs of the Visual Basic program are shown in the following displays. The first is the output of the program run from within the programming environment and the second is the output of the executable file.

As noted in the previous problem, the percentage of the games played that are won is more accurate in the Visual Basic program compared to the C++ program. This is due to less than perfect use of the modulus operator used to determine the value of each die in the C++ program. This inaccuracy can be seen to be minor but, nevertheless, will be corrected in Chapter 7.

Output of the Visual Basic Program—From Within the Programming Environment

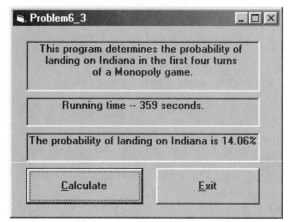

Output of the Visual Basic Program—From the Executable File

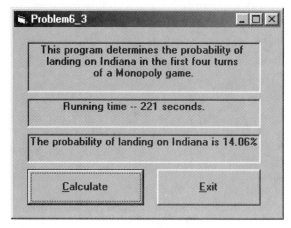

6.3   THE "WHAT IF" SCENARIO

The simulations of the previous three problems involved random occurrences to calculate odds for common events. Simulations are also useful in examining events that are not so easily reproduced in reality. Flight simulators allow pilots to practice controlling new aircraft designs from the safety of the ground. Fission and fusion reactions can be simulated without the destruction or the radiation of a real detonation. Less dramatic but still rather interesting is the shuffling of a deck of cards.

The purpose of shuffling cards is to randomize their order. It would seem that the better the cards are interleaved the fewer the shuffles that would be required to randomize the cards. That is, interleaving the cards, taking one at a time from each half of the deck, should produce better randomization than interleaving clumps of ten cards from each half of the deck. This is difficult to test in practice. Even professional, slight-of-hand magicians have difficulty in repeatedly producing a perfect shuffle. Restacking the cards one at a time is a rather tedious process and errors still might creep in if cards stick together.

On the other hand, a computer can easily simulate the perfect shuffle, repeatedly and virtually instantly, for as long as we choose to continue the simulation.

PROBLEM 6.4   *What would happen if a deck of cards were shuffled perfectly? Twice? Three or more times? Would the cards randomize? How quickly?*

The problem itself requires that some clarity be added by defining the terms used. If the conditions of the problem are not clear or the end point is not clear, there is little hope of finding a solution. In this case a perfect shuffle results if the deck is exactly cut in half, 26 cards in each half, and the cards are interleaved one from alternate half decks. If the cards are initially numbered from the top down from 1 to 52, a perfect shuffling of the deck would order the cards 1, 27, 2, 28, 3, 29, and so on.

The second item is how the condition of randomization can be recognized. The cards are randomized if the number of the next card cannot be predicted by pattern of previous cards. This is less than satisfactory. Just because an individual can find no pattern doesn't mean that no pattern exists. For the moment let's reverse the issue. The cards are *not* randomized if a pattern is discernable. In short we will look for the possibility of randomization.

Initial Data:
1. There are 52 cards in a deck.
2. The cards are initially in some order.
3. The initial order is unimportant but for convenience the cards can be numbered 1 through 52 with 1 on the top. It doesn't matter whether card 1 is the three of hearts or the king of spades, it is the first card at the top of the deck.
4. A perfect shuffle cuts the deck exactly in half and interleaves the cards one at a time from alternate halves of the deck.
5. The perfect shuffle will have to be repeated since it is clear that the first perfect shuffle will leave the cards ordered, that is, 1, 27, 2, 28, 3, 29, and so on.

Output: The output is the order of the deck after each shuffle. Examining the cards for order will be left to the human controlling the program for determination of whether a pattern exists.

In this problem the logic is simple because the action of shuffling the cards is simple. An outer loop will control the number of times the deck is shuffled. Because this number is unknown to the programmer and will be determined by the user of the program at runtime, a do/while loop is called for. Within this loop the cards must be cut into two halves and a new stack made by alternately taking cards from the two half decks.

Of course, in a simulation there is no real cutting of the deck. Creating the new stack from the old is just a matter of choosing the first card of the source deck and then the 27th card from the same deck. It is much easer to take out the 27th card of a simulated deck than a real one. The next card is the second from the top and the fourth card is the 28th card. When 52 cards have been moved, the results can be displayed and examined.

Pseudocode

1. Begin
2.   Declare and initialize variables.
3.   Begin loop to put the deck in order.
4.   Initialize the array deck1[52] to hold the numbers 1, 2, 3, 4, 5, ...
5.   End ordering loop.
6.   Begin the shuffling routine.
7.   On odd-numbered cycles deck1 is shuffled into deck2.
8.   On even-numbered cycles deck2 is shuffled into deck1.
9.   Display cycle number.
10.   Set front pointer to card 1 of source.
11.   Set back pointer to card 27 of source.
12.   For 52 cards
13.   Put card pointed to by front pointer into target deck.
14.   Increment front pointer to next card.

15.   Increment target deck pointer to next position.
16.   Put card pointed to by back pointer into target deck.
17.   Increment back pointer to next card.
18.   Increment target deck pointer to next position.
19.   End shuffle loop.
20.   Display results.
21.   Prompt user—new shuffle or end.
22.   End shuffle routine.
23. End

Flowchart

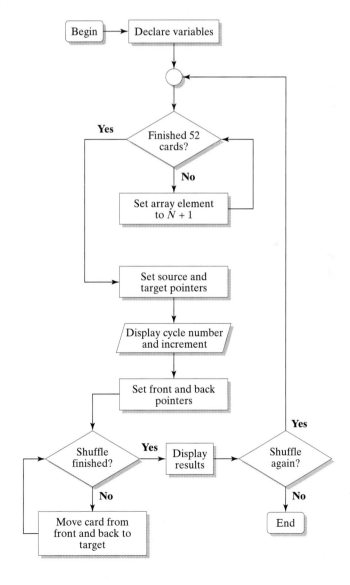

Solution Implemented in C++

```
1    //  Problem 6.4
2    #include <iostream.h>
3    #include <iomanip.h>
4    #include <conio.h>
5
6    void main(void)
7    {
8       int deck1[52], deck2[52], *frontptr, *backptr, *source, *target;
9       int counter, cycle = 1;
10      char ans;
11         ////////  Order deck1    1, 2, 3, 4, 5, ...
12      for (counter = 0; counter < 52; counter++)
13         deck1[counter] = counter + 1;
14      do
15      {
16         if (cycle % 2 == 1)     // deck1 is the source for
17         {                   //   odd-numbered shuffles
18            source = deck1;
19            target = deck2;
20         }
21         else               // deck2 is the source for
22         {                   //   even-numbered shuffles
23            source = deck2;
24            target = deck1;
25         }
26         cout << "Cycle " << cycle++ << endl;
27         frontptr = source;
28         backptr  = source + 26;
29            //////////    Make the perfect shuffle
30         for (counter = 0; counter < 52;)
31         {
32            *(target + counter++) = *frontptr++;
33            *(target + counter++) = *backptr++;
34         }
35         for (counter = 0; counter < 52; counter++)
36            cout << setw(5) << *(target + counter);
37         cout << endl;
38         cout << "Another shuffle? (Any key to continue / <Esc> to end)";
39         cout << endl << endl;
40         ans = getch();
41      }while(ans != 27);
42   }
```

The use of pointers is not necessary in this program but they considerably simplify the code. Without the pointers the bulk of the program would need to be written twice, once to shuffle from deck1 to deck2, and again to shuffle from deck2 to deck1. By using pointers the shuffle is always from the source to the target. The array that is considered the source deck is changed each cycle by the if-else construction on lines 16 through 25.

The pointers also make moving through each deck simpler and executed in less code than the pseudocode required. The shuffling of the deck is compacted to the two lines within the for() loop because of the ability to move the pointer to the next element of the array.

```
30              for (counter = 0; counter < 52;)
31              {
32                  *(target + counter++) = *frontptr++;
33                  *(target + counter++) = *backptr++;
34              }
```

Notice that the third field in the for() statement that typically increments the counter is empty. By incrementing the counter on lines 32 and 33 the counter increments twice in one cycle of the loop, once for each of the cards supplied by the frontptr and backptr.

Once the ability to create perfect shuffles is created, the question remains as to what repeated perfect shuffles tell us. This requires running the program several times.

Output of the C++ Program

```
Cycle 1
    1    27    2    28    3    29    4    30    5    31    6    32    7    33    8
34     9   35    10   36    11   37    12   38    13   39    14   40    15   41    16
42    17   43    18   44    19   45    20   46    21   47    22   48    23   49    24
50    25   51    26   52
Another shuffle? (Any key to continue / <Esc> to end)


Cycle 2
    1    14   27    40    2    15   28    41    3    16   29    42    4    17    30
43     5   18    31   44     6   19    32   45     7   20    33   46     8   21    34
47     9   22    35   48    10   23    36   49    11   24    37   50    12   25    38
51    13   26    39   52
Another shuffle? (Any key to continue / <Esc> to end)


Cycle 3
    1    33   14    46   27     8   40    21    2    34   15    47   28     9   41
22     3   35    16   48    29   10    42   23     4   36    17   49    30    11   43
24     5   37    18   50    31   12    44   25     6   38    19   51    32    13   45
26     7   39    20   52
Another shuffle? (Any key to continue / <Esc> to end)
```

Even though some order still exists, it appears that the numbers are becoming less ordered. Continuing the shuffles:

```
Cycle 4
    1    17   33    49   14    30   46    11   27    43    8    24   40     5   21
37     2   18    34   50    15   31    47   12    28   44     9   25    41     6   22
38     3   19    35   51    16   32    48   13    29   45    10   26    42     7   23
39     4   20    36   52
```

Another shuffle? (Any key to continue / <Esc> to end)

Cycle 5
```
       1    9   17   25   33   41   49    6   14   22   30   38   46    3   11
 19   27    5   43   51    8   16   24   32   40   48    5   13   21   29   37
 45    2    0   18   26   34   42   50    7   15   23   31   39   47    4   12
 20   28   36   44   52
```
Another shuffle? (Any key to continue / <Esc> to end)

Cycle 6
```
       1    5    9   13   17   21   25   29   33   37   41   45   49    2    6
 10   14   18   22   26   30   34   38   42   46   50    3    7   11   15   19
 23   27   31   35   39   43   47   51    4    8   12   16   20   24   28   32
 36   40   44   48   52
```
Another shuffle? (Any key to continue / <Esc> to end)

Cycle 7
```
       1    3    5    7    9   11   13   15   17   19   21   23   25   27   29
 31   33   35   37   39   41   43   45   47   49   51    2    4    6    8   10
 12   14   16   18   20   22   24   26   28   30   32   34   36   38   40   42
 44   46   48   50   52
```
Another shuffle? (Any key to continue / <Esc> to end)

Cycle 8
```
       1    2    3    4    5    6    7    8    9   10   11   12   13   14   15
 16   17   18   19   20   21   22   23   24   25   26   27   28   29   30   31
 32   33   34   35   36   37   38   39   40   41   42   43   44   45   46   47
 48   49   50   51   52
```
Another shuffle? (Any key to continue / <Esc> to end)

Unfortunately, further shuffles begin to undo the effects of the initial shuffles until by cycle 8 the cards are returned to their original order. Perfect shuffles have been discovered to be ineffective for randomizing cards. However, the program does raise some new, rather interesting "what if" questions. What if card 27 was made the top card in the target deck? Would that produce a randomized deck? To simulate this condition only a small change is required in the program. If lines 32 and 33 are reversed,

```
32                  *(target + counter++) = *backptr++;
33                  *(target + counter++) = *frontptr++;
```

each card from the lower half of the deck is raised one position. The result appears to show more promise for randomizing.

Cycle 1
```
      27    1   28    2   29    3   30    4   31    5   32    6   33    7   34
  8   35    9   36   10   37   11   38   12   39   13   40   14   41   15   42
 16   43   17   44   18   45   19   46   20   47   21   48   22   49   23   50
 24   51   25   52   26
```

Another shuffle? (Any key to continue / <Esc> to end)
Cycle 2

```
     40   27   14    1   41   28   15    2   42   29   16    3   43   30   17
 4   44   31   18    5   45   32   19    6   46   33   20    7   47   34   21
 8   48   35   22    9   49   36   23   10   50   37   24   11   51   38   25
12   52   39   26   13
```

Another shuffle? (Any key to continue / <Esc> to end)

Cycle 3

```
     20   40    7   27   47   14   34    1   21   41    8   28   48   15   35
 2   22   42    9   29   49   16   36    3   23   43   10   30   50   17   37
 4   24   44   11   31   51   18   38    5   25   45   12   32   52   19   39
 6   26   46   13   33
```
Another shuffle? (Any key to continue / <Esc> to end)

Notice that the top card is no longer 1 and the bottom card is no longer 52 as in the previous run. By cycle 11 the change seems to have improved the shuffle.

Cycle 11

```
     39   25   11   50   36   22    8   47   33   19    5   44   30   16    2
41   27   13   52   38   24   10   49   35   21    7   46   32   18    4   43
29   15    1   40   26   12   51   37   23    9   48   34   20    6   45   31
17    3   42   28   14
```
Another shuffle? (Any key to continue / <Esc> to end)

However, by cycle 26 it is apparent we have a problem.

Cycle 25

```
     51   49   47   45   43   41   39   37   35   33   31   29   27   25   23
21   19   17   15   13   11    9    7    5    3    1   52   50   48   46   44
42   40   38   36   34   32   30   28   26   24   22   20   18   16   14   12
10    8    6    4    2
```
Another shuffle? (Any key to continue / <Esc> to end)

Cycle 26

```
     52   51   50   49   48   47   46   45   44   43   42   41   40   39   38
37   36   35   34   33   32   31   30   29   28   27   26   25   24   23   22
21   20   19   18   17   16   15   14   13   12   11   10    9    8    7    6
 5    4    3    2    1
```
Another shuffle? (Any key to continue / <Esc> to end)

This second failure to randomize leads to further questions. What if the two schemes are combined and on even-numbered cycles the first shuffle order is used and on odd-numbered cycles the second shuffle is used? The change to the program is quite simple.

```
30          for (counter = 0; counter < 52;)
31          {
32              if (cycle % 2 == 0)
```

```
33              {
34                  *(target + counter++) = *frontptr++;
35                  *(target + counter++) = *backptr++;
36              }
37              else
38              {
39                  *(target + counter++) = *backptr++;
40                  *(target + counter++) = *frontptr++;
41              }
42          }
```

Further variations are possible but in general we find that perfection is not quite as useful as we might have imagined. In the end it is discovered that it is the errors made in shuffling the deck, the deviations from the perfect shuffle, that produce the randomizing that is the purpose of shuffling.

Solution Implemented in Visual Basic

```
1   Option Explicit
2
3   Private Sub cmdExit_Click()
4       Unload Me
5   End Sub
6
7   Private Sub cmdShuffle_Click()
8       Static deck1(1 To 52) As Long
9       Static target(1 To 52) As Long
10      Static click As Integer
11      Dim counter, place As Integer
12      Dim cycle, hold As Integer
13      Dim place_counter As Integer
14
15      click = click + 1
16      If click = 1 Then
17          For counter = 1 To 52
18              deck1(counter) = counter
19          Next counter
20      Else
21          For counter = 1 To 52
22              deck1(counter) = target(counter)
23          Next counter
24      End If
25
26      cycle = 1
27      counter = 1
```

```
28        For place = 1 To 26
29            target(counter) = deck1(place)
30            target(counter + 1) = deck1(26 + place)
31            counter = counter + 2
32        Next place
33        place_counter = 0
34        place = 0
35
36        msgTable.Rows = 4
37        msgTable.Row = 0
38        msgTable.Col = 0
39
40        lblCycle.Caption = "Cycle " & click
41
42        For counter = 0 To 51
43            place = counter Mod 16
44            If counter > 1 And place = 0 Then
45                msgTable.Row = msgTable.Row + 1
46            End If
47            hold = target(counter + 1)
48            msgTable.Col = place
49            msgTable.Text = hold
50            place_counter = place_counter + 1
51        Next counter
52    End Sub
53
54    Private Sub Form_Load()
55        Dim Index As Integer
56
57        lblTitle.Caption = "This program demonstrates the perfect shuffle"
58        For Index = 0 To 15
59            msgTable.ColWidth(Index) = 400
60        Next Index
61    End Sub
```

Because Visual Basic does not use pointers, the algorithm is slightly different from the one used in the C++ solution. Where the pointers in the C++ program allow the shuffling to go from deck1 to deck2 on one cycle and deck2 to deck1 on the next cycle, in the Visual Basic program deck1 always shuffles into the target deck. This takes place in the for loop beginning on line 28. However, this requires that for every new shuffling the target deck must be recopied back into deck1. This reloading of deck1 has been packaged in the if/else construction beginning on line 16, which either provides the initial ordering of the deck (before the first shuffle) or reloads the target deck into deck1 on every other cycle.

Output of the Visual Basic Program

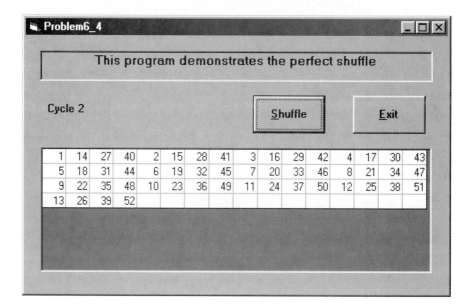

6.4 GEOMETRIC PROBABILITY

By combining the "what if" scenario with probability we can explore the question of what would happen if a needle were repeatedly dropped to the floor and it landed on lined paper. It's not a problem that would have kept Voltaire, Kant, or Neitzsche up late at night but it has been of interest to mathematicians for over 200 years because of the absolutely fascinating answer. The problem is called Buffon's Needle.

PROBLEM 6.5   *What would happen if a needle were dropped onto lined paper, given that the needle is one unit in length and the lines on the paper are one unit apart?*

As always there is a need for clarity. "What would happen" should be replaced with a more testable and interesting question such as: What are the odds that the dropped needle will land on one of the lines? The odds could be calculated, with some difficulty, but in keeping with the theme of creating simulations we might have the computer, in simulation, drop the needle a million or more times and count the number of times it lands on a line. Hopefully the answer will be sufficiently fascinating to make the effort worthwhile.

To make the problem slightly more tractable the next step is to search for ways to limit the problem (Rule 7—The Limitations Rule) in ways that will make it easier to model but will still provide useful information. The general case would have no definite ratio between the length of the needle and the distance between the lines; however, the problem is simpler (and the answer more interesting) if the needle is considered to be of one unit in length and the distance between the lines is also one unit.

The problem can also be restricted to a single pair of lines and the requirement that the center of the needle will always fall on or between the lines.

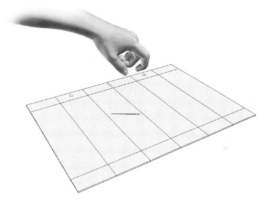

This restriction does not really limit the accuracy of the simulation. If the experiment were actually performed, the restriction would require the dropper of the needle to aim the drop so the center of the needle would not fall outside the lines. The aiming would remove the random factor from the dropping and invalidate the experiment. In simulation the randomness within the restricted space is not destroyed and the results are unaffected. The limited simulation will still reflect the more general reality of many spaced lines because a needle that falls outside of the limited range will still fall between some pair of lines and that result can be summed with the needle drops within the two chosen lines.

Initial Data: **1.** A needle is dropped on a lined sheet of paper.
                   2. The needle is one unit in length.
                   3. The lines on the paper are one unit apart.
                   4. The position of the center of the needle will be randomly chosen but will be on or between the lines.
                   5. The angle of the needle relative to the parallel lines will be randomly chosen.

Output: Determine the odds that the needle will land on a line.

An attempt to model the dropping of the needle quickly reveals that the initial information of the problem lacks any clue as to how the landing position of the needle should be described. If the position of the needle can be described, then randomizing the factors that describe its position i.e., the location of the needle center and its relative angle can be accomplished with the pseudorandom number generator. Counting the hits is simple and is a well-practiced task.

The description of the resting position of the fallen needle becomes the problem within the problem. Fortunately, focusing on this problem and the preceding picture of the fallen needle (Rule 3—The Picture Rule) reveals that only two numbers are needed: the location of the needle center relative to the lines (read: perpendicular distance from the center of the needle to the nearest line) and the angle that the needle makes with the parallel lines. These two numbers will describe the position of the needle and can be limited and randomized.

The distance of the center of the needle to the closest line must be between zero units if the center of the needle falls on the line and .5 units if the center of the needle is exactly at the center point between the lines. Therefore, the position of the center of the needle can be described by a random number between zero and one half, inclusive.

The angle that the needle makes with lines is similarly simple to model. Since there is no difference between the two ends of the needle (ignore the eye, it isn't relevant), the angle must be between zero and 180°. Actually only one limiting number should be included since zero and 180° are the same and should not be counted twice.

Now that the problem of modeling the needle drop is solved, the pseudocode for the problem can be written.

Pseudocode

1. Begin
2.   Declare and initialize variables.
3.   Seed random number generator with system time.
4.   Message to user—prompt for number of drops.
5.   Start timer.
6.   Begin dropping loop.
7.   Get random distance from line.
8.   Get random angle.
9.   If needle hits line
10.   Increment hit counter.
11.   End loop.
12.   Calculate odds for hit.
13.   End timer.
14.   Display odds for hit and double the quotient of drops divided by hits.
15. End

Flowchart

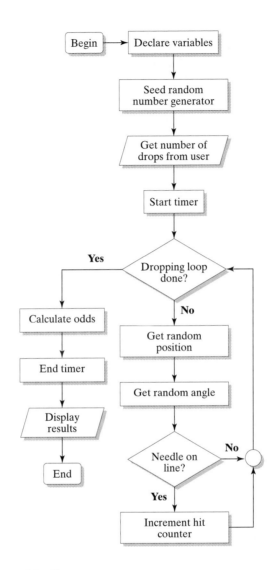

Solution Implemented in C++

```cpp
1    //  Problem 6.5
2    #include <iostream.h>
3    #include <stdlib.h>
4    #include <time.h>
5    #include <math.h>
6
7    void main(void)
8    {
9        double alpha, distance, ans, drops, counter, hits = 0;
10       long start, end;
```

```
11      const double PI = 3.14159265358979323;
12      srand((unsigned) time(0));
13      cout << "This program calculates the odds of Buffon's Needle \n"
14         << "        landing on a line\n"
15         << "\tEnter the number of needles dropped --   " << flush;
16      cin >> drops;
17      time(&start);
18      for (counter = 1; counter <= drops; counter++)
19      {
20         distance = .5 * rand() / 32767.0;
21         alpha = PI * rand() / 32768.0;
22         if (distance <= .5 * sin(alpha))
23            hits++;
24      }
25      ans = 2 * drops / (hits);
26      time(&end);
27      cout.precision(8);
28      cout << "\n\nThe odds of the needle hitting a line are "
29         << hits / drops << endl << endl
30         << "Twice the drops divided by the hits equals "
31         << ans << endl << endl
32         << "\tElapsed time -- " << end - start << " seconds"
33         << endl << endl;
34 }
```

Output of the C++ Program

```
This program calculates the odds of Buffon's Needle
        landing on a line

        Enter the number of needles dropped --    1e9

The odds of the needle hitting a line are 0.63661771

Twice the drops divided by the hits equals 3.1416028

        Elapsed time -- 529 seconds
```

The odds of the needle hitting one of the lines are not really the point of interest for the problem. The item that is fascinating (at least for those with a mathematical bent) is that if the odds of hitting the line are divided by two and inverted the value is quite close to the value of π. The error for the foregoing simulation is only three parts in 100,000 or .003 percent. Of course, this level of accuracy required dropping one billion needles. The simulation took nearly nine minutes but actually dropping one billion needles would take much longer.

The interpretation of the results requires some caution. If the real experiment is carried out for a large number of drops, the value of π can be calculated. The reason this works is because whether the needle lands on the line or not depends on the angle that the needle makes relative to the lines. The possible angles span a range of 0 to π radians. However, if the problem is simulated, the value of π must already be known. The range for random numbers for the angle (line 21) requires a value for π.

There is one more curious feature to the program. The denominators in lines 20 and 21 are slightly different.

```
20          distance = .5 * rand() / 32767.0;
21          alpha = PI * rand() / 32768.0;
```

The range of integers generated by the pseudorandom number generator is from 0 to 32,767. This indicates that rand() / 32767.0 can take fractional values from 0 to 1 inclusive. The fraction rand() / 32768.0 on line 21 can have the value of zero but will fall just short of one. But this is precisely what is needed to avoid doubling the number of times the needle landed exactly parallel to the border lines.

It should also be noted that lines 20 and 21 are the crux of the problem. The simulation of the dropping needle was new to this program. Every other element of the simulation has been encountered in previous problems. Building experience is crucial to problem solving.

Solution Implemented in Visual Basic

```
1    Option Explicit
2    Const PI = 3.14159265358979
3
4    Private Sub cmdCalculate_Click()
5        Dim alpha, distance, drops As Double
6        Dim counter, hits, ans As Double
7        Dim start, temp, finish As Long
8        Dim message As String
9        Randomize
10
11       message = "Elapsed time -- "
12       start = Timer
13       drops = CDbl(txtInput.Text)
14       For counter = 1 To drops
15           If (counter + 1) Mod 200000 = 0 Then
16               temp = Timer
17               lblTime.Caption = message & CStr(Int(temp - start)) & _
18                   " seconds"
19               DoEvents
20           End If
21           distance = 0.5 * Int((32768 * Rnd)) / 32767
22           alpha = PI * Int((32768 * Rnd)) / 32768
23           If distance <= 0.5 * Sin(alpha) Then
24               hits = hits + 1
25           End If
26       Next counter
27       finish = Timer
28       ans = 2 * drops / (hits)
29       lblOutput.Caption = CStr(hits / drops)
30       lblAns.Caption = "Twice the drops divided by the " & _
31           "hits equals " & CStr(ans)
32       DoEvents
33       lblTime.Caption = "Elapsed time " & _
34           Format((finish - start), "##.##") & " seconds."
35   End Sub
36
```

```
37   Private Sub cmdExit_Click()
38       Unload Me
38   End Sub
39
40   Private Sub Form_Load()
41       lblTitle.Caption = "This program calculates the odds on" & _
42               "Buffon's needle landing on a line."
43       lblInput.Caption = "Enter the number of needles dropped"
44       lblAnswer.Caption = "The odds of the needle hitting a line are "
45   End Sub
46
```

Two elements in the Visual Basic program deserve comment. The first is the manner in which the random numbers for the distance to the lines and the angle of the needle are generated. Lines 21 and 22 determine values for `distance` and `alpha` based on random numbers chosen between zero and one (excluding one). The factor 32,768 is used to scale the values to a zero to 32,767 range. This range was chosen somewhat arbitrarily. Any suitably wide range would also work. Zero to 32,767 was chosen to make the program similar to the C++ program.

The second item is the improvement over the expanding bar that indicated the previous programs were still conducting the simulations. The `if` statement on line 15 is familiar but, rather than merely writing a character, a message is generated indicating elapsed time since the *Calculate* button was clicked. With little difficulty the time elapsed message could be changed to a time remaining message, but as expected that is an exercise left to the reader.

Output of the Visual Basic Program

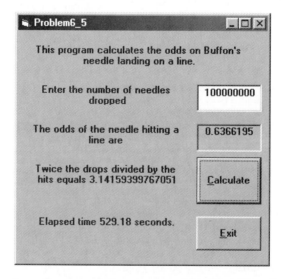

The number of needles dropped was reduced to 100 million from the one billion trials from the C++ program. Extrapolating from the nearly nine minutes for 100 million trials indicates that one billion trials would require a runtime of nearly $1\frac{1}{2}$ hours. Still the value generated is only one part in nearly 286,000 deviant from the value of π. Not bad for dropping needles.

6.5 INTEGRAL CALCULUS

While physicists, astronomers, engineers, economists, mathematicians, and professionals in many other fields find integral calculus an absolute necessity, this branch of mathematics is difficult and may be beyond the skill of the average problem solver. However, in many cases the integration itself can be very simply simulated, making the power of calculus available to anyone who can write a for() loop.

Integration allows us to find the area under a curve or even the volume under a surface. This means that the area of any figure can be calculated, no matter how irregular, as long as its borders can be described by an equation. The difficulty lies in finding the equation for the border and then performing the integration on what can potentially be a rather nasty equation.

For some figures calculus is unnecessary. The formula for the area of a circle is well known. But if the circle is distorted into an ellipse or some other conic section, there may be no common formula and the level of difficulty rises. Problem 6.6 involves an ellipse and its solution illustrates the simulation of integration.

PROBLEM 6.6 *Position the forms for a backyard basketball court and calculate the amount of concrete needed to pour the slab.*

The problem would be simple if the court were to be rectangular. Unfortunately, the placement of two fir trees and the homeowner's sense of aesthetics require that the court be a semi-ellipse. This complicates the problem in that the positions of the forms are more difficult to determine than they would be for a more straight-sided figure and the calculations for the surface area of the court requires calculus to find the area under the curve. At this point a picture is advisable.

With this in mind, Problem 6.6 needs to be restated.

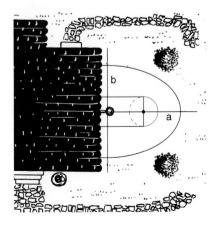

PROBLEM 6.6   *Find a general solution that will determine sufficient coordinate points on the semi-ellipse so the forms can be positioned and also determine the amount of concrete required to pour the slab for a backyard basketball court.*

Drawing the picture provides considerable insight into the problem, which, for the sake of clarity, should be carefully listed.

Initial Data:

1. The basketball court will be in the shape of a semi-ellipse.

2. The user will provide the dimensions a and b. a is one half of the major axis and b is one half of the minor axis.

3. We can imagine the ellipse drawn on a coordinate system where the intersection of the major and minor axes is the origin, the horizontal vertex is the point $(a,0)$ and the vertical vertex is the point $(0,b)$.

4. The general formula for an ellipse centered at the origin is known to be

$$\frac{x^2}{a^2} + \frac{y^2}{b^2} = 1 \quad \text{or} \quad y = \left(b^2 - \frac{b^2}{a^2} x^2 \right)^{.5}$$

where a is one half of the major axis and b is one half of the minor axis. The equation for the ellipse can be derived from the definition of the ellipse, but this chapter focuses on simulations and the derivation has been relegated to Appendix B.

5. By substituting values for x into the second equation, points can be determined for plotting the ellipse or, in this case, placing the forms in the backyard relative to two perpendicular lines acting as the axes.

6. The area under the curve can be calculated using a definite integral from zero to a, which we will simulate rather than calculate.

7. Once the area under the curve is calculated, it should be doubled to add the area of the lower half of the court.

8. Once the total area is calculated, the volume of concrete can be calculated using the user-supplied depth for the slab.

Output:

1. Generate a sufficient number of coordinate points so the forms can be placed.

2. Determine the amount of concrete required.

Assuming that the general formula for an ellipse is known and that the equation can be manipulated algebraically to solve for y, there is a surprisingly large amount of initial information. The only element that is missing before the pseudocode is written is the routine for finding the area under the curve, i.e., the upper half of the semi-ellipse. Fortunately, this is extremely simple.

Consider an approximation for the area under the curve. The four rectangles superimposed on the court have a total area that is close to the area of the top half of the court. The area of each rectangle is simple to calculate, i.e., length times width. The difference between the correct answer for the area under the curve and the area of the rectangles is represented by the upper right-hand corners of the rectangles. We would like to make this error small enough to be inconsequential.

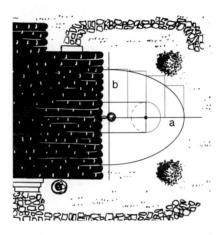

Rule 15   The Approximation Rule

Look for approximations that simplify a problem but do not appreciably affect the accuracy of the solution.

Using more rectangles by reducing the width of each will reduce the error but using 8, or 100, or 1,000,000 rectangles will increase the amount of calculating that has to be done. With the computer doing the work the amount of calculation is irrelevant, assuming we don't choose 10^{200} rectangles. Solving the basketball court problem using 10,000,000 rectangles will produce an answer that is not exact but is extremely close to the correct, calculus-derived answer. In effect the curve of the ellipse has been approximated by stair step lines made of extremely small steps.

Pseudocode

1. Begin
2.   Declare and initialize variables.
3.   Message to user and prompt for input.

4. Begin loop for 20 values along *x*-axis.
5.   Calculate *y* values for the *x* positions.
6.   Display (*x*, *y*) coordinates.
7. End loop.
8. Begin loop to calculate the area for 10,000,000 rectangles.
9.   Calculate the *x* position.
10.   Calculate the *y* value for each *x* position.
11.   Keep a running sum of the areas of the rectangles.
12. End loop.
13. Double the area to include the lower half of the ellipse.
14. Calculate the volume of the concrete and convert to cubic yards.
15. Display the results.
16. End

Flowchart

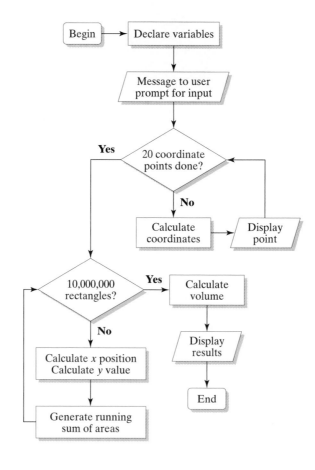

There are a number of bookkeeping details for this program that, for the sake of clarity, are better left out of the pseudocode. These details concern the handling of units. Typically the length and width of a concrete slab are given in feet and the depth in inches. Since the volume will be calculated in cubic feet, the depth should be converted to feet. Concrete is purchased in cubic yards, necessitating another conversion from cubic feet to cubic yards.

Solution Implemented in C++

```
1    //  Problem 6.6
2    #include <iostream.h>
3    #include <iomanip.h>
4    #include <math.h>
5
6    int main(void)
7    {
8        double major, minor, depth, area = 0, volume;
9        double x_value, y_value, step, a, b, c;
10       int counter;
11       cout.setf(ios::fixed|ios::showpoint);
12       cout << "This program calculates the shape of a semielliptical "
13           << "basketball\ncourt and the amount of concrete required "
14           << "to pour the slab."
15           << "\n\n\tEnter half of the major axis (ft) . .   " << flush;
16       cin >> major;
17       cin.ignore(3,'\n');
18       cout << "\n\tEnter half of the minor axis (ft) . .   " << flush;
19       cin >> minor;
20       cout << "\n\tEnter the depth of the slab (in) . .   " << flush;
21       cin >> depth;
22       depth /= 12;   //   Convert the depth of slab to feet
23       cout << endl;
24       step = major / 20;
25       a = minor * minor;  //  speed up variables
26       b = major * major;
27       c = a / b;
28       for (counter = 0; counter <= 20; counter++)
29       {
30           x_value = counter * step;
31           y_value = sqrt(a - c * x_value * x_value);
32           cout << setw(10) << x_value << setw(10) << y_value << endl;
33       }
34       step = major / 1e7;
35       for (counter = 0; counter <= 1e7; counter++)
36       {
37           x_value = counter * step;
```

```
38          y_value = sqrt(a - c * x_value * x_value);
39          area += step * y_value;
40      }
41      area *= 2;
42      volume = area * depth / 27;
43      cout << endl << "The surface area of the court is " << area
44          << " sq. ft. " << endl << "The amount of concrete required is "
45          << volume << " cu. yd." << endl;
46      return(0);
47  }
```

The only curious feature in this program is the use of the variables a, b, and c to speed up the program. Line 38 could have been written more descriptively as

```
38          y_value = sqrt(minor * minor - ((minor* minor) / (major * major)) *
                x_value * x_value);
```

However, this would entail making several arithmetic operations during each of 10,000,000 cycles. The program runs considerably faster if the lines

```
25      a = minor * minor;  //  speed up variables
26      b = major * major;
27      c = a / b;
```

are executed just once prior to the first loop and line 38 is written in its shorter form.

```
38          y_value = sqrt(a - c * x_value * x_value);
```

Output of the C++ Program

```
This program calculates the shape of a semielliptical basketball
court and the amount of concrete required to pour the slab.

        Enter half of the major axis (ft) . .    30

        Enter half of the minor axis (ft) . .    20

        Enter the depth of the slab (in) . .     5

 0.000000 20.000000
 1.500000 19.974984
 3.000000 19.899749
 4.500000 19.773720
 6.000000 19.595918
 7.500000 19.364917
 9.000000 19.078784
10.500000 18.734994
12.000000 18.330303
13.500000 17.860571
15.000000 17.320508
16.500000 16.703293
```

```
18.000000 16.000000
19.500000 15.198684
21.000000 14.282857
22.500000 13.228757
24.000000 12.000000
25.500000 10.535654
27.000000  8.717798
28.500000  6.244998
30.000000  0.000000
```

```
The surface area of the court is 942.477856 sq. ft.
The amount of concrete required is 14.544411 cu. yd.
```

The coordinates for determining where to place the forms are given for every 1.5 feet along the *x*-axis. Only the positions for the top half of the semi-ellipse have been calculated. The coordinates for the lower half would be the same except each *y*-axis value would have to be multiplied by −1.

There is some small difficulty in verifying the accuracy of the output of the program. Theoretical solution requires the solution to the integral

$$I = \int_0^{30} \sqrt{1 - \left(\frac{x}{30}\right)^2} \, dx$$

which involves an interesting substitution and integration by parts. The solution to this integral is provided in Appendix C for the mathematically curious. For now the reader is asked to trust that the theoretical solution to the area of the court is 300π or 942.477796. Comparing this answer to the one provided by the simulation, we find that the simulation error is one part in about 15.7 million—more than close enough when pouring concrete.

There are a couple less valid ways to confirm the accuracy of the simulation. One option involves running the program for a semicircular court, i.e., limiting the scope of possible values for the axes. If 30 feet is used for both the major and minor axes, the ellipse becomes a circle and the program produces

```
The surface area of the court is 1413.716784 sq. ft.
The amount of cement required is 21.816617 cu. yd.
```

The surface area for the semicircle can be compared to the area calculated by

$$A = \frac{1}{2} \pi r^2 = .5(3.14159265)(30)(30) = 1{,}413.716694$$

again a number very close to the value produced by the simulation.

More crude and less valid but still slightly useful is to assume that a circle of radius 25 would be somewhat close in area to an ellipse with axes of 20 and 30. The area of a semicircle of radius 25 is 981.7. This approximation is more like a ballpark guess than a real solution. The error in using a compromise circle to approximate an ellipse grows larger as the ellipse becomes more elongated. In this case the error of almost 40 square feet looks bad but when buying concrete translates into only .6 cubic yards for a slab five inches thick.

Solution Implemented in Visual Basic

```
1    Option Explicit
2
3    Private Sub cmdCalculate_Click()
4        Dim depth, area, volume As Double
5        Dim x_value, y_value, step As Double
6        Dim a, b, c As Double
7        Dim counter As Long
8        Dim start, temp, finish As Single
9        Dim Message As String
10       Message = "Elapsed Time -- "
11
12       a = CDbl(txtMinor.Text) * CDbl(txtMinor.Text)
13       b = CDbl(txtMajor.Text) * CDbl(txtMajor.Text)
14       c = a / b
15       depth = CDbl(txtDepth.Text) / 12
16       step = CDbl(txtMajor.Text) / 20
17       start = Timer
18       For counter = 0 To 20
19           msgTable.Rows = counter + 2
20           msgTable.Col = 0
21           x_value = counter * step
22           y_value = Sqr(a - c * x_value * x_value)
23           msgTable.Row = counter + 1
24           msgTable.Text = Format(x_value, "0.000000")
25           msgTable.Col = 1
26           msgTable.Text = Format(y_value, "0.000000")
27       Next counter
28
29       step = CDbl(txtMajor.Text) / 10000000
30       For counter = 0 To 10000000
31           If (counter + 1) Mod 100000 = 0 Then
32               temp = Timer
33               lblAnswer.Caption = Message & CStr(Int(temp - start)) & _
34                   " seconds"
35               DoEvents
36           End If
37           x_value = counter * step
38           y_value = Sqr(a - c * x_value * x_value)
```

```
39              area = area + step * y_value
40        Next counter
41
42        area = area * 2
43        volume = area * depth / 27
44        finish = Timer
45        lblAnswer.Caption = "The surface area of the court is " & _
46            Format(area, "0.000000") & " sq. ft." & vbCr & _
47            "The amount of concrete required is " & _
48            Format(volume, "0.000000") & " cu. yd." & vbCrLf & _
49            "Total run time -- " & CStr(finish - start) & " seconds"
50    End Sub
51
52    Private Sub cmdExit_Click()
53        Unload Me
54    End Sub
55
56    Private Sub Form_Load()
57        lblTitle.Caption = "This program calculates the shape of " & _
58            "a semi-elliptical basketball court and the amount " & _
59            "of concrete required to pour the slab."
60        lblMinor.Caption = "Enter half of the minor axis (ft)"
61        lblMajor.Caption = "Enter half of the major axis (ft)"
62        lblDepth.Caption = "Enter the depth of the slab (in)"
63
64        msgTable.Row = 0
65        msgTable.Col = 0
66        msgTable.Text = "X_Value"
67        msgTable.Col = 1
68        msgTable.Text = "Y_Value"
69        msgTable.ColWidth(0) = 1200
70        msgTable.ColWidth(1) = 1200
71    End Sub
```

Even though there was no elapsed time feature in the C++ program, it was added to the Visual Basic program to inform the user that the program was in fact still running as it made its calculations. The only programming feature worth special notice is the use of the `step` variable. For the `for` loop beginning on line 18, `step` has a value of one twentieth of the length of the major axis. In this loop determining coordinate points every 1.5 feet is satisfactory for determining the curve for placing the cement forms. To increase the accuracy of the surface area calculations, `step` was reset to one ten-millionth for the loop beginning on line 30.

Output of the Visual Basic Program

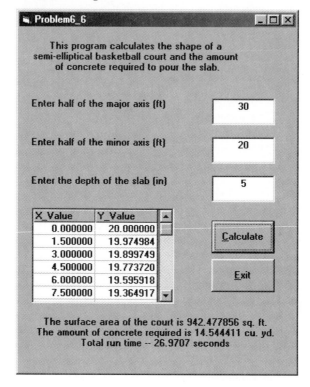

The basketball court problem illustrates that limits imposed on our problem solving can often be overcome with imagination or brute force or both. In this case the limit was the user's mathematical training. Chapter 7 is dedicated to removing many of the limits that have so far been used to make the problems in this book more manageable.

CHAPTER 7

Removing the Limits

7.1 LIMITATIONS IN ACCURACY

In the quest to find solutions to a wide variety of problems compromises are often made. In many cases a solution is acceptable if it is very close to the correct answer even though the solution is not exact. For each of the probability problems presented in the previous chapters an exact answer can be calculated. However, the mathematical talent required to make those calculations is typically beyond that of the average problem solver. More importantly the exact solution is often of no greater value to the problem solver than an arbitrarily close answer. The odds of winning a game rarely need to be calculated to better than five decimal places. The odds for winning a game of craps can be calculated exactly, but to what purpose? Despite its lack of mathematical purity, an arbitrarily close value is usually as useful as an exact value.

The successive approximation problems also fall into this category of limited accuracy except that in these problems there may be no exact answer. In the program for calculating square roots the user entered the tolerance or the amount of error that would be considered acceptable. If the user runs the program in order to calculate the square root of 144 to a tolerance of .000001, the output of the program will closely approximate the true answer. If the user tries to calculate the square root of 2, there can be no comparison to the true answer because the square root of 2 is an irrational number and no exact answer exists. Arbitrary accuracy is the best that can be achieved.

Similarly, finding the sum of an infinite series of numbers may or may not have a true answer. Summing the infinite number of segments of Superfly's last flight is a summation that has an exact answer that can be approximated by a more limited summing. On the other hand, finding the value of the sine function for an arbitrary angle is more problematic. The sine function and all other trigonometric functions are transcendental functions, meaning that they cannot be expressed algebraically. Solutions are necessarily approximate, but the approximation can be of whatever accuracy is required.

In all of these problems in which the accuracy has been limited, the accuracy can be increased by merely running the loop that generates the terms to be summed or the events to be examined for a greater number of cycles. In practice the factor limiting the accuracy in most of our programs is the 15-digit storage capacity of the double-precision, floating-point variable. Even this limit can be circumvented with a little imagination. In Problem 5.2, 50-digit integers were added.

For real-world problems involving measurements, the limitations to accuracy are almost always irrelevant. As long as the accuracy is arbitrarily close to the theoretically correct answer, the problem can be considered to be solved.

7.2 LIMITATIONS IN SCOPE

Limitations in scope are potentially more relevant to the solution of a problem. The initial program to calculate square roots using the divide by two, successive approximation method was limited in scope to positive numbers greater than one. Negative numbers were not considered because the square root of a negative number results in an imaginary answer. For numbers between zero and one the program will fall into an infinite loop and fail to provide a solution. The reason for this problem is the successive guessing algorithm that makes the initial guess at one half of the number whose square root is needed. This is reasonable for numbers greater than one but for proper fractions the square root is larger than the number itself.

PROBLEM 7.1 *Find the square root of any rational number.*

The solution to the original square root problem that limited the scope to numbers greater than one suggests the adaptations that are needed for a more general solution and also suggests Rule 16.

> **Rule 16 The Expansion Rule**
> When generalizing a solution to encompass greater range, greater complexity, broader conditions, or greater utility, focus on the differences between the conditions under which the old solution works and the new conditions.

To make the square root program work for negative numbers, the negative number can be detected and changed to a positive number by merely multiplying by −1. Of course, a flag must be set to indicate that this change has been made. After the square root of the positive number is determined, the solution can be displayed with a trailing *i* that indicates the square root is an imaginary number. Except for the sign change of the input, the setting of the flag, and the *i* to indicate an imaginary answer, the algorithm for calculating the square root is unchanged.

   The second difference in the expanded scope is related to the size of the square root compared to the original number. For numbers greater than one the square root is the smaller of the two numbers. For fractions from zero to one the square root is larger than the starting number. This indicates that a change is needed for the initial guess. Consider the fact that the square root of every fraction between zero and one is another fraction in the same range but larger. That range of guesses can be covered completely if the initial guess is one and the initial adjustment is one half.

   Much of the pseudocode and the programming for the solution to the general case is identical to the code for Problem 3.1, the limited case. The adaptations required to expand the solution are indicated in gray.

Pseudocode Solution

1. Begin
2.   Declare and initialize variables.
3.   Prompt user for input and tolerance.
4.   Test for negative number.
5.   If negative, multiply input by −1, set flag.
6.   Test for zero to one range.
7.   If in range, set guess to 1.
8.   Else
9.   Set guess to .5 times input.
10.   Set adjustment.
11.   Begin loop.
12.   Generate the error value.
13.   Make appropriate adjustment to guess.
14.   Make appropriate adjustment to adjust.
15.   End loop if absolute value of error is less than required tolerance.
16.   Test for flag.
17.   If set, display imaginary root.
18.   Else
19.   Display real square root.
20. End

Solution Implemented in C++

```
1    //    Problem 7.1
2    #include <iostream.h>
3    #include <iomanip.h>
4    #include <conio.h>
5    #include <math.h>
6
7    void main(void)
8    {
9       double input, guess, tolerance, adjust, error;
10      int counter = 1, negative_flag = 0;
11      cout << "This program calculates the square root of any number"
12         << "\n\n\t\tEnter a number . .    ";
13      cin >> input;
14      cout << "\n\tEnter the tolerance . .    ";
15      cin >> tolerance;
16      cout.precision(12);
17      cout.setf(ios::fixed|ios::showpoint);
18      if ( input < 0)
19         input = -input, negative_flag = 1;
20      if ( input > 0 && input < 1)
21         guess = 1;
```

```
22      else
23         guess = .5 * input;
24      adjust = .5 * guess;
25      do
26      {
27         error = input - guess * guess;
28         if ( fabs(error) < tolerance)
29              break;
30         if ( error < 0)
31            guess -= adjust;
32         else
33            guess += adjust;
34         adjust *= .5;
35         counter++;
36      }while (fabs(error) > tolerance);
37      if (negative_flag == 0)
38         cout << "\nThe square root of " << input << " is " << setw(18)
39            << guess << "  \n\twith an error of "
40            << setw(18) << error << endl;
41      else
42         cout << "\nThe square root of " << -input << " is " << setw(18)
43            << guess << "i  \n\twith an error of "
44            << setw(18) << error << endl;
45  }
```

Lines 18 and 19 convert the input from negative to positive if necessary. If the conversion takes place, the `negative_flag` is set and tested later on line 37 to determine which of the output messages should be used.

The special cases of zero and one for the user input have not been specifically addressed. Zero is not included in the negative test (line 18) or in the test for numbers between zero and one (line 20). This leaves zero to be handled as though it were a positive number greater than one. The initial guess is calculated to be one half of the input or zero. Line 27 calculates the error to be `input - guess * guess` or zero. The loop fails after the first cycle with guess still equal to zero. If the zero to one test had been made to include zero, that is,

```
20      if ( input >= 0 && input < 1)
```

the initial guess would have been one and the do loop would have reduced the guess by one half each cycle until the error was sufficiently small *but nonzero*. This would make the square root of zero some small positive number, which would seem odd.

The special case of the input equal to one is even more crucial. One must be handled in the same manner as the numbers greater than one. If line 20 were changed to include one,

```
20      if ( input > 0 && input <= 1)
```

the initial guess would be one and the calculation for the error would be zero. This would make the loop fail after one cycle but not before the adjustment of one half was added to the guess. Consequently, the output would show the square root of one to be 1.5. This should be avoided.

Remember that the error returned by the program is not the difference between the calculated square root and the true square root. The true square root is not available for making that test. Instead the error is the difference between the calculated square root squared and the user input.

There is one other small difference between the general square root program and the limited solution from Chapter 3. Because the output message was moved from inside the loop (immediately following the calculation of `error`) to its position after the loop, two new lines were needed. Without lines 28 and 29 an incorrect solution will be calculated for values that have an integer square root e.g., 4, 9, 16. Line 28 tests whether the current error is within tolerance and, if it is, the loop breaks before a new and incorrect guess can be generated.

Output of the C++ Program

```
This program calculates the square root of any number

            Enter a number . .     -2

        Enter the tolerance . .    1e-6

The square root of -2.000000000000 is     1.414213418961i
        with an error of    -0.000000268718


This program calculates the square root of any number

            Enter a number . .     .36

        Enter the tolerance . .    1e-9

The square root of 0.360000000000 is     0.600000000559
        with an error of    0.000000000447
```

Solution Implemented in Visual Basic

```
1    Option Explicit
2
3    Private Sub cmdCalculate_Click()
4        Dim number, guess, tolerance, adjust, error As Double
5        Dim counter, negative_flag As Integer
6        counter = 1
7        negative_flag = 0
8        number = CDbl(txtNumber.Text)
9        If txtTolerance.Text <> "" Then
10           tolerance = CDbl(txtTolerance.Text)
11       Else
12           tolerance = 0.000001
13       End If
14       If number < 0 Then
```

```
15              number = -number
16              negative_flag = 1
17          End If
18
19          If number > 0 And number < 1 Then
20              guess = 1
21          Else
22              guess = 0.5 * number
23          End If
24
25          adjust = 0.5 * guess
26
27          Do
28              error = number - guess * guess
29              If Abs(error) < tolerance Then
30                  Exit Do
31              Else
32                  If error < 0 Then
33                      guess = guess - adjust
34                  Else
35                      guess = guess + adjust
36                  End If
37              End If
38              adjust = adjust * 0.5
39              counter = counter + 1
40
41          Loop While (Abs(error) > tolerance)
42
43          If negative_flag = 0 Then
44              lblAnswer.Caption = "The square root of " & number & _
45                  " is " & guess & " with an error of " & error
46          Else
47              lblAnswer.Caption = "The square root of " & -number & _
48                  " is " & guess & " i with an error of " & error
49          End If
50      End Sub
51
52      Private Sub cmdExit_Click()
53          Unload Me
54      End Sub
55
56      Private Sub Form_Load()
57          lblTitle.Caption = _
58              "This program calculates the square root of any number"
59          lblNumber.Caption = "Enter a number   "
60          lblTolerance.Caption = "Enter a tolerance   "
61      End Sub
```

The Visual Basic program mirrors the C++ program closely with one notable exception. A default tolerance was added to the program in case the user should hit <Enter> after entering the number instead of <Tab> to move to the txtTolerance box.

Because the *Calculate* command button is activated by the <Enter> key, the lack of a tolerance value will cause an unexpected program interruption if the default value is not in place. Lines 9 through 13 test the txtTolerance box for a string and, if one is not available, the default value of one millionth is used.

Output of the Visual Basic Program

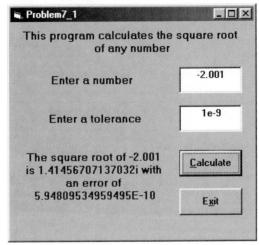

Another program that contained an unfortunate limitation in its scope was the binary conversion program. This program converted only positive integers into their binary equivalents.

PROBLEM 7.2   *Convert any rational decimal number into binary.*

This problem requires the scope to be expanded from positive integers to include negative numbers and fractions. Experience in expanding the square root problem to include negative numbers suggests that changing the sign of the input to positive and altering the output display might be all that is needed to handle negative numbers. In Problem 2.4 the output was constructed in a character array. In this expanded case the output message could be changed to include a negative sign before the array storing the binary number is printed. On the other hand, it might be simpler to merely include the negative sign as the first element of the binary array and increment the index counter to the next position. This eliminates the need for a flag variable to track the sign of the original number.

To include fractions in the conversion examine the difference between integers and fractions, that is, the difference between the scope in which the program already works and the new range that must be included. The difference is more apparent if concrete examples are used (Rule 8—Concrete Examples). What is the difference between 100 and .1? In the number 100 the digit 1 is in the hundreds place or 10^2. In the number .1 the digit 1 is in the tenths place or 10^{-1}. The difference between integers and numbers containing decimals is that numbers containing fractional parts have some digits that have values based on negative powers of the base. The same is true in any number system. In the binary number 1000.001 the first bit indicates 2^3 or 8. The final bit indicates 2^{-3} or one eighth. The relevant issue is that including fractional numbers requires the program to handle negative powers of the base where the original program terminated its calculation when the variable `power` reached zero.

The next question is how many negative powers we should include. This raises the issue of accuracy and what limit we should place on it. We found in the previous section that it is often the case that we can have as much accuracy as we want and the real question is how much do we need. We'll choose, rather arbitrarily, 16 bits past the binary point (the binary equivalent of the more familiar decimal point).

The pseudocode from Problem 2.4 is reproduced here with the adaptation necessary for the expanded case shown in gray.

Pseudocode

1. Begin
2.   Declare variables.
3.   Get the number to be converted from the user and store in "input."
4.   If input is negative
5.   Multiply input by −1.
6.   Place negative sign in first position of binary array and increment index.
7.   Determine the highest power of two that is less than the input number.
8.   Initialize "power" to highest power of two that is less than the input number.
9.   Begin conversion loop.
10.   If there is a fractional part to the number
11.   Place a binary point in the binary array and increment index.
12.   Divide decimal by 2 raised to power.
13.   Store the integer quotient (1 or 0) in the "binary" character array.
14.   If the integer result is 1, create new value for decimal equal to decimal −2 raised to power.
15.   If power is evenly divisible by 4, add a space to the binary array to separate nibbles.
16.   Decrement power.
17.   Increment index for binary array.
18.   Continue if power is greater than or equal to −16.
19.   Display the result.
20. End

The changes to the pseudocode indicate that expanding the program to include negative numbers and fractions is rather straightforward.

1. Store a negative sign if necessary.
2. Store a period (binary point) if necessary.
3. Run the loop 16 more times.

Notice that increasing the accuracy from 16 bits past the binary point to 32 bits past the binary point would only require one change to the terminating test of the loop. Accuracy could be increased still further until the storage capacity of the binary array was reached, which could also be increased.

Solution Implemented in C++

```
1    //  Problem 7.2
2    //  Binary conversion problem based on weighted values.
3    #include <iostream.h>
4    #include <math.h>
5
6    void main(void)
7    {
8        double input;
9        int counter = 0, power = 0;
10       char binary[100] = {0};
11       cout << "Enter the number to be converted to binary    "  << flush;
12       cin >> input;          // Get number from user
13       cout << endl;
14       if ( input < 0)
15       {
16          binary[counter++] = '-';
17          input = -input;
18       }
19       while ( pow(2,power++) <= input);
20       power = power - 2;
21       do
22       {
23          if ( power == -1)
24             binary[counter++] = '.';
25          binary[counter++] = (int)(input / pow(2, power)) + 48;
26                   // Determine whether binary[counter] is 1 or 0
27          if (binary[counter - 1] == '1')
28             input = input - pow(2, power);
29                   // If bit is 1 reduce input appropriately
30          if (power % 4 == 0)
31             binary[counter++] = 32;
32       }while (--power >= -16);
33       cout << "\n\n\tBinary -->    "  << binary << endl;
34   }
```

Line 14 makes the test to determine if the input is negative. If it is, the two following lines store the negative sign, increment the index for the array, and convert the input to a positive number. No other changes for negative numbers are required.

Positioning of the binary point is controlled by lines 23 and 24. This is slightly tricky. The binary point must be placed before the bit in the 2^{-1} position, not after the bit in the 2^0 position. The two positions are only identical if the input number is greater than one. For fractions between one and zero there is no bit in the 2^0 position and, therefore, that bit cannot be used to position the binary point.

Line 32 controls the accuracy of the binary conversion. A negative 16 powers of two gives an accuracy to one 65,536th. Changing the test condition to a negative 32 powers of two would provide an accuracy to nearly one 4.3 billionth.

Output of the C++ Program

```
Enter the number to be converted to binary    -32769.25

        Binary -->    -1000 0000 0000 0001 .0100 0000 0000 0000

Enter the number to be converted to binary    .0626

        Binary -->    .0001 0000 0000 0110
```

In the first example, 32,769.25 has an integer value that is clearly one greater than 15 powers of two. The decimal part is one quarter or two raised to the negative second power. In the second example .0626 was chosen as being only slightly larger than one sixteenth or a negative four powers of two. Binary $.0001_2$ is equivalent to one sixteenth and the two bits in the 2^{-14} and 2^{-15} positions add to slightly less than the extra one ten thousandth.

While these binary conversions are mathematically correct, they are not the binary numbers that would be stored in computer memory. Negative integers are stored in memory as two's complement numbers. Floating-point numbers, both positive and negative, are stored as a combination of a power of two and a fraction. Both topics are absolutely fascinating but unfortunately not relevant to problem-solving techniques.

Solution Implemented in Visual Basic

```
1    Option Explicit
2
3    Private Sub cmdCalculate_Click()
4        Dim number As Double
5        Dim counter, power, saved_power, x As Integer
6        Dim neg_flag, fraction_flag As Integer
7        Dim binary(0 To 100) As Byte
8        Dim y As Integer
9        Dim temp As Double
10
11       txtOutput = ""
12       temp = 0
13       counter = 0
14       power = 0
15       number = CDbl(txtNumber.Text)
16       neg_flag = 0
17       If number < 0 Then
18           number = -number
19           neg_flag = 1
20       End If
21       If number >= 0 And number < 1 Then
22           fraction_flag = 1
23       End If
24       Do While (2 ^ power <= number)
```

```
25            power = power + 1
26        Loop
27        power = power - 1
28        saved_power = power
29        Do
30            binary(counter) = Int(number / (2 ^ power))
31            counter = counter + 1
32            If binary(counter - 1) = 1 Then
33                number = number - (2 ^ power)
34            End If
35            power = power - 1
36        Loop While (power >= -16)
37        If neg_flag = 1 Then
38            txtOutput = "-"
39        End If
40        For x = 0 To saved_power + 16
41            If fraction_flag = 1 Then
42                txtOutput = txtOutput & "."
43                fraction_flag = 0
44            End If
45            txtOutput = txtOutput & Trim(Str(binary(x)))
46            If x = saved_power Then
47                txtOutput = txtOutput & "."
48            End If
49            If (saved_power - x) Mod 4 = 0 Then
50                txtOutput = txtOutput & " "
51            End If
52        Next x
53    End Sub
54
55    Private Sub cmdExit_Click()
56        Unload Me
57    End Sub
58
59    Private Sub Form_Load()
60        lblTitle.Caption = "This is a binary conversion program " & _
61          "based on weighted values. "
62        lblNumber.Caption = "Enter the number to be converted to binary "
63    End Sub
```

The logic of the original Visual Basic solution to the problem has been preserved in this expanded version. The modifications necessary for accommodating fractions and negative numbers have been highlighted in gray. These modifications primarily concern two features of the program: the use of the two flag variables to indicate negative and/or fractional numbers, and the changes in limits to the loops. Where the original program contained loops that ended after the zero power of two was reached, the expanded program handles the positioning of the binary point and continues until the negative sixteenth power of two is reached.

The single, less obvious feature of the program is the use of saved_power on line 28. As the power variable is used in determining the position of bits in the binary array, the original value of power must be saved for use later in the loop that controls the output display.

Output of the Visual Basic Program

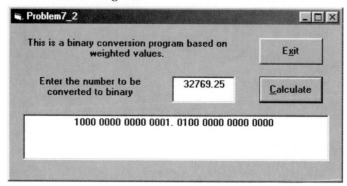

7.3 LIMITATIONS IN CONDITIONS

The falling ball problem, Problem 2.1, was an example of a problem whose conditions were limited in order to find a partial solution. That problem was solved as though the force of gravity was the only factor in determining the position and velocity of the ball after it was released. In reality the shape of the falling object, the air density, the height from which it is released, and many other factors compound the problem. The more factors that are included in the program the greater the accuracy of the results.

Expanding the falling ball problem would quickly lead to nonlinear equations that could be described as difficult. Other problems more easily lend themselves to expanding conditions without the need for a doctorate in mathematics. In general these problems are approached with the hope that solving the problem under limited conditions will provide some insight as to how the more general problem can be attacked. The craps problem provides a reasonable example.

The original problem asked for the odds of winning a game of craps on the first roll. Limiting the conditions of the problem to the first roll made the game reasonably easy to simulate with the game either being won or not. However, including successive rolls brings the possibility that the game will be won, lost, or continued after each roll.

PROBLEM 7.3 *What are the odds of winning a game of craps?*

Attacking the problem involves examining the differences between the problem already solved, i.e., winning on the first roll, and the expanded problem. The odds of winning a game of craps are the odds of winning on the first roll plus the odds of winning on subsequent rolls. Since the limited game has already been simulated, it is necessary to add the simulation for the subsequent rolls.

There is a second difference between the limited and the general cases. Not only are the rules for subsequent rolls different from the rules for the first roll but more outcomes of the first roll must be considered. In the limited case only winning scenarios were of interest and rolls of seven or eleven were detected and counted. In the general case losing rolls of two, three, and twelve must also be detected because these rolls end the game and there are no subsequent rolls. If the first roll is not two, three, seven, eleven, or twelve, the game continues.

Any other roll (four, five, six, eight, nine, or ten) continues the game with the number rolled called the "point." On subsequent rolls, rolling the "point" value produces a win, rolling a seven is a loss, and rolling any other number produces neither win nor loss but merely allows the player to roll again. This implies the use of nested loops. The outer loop controls the 100 million games that will be simulated and the inner loop controls the variable number of rolls in each game.

For each game a roll counter is needed to keep track of whether a roll is the first roll or a subsequent roll. These are the only two possibilities. The first roll is the only roll with rules different from the other rolls. Setting the roll counter to one must take place at the beginning of every game.

Each game consists of at least one but possibly an unknown number of rolls. This suggests that a do/while loop should be used to simulate the play of each game. Every roll of the game requires that the dice be rolled and their counts totaled just as in the limited version of the problem. After the dice are rolled, there are two possibilities—either it was the first roll or not, indicating an if/else construction.

Nested within the first roll occurrences are three possibilities: The dice show a winning roll and the game ends, a losing roll and the game ends, or some other roll and the game continues. On subsequent rolls there are also three possibilities: A seven produces a loss and the game ends, matching the first roll produces a win and the game ends, or neither is rolled and the player rolls again. Whether any given roll ends or continues the game is key to creating the simulation.

Pseudocode

1. Begin
2.   Declare and initialize variables.
3.   Seed the pseudorandom number generator from the system clock.
4.   Message to user.
5.   Start the timer.
6.   Begin loop for 100 million games.
7.   Set rolls counter to 1.
8.   Begin a loop of unknown number of rolls (the game loop).
9.   Get random number for first die.
10.   Get random number for second die.
11.   Total the dice.
12.   If rolls counter is 1
13.   If the total is 7 or 11
14.   Increment wins counter and break out of the game loop.
15.   If the total is 2, 3, or 12
16.   Break out of the game loop.

17.	Any other total
18.	Set point equal to total, increment rolls counter, and continue.
19.	If rolls counter is not 1
20.	If total equals 7.
21.	Break out of game loop.
22.	If total equals point
23.	Increment wins counter and break out of game loop.
24.	If total equals anything else
25.	Continue game.
26.	Return to beginning of game loop.
27.	End loop.
28.	End timer.
29.	Display results.
30.	End

Much of the code in the expanded solution is reused from the original solution. The use of the timer, the randomization of the dice, and the idea of trapping certain rolls and acting on them have already been thought-out and coded. The expansion of the program required separating the first roll from the other rolls and the trapping of more roll values.

```
1    // Problem 7.3
2    #include <iostream.h>
3    #include <time.h>
4    #include <stdlib.h>
5    #include <iomanip.h>
6
7    int main (void)
8    {
9       long counter, wins = 0, point, first_die, second_die, total, roll;
10      long start, end;
11      cout.setf(ios::fixed|ios::showpoint);
12      cout.precision (4);
13      srand((unsigned)time(NULL));
14      cout << "This program calculates the odds of winning a game of craps."
15         << endl;
16      time(&start);
17      for (counter = 0; counter < 1e8; counter++)
18      {
19         roll = 1;
20         do
21         {
22            first_die = rand() % 6 + 1;
23            second_die = rand() % 6 + 1;
24            total = first_die + second_die;
25            if (roll == 1)
```

```
26                if(total == 7 || total == 11)
27                {
28                    wins++;
29                    break;
30                }
31                else if (total == 2 || total == 3 || total == 12)
32                    break;
33                else
34                {
35                    point = total;
36                    roll++;
37                    continue;
38                }
39            else
40                if (point == total)
41                {
42                    wins++;
43                    break;
44                }
45                else if (total == 7)
46                    break;
47        }while (1);
48    }
49    time(&end);
50    cout << "\nThe game was won " << wins
51        << " times out of 100,000,000"
52        << "\n\t or " << wins / 1000000.0 << " % of the time."
53        << endl << endl
54        << "The program required " << (int)difftime(end, start)
55        << " seconds to complete." << endl;
56    return(0);
57 }
```

There are several ways that the do/while loop can be written. The use of the always true test condition on line 47 was chosen because it reflects the idea that the game continues indefinitely until a winning or a losing roll is thrown. Similarly, the continue on line 37 is unnecessary. It is only included to make the logic of the simulated game more apparent.

Output of the C++ Program

```
This program calculates the odds of winning a game of craps.

The game was won 49230171 times out of 100,000,000
        or 49.2302 % of the time.

The program required 91 seconds to complete.
```

The theoretical odds for winning a game of craps are 49.292929 percent and are calculated in detail in Appendix D. The results of the simulation are consistently low by roughly .07 percent. This reflects the bias already noted in using the modulus operator for generating random numbers when the divisor does not evenly divide into 32,768.

Solution Implemented in Visual Basic

```
1    Option Explicit
2
3    Private Sub cmdCalculate_Click()
4        Dim counter, wins, point, first_die, second_die, total, roll As Long
5        Dim start, finish, temp As Single
6        Dim flag, lap As Integer
7        Randomize
8        start = Timer
9        lap = 0
10       counter = 0
11       Do While counter < 10000000
12           If (counter + 1) Mod 100000 = 0 Then
13               temp = Timer
14               lap = lap + 1
15               lblTime.Caption = "Elapsed time is " & _
16                   Int(temp - start) & " seconds." & vbCrLf & _
17                   "Expected completion in " & _
18                   Int((temp - start) * 100 / lap) & " seconds."
19               DoEvents
20           End If
21
22           first_die = Int(6 * Rnd + 1)
23           second_die = Int(6 * Rnd + 1)
24           total = first_die + second_die
25           If total = 7 Or total = 11 Then
26               wins = wins + 1
27           ElseIf total <> 2 And total <> 3 And total <> 12 Then
28               point = total
29               Do
30                   first_die = Int((6 * Rnd) Mod 6) + 1
31                   second_die = Int((6 * Rnd) Mod 6) + 1
32                   total = first_die + second_die
33                   If point = total Then
34                       wins = wins + 1
35                       Exit Do
36                   ElseIf total = 7 Then
37                       Exit Do
38                   End If
39               Loop While (1)
40           End If
41           counter = counter + 1
42       Loop
43
44       finish = Timer
45       lblOutput.Caption = "The game was won " & wins & _
```

```
46          " times out of 10,000,000  or " & _
47             wins / 100000# & "% of the time."
48   End Sub
49
50   Private Sub cmdExit_Click()
51        Unload Me
52   End Sub
53
54   Private Sub Form_Load()
55        lblTitle.Caption = "This program calculates the odds on winning " & _
56           "a game of craps."
57   End Sub
```

One new feature was added to the Visual Basic program. In the ongoing quest to keep the user informed as to the status of a long-running program an expected completion time was added to the time information box. Estimating when the program will finish the simulation can be considered to be another problem within the problem. Since the first time information will occur when the program is one hundredth of the way to completion, the total time will be 100 times longer. However, this value can be refined and rounding error reduced if it is recalculated with more accurate time data as the program proceeds toward completion.

Line 18 determines a new elapsed time every 100,000 games played. This number is multiplied by 100 and divided by the number of 100,000 game cycles. The estimated time is added to the message in the lblTime label box.

Output of the Visual Basic Program

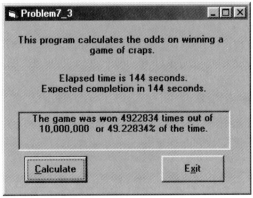

7.4   ELIMINATION OF THE RANDOM NUMBER BIAS

In Chapter 6 during the original discussion of Problem 6.2 it was pointed out that if each number from 0 to 32,767 is divided by 6 the remainders of 0 and 1 will occur 5,462 times but the remainders 2, 3, 4, and 5 will occur only 5,461 times. The obvious question as we expand the complexity of the problem is whether we can remove this bias and generate a more accurate answer. Of course, this discussion is only relevant for C++ programs.

Because Visual Basic uses an algorithm that produces single-precision floating-point numbers from zero to one, including zero but not one, the problem does not exist.

If the problem in C++ is due to the range of random numbers not being evenly divisible by the number of random numbers required, then the solution is to create a new range that is evenly divisible by that number. In this case the requirement is for a range that is evenly divisible by six. If the last two numbers of the normal random number range were removed, the range of 32,766 remaining numbers would be evenly divisible by six, eliminating the bias problem.

While it is not possible to alter the range of the random number generator we can trap the times when the numbers 32,766, and 32,767 occur and request that the random number generator provide a different number. If the code using the modulus operator, lines 30 and 31 in Problem 7.3, were replaced by

```
30    do
31            first_die = rand();
32    while(first_die > 32765);
33    first_die /= 5461;
34    do
35            second_die = rand();
36    while(second_die > 32765);
37    second_die /= 5461;
38    total = first_die + second_die + 2;
```

the variables `first_die` and `second_die` would not be allowed to leave the do/while loops if their values were 32,766 or 32,767. If these values were generated the loop test would evaluate to true and the loop would repeat generating a new value. Lines 4 and 8 divide the properly ranged variables by 5461 bringing the values of `first_die` and `second_die` to the range of zero to five. Line 9 adds two to the sum of `first_die` and `second_die` so the range for `total` is adjusted from two to twelve.

This scheme does raise the question of whether either of the loops could become an infinite loop causing the program to stop running. An infinite loop is possible but the odds are astronomically remote. The odds for the test causing the loop to repeat are 1 in 16,384 (or 2 chances in 32,768 numbers). The odds for this happening twice in a row are 1 in $16,384^2$ or 1 in 268,435,456. The odds on the test being true ten times in a row are 1 in 1.39×10^{42}. We can be absolutely sure that the loops will never repeat 1,000 times much less produce an infinite loop.

The altered coded produces the following output.

```
The game was won 492964423 times out of 1,000,000,000
or 49.2964 % of the time.
```

The result differs from the theoretical value calculated in Appendix D by only .0071%.

7.5   LIMITATIONS IN OPTIONS

The binary conversion program has been adjusted to handle any positive or negative integer, or floating-point number. However, the program only operates in one direction. Decimal, base 10, numbers can be converted to binary but the reverse process of converting binary numbers to decimal is missing. It would be reasonable for a conversion program to go in both directions.

PROBLEM 7.4   *Create a complete binary/decimal conversion routine.*

The first step is to be clear about what needs to be done. The program that makes the binary/decimal conversions will have to handle three tasks:

1. Control the program by offering a menu choice to convert binary to decimal, decimal to binary, or to quit the program.
2. Make the binary to decimal conversion.
3. Make the decimal to binary conversion.

The decimal to binary conversion routine has already been written and can be incorporated into the new program as a function almost without change. The program control is the `main` function of the program and represents a simple task of presenting a menu, getting the user's choice of operation, and calling the correct function. The only real work is determining how to convert binary numbers to decimal numbers.

Since binary to decimal conversion is the opposite of decimal to binary conversion, there is some expectation that reversing the steps of the decimal to binary conversion would be successful. Notice the similarities in the operation of the decimal to binary conversion compared to what needs to be done to convert binary to decimal.

1. The decimal to binary function gets the user input as a number and creates a string of binary bits.
   The binary to decimal function should get a string of binary bits and create a number.
2. The decimal to binary function determines whether the weight of a bit is contained in the number and if so sets the bit in the string.
   The binary to decimal function should determine if a bit is set in the string and calculate its weighted value.
3. The decimal to binary function subtracts the weighted value from the input to create the next value to be tested.
   The binary to decimal function should add the weighted value of each bit to a running sum that is the converted number.

With a general idea of what needs to be done the pseudocode can be written for the binary to decimal function filling in the details.

Pseudocode

1. Begin binary to decimal function.
2. Declare and initialize variables.
3. Prompt user for input.
4. Store input in a character array.
5. Scan the string for a binary point.

   The binary number may or may not have a fractional part. If it does not, then the bit weighted 2^0 is the last bit (the one just to the left of the NULL). If there is a binary point, then the bit weighted 2^0 is just to the left of the binary point.
6. If the binary point is found, save the position of the binary point i.e., the value of the array index and set a flag.

7. If the flag is not set (the binary number is an integer),

8.   Back up the index so it points to the least significant bit instead of the NULL.

9.   Begin a loop that searches backward through the array searching for 1s.

10.   If a 1 is found

11.   Add its weight to the running sum, adjust index.

12.   End loop when index is 0.

13.   Display the final sum.

14.   If the first bit in the binary array is "−"

15.   Display minus sign before the sum.

16. If the flag is set (the binary number is floating point)

17.   Set one index to the left of the binary point to get the integer part.

18.   Set another index to the right of the binary point to get the fraction.

19.   Begin a loop that searches backward through the array searching for 1s.

20.   If a 1 is found

21.   Add its weight to the running sum, adjust index.

22.   End loop when index is 0.

23.   Adjust counter for the power of 2.

24.   Begin loop that searches forward from binary point searching for 1s.

25.   If a 1 is found

26.   Add its weight to the running sum, adjust index, adjust power control variable.

27.   End the loop at the NULL.

28.   Display the final sum.

29.   If the first bit in the binary array is "−"

30.   Display minus sign before the sum.

31. End the binary to decimal function.

There is little difficulty in summing a series of numbers that are all powers of two. The question is what power of two each bit represents. The key to this solution is in step 5. There must be a search for the binary point. If there is no binary point, the number is an integer and the least significant bit is just before the NULL. If there is a binary point, then the number has potentially an integer and fractional part. The zero power of two is just to the left of the binary point and the weights of the bits grow larger as the loop moves to the beginning of the array. The value of 2^{-1} is just to the right of the binary point and the power grows smaller as the index moves toward the end of the string.

While the game plan for solving the problem is straightforward, implementing the program requires considerable attention to details. Particular attention should be given to the index variables used to take bits from the array. Going off either end of the array causes significant errors. If there is an error in one of the index variables and the programmer is fortunate enough to have the program merely produce an incorrect result instead of crashing, the index error tends to show up in a result that is wrong by one or more powers of two. This tells the programmer how the index must be adjusted to correct the problem.

Solution Implemented in C++

```
1    //  Problem 7.4
2    #include <iostream.h>
3    #include <math.h>
4
5    void decimal_to_binary(void)
6    {
7        double input;
8        int counter = 0, power = 0, flag = 0;
9        char binary[100] = {0};
10
11       cout << "Enter the number to be converted to binary   "  << flush;
12       cin >> input;          // Get number from user
13       cout << endl;
14       cin.ignore(1,'\n');
15       if ( input < 0)
16       {
17           binary[counter++] = '-';
18           input = -input;
19       }
20       while ( pow(2,power++) < input);
21       power = power - 2;
22       do
23       {
24           if ( power == -1)
25               binary[counter++] = '.';
26           binary[counter++] = (int)(input / pow(2, power)) + 48;
27                       // Determine whether binary[counter] is 1 or 0
28           if (binary[counter - 1] == '1')
29               input = input - pow(2, power);
30                       // If bit is 1 reduce input appropriately
31           if (power % 4 == 0)
32               binary[counter++] = 32;
33       }while (--power >= -16);
34       cout << "\n\n\tBinary -->   " << binary << endl;
35    }
36    void binary_to_decimal(void)
37    {
38        char binary[100];
39        double flt_number = 0;
40        long int_number = 0, power, index, point, flag = 0, counter, fraction;
41        cout << "Enter the binary number to be converted" << endl << endl;
42        cin.getline(binary, 99, '\n');
43        index = 0;
44        while(binary[index] != 0)   // find the binary point if there is one
45        {
46            if (binary[index] == '.')
47                point = index, flag = 1;
48            index++;
```

```
49      }
50      if (flag == 0)
51      {
52          point = index - 1;
53          for (counter = point, power = 0; counter >= 0; counter--)
54              if (binary[counter] == '1')
55                  int_number += pow(2, point - counter);
56          cout << endl << "The decimal equivalent is ";
57          if (binary[0] == '-')
58              cout << "-";
59          cout << int_number
60              << endl << endl;
61      }
62      else
63      {
64          fraction = point + 1;
65          counter = 0;
66          point--;
67          while (point >= 0)
68          {
69              if (binary[point--] == '1')
70                  flt_number += pow(2, counter);
71              counter++;
72          }
73          counter = -1;
74          while (binary[fraction] != 0)
75          {
76              if (binary[fraction] == '1')
77                  flt_number += pow(2,counter);
78              fraction++, counter--;
79          }
80          cout << endl << "The decimal equivalent is ";
81          if (binary[0] == '-')
82              cout << "-";
83          cout << flt_number
84              << endl << endl;
85      }
86  }
87  int main(void)
88  {
89      char input;
90      do
91      {
92          cout << "Select from the menu" << endl << endl;
93          cout << "  1) Convert decimal to binary " << endl
94              << "  2) Convert binary to decimal " << endl
95              << "  3) Quit " << endl << endl;
96          input = cin.get();
97          cin.ignore(1,'\n');
98          switch(input)
```

```
99         {
100            case '1':
101                decimal_to_binary();
102                break;
103            case '2':
104                binary_to_decimal();
105                break;
106            case '3':
107                break;
108            default:
109                break;
110        }
111    }while (input != '3');
112    return(0);
113 }
```

The program has been divided into three units: the main function, the binary_to_decimal function, and the decimal_to_binary function. It is also reasonable to place the menu display and to get the user's menu choice in a menu function. The two conversion functions could also be broken down into subfunctions but that would not be advisable. Functions should not be created for the sake of creating functions. Functions are created to group a logical process for the purposes of clarity and reusability.

As mentioned earlier the decimal_to_binary function is nearly identical to the solution to Problem 7.2. The only difference is on line 14. Using cin and cin.get() to bring in information from the user can leave a buffered character that will cause the next input routine to grab the buffered character. This has the effect of making the input function appear not to execute. The use of cin.ignore(1, '\n') clears out the buffered character roughly corresponding to the C function fflush(stdin).

Output of the C++ Program

```
Select from the menu

   1) Convert decimal to binary
   2) Convert binary to decimal
   3) Quit

1
Enter the number to be converted to binary   65537.125

        Binary -->   1 0000 0000 0000 0001 .0010 0000 0000 0000
Select from the menu

   1) Convert decimal to binary
   2) Convert binary to decimal
   3) Quit

2
Enter the binary number to be converted
```

```
-11111110.011
```

The decimal equivalent is -254.375

Select from the menu

    1) Convert decimal to binary
    2) Convert binary to decimal
    3) Quit

3

Solution Implemented in Visual Basic

```
1    Option Explicit
2
3    Private Sub cmdConvert_Click()
4        Dim number As Double
5        Dim counter, power, saved_power, x, decimalFlag As Integer
6        Dim neg_flag, fraction_flag, length, point As Integer
7        Dim binary(0 To 100) As Byte
8        Dim temp As Double
9        Dim binaryString As String
10       fraction_flag = 0
11       neg_flag = 0
12       If txtBinary.Text = "" And txtDecimal = "" Then
13           Call MsgBox("Input either a decimal" & vbCrLf & _
14               "or a binary number", vbExclamation, _
15                   "Decimal/Binary Conversion")
16           txtDecimal.SetFocus
17           Exit Sub
18       End If
19       If txtBinary = "" Then
20           decimalFlag = 1
21           lblOutput = ""
22           temp = 0
23           counter = 0
24           power = 0
25           number = CDbl(txtDecimal.Text)
26
27           If number < 0 Then
28               number = -number
29               neg_flag = 1
30           End If
31           If number >= 0 And number < 1 Then
32               fraction_flag = 1
33           End If
34           Do While (2 ^ power <= number)
35               power = power + 1
```

```
36          Loop
37          power = power - 1
38          saved_power = power
39          Do
40              binary(counter) = Int(number / (2 ^ power))
41              counter = counter + 1
42              If binary(counter - 1) = 1 Then
43                  number = number - (2 ^ power)
44              End If
45            power = power - 1
46          Loop While (power >= -16)
47          lblOutput = txtDecimal.Text & " converted to binary is" & _
48              vbCrLf
49          If neg_flag = 1 Then
50              lblOutput = "-"
51          End If
52          For x = 0 To saved_power + 16
53              If fraction_flag = 1 Then
54                  lblOutput = lblOutput & "."
55                  fraction_flag = 0
56              End If
57              lblOutput = lblOutput & Trim(Str(binary(x)))
58              If x = saved_power Then
59                  lblOutput = lblOutput & "."
60              End If
61              If (saved_power - x) Mod 4 = 0 Then
62                  lblOutput = lblOutput & " "
63              End If
64          Next x
65      Else
66          If txtDecimal.Text = "" Then
67              length = Len(txtBinary.Text)
68              If Mid(txtBinary.Text, 1, 1) = "-" Then
69                  neg_flag = 1
70                  binaryString = Right(txtBinary.Text, length - 1)
71              Else
72                  binaryString = txtBinary.Text
73              End If
74              length = Len(binaryString)
75              For counter = 1 To length
76                  If Mid(binaryString, counter, 1) = "." Then
77                      point = counter
78                      fraction_flag = 1
79                  End If
80              Next counter
81              number = 0
82              If fraction_flag = 0 Then
83                  For counter = length To 1 Step -1
84                      temp = CInt(Mid(binaryString, counter, 1))
```

```
85                        If temp = 1 Then
86                            number = number + 2 ^ (length - counter)
87                        End If
88                    Next counter
89                Else
90                    point = point - 1
91                    For counter = point To 1 Step -1
92                        temp = CInt(Mid(binaryString, counter, 1))
93                        If temp = 1 Then
94                            number = number + 2 ^ (point - counter)
95                        End If
96                    Next counter
97                    point = point + 1
98                    For counter = (point + 1) To length
99                        temp = CInt(Mid(binaryString, counter, 1))
100                       number = number + temp * (2 ^ (point - counter))
101                   Next counter
102               End If
103           End If
104           lblOutput = txtBinary.Text & " converted to binary is" & _
105               vbCrLf
106           If neg_flag = 1 Then
107               lblOutput = lblOutput & "-"
108           End If
109           lblOutput = lblOutput & number
110       End If
111   End Sub
112
113   Private Sub cmdExit_Click()
114       Unload Me
115   End Sub
116
117   Private Sub cmdReset_Click()
118       txtDecimal.Text = ""
119       txtBinary.Text = ""
120       lblOutput.Caption = ""
121       txtDecimal.SetFocus
122   End Sub
123
124   Private Sub Form_Load()
125       lblMessage.Caption = "This program performs decimal/binary " & _
126           "conversions.  Enter a number in the appropriate box " & _
127           " and click convert."
128       lblDecimal.Caption = "Enter a decimal number."
129       lblBinary.Caption = "Enter a binary number."
130   End Sub
```

Even though both the C++ and the Visual Basic programs extend to over 100 lines of code, the problem is far easier to solve than the program lengths would indicate. It has been pointed out several times that for programming there is no substitute for experience. The comparable axiom in programming is "Reuse. Reuse. Reuse." In the solution to Problem 7.4, the code to Problem 7.2 has been lifted intact. The only new code involves reversing the weighted value process.

Output of the Visual Basic Program

7.6   LIMITATIONS IN UTILITY

Rather than tackle a large, complex project, it is often reasonable to scale back the effort to demonstrate a "proof of concept." Once the plan is shown to be viable, the extra features that make the concept, device, or program useful are added later. The encryption program (Problem 5.1) verified that the scheme for encoding and decoding could be implemented and that the encoded message was apparently without pattern.

Unfortunately, a program that stores the encrypted message in a string that is destroyed when the program ends is not terribly useful. To be a reasonable encryption program the program must write the encrypted message to a file that can be sent by LAN, Internet, or sneaker net to the person for whom the information is intended. It would also be handy if the person who receives the file, and who presumably has a copy of the encryption program, is able to read the file and decrypt the message.

PROBLEM 7.5   *Encode a message with an unbreakable code and write the encrypted message to a file. Open the file and retrieve the original message.*

Again it is important to focus on the differences between the limited and expanded problems. The first and obvious difference is that the encrypted message should be written to a file and the message to be decrypted should be read from a file. The second and implicit difference is that the length of the message should no longer be limited to a fixed number of characters but instead should be virtually unlimited in length.

Both C++ and Visual Basic provide for input strings of indeterminate length. However, the string object in C++ is usually considered an advanced topic and C-style strings, stored in fixed arrays, are more commonly taught in introductory classes. The need for string objects can be circumvented in the C++ program by getting, encrypting, and writing to the output file each character as it is entered by the user. This eliminates the need for a character array to store the incoming message.

Since string objects are more common in Visual Basic, the input message is entered as a string and scanned character by character in the encode function. As each character is identified, it is encoded and written to the output file.

Because the look-up table and the system of random shifts through the table worked well in Problem 5.1, these are retained in the expanded program. It is also reasonable to retain the logical division into the main function and three other functions to handle the menu operation, the encode and write operations, and the read and decode operations. Unlike Problem 5.1, the user input will be handled by the encoding function in the C++ program.

The logical order of events for the encoding routine is to get a name for the file that will store the encoded message, create a file by that name, get the seed number for the pseudorandom number generator from the user, and then begin a loop to get the message one character at a time, encode the character, and write it to the file. Actually the write to the file doesn't take place one character at a time even though the program will be written that way. Instead the program negotiates a buffer with the operating system and the write takes place when the buffer is full. This is a considerable time saver because writing to a disk is incredibly slow compared to microprocessor speeds.

Since the operations of the main() function and the menu() function are elemental and are similar to the limited solution, only the pseudocode for the encoding and decoding functions will be written.

Writing characters to a file emphasizes another difference in the two programs, which is really a difference between the C++ language and Windows (actually DOS because we are working in a command window provided by Windows). C++ and DOS handle the new line character in two different ways. This is an historical problem. Because C was developed on a UNIX platform, C handles the new line character as a single character as does UNIX. Windows uses two characters for the new line character, a carriage return (ASCII 13) and a linefeed (ASCII 10).

This difference was not encountered in the limited version of the encryption problem because no call to the operating system was made for a disk write. In this version the issue must be addressed. The details will be explained after the C++ code is provided.

Pseudocode for the Encode/Write Function

1. Begin encode/write function.
2. Declare variables.
3. Prompt user for file name and get name.
4. Create the file.
5. Prompt user for the encryption key and get the key, i.e., the pseudorandom number generator seed number.
6. Seed the pseudorandom number generator.
7. Prompt for the text to be encoded.
8. Begin loop for message.
9.   Get a character.
10.   If the character is a new line
11.   Move the screen display down one line.
12.   If the character is the <Esc>
13.   Break out of the loop.
14.   If the character is uppercase.
15.   Make it lowercase.
16.   Reset table index to zero.
17.   Begin TABLE scan loop.
18.   If the character is a new line
19.   Manually set the table_index to 40 and break.
20.   If the character is found in the table scan
21.   Break saving the current value of table index.
22.   Increment table index to continue scan until character is found.
23.   End loop if the last character in the table is reached.
24.   If the end of the table is reached without finding the character
25.   Continue i.e., get the next character from the message without writing to the file.
26.   Shift the table index a random amount to the right.
27.   Replace the message character with the encrypted letter.
28.   Write the encrypted letter to the file.
29. End the loop if the <Esc> key is entered.
30. Close the file.
31. End the function.

Pseudocode for the Read/Decode Function

1. Begin encode/write function.

2.   Declare variables.

3.   Prompt user for file name and get name.

4.   Open the file.

5.   Prompt user for the encryption key and get the key, i.e., the pseudorandom number generator seed number.

6.   Seed the pseudorandom number generator.

7.   Begin loop to get characters from the file.

8.   Get a character from the file.

9.   If the character is the End Of File

10.   Break.

11.   Reset the table index to zero.

12.   Begin loop to scan TABLE for the character.

13.   If the character is found

14.   Break and save the table index.

15.   Increment table index to check next character in table.

16.   End loop when end of TABLE is reached.

17.   Shift the table index a random amount to the left.

18.   Replace the encrypted character with the decrypted character.

19.   If the character is the new line character

20.   Move the display to the next line.

21.   Else

22.   Display the character.

23.   End the read loop at the End Of File or other error.

24.   Close the file.

25. End the function.

Solution Implemented in C++

```
1   // Problem 7.5
2   #include <conio.h>
3   #include <iostream.h>
4   #include <fstream.h>
5   #include <stdlib.h>
6
7   char menu(void);
8   void make_file(void);
9   void read_file(void);
10  const char TABLE[42] = "abcdefghijklmnopqrstuvwxyz .,1234567890?\n";
11
12  int main(void)
13  {
```

```
14      char choice;
15      do
16      {
17         choice = menu();
18         switch (choice)
19         {
20            case '1':
21               make_file();    // Create the encrypted file
22               break;
23            case '2':
24               read_file();    // Open and decrypt the file
25               break;
26            case '3':
27               break;          // End program
28            default:
29               break;          // Repeat menu for improper input
30         }
31      }while (choice != '3');
32      return(0);
33  }
34  char menu(void)
35  {
36      char choice;
37      cout << endl << "Choose a menu item" << endl
38         << "\t1) Make a file\n\t2) Read a file\n\t3) Quit        " << flush;
39      choice = cin.get();
40      cin.ignore(1,'\n');
41      return choice;
42  }
43  void make_file(void)
44  {
45      char name[50], letter = 0;
46      int key, table_index;
47      cout << endl << "Enter the file name . .    " << flush;
48      cin.getline(name, 49, '\n');
49      ofstream out(name);
50      cout << "Enter the key  . .    " << flush;
51      cin >> key;
52      cin.ignore (1,'\n');
53      srand(key);
54      cout << "Enter the text . ." << endl;
55      do
56      {
57         letter = getche();
58         if (letter == 13)
59            cout << endl;
60         if (letter == 27)
61            break;
62         if (letter > 64 && letter < 93)
63            letter += 32;
```

```
64       table_index = 0;
65       do
66       {
67          if (letter == 13)
68          {
69             table_index = 40;
70             break;
71          }
72          if (letter == TABLE[table_index])
73             break;
74          table_index++;
75       }while (table_index < 42);
76       if (table_index == 42)
77          continue;
78       table_index = (table_index + (rand() % 41 + 1)) % 41;
79       letter = TABLE[table_index];
80       out.put(letter);
81    }while (letter != 27);
82    out.close ();
83    cin.ignore (3,'\n');
84 }
85 void read_file(void)
86 {
87    char name[50], letter;
88    int key, table_index;
89    cout << endl << "Enter the file name . .   " << flush;
90    cin.getline(name, 49, '\n');
91    ifstream in(name);
92    cout << "Enter the key  . .   " << flush;
93    cin >> key;
94    cin.ignore (1,'\n');
95    srand(key);
96    while (in.good())
97    {
98       in.get(letter);
99       if (letter == EOF)
100         break;
101      table_index = 0;
102      do
103      {
104         if (letter == TABLE[table_index])
105            break;
106         table_index++;
107      }while (table_index < 42);
108      table_index = ((table_index - (rand() % 41 + 1)) + 41) % 41;
109      letter = TABLE[table_index];
110      if (letter == 10)
111         cout << endl;
112      else
```

```
113            cout << letter;
114    }
115    in.close ();
116    cout << endl;
117 }
```

The `main()` function organizes the program at the highest level. It calls `menu()` to display the options to the user, gets the user's choice, and directs the flow to create the encrypted file, read an encrypted file, or exit.

The new item in this program is the command to create a file. Actually the program doesn't really create the file, rather it creates an object (C++ is object oriented) that communicates with the operating system to create the file. The line

```
49    ofstream out(name);
```

creates an object called `out` of class `ofstream`. `Ofstream` is a class of objects built into Visual C++. Objects of this class know how to output information to a file. The details are complex and thankfully are handled without the awareness or intervention of the programmer. `Out` is an object or an instance of the class and, therefore, knows about sending information to a file. `Name` is an argument of the constructor of the object. All communication with the file is done through the object `out`; for example, sending the characters to the file is done by `out.put(letter)`. `Put` is a function of the object `out` and `letter` is the argument of `put()`. Similarly

```
91    ifstream in(name);
```

creates an object `in` of class `ifstream` that knows how to get information from a file. The `get` function of the object `in` extracts a character from the file and stores it in the variable `letter`.

```
98    in.get(letter);
```

The `make_file()` function prompts the user for the name of the file to hold the encrypted message, the key for the encryption, and the message itself. The input commands in this function deserve a word of warning. The use of an input function (getline), the insertion operator (`<<`), and a C-style input function (getche) in a single program can cause problems. The insertion operator tends to leave a character in the input stream that needs to be removed with `cin.ignore(1,'\n')`. If the extra character is not removed, the `getche()` function will work properly because as a C-style function it does not use the same input stream, but the next input call in `menu()` will not work.

`Getche()` has a few unexpected qualities of its own. First, it does not handle the <Enter> key well. The <Enter> key will return the input to the left-hand margin but will not move to the next line. Lines 58 and 59 correct this problem. `Getche()` has a similar problem with the backspace key. The display shows the backspace but the backspace key itself is a character with an ASCII value that is sent to the encoding routine. This is trapped by lines 76 and 77. Any character that is not found in the look-up table is detected and the encoding and the write to the file are bypassed. The problem is that the letters that were backspaced over have already been encoded and written to the file. This is more difficult to correct and requires handling a position pointer in the file object. Since this is an advanced feature, it has been ignored here.

Lines 67 through 71 detect the new line character and manually set the `table_index` to the proper value. In the read function the new line is decoded and line 110 detects the character. Line 111 causes the display to advance one line.

Output of the C++ Program

```
Choose a menu item
        1) Make a file
        2) Read a file
        3) Quit          1


Enter the file name . .    beauty.txt
Enter the key  . .    321
Enter the text . .
She walks in Beauty, like the night
Of cloudless climes and starry skies;
And all that's best of dark and bright
Meet in her aspect and her eyes:
Thus mellowed to that tender light
Which Heaven to gaudy day denies.

Choose a menu item
        1) Make a file
        2) Read a file
        3) Quit          2


Enter the file name . .    beauty.txt
Enter the key  . .    5
z2hmljo?pt.xilgvzsxhrcrc9.iy24ha blhux9gf?g54q?val?y alefj8w7?rl9mfe4
s4halsl0  nq4xyb31.d.n.wyk9ns2ph2rja7d3x?7n,v5ijo?0,tn5ff,,zc
5dqty016qz5.4btlzt
uei fkle718ou5,4vr hm?q0iaxy2jmuces?zfifl9ff tz 0?b
77562rg5

Choose a menu item
        1) Make a file
        2) Read a file
        3) Quit          2


Enter the file name . .    beauty.txt
Enter the key  . .    321
she walks in beauty, like the night
of cloudless climes and starry skies
and all thats best of dark and bright
meet in her aspect and her eyes
thus mellowed to that tender light
which heaven to gaudy day denies.

Choose a menu item
        1) Make a file
        2) Read a file
        3) Quit          3
```

The poem is the first verse of *She Walks in Beauty* by Byron. The first attempt to decode it with an incorrect key resulted in random text. The second attempt using the correct key reproduced the original verse except for the capitalization, the colon, the semicolon, and the apostrophe. The file beauty.txt contains the encrypted text

```
?ye 06?ssyrom
xyr80j2hkgvppcqh6qz
i.8n0?n1ox9reot33hkvv5qgb uqrqnj1zvg4m9u4ee33mueq9eq87q 223izy1j
k.1,g?upb81bemcyfiv7gig0om,,sv14ka1?ojo2x.g,ihjxspi0ct1hxxk3pt8,, 94onu71b
15ndrpn?0eom4rgfawgs?w2aow
c1,fkker99
```

Actually there were only five lines in the encrypted file. The preceding fourth and fifth lines are a single line that would not fit across this page and was broken at the space following the 94onu71b. The author of this text would be interested in hearing from any reader who can find a way to decode the encrypted text without the key, the program, and the knowledge that the C++ random number generator was used in the encryption.

The logic of the expanded encryption program is identical to the limited version developed as the solution to Problem 5.1. The only difference is in the destination of the encrypted message (to a file) and the source of the message to be decrypted (from a file). The alterations to both the C++ and Visual Basic solutions to Problem 5.1 have been highlighted.

Solution Implemented in Visual Basic

```
1   Option Explicit
2   Private Table(0 To 41) As Byte
3
4   Private Sub cmdExit_Click()
5       Unload Me
6   End Sub
7
8   Private Sub cmdGo_Click()
9       Static Message As String
10      Dim Num, Count As Integer
11      If optEncode.Value = True Then
12
13          Message = txtInOut.Text
14          Call encode(Message)
15      Else
16
17          Message = decode()
18      End If
19      txtInOut.Text = ""
20      For Count = 1 To Len(Message)
21          If Mid(Message, Count, 1) = Chr(13) Then
22              Count = Count + 1
23              txtInOut.Text = txtInOut.Text & vbCrLf
24          Else
25              txtInOut.Text = txtInOut.Text & _
26                  Mid(Message, Count, 1)
```

```
27              End If
28          Next
29      End Sub
30
31      Private Sub cmdReset_Click()
32          txtInOut.Text = ""
33          txtKey.Text = ""
34          txtFileName.Text = ""
35      End Sub
36
37      Private Sub Form_Load()
38          Dim Index As Long
39
40          lblMessage.Caption = "This program encodes a message and " & _
41              "writes it to a file or opens a file and decodes the message."
42          lblFileName.Caption = "Output file name"
43          lblinput = "Message box"
44          For Index = 0 To 25      ' Build the Look-Up Table
45              Table(Index) = Index + 97
46          Next Index
47
48          For Index = 26 To 35
49              Table(Index) = Index + 49 - 26
50          Next Index
51
52          Table(36) = Asc("?")
53          Table(37) = Asc(".")
54          Table(38) = Asc(",")
55          Table(39) = Asc(" ")
56          Table(40) = 13 'the return char
57          Table(41) = 0   'the null
58          optEncode.Value = True
59      End Sub
60
61      Public Sub encode(ByRef Msg As String)
62          Dim Key As Single
63          Dim msg_index As Integer
64          Dim letter, name As String
65          Dim asc_val As Long
66          Dim table_index, fileNumber As Integer
67          Dim temp As Integer
68
69          If IsNumeric(txtKey.Text) = False Then
70              Call MsgBox("Enter a valid key", vbOKOnly + vbInformation)
71              Exit Sub
72          End If
73          name = txtFileName
74          fileNumber = FreeFile
75          name = App.Path & "\" & name
76          Open name For Output As #fileNumber
77          Key = CSng(txtKey.Text)
```

```
78      msg_index = 1
79      Rnd (-1)
80      Randomize (Key)
81      Do While msg_index <= Len(Msg)
82          letter = Mid(Msg, msg_index, 1)
83          asc_val = Asc(letter)
84          If asc_val > 64 And asc_val < 93 Then
85              asc_val = asc_val + 32
86              Mid(Msg, msg_index, 1) = Chr(asc_val)
87          End If
88          table_index = 0
89          Do While table_index < 40
90              If asc_val = Table(table_index) Then
91                  Exit Do
92              End If
93              table_index = table_index + 1
94          Loop
95          temp = 41 * Rnd()
96          table_index = (table_index + (temp Mod 41) + 1) Mod 41
97          Mid(Msg, msg_index, 1) = Chr(Table(table_index))
98          Write #fileNumber, Table(table_index)
99          msg_index = msg_index + 1
100     Loop
101     Close #fileNumber
102 End Sub
103
104 Public Function decode() As String
105     Dim Key As Single
106     Dim msg_index, temp, table_index, fileNumber As Integer
107     Dim letter, name, Msg As String
108     Dim asc_val As Long
109     Dim inByte As Byte
110
111     name = txtFileName.Text
112     fileNumber = FreeFile
113     name = App.Path & "\" & name
114     Open name For Input As #fileNumber
115
116     If IsNumeric(txtKey.Text) = False Then
117         Call MsgBox("Enter a valid key", vbOKOnly + vbInformation)
118         Exit Function
119     End If
120     Key = CSng(txtKey.Text)
121     Rnd (-1)
122     Randomize (Key)
123     msg_index = 1
124     Do While Not EOF(fileNumber)
125         table_index = 0
126         Input #fileNumber, inByte
127         Do While table_index < 40
128
```

```
129                    If inByte = Table(table_index) Then
130                     Exit Do
131                    End If
132                    table_index = table_index + 1
133               Loop
134               temp = 41 * Rnd()
135               table_index = ((table_index - ((temp Mod 41) + 1)) + 41) Mod 41
136               Msg = Msg & Chr(Table(table_index))
137               msg_index = msg_index + 1
138          Loop
139          Close #fileNumber
140          decode = Msg
141 End Function
142
143 Private Sub optDecode_Click()
144      lblFileName.Caption = "Input file name"
145 End Sub
146
147 Private Sub optEncode_Click()
148      lblFileName.Caption = "Output file name"
149 End Sub
```

The first difference between the solutions to Problem 7.5 and Problem 5.1 shows up on line 17. In the limited program Message could be passed by reference to the function *because message existed*. In the expanded version there is no message until it is created in the decode() function. This takes place on line 136 as Msg is built character by character. On line 140 Msg is returned to cmdGo and stored in Message. Of course, returning a value implies the call routine cannot be used and decode() must be written as a function that returns a string (line 104).

File handling requires a few other alterations to the encode() and decode() functions. Because there was no message for the decode() function to work with prior to the reading of characters from the file, the do loop cannot use the message length as the terminating characteristic for the loop. Instead the characters are read from the file until the EOF (End Of File) character is read (line 124). In the encode() function there are two different outputs for the message. Line 97 creates the same Msg string that was created in the limited version but the next line outputs the byte value of the character to the function named in the txtFileName box. The byte value for each character was used because, if a character is sent, Visual Basic will enclose the Chr() value in quotations marks, which wreaks havoc when the message is decoded.

Of course, for encoding and decoding the file must be opened before character values can be either written or read. In the encoding routine the file is opened for writing by the code contained on lines 73 to 76. For the decoding function the file is open for input by the lines 111 to 114.

The only truly cute part of the program is listed on lines 143 to 149. This code changes the prompt ahead of the txtFileName box from a request for an output file name to an input file name depending on whether the optEncode or optDecode button is clicked.

Output of the Visual Basic Program

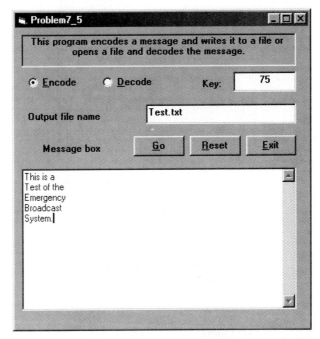

Now that we have some experience at opening files and examining their contents we might consider adjusting the letter frequency program. The original program was limited to examining just the string entered by the user. The solution would be more accurate and the program more generally useful if it could open a file containing a large amount of text. With this adaptation the program could scan an entire book and could provide a comparison of letter frequencies in modern English compared to the dialectic English used by Mark Twain in *The Adventures of Huckleberry Finn*.

PROBLEM 7.6   *Determine the frequency of occurrence for each letter in an entire book.*

In this case there is little reason to write the pseudocode. The problem requires that a file be opened and read one character at a time, which was done in Problem 7.5, and the ability to count how many times each letter occurred, which was done in Problem 4.5. In short, there is nothing really new here and the solution is a product of experience.

Solution Implemented in C++

```
1    // Problem 7.6
2    #include <stdio.h>
3    #include <conio.h>
4    #include <iomanip.h>
5    #include <fstream.h>
6
7    void main(void)
```

```
8   {
9       int letters[26] = {0}, counter, total_letters = 0;
10      char incoming, name[100];
11      cout << "This program will calculate the frequency of "
12          << "\n\tthe letters 'a' through 'z' in a text file."
13          << "\n\nEnter the file to be opened    " << flush;
14      cin.getline(name,99,'\n');
15      cout.precision(2);
16      cout.setf(ios::fixed|ios::showpoint);
17      ifstream in(name);
18      while(in.good())
19      {
20          in.get(incoming);
21          if (incoming >= 'a' && incoming <= 'z')
22              letters[incoming - 97]++, total_letters++;
23          if (incoming >= 'A' && incoming <= 'Z')
24              letters[incoming - 65]++, total_letters++;
25      }
26      cout << endl;
27      for (counter = 0; counter < 13; counter++)
28      {
29          cout << setw(2) << static_cast<char>(counter + 97) << " -> "
30              << setw(7) << letters[counter] << " -> "
31              << setw(7) << letters[counter] * 100.0 / total_letters << "%"
32              << setw(2) << static_cast<char>(counter + 110) << " -> "
33              << setw(7) << letters[counter + 13] << " -> "
34              << setw(7) << letters[counter + 13] * 100.0 / total_letters
35              << "%"
36              << endl;
37      }
38      cout << endl << "Total letters in text --    " << total_letters
            << endl;
39      in.close();
40  }
```

The changes made to the solution program of Problem 4.5 are minor. The first change is on line 5 where the header file was included for the objects that allow output to and input from a file. The name of a file entered by the user on line 14 replaced the name of the string. On line 17 the name entered for the file was used in creating the object that communicates with the file. The scanning loop continued until it encountered the End Of File marker instead of stopping at the NULL at the end of the string. Otherwise the programs are nearly identical. However, this revised program is far more useful than the limited version.

Jack London's book *The Call of the Wild* can be used as an example of modern English. An example of slightly nonstandard English is provided by Samuel Clemens who described the dialects used in *The Adventures of Huckleberry Finn* by explaining:

```
In this book a number of dialects are used, to wit: the Missouri negro
dialect; the extremest form of the backwoods Southwestern dialect; the
ordinary "Pike County" dialect; and four modified varieties of this last.
```

Output of the C++ Program

```
This program will calculate the frequency of
        the letters 'a' through 'z' in a text file.

Enter the file to be opened    call.txt
```

a ->	11101 ->	8.05%			n ->	9901 ->	7.18%
b ->	2305 ->	1.67%			o ->	9413 ->	6.83%
c ->	3419 ->	2.48%			p ->	2265 ->	1.64%
d ->	7365 ->	5.34%			q ->	94 ->	0.07%
e ->	17235 ->	12.50%			r ->	7799 ->	5.65%
f ->	3222 ->	2.34%			s ->	8230 ->	5.97%
g ->	3314 ->	2.40%			t ->	12604 ->	9.14%
h ->	9801 ->	7.11%			u ->	3753 ->	2.72%
i ->	8617 ->	6.25%			v ->	1073 ->	0.78%
j ->	163 ->	0.12%			w ->	3673 ->	2.66%
k ->	1634 ->	1.18%			x ->	146 ->	0.11%
l ->	5518 ->	4.00%			y ->	2113 ->	1.53%
m ->	2984 ->	2.16%			z ->	172 ->	0.12%

```
Total letters in text --    137914


This program will calculate the frequency of
        the letters 'a' through 'z' in a text file.

Enter the file to be opened    finn.txt
```

a ->	25828 ->	8.45%			n ->	22771 ->	7.45%
b ->	5329 ->	1.74%			o ->	25448 ->	8.33%
c ->	5628 ->	1.84%			p ->	4034 ->	1.32%
d ->	16965 ->	5.55%			q ->	141 ->	0.05%
e ->	34448 ->	11.27%			r ->	13985 ->	4.58%
f ->	5499 ->	1.80%			s ->	17448 ->	5.71%
g ->	7519 ->	2.46%			t ->	29280 ->	9.58%
h ->	18745 ->	6.13%			u ->	9672 ->	3.16%
i ->	19350 ->	6.33%			v ->	2070 ->	0.68%
j ->	793 ->	0.26%			w ->	9402 ->	3.08%
k ->	4099 ->	1.34%			x ->	296 ->	0.10%
l ->	12292 ->	4.02%			y ->	7306 ->	2.39%
m ->	7121 ->	2.33%			z ->	130 ->	0.04%

```
Total letters in text --    305599
```

Solution Implemented in Visual Basic

```
1   Option Explicit
2   Private Sub cmdCount_Click()
3       Dim FileName, OutputStr, ptr, Str As String
4       Dim Letter(0 To 25) As Long
5       Dim TotalLetters, FileNumber, Ctr, strLen As Integer
6       Dim AsciiVal As Byte
```

```
7
8        Ctr = 1
9        TotalLetters = 0
10       FileName = txtFileName.Text
11       FileNumber = FreeFile
12       FileName = App.Path & "\" & FileName
13       Open FileName For Input As #FileNumber
14
15       Do While Not EOF(FileNumber)
16           Line Input #FileNumber, Str
17           strLen = Len(Str)
18           For Ctr = 1 To strLen
19               ptr = Mid(Str, Ctr, 1)
20               AsciiVal = Asc(ptr)
21               If ptr >= "a" And ptr <= "z" Then
22                   Letter(AsciiVal - 97) = Letter(AsciiVal - 97) + 1
23                   TotalLetters = TotalLetters + 1
24               ElseIf ptr >= "A" And ptr <= "Z" Then
25                   Letter(AsciiVal - 65) = Letter(AsciiVal - 65) + 1
26                   TotalLetters = TotalLetters + 1
27               End If
28           Next Ctr
29       Loop
30
31       lstOutput1.Clear
32       If TotalLetters > 0 Then
33           For Ctr = 0 To 12
34               Str = Space(6)
35               RSet Str = Format(Letter(Ctr))
36               OutputStr = Chr(Ctr + 97) & " -> " & Str & " -> "
37               Str = Space(6)
38               RSet Str = Format((Letter(Ctr) / TotalLetters), "0.00%")
39               OutputStr = OutputStr & Str
40               Str = Space(6)
41               RSet Str = Format(Letter(Ctr + 13))
42               OutputStr = " " & OutputStr & "     " & Chr(Ctr + 110) & _
43                   " -> " & Str & " -> "
44               Str = Space(6)
45               RSet Str = Format((Letter(Ctr + 13) / TotalLetters), "0.00%")
46               OutputStr = OutputStr & Str
47               lstOutput1.AddItem (OutputStr)
48           Next Ctr
49           Str = "There were " & TotalLetters & _
50               " letters in the file."
51           lblTotal.Caption = Str
52       End If
53       Close #FileNumber
54   End Sub
55
56   Private Sub cmdExit_Click()
57       Unload Me
58   End Sub
```

```
59
60   Private Sub cmdReset_Click()
61       txtFileName.Text = ""
62       Call lstOutput1.Clear
63       lblTotal.Caption = ""
64       txtFileName.SetFocus
65   End Sub
66
67   Private Sub Form_Activate()
68       txtFileName.SetFocus
69   End Sub
70
71   Private Sub Form_Load()
72       lblMessage.Caption = "This program will calculate the " & _
73           "frequency of the letters 'a' through 'z' in a file."
74       lblFileName.Caption = "Enter the name of the file to be opened."
75   End Sub
```

The changes to the original program are minor and are contained in a very few lines of code. Lines 10 through 13 open the file to be read. Importing the text is handled a line at a time (line 16) with the line being stored in the string Str. This allows the reading of the individual letters to be examined in the same fashion as the limited program, which also examined a string. Importing one line of text at a time requires nested loops with the inner loop counting letters and the outer loop reading in lines of text from the file until the EOF (End Of File) is reached.

Output of the Visual Basic Program—The Call of the Wild

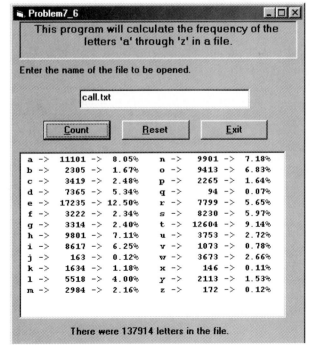

Output of the Visual Basic Program—The Adventures of Huckleberry Finn

Problem7_6					_ □ ✕

This program will calculate the frequency of the
letters 'a' through 'z' in a file.

Enter the name of the file to be opened.

finn.txt

Count	Reset	Exit

a ->	25828 ->	8.45%		n ->	22771 ->	7.45%
b ->	5329 ->	1.74%		o ->	25448 ->	8.33%
c ->	5628 ->	1.84%		p ->	4034 ->	1.32%
d ->	16965 ->	5.55%		q ->	141 ->	0.05%
e ->	34448 ->	11.27%		r ->	13985 ->	4.58%
f ->	5499 ->	1.80%		s ->	17448 ->	5.71%
g ->	7519 ->	2.46%		t ->	29280 ->	9.58%
h ->	18745 ->	6.13%		u ->	9672 ->	3.16%
i ->	19350 ->	6.33%		v ->	2070 ->	0.68%
j ->	793 ->	0.26%		w ->	9402 ->	3.08%
k ->	4099 ->	1.34%		x ->	296 ->	0.10%
l ->	12292 ->	4.02%		y ->	7306 ->	2.39%
m ->	7121 ->	2.33%		z ->	130 ->	0.04%

There were 305599 letters in the file.

Now we have reliable information about letter frequency in a large body of text. The program can answer questions such as what the eighth most common letter is or how many more times the sixth most common letter occurs than the seventh most common letter, but not conveniently. The program would be more useful if the data were sorted and numbered with the most frequently occurring letter first.

PROBLEM 7.7 *Determine the frequency of occurrence for each letter in an entire book and sort the information.*

Again there is no new problem to solve. Sorting is an operation that has already been developed in other programs. Tying the name of a letter to its count is merely a matter of putting the data into a structure variable. The greater utility is a product of adding features that are familiar and practiced. As in the previous programs the changes to the program are highlighted.

Solution Implemented in C++

```
1    // Problem 7.7
2    #include <stdio.h>
3    #include <conio.h>
4    #include <iomanip.h>
5    #include <fstream.h>
6
7    struct info
```

```
8    {
9       char name;
10      int count;
11   };
12   void main(void)
13   {
14      int counter, total_letters = 0, flag;
15      struct info sort[26], temp;
16      char incoming, name[100];
17      cout << "This program will calculate the frequency of "
18         << "\n\tthe letters 'a' through 'z' in a text file."
19         << "\n\nEnter the file to be opened    " << flush;
20      cin.getline(name,99,'\n');
21      cout.precision(2);
22      cout.setf(ios::fixed|ios::showpoint);
23      ifstream in(name);
24      for (counter = 0; counter < 26; counter++)
25      {
26         sort[counter].name = counter + 97;
27         sort[counter].count = 0;
28      }
29      while(in.good())
30      {
31         in.get(incoming);
32         if (incoming >= 'a' && incoming <= 'z')
33            sort[incoming - 97].count++, total_letters++;
34         if (incoming >= 'A' && incoming <= 'Z')
35            sort[incoming - 65].count++, total_letters++;
36      }
37      cout << endl;
38      do
39      {
40         flag = 0;
41         for (counter = 0; counter < 25; counter++)
42            if (sort[counter].count < sort[counter + 1].count)
43            {
44               temp = sort[counter];
45               sort[counter] = sort[counter + 1];
46               sort[counter + 1] = temp;
47               flag = 1;
48            }
49      }while(flag == 1);
50      for (counter = 0; counter < 13; counter++)
51      {
52         cout << setw(2) << counter + 1 << ")"
53            << setw(3) << sort[counter].name << " -> "
54            << setw(7) << sort[counter].count << " -> "
55            << setw(7) << sort[counter].count * 100.0 / total_letters << "%"
56            << setw(5) << counter + 14 << ")"
57            << setw(3) << sort[counter + 13].name << " -> "
58            << setw(7) << sort[counter + 13].count << " -> "
59            << setw(7) << sort[counter + 13].count * 100.0 / total_letters
```

```
60      }
61      cout << endl << "Total letters in the file --     "
62          << total_letters << endl;
63      in.close();
64  }
```

The greater utility is the result of only three changes to the program. Lines 7 through 11 plus 15 define the structure that will hold the information and declare the variables of this type. The loop on lines 24 through 28 initialize the structure variables with the name of the letter stored and the initial count of zero. The do/while loop on lines 38 through 49 performs the bubble sort on the data.

Output of the C++ Program

```
This program will calculate the frequency of
        the letters 'a' through 'z' in a text file.

Enter the file to be opened     2city.txt


 1)   e ->    72881 ->    12.49%    14)   w ->    13835 ->    2.37%
 2)   t ->    52397 ->     8.98%    15)   c ->    13223 ->    2.27%
 3)   a ->    47072 ->     8.07%    16)   f ->    13152 ->    2.25%
 4)   o ->    45116 ->     7.73%    17)   g ->    12121 ->    2.08%
 5)   n ->    41316 ->     7.08%    18)   y ->    11849 ->    2.03%
 6)   i ->    39773 ->     6.82%    19)   p ->     9452 ->    1.62%
 7)   h ->    38334 ->     6.57%    20)   b ->     8163 ->    1.40%
 8)   s ->    36770 ->     6.30%    21)   v ->     5065 ->    0.87%
 9)   r ->    35946 ->     6.16%    22)   k ->     4631 ->    0.79%
10)   d ->    27487 ->     4.71%    23)   x ->      666 ->    0.11%
11)   l ->    21479 ->     3.68%    24)   q ->      655 ->    0.11%
12)   u ->    16218 ->     2.78%    25)   j ->      623 ->    0.11%
13)   m ->    14928 ->     2.56%    26)   z ->      213 ->    0.04%

Total letters in the file --     583365
```

For this run of the program *A Tale of Two Cities* by Charles Dickens was chosen as the text to be examined. Notice that the relative letter frequency closely matches that of the other two books but not exactly. It might be more useful to have the program open two books at the same time, determine the letter frequencies for both, and display the results side by side for easy comparison. Could this be done with one more adaptation of the program? Of course it could. The task has been left as an exercise for the reader.

Solution Implemented in Visual Basic

```
1    Option Explicit
2    Private Type udtItem        ' User defined data type to combine
3         letter As Byte         ' a letter and it count in a single unit
4         count As Long
5    End Type
6    Dim Letters(0 To 25) As udtItem
7    Dim TotalLetters As Long
8
```

```
9    Private Sub cmdCount_Click()
10       Dim FileName, OutputStr, ptr, Str As String
11       Dim FileNumber, Ctr, strLen As Integer
14       Dim AsciiVal As Byte
15
16       Ctr = 1
17       TotalLetters = 0
18       FileName = txtFileName.Text
19       FileNumber = FreeFile
20       FileName = App.Path & "\" & FileName
21       Open FileName For Input As #FileNumber
22
23       For Ctr = 0 To 25
24           Letters(Ctr).letter = Ctr + 97
25           Letters(Ctr).count = 0
26       Next Ctr
27
28       Do While Not EOF(FileNumber)
29           Line Input #FileNumber, Str
30           strLen = Len(Str)
31           For Ctr = 1 To strLen
32               ptr = Mid(Str, Ctr, 1)
33               AsciiVal = Asc(ptr)
34               If ptr >= "a" And ptr <= "z" Then
35                   Letters(AsciiVal - 97).count = _
36                       Letters(AsciiVal - 97).count + 1
37                   TotalLetters = TotalLetters + 1
38               ElseIf ptr >= "A" And ptr <= "Z" Then
39                   Letters(AsciiVal - 65).count = _
40                       Letters(AsciiVal - 65).count + 1
41                   TotalLetters = TotalLetters + 1
42               End If
43           Next Ctr
44       Loop
45
46       lstOutput1.Clear
47       If TotalLetters > 0 Then
48           Call display
49           Str = "There were " & TotalLetters & _
50               " letters in the file."
51           lblTotal.Caption = Str
52       End If
53       Close #FileNumber
54   End Sub
55   Private Sub cmdExit_Click()
56       Unload Me
57   End Sub
58
59   Private Sub cmdReset_Click()
60       txtFileName.Text = ""
61       Call lstOutput1.Clear
62       lblTotal.Caption = ""
```

```
63        txtFileName.SetFocus
64   End Sub
65
66   Private Sub cmdSort_Click()
67        Dim inloop, outloop As Integer
68        Dim temp As udtItem
69        For outloop = 0 To 24
70            For inloop = (outloop + 1) To 25
71                If Letters(outloop).count < Letters(inloop).count Then
72                    temp = Letters(outloop)
73                    Letters(outloop) = Letters(inloop)
74                    Letters(inloop) = temp
75                End If
76            Next inloop
77        Next outloop
78        Call display
79   End Sub
80   Private Sub display()
81        Dim Ctr As Integer
82        Dim Str, OutputStr As String
83        lstOutput1.Clear
84        For Ctr = 0 To 12
85            Str = Space(6)
86            RSet Str = Format(Letters(Ctr).count)
87            OutputStr = Chr(Letters(Ctr).letter) & " -> " & Str & " -> "
88            Str = Space(6)
89            RSet Str = Format((Letters(Ctr).count / TotalLetters), _
90                "0.00%")
91            OutputStr = OutputStr & Str
92            Str = Space(6)
93            RSet Str = Format(Letters(Ctr + 13).count)
94            OutputStr = " " & OutputStr & "     " & _
95                Chr(Letters(Ctr + 13).letter) & " -> " & Str & " -> "
96            Str = Space(6)
97            RSet Str = Format((Letters(Ctr + 13).count / _
98                TotalLetters), "0.00%")
99            OutputStr = OutputStr & Str
100           lstOutput1.AddItem (OutputStr)
101       Next Ctr
102
103  End Sub
104  Private Sub Form_Activate()
105       txtFileName.SetFocus
106  End Sub
107
108      Private Sub Form_Load()
109      lblMessage.Caption = "This program will calculate the " & _
110          "frequency of the letters 'a' through 'z' in a file" & _
111          " and sort the information by letter count."
112      lblFileName.Caption = "Enter the name of the file to be opened."
113  End Sub
```

A user-defined data type called Item was declared and defined on lines 2 through 5. The array of variables of the type Item was also declared globally as a matter of convenience on line 6. The use of the data type made certain adjustments necessary in naming throughout the programs, although the logic was identical to the logic developed in the Visual Basic solution to the previous problem.

Since the objective of the program was to sort the data read from the input file, the code associated with the cmdSort command button on lines 66 through 79 is new to the program. However, the logic of the sort routine is merely the select sort that was described in Chapter 4. Notice that on line 71 it is the information in the count members of the Letters variables that is compared for sorting purposes; however, it is the entire Letters variables that are actually sorted (lines 72 to 74).

One other change has been made in the program. Because the output display is created twice, once for the cmdCount and again within the cmdSort, it is reasonable to create a display() function rather than to write the code twice. Line 48 calls the display() function in the count code and line 78 calls display() after the sorting is finished. The display code is identical to the display code for Problem 7.7 except for the variable naming that was changed to reference the Letters variables.

Output of the Visual Basic Program

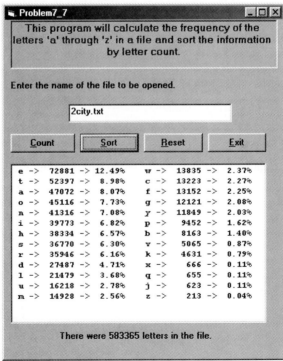

Looking back to Problem 1.5, which posed a question concerning the pull of gravity on an astronaut aboard the space shuttle, the problem appears to have very little utility. After all, regardless of the pull of gravity, the forward motion of the space shuttle causes the astronaut to float as though there were no gravity. But the question can be turned around. It would be more interesting to know how fast the shuttle must go to produce the floating effect. However, astronauts are not sent into space so they can float and the problem and its solution are still not very useful. This suggests that the focus should not be on the astronaut at all.

The real question is how fast the shuttle must go in order for the shuttle to float. Or, stated more properly,

---

PROBLEM 7.8   *How fast must a satellite travel in order to stay in orbit?*

This represents a considerable step beyond the astronaut problem and it would be good to reexamine the information we have to work with.

Initial Data: **1.** The altitude of the satellite is provided by the user.
   2. The force of gravity is inversely proportional to the altitude.
   3. The radius of the earth is 3,960 miles.
   4. The acceleration due to gravity at sea level is approximately 32.174 ft/sec^2.
   5. An object in motion stays in motion until acted upon by an outside force.
   6. The velocity of the satellite is tangential to the orbit.
   7. To stay in orbit the satellite must travel forward along that tangential path sufficiently far so that, after it falls due to gravity, the net difference in distance from the center of the earth is zero.

Output: Find the velocity that offsets the pull of gravity.

Items 6 and 7 may not be immediately obvious. An expansion of the illustration used for the astronaut problem will help (Rule 3—The Picture Rule).

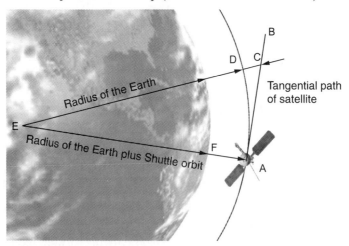

The forward motion on a satellite at position *A* would cause it to travel along the straight line path *AB* if it were not for the pull of earth's gravity (an outside force). *CD* represents the falling path that the satellite would take if it were motionless at point *C*. The distance *AC* is approximately the same distance as the curved path *AD*. The shorter the distances are the better this approximation is.

If the distances between points are added to the foregoing information:

1. *EF* = 3,960 miles
2. *FA* = a known distance entered by the user
3. *CD* = the distances a motionless object would fall from point *C* in a given amount of time
4. *AD* ≈ *AC*

a picture begins to develop of a right triangle and enough information to use the Pythagorean Theorem. *EA* is the radius of the earth plus the altitude of the satellite. *EC* is the distance *EA* plus the fall distance *CD*. It is also the hypotenuse of the right triangle. *AC* is the distance we're looking for. The only missing piece is *CD*.

But the distance *CD* is based on the time an object is allowed to fall from point *CD*, which can be any amount of time we choose as long as it's small. We can choose 30 seconds and base all the calculations on that time unit. *CD* is the distance fallen in 30 seconds; *AC* is the forward distance of the satellite in 30 seconds; and *EC* is the distance of the satellite from the center of the earth if it did not fall for 30 seconds.

Calculating the distance fallen in 30 seconds is simple. The formula was developed in Problem 1.7, the falling ball problem.

$$\text{distance} = .5 \times \text{gravity} \times \text{time}^2$$

There is the slight problem that gravity at the altitude of the satellite is not the same as gravity at sea level but the new value for gravity can be calculated as it was in Problem 1.5, the astronaut problem.

$$\text{gravity\_at\_altitude} = 32.174 \times \frac{(\text{earth\_radius})^2}{(\text{earth\_radius} + \text{altitude})^2}$$

The preceding logic can be restated in terms of working the problem backward. Consider the end point: The speed of the satellite is required.

1. We can determine the speed if we have a distance and a time; that is, $D = rt$.
2. We can set any time frame that is convenient. By choosing 30 seconds we have a value for time, which means the problem can be solved if we can find the distance *AC*. Over 30 seconds, *AC* is virtually identical to *AD*.
3. Distance *AC* is one arm of a right triangle. We can find that distance by using the Pythagorean theorem if we have the other two arms.
4. We have the distance *EA*, which means we can solve the problem if we have the hypotenuse.
5. We can find the distance *EC* if we have the distances *ED* and *DC*. We have the distance *ED*, which means we can solve the problem if we can find the distance *DC*.

6. We have the formula for finding the distance traveled by a falling object; that is, $d = .5 \times g \times t^2$. We have the time, 30 seconds, so we can solve the problem if we can find the value of the acceleration due to gravity at the orbital altitude.

7. We can find the acceleration due to gravity because we've already solved the problem involving the reduction in acceleration due to gravity based on the inverse square law (Problem 1.5).

8. So, the value for g at the orbital altitude makes possible the calculation for the distance DC, which makes possible the calculation for the distance EC, which makes possible the calculation for the distance AC, which makes possible the calculation for the speed of the satellite, which solves the problem.

This is the last piece of information needed and the pseudocode can be written.

Pseudocode

1. Begin
2.   Declare variables.
3.   Begin loop.
4.   Prompt user for altitude.
5.   Calculate radius of orbit.
6.   Calculate gravity at altitude.
7.   Calculate fall distance for 30 seconds.
8.   Calculate satellite distance for 30 seconds.
9.   Calculate satellite speed.
10.   Display results.
11.   Calculate time for orbit.
12.   Display results.
13.   Prompt user for continue.
14.   End loop.
15. End

Flowchart

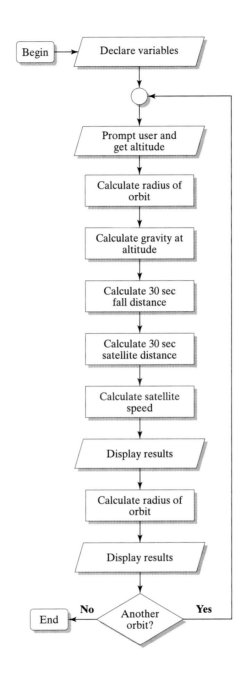

Solution Implemented in C++

```
1    //  Problem 7.8
2    #include <iostream.h>
3    #include <math.h>
4    #define PI 3.1415926536
5
6    void main(void)
7    {
8       double orbital_radius, fall, orbital_distance, satellite_speed;
9       double orbit, time_for_orbit, gravity, altitude;
10      char input[20], again;
11      do
12      {
13        cout << "This program calculates the speed required to "
14           << endl << "     keep a satellite in orbit." << endl << endl
15           << "          Enter the orbital altitude in miles . .    "
16           << flush;
17        cin.getline(input, 19, '\n');
18        altitude = atof(input);
19        cout.setf(ios::fixed|ios::showpoint);
20        cout.precision(2);
21        orbital_radius = 3960 + altitude;   // in miles
22        gravity = 32.174 * (3960 * 3960) / (orbital_radius *
23           orbital_radius);      // in feet/sec^2
24        fall = .5 * gravity * 30 * 30;
25        fall /= 5280;            // in miles per 30 sec
26        orbital_distance = sqrt(pow(fall + orbital_radius, 2) -
27           pow(orbital_radius,2));      // in miles per 30 sec
28        satellite_speed = orbital_distance * 60 * 2;   // miles / hour
29        cout << "\n        The satellite must travel at "
30           << satellite_speed  << " miles per hour." << endl << endl;
31        orbit = PI * 2 * orbital_radius;
32        time_for_orbit = orbit / satellite_speed;
33        cout << "The satellite orbits the earth in " << time_for_orbit
34           << " hours." << endl << endl;
35        cout << "Calculate another orbit?  (y/n)     " << flush;
36        cin.get(again);
37        cin.ignore (1, '\n');
38        cout << endl;
39      }while(again == 'y' || again == 'Y');
40    }
```

The critical element in solving this problem is Rule 2—The Units Rule. The calculations involve miles and feet. Acceleration is given in ft/sec^2 and speed is in miles per hour. There is also the time frame to consider, which uses distances in feet per 30 seconds and miles per 30 seconds. The conversions are simple; the danger is in not keeping the units with the numbers.

Output of the C++ Program

```
This program calculates the speed required to
    keep a satellite in orbit.

        Enter the orbital altitude in miles . .   200

        The satellite must travel at 17256.45 miles per hour.

The satellite orbits the earth in 1.51 hours.

Calculate another orbit?  (y/n)    y

This program calculates the speed required to
    keep a satellite in orbit.

        Enter the orbital altitude in miles . .   400

        The satellite must travel at 16855.68 miles per hour.

The satellite orbits the earth in 1.63 hours.

Calculate another orbit?  (y/n)    n
```

The intriguing feature of this problem is that it began as a problem with no data to work with and no apparent starting point. The solution began with a picture (Rule 3). The picture indicated that gravity would be involved and our experience with the falling ball problem (Problem 1.7) would likely be part of the solution. Since the problem involved the force of gravity at a significant distance above sea level, our experience with the astronaut problem (Problem 1.5) would also come into play. And lastly the picture showed a right triangle that involved some known values and the one we were trying to determine, which suggested working the problem backward (Rule 4). Knowledge of the Pythagorean Theorem finished the solution.

Actually one more feature was thrown into the program that doesn't apply to the original problem. The calculations include the time required for the satellite to circle the earth. This orbital time is of interest because it raises new questions. What would happen if the satellite circled the earth in exactly 24 hours? And what altitude and speed would enable the satellite to make the trip in one day?

A satellite that circles the earth in one day is in geosynchronous orbit. Satellites in this orbit, assuming they are traveling west to east and circle the earth above the equator, appear to observers on the earth to be stationary or parked above a single spot. A satellite that (apparently) never moves is extremely useful for relaying communications signals.

Solution Implemented in Visual Basic

```
1    Option Explicit
2    Private Const PI As Double = 3.14159265358979
3
4    Private Sub cmdCalculate_Click()
```

```
5      Dim altitude, orbital_radius, orbital_distance As Double
6      Dim orbit, gravity, time_for_orbit, fall As Double
7      Dim satellite_speed As Double
8
9      altitude = CDbl(txtInput.Text)
10     orbital_radius = 3960 + altitude
11     gravity = 32.174 * (3960# * 3960#) / _
12         (orbital_radius * orbital_radius)
13     fall = 0.5 * gravity * 30 * 30    'distance that the satellite
14                                       'falls due to gravity in 30 sec
15     fall = fall / 5280          'fall converted to miles per 30 sec
16     orbital_distance = (((fall + orbital_radius) ^ 2) - _
17         (orbital_radius ^ 2)) ^ 0.5
18     satellite_speed = orbital_distance * 60 * 2 'Convert to mph
19     lblSpeed.Caption = "The satellite must travel " & _
20         Format(satellite_speed, "##.###") & _
21         " miles per hour to remain in orbit."
22     orbit = PI * 2 * orbital_radius
23     time_for_orbit = orbit / satellite_speed
24     lblTime.Caption = "The satellite orbits the earth in " & _
25         Format(time_for_orbit, "##.###") & " hours"
26 End Sub
27
28 Private Sub cmdExit_Click()
29     Unload Me
30 End Sub
31
32 Private Sub cmdReset_Click()
33     txtInput.Text = ""
34     lblSpeed.Caption = ""
35     lblTime.Caption = ""
36     txtInput.SetFocus
37 End Sub
38
39 Private Sub Form_Activate()
40     txtInput.SetFocus
41 End Sub
42
43 Private Sub Form_Load()
44     lblMessage.Caption = "This program calculates the speed " & _
45         "required to keep a satellite in orbit."
46     lblInput.Caption = "Enter the altitude of the satellite " & _
47         "in miles."
48 End Sub
```

Output of the Visual Basic Program

```
┌─────────────────────────────────────────────┐
│ ▪ Problem7_8                        _ □ X     │
├─────────────────────────────────────────────┤
│                                               │
│   This program calculates the speed required to│
│          keep a satellite in orbit.           │
│                                               │
│    Enter the altitude of the    ┌───────────┐ │
│       satellite in miles.       │   200|     │ │
│                                 └───────────┘ │
│                                               │
│     The satellite must travel    ┌──────────┐ │
│    17256.449 miles per hour to   │ Calculate│ │
│          remain in orbit.        └──────────┘ │
│                                               │
│                                  ┌──────────┐ │
│   The satellite orbits the earth in│  Reset  │ │
│             1.515 hours          └──────────┘ │
│                                  ┌──────────┐ │
│                                  │  Exit    │ │
│                                  └──────────┘ │
└─────────────────────────────────────────────┘
```

PROBLEM 7.9   *What is the altitude and speed of a satellite that orbits the earth once in exactly 24 hours?*

The problem as stated contains little information beyond the 24-hour orbital time but, because of our experience in solving other problems, there is really much more to work with.

Initial Data: **1.** The orbital time is required to be 24 hours.

2. The solution to Problem 7.8 allows us to calculate the time for a satellite to orbit the earth once at any given altitude.

3. We can zero in on the solution by guessing an altitude, finding the time required for one orbit, and revising the guess higher or lower depending on whether the time is less than or greater than 24 hours.

4. If the orbital time is less than 24 hours, the orbit should be higher. If the orbital time is more than 24 hours, the orbit should be lower.

5. To make our system of guessing work we need upper and lower limits for our guessing range.

6. The altitude must be greater than zero.

7. The moon goes around the earth in 28 days, which is more than one day, so the distance from the earth to the moon can be an upper limit.

8. While the lunar orbit is elliptical, the average distance from the earth is approximately 239,000 miles. This number is easy to find on the Internet but, assuming we don't know it and want to be on the safe side for the upper limit of the guessing, we can use 1 million miles for an upper limit.

Output: Find the altitude at which a satellite will circle the earth once per day.

A first pass on the pseudocode would be:

1. Make an initial guess for the orbit of 1,000,000 miles and an initial adjustment of 500,000 miles.
2. Use the solution to Problem 7.8 to calculate the time required to circle the earth.
3. Compare the time to 24 hours. If the difference is small, end the loop; if not, adjust the altitude.
4. Divide the adjustment by two.
5. Go to step 2.

Step 3 indicates that the problem is solved when the difference between 24 hours and the calculated time for one orbit is small. Small is an arbitrary number but can be set at one second or 1/86,400 of a day. This number is particularly unimportant since the solution to the problem is not really the speed of the satellite but the average speed of the satellite. Several factors cause satellites to speed up and slow down in the course of a single orbit.

Pseudocode

1. Begin
2.   Declare variables and initialize.
3.   Initialize altitude to 1,000,000, adjustment to 500,000, and tolerance to 1/86,400.
4.   Message to user.
5.   Begin calculating loop.
6.   Calculate orbital radius.
7.   Calculate force of gravity at altitude.
8.   Calculate the 30 second fall distance.
9.   Calculate the 30 second satellite distance.
10.   Calculate the satellite speed.
11.   Calculate orbit circumference.
12.   Calculate the time for one orbit.
13.   Calculate the error (24–orbit_time).
14.   If error is negative
15.   Subtract adjustment from altitude.
16.   Else
17.   Add adjustment to altitude.
18.   Make new adjustment.
19.   Display results.
20.   End loop if error is less than tolerance.
21.   Display final results.
22. End

Solution Implemented in C++

```
1   //  Problem 7.9
2   #include <iostream.h>
3   #include <iomanip.h>
```

```
4   #include <math.h>
5   #define PI 3.1415926536
6
7   void main(void)
8   {
9       double altitude = 1e6, tolerance = 1 / 86400.0, adjustment = 500000;
10      double orbital_radius, fall, orbital_distance, satellite_speed, error;
11      double orbit, time_for_orbit, gravity;
12      int counter = 0;
13      cout << "This program calculates the speed and altitude required to "
14          << endl << "   keep a satellite in geosynchronous orbit.\n\n";
15      cout.setf(ios::fixed|ios::showpoint);
16      cout.precision(4);
17      cout << "      Altitude       Speed        Time" << endl << endl;
18      do
19      {
20          orbital_radius = 3960 + altitude;       // in mile
21          gravity = 32.174 * (3960 * 3960) / (orbital_radius *
                orbital_radius);
22          fall = .5 * gravity * 30 * 30;
23          fall /= 5280;            // miles in 30 sec
24          orbital_distance = sqrt(pow(fall + orbital_radius, 2) -
25              pow(orbital_radius,2));          // in miles
26          satellite_speed = orbital_distance * 60 * 2;   // miles / hour
27          orbit = PI * 2 * orbital_radius;
28          time_for_orbit = orbit / satellite_speed;
29          error = 24 - time_for_orbit;
30          if (error < 0)
31              altitude -= adjustment;
32          else
33              altitude += adjustment;
34          adjustment *=.5;
35          counter++;
36          cout << setw(3) << counter << setw(13) << altitude << setw(13)
37              << satellite_speed << setw(13) << time_for_orbit << endl;
38      }while(fabs (error) > tolerance);
39      cout << endl <<"Geosynchronous orbit is " << altitude
40          << " miles above the earth."
41          << endl << "   The satellite travels " << satellite_speed
42          << " miles per hour " << endl
43          << "   and circles the earth in 24 hours." << endl;
44  }
```

The process of zeroing in on the solution is very similar to the solution of the square root problem. In both problems it was necessary to be able to test the accuracy of the guess. The test in the square root problem involved squaring the guess and comparing the result to the input number. Here the test involves more calculations but the idea is the same. The guessed altitude implied a definite satellite speed and a definite orbit circumference, which implied a definite time for one orbit, which could be compared to 24 hours.

Output of the C++ Program

This program calculates the speed and altitude required to
keep a satellite in geosynchronous orbit.

	Altitude	Speed	Time
1	500000.0000	1110.6451	5679.6420
2	250000.0000	1567.5999	2019.9504
3	125000.0000	2208.2620	722.5944
4	62500.0000	3098.8870	261.4744
5	31250.0000	4316.7123	96.7358
6	15625.0000	5930.6234	37.3032
7	23437.5000	7951.9216	15.4750
8	19531.2500	6723.2307	25.6043
9	21484.3750	7260.7344	20.3285
10	22460.9375	6976.5007	22.9157
11	21972.6563	6846.3547	24.2476
12	22216.7969	6910.5087	23.5785
13	22338.8672	6878.2073	23.9123
14	22277.8320	6862.2256	24.0797
15	22308.3496	6870.2025	23.9960
16	22293.0908	6866.2106	24.0378
17	22285.4614	6868.2057	24.0169
18	22281.6467	6869.2039	24.0064
19	22279.7394	6869.7031	24.0012
20	22280.6931	6869.9528	23.9986
21	22281.1699	6869.8280	23.9999
22	22280.9315	6869.7656	24.0005
23	22280.8123	6869.7968	24.0002
24	22280.7527	6869.8124	24.0001
25	22280.7825	6869.8202	24.0000
26	22280.7676	6869.8163	24.0000
27	22280.7750	6869.8182	24.0000

Geosynchronous orbit is 22280.7750 miles above the earth.
The satellite travels 6869.8182 miles per hour
and circles the earth in 24 hours.

Solution Implemented in Visual Basic

```
1    Option Explicit
2    Private Const PI As Double = 3.14159265358979
3
4    Private Sub cmdCalculate_Click()
5        Dim altitude, tolerance, adjustment As Double
6        Dim orbital_radius, fall, orbital_distance As Double
7        Dim satellite_speed, error, orbit As Double
8        Dim time_for_orbit, gravity As Double
9        Dim counter As Integer
10
11       counter = 0
12       altitude = 1000000#
13       tolerance = 1# / 86400#
```

```
14      adjustment = 500000
15      Do
16          orbital_radius = 3960 + altitude
17          gravity = 32.174 * (3960# * 3960#) / _
18              (orbital_radius * orbital_radius)
19          fall = 0.5 * gravity * 30 * 30
20          fall = fall / 5280
21          orbital_distance = ((fall + orbital_radius) * _
22          (fall + orbital_radius) - (orbital_radius ^ 2)) ^ 0.5
23          satellite_speed = orbital_distance * 60 * 2
24          orbit = PI * 2 * orbital_radius
25          time_for_orbit = orbit / satellite_speed
26          error = 24# - time_for_orbit
27          msgTable.Row = counter + 1
28          msgTable.Col = 0
29          msgTable.Text = Format(counter + 1, "@@@@")
30          msgTable.Col = 1
31          msgTable.Text = Format(FormatNumber(altitude, 0), _
32              "@@@@@@@@@@@@@@@@")
33          msgTable.Col = 2
34          msgTable.Text = Format(FormatNumber(satellite_speed, 2), _
35              "@@@@@@@@@@@@@@@@")
36          msgTable.Col = 3
37          msgTable.Text = Format(FormatNumber(time_for_orbit, 6), _
38              "@@@@@@@@@@@@@@@@")
39
40          If error < 0 Then
41              altitude = altitude - adjustment
42          Else
43              altitude = altitude + adjustment
44          End If
45          adjustment = adjustment * 0.5
46          counter = counter + 1
47      Loop While Abs(error) > tolerance
48      lblOutput.Caption = "Geosynchronous orbit is " & _
49          Format(altitude, "#.####") & _
50          " miles above the earth.  The satellite travels at " & _
51          Format(satellite_speed, "#.##") & _
52          " miles per hour and circles the earth in " & _
53          "precisely 24 hours."
54  End Sub
55
56  Private Sub cmdExit_Click()
57      Unload Me
58  End Sub
59
60  Private Sub Form_Load()
61      lblMessage.Caption = "This program calculates the speed and " & _
62          "altitude required to keep a satellite in geosynchronous " & _
63          "orbit."
64      msgTable.Rows = 30
65      msgTable.Cols = 4
```

```
66      msgTable.ColWidth(0) = 600
67      msgTable.ColWidth(1) = 2200
68      msgTable.ColWidth(2) = 2200
69      msgTable.ColWidth(3) = 2100
70      msgTable.Row = 0
71      msgTable.Col = 1
72      msgTable.Text = "      Altitude in miles"
73      msgTable.Col = 2
74      msgTable.Text = "        Speed in MPH"
75      msgTable.Col = 3
76      msgTable.Text = "        Time in hours"
77  End Sub
```

Output of the Visual Basic Program

Problem7_9

This program calculates the speed and altitude required
to keep a satellite in geosynchronous orbit.   [Calculate]   [Exit]

	Altitude in miles	Speed in MPH	Time in hours
1	1,000,000	1,110.65	5,679.641966
2	500,000	1,567.60	2,019.950359
3	250,000	2,208.26	722.594395
4	125,000	3,098.89	261.474384
13	22,217	6,878.21	23.912287
14	22,339	6,862.23	24.079747
15	22,278	6,870.20	23.995968
16	22,308	6,866.21	24.037845
17	22,293	6,868.21	24.016904
18	22,285	6,869.20	24.006435
19	22,282	6,869.70	24.001201
20	22,280	6,869.95	23.998585
21	22,281	6,869.83	23.999893
22	22,281	6,869.77	24.000547
23	22,281	6,869.80	24.000220
24	22,281	6,869.81	24.000057
25	22,281	6,869.82	23.999975
26	22,281	6,869.82	24.000016
27	22,281	6,869.82	23.999995

Geosynchronous orbit is 22280.775 miles above the earth. The
satellite travels at 6869.82 miles per hour and circles the earth in
precisely 24 hours.

Clearly, there is nothing new in the solution to Problem 7.9. The solution is a combination of two already solved problems. By combining the calculations involved in the satellite problem (Problem 7.8) and the successive approximation routine of the square root problem (Problems 3.1 and 7.1), the orbital characteristics of a geosynchronous satellite are found.

In the end problem solving, like programming, is seen to be an iterative process. Solutions that were limited in order to make the problem manageable often lead to insight that leads to a plan for removing those limitations and for expanding the solution to be more encompassing. On subsequent revisions the solutions may become more accurate, wider in scope, more inclusive, more useful, or more expansive.

CHAPTER 8

Advanced Techniques

8.1 ERROR TRAPPING

To this point an assumption has been made in each problem examined. The assumption has been that the user of the program would behave properly and, if prompted for an integer, would not enter 4.567 and, if prompted for a number, would not enter "bird." This is a fairly safe assumption if the programmer and the user are the same person but that is often not the case.

But for any user, even the programmer (problem solver) himself, things can go wrong. Consider the following code designed to provide the width of a rectangle after the user enters the area and length.

```
#include <iostream.h>


void main (void)
{
    double area, length, width;
    cout << "Enter the area    " << flush;
    cin >> area;
    cout << "Enter the length  " << flush;
    cin >> length;
    cout << "The width is      " << area / length << endl;
}
```

The program works without a problem unless the user makes a mistake and hits the 'r' key instead of the '5' key for the length.

```
Enter the area    10
Enter the length  r
The width is     -1.08038e-061
```

Now the program provides an answer that makes no sense. Of course, the problem here is obvious and no one would expect a reasonable answer if the length of the rectangle were 'r'. On the other hand, the problem may be more subtle. Consider a program that is sequencing through a series of numbers, taking the reciprocal of each number.

```
#include <iostream.h>

void main (void)
{
    double number, x;
    cout << "Enter the number    " << flush;
    cin >> number;
    for (x = number; x < number + 10; x++)
        cout << "The reciprocal of " << x << " is " << 1 / x << endl;
}
```

The program properly delivers the expected reciprocals,

```
Enter the number    5
The reciprocal of 5 is 0.2
The reciprocal of 6 is 0.166667
The reciprocal of 7 is 0.142857
The reciprocal of 8 is 0.125
The reciprocal of 9 is 0.111111
The reciprocal of 10 is 0.1
The reciprocal of 11 is 0.0909091
The reciprocal of 12 is 0.0833333
The reciprocal of 13 is 0.0769231
The reciprocal of 14 is 0.0714286
```

unless the starting number is a negative integer between −10 and zero. For these cases the program will encounter division by zero, which is undefined. Newer versions of Windows have built-in error trapping that handles the divide by zero error. Under other operating systems the program may terminate unexpectedly and represent a problem to be solved by the programmer.

Error trapping of this type usually involves an if() statement that handles the special case that might cause a problem.

PROBLEM 8.1   *Determine the reciprocals of 10 integers starting at a number chosen by the user.*

In this case the problem of determining reciprocals is trivial. The objective is to ensure that the program runs correctly even if the user enters a starting value that leads to a division by zero. The important item to remember about error trapping is that to successfully solve the problem and avoid the error, the program must catch the error *before* the error occurs. That is, the error must be anticipated, not reacted to.

The relevant initial data is that division will take place and that a divisor of zero will cause a problem. The solution is to test the divisor and, if it is not zero, proceed with the division. If it is zero, something else must be done. Typically this would be a message to the user that something irregular has occurred.

Pseudocode

1. Begin
2. Declare variables.
3. Message to user and prompt for input.

4.   Begin loop for 10 cycles.
5.   If taking the reciprocal will result in division by zero
6.   Display division by zero message.
7.   Else
8.   Perform the division and display the result.
9.   End the loop.
10. End

Flowchart

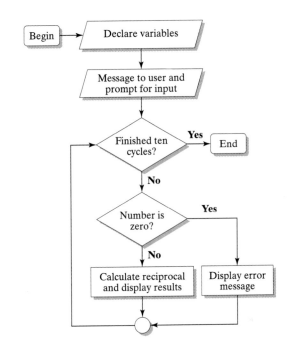

Solution Implemented in C++

```
1   //  Problem 8.1
2   #include <iostream.h>
3
4   void main (void)
5   {
6       int number, x;
7       cout << "Enter the number     " << flush;
8       cin >> number;
9       for (x = number; x < number + 10; x++)
10      {
11          if ( x == 0)
12              cout << "Division by zero is undefined." << endl;
13          else
14              cout << "The reciprocal of " << x << " is " << 1.0 / x << endl;
15      }
16  }
```

Output of the C++ Program

```
Enter the number     -5
The reciprocal of -5 is -0.2
The reciprocal of -4 is -0.25
The reciprocal of -3 is -0.333333
The reciprocal of -2 is -0.5
The reciprocal of -1 is -1
Division by zero is undefined.
The reciprocal of 1 is 1
The reciprocal of 2 is 0.5
The reciprocal of 3 is 0.333333
The reciprocal of 4 is 0.25
```

Solution Implemented in Visual Basic

```
1    Option Explicit
2
3    Private Sub cmdCalc_Click()
4        Dim x As Double
5        lblAnswer.Caption = " "
6        x = CDbl(txtInput.Text)
7        Do While x < txtInput.Text + 10
8            If x = 0 Then
9                lblAnswer.Caption = lblAnswer.Caption & vbCr & _
10                    "        Division by zero is undefined"
11            Else
12                lblAnswer.Caption = lblAnswer.Caption & vbCr & _
13                    "        The reciprocal of " & x & _
14                        " is " & Format(1 / x, ".000000")
15            End If
16            x = x + 1
17        Loop
18   End Sub
19
20   Private Sub cmdExit_Click()
21       Unload Me
22   End Sub
23
24   Private Sub Form_Activate()
25       Call txtInput.SetFocus
26   End Sub
27
28   Private Sub Form_Load()
29       lblTitle.Caption = "This program calculates the reciprocal " & _
30           "of the number entered and the next nine integers."
31       lblInput.Caption = "Enter the number"
32   End Sub
```

Output of the Visual Basic Program

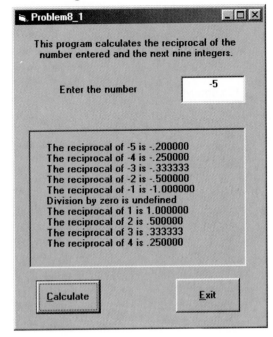

Division by zero can make a program terminate unexpectedly. Still worse is a program that makes an error and merely continues. This is more insidious, leading the user to believe he has a correct answer when the program ends, when in fact that is not the case. Problem 6.6, the basketball court problem, provides an example.

8.2   HANDLING INPUT

If the axes for the semiellipse in the basketball court problem are 71 and 93, the program produces the following output.

```
This program calculates the shape of a semielliptical basketball
court and the amount of cement required to pour the slab.
        Enter half of the major axis (ft) . . 71

        Enter half of the minor axis (ft) . . 93
The surface area of the court is 10371.968806 sq. ft.
The amount of cement required is 160.061247 cu. yd.
```

If the user makes an error in entering the information and enters 71 and 9w for the axes, the result is quite different.

```
This program calculates the shape of a semielliptical basketball
court and the amount of cement required to pour the slab.

        Enter half of the major axis (ft) . . 71
```

```
     Enter half of the minor axis (ft) . . 9w

     Enter the depth of the slab (in) . . 5
```

```
The surface area of the court is 1003.738917 sq. ft.
The amount of cement required is 15.489798 cu. yd.
```

A result of 15 cubic yards is considerably different than 160 cubic yards. The problem is that the 9w was accepted as input without a warning to the user that something was wrong. Actually there are two alternatives, both bad, that might have resulted from the input of 9w. If the variable storing the input is defined as a floating-point number, the input read by the program actually ends with the first nonproper key hit by the user. If the nonproper input, the 'w', is not removed from the input stream, then the third request for input, the depth, is given the 'w'. When the program attempts to make calculations without a proper value for depth, it terminates unexpectedly.

The second possibility is far worse. If the inappropriate character is removed by the `cin.ignore(3,'\n')` statement, as it has been in the basketball court problem, then the program proceeds normally, except the value stored for the minor axis is 9 instead of the intended 93. This is a more significant problem because an incorrect answer is given with no indication that a mistake has been made. Problem 8.2 addresses the issue of user errors in entering data.

PROBLEM 8.2   *How can we determine if the input for a program is correct?*

The first step is to be clear about the meaning of the problem. If the user enters 92 when he intends 93, there is little that the program can do. Computers are not yet sophisticated enough to read minds. However, the program can guard against accidental keystrokes that would invalidate the data. This type of error checking is commonly seen in computerized forms that will not allow the user to continue unless the previous data, e.g., a social security number, a zip code, or an e-mail address, is correct.

The immediate problem here is how to ensure that the input values for the basketball court dimensions are proper floating-point numbers. The definition of a floating-point number provides a significant amount of initial data.

Initial Data: **1.** Acceptable characters for floating-point numbers are the digits 0 through 9.

2. Plus and minus signs are acceptable only in the first position.

3. There may or may not be a decimal point but there may not be more than one.

4. In order to check the validity of each character the input should be accepted as a character array.

5. If all the elements of the input string prove to be valid characters, a function exists to convert a string into a floating-point number.

Outcome: Guarantee that the input is a proper floating-point number.

There are a number of approaches that can be taken toward a solution of this problem. The simplest is to be clear about which characters are allowed to appear in a floating-point number and which are not. This information becomes the basis for the test conditions.

1. Clearly, the digits zero through nine are permitted.
2. A plus sign or a minus sign is permitted as the first character but nowhere else in the number.
3. A decimal point is permitted but only once. A second decimal point is invalid.

The format of the solution should be to prompt the user for a floating-point number but to accept the input as a string. After the user has completed the input, the program should examine the input string and determine if the string contains only valid characters. If no invalid characters are found, the string is converted into a floating-point number that can be used in making calculations. If even one invalid character is found, the program should print an error message to the screen and prompt the user for another number. Some sophistication can be added to the program and customized error messages displayed to tell the user just what mistake has been made, but here we'll keep it simple and merely display a general error message and prompt for another input.

The validity tests can be made to check for valid characters or invalid characters. Since there are fewer valid characters and most of them are consecutive (zero through nine) in the ASCII table, it will be easier to test for valid characters. If a character is found that is not in this set, a flag should be set that indicates the user should reenter the number.

Pseudocode

1. Begin
2.   Declare variables.
3.   Begin do/while loop that runs until a valid string is entered.
4.   Initialize variables (reset to zero the counter and the flags).
5.   Prompt the user for input and get input.
6.   Begin a while loop that runs until the NULL is found or the flag is set indicating an invalid character.
7.   Test the character for zero through nine.
8.   Test for first character and either '+' or '−'.
9.   Test for decimal point and no previous decimal point.
10.   If all the tests fail, set the flag indicating an invalid character was found.
11.   Increment the counter.
12.   End the scanning loop.
13.   If the bad character flag was never set

14.   Convert to a floating-point number and display.

15.   Else

16.   Display error message.

17.   End input loop.

18. End

Notice that all the tests were made for valid characters. The flag to end the scan loop and to prompt for another input was based on finding a character that was not in the valid character set.

Flowchart

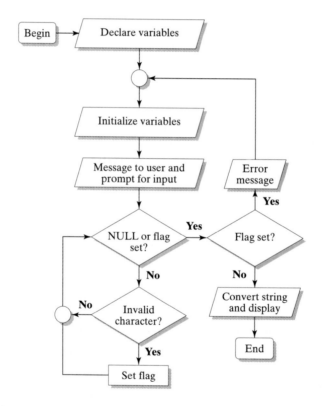

Solution Implemented in C++

```
1    //  Program 8.2
2    #include <iostream.h>
3    #include <math.h>
4
5    void main(void)
6    {
7        char input[20];
```

```
8       double number;
9       int counter, decimal_flag, out_flag;
10      cout.precision(15);
11      do
12      {
13          counter = 0, decimal_flag = 0, out_flag = 0;
14          cout << "\nEnter a floating-point number  -->  " << flush;
15          cin.getline(input,20,'\n');
16          while (input[counter] != 0 && out_flag == 0)
17          {
18              if (input[counter] >= '0' && input[counter] <= '9'){}
19              else if (counter == 0 && (input[0] == '-' ||
20                      input[0] == '+')){}
21              else if (input[counter] == '.' && decimal_flag == 0)
22                      decimal_flag = 1;
23              else
24                      out_flag = 1;
25              counter++;
26          }
27          if (out_flag == 0)
28          {
29              number = atof(input);
30              cout << "The floating-point number is " << number << endl;
31          }
32          else
33              cout << "There is an error in the input. " << endl;
34      }while (out_flag != 0);
35  }
```

The while() loop consisting of lines 16 to 26 scans each letter of the string until the end of the string is found or the out_flag is set, indicating that an invalid character has been found. The if/else structure within the loop makes three tests, which trap all valid characters. If the character being examined is not identified by one of these tests, then it must be invalid and the else condition sets the out_flag.

There are two test conditions that can end the while() loop. If the end of the string is found or the out_flag is set, the loop ends. If the loop ends without the out_flag being set, then the if() statement on line 27 is true and the floating-point number is displayed. If out_flag is set by an invalid character, then line 33 displays the error message. The out_flag set to one also makes the test on line 34 true and the outer loop repeats requiring the user to reenter the number.

It should be noted that a program that gets a number from the user and prints it on the screen is not a terribly useful program. The program should be thought of as a function that can be added to other programs. Whenever the user is asked for input, there is the possibility that the program can behave badly if the user makes a mistake. This possibility should be eliminated by putting the input through a testing function before the input is used.

Output of the C++ Program

```
Enter a floating-point number  -->  9.8.76
There is an error in the input.


Enter a floating-point number  -->  +-88
There is an error in the input.


Enter a floating-point number  -->  +6.6t66
There is an error in the input.


Enter a floating-point number  -->  75.7575
The floating-point number is 75.7575
```

Solution Implemented in Visual Basic

```
1    Option Explicit
2
3    Private Sub cmdExit_Click()
4        Unload Me
5    End Sub
6
7    Private Sub cmdReset_Click()
8        txtInput.Text = ""
9        lblMessage.Caption = ""
10       txtInput.SetFocus
11   End Sub
12
13   Private Sub cmdTest_Click()
14       Dim inputString, temp As String
15       Dim number As Single
16       Dim decimalFlag, outFlag, character As Byte
17       Dim length, counter As Integer
18       inputString = txtInput.Text
19       length = Len(txtInput.Text)
20       decimalFlag = 0
21       outFlag = 0
22       counter = 1
23
24       Do While counter <= length And outFlag = 0
25           temp = Mid(inputString, counter, 1)
26           character = Asc(temp)
27           If character >= 48 And character <= 57 Then
28           Else
29               If counter = 0 And character = 43 Or character = 45 Then
30               Else
31                   If character = 46 And decimalFlag = 0 Then
32                       decimalFlag = 1
33                   Else
```

```
34                        outFlag = 1
35                    End If
36                End If
37            End If
38            counter = counter + 1
39        Loop
40        If outFlag = 0 Then
41            number = txtInput.Text
42            lblMessage.Caption = "The input is a floating point " & _
43                "number with a value of " & number
44        Else
45            txtInput.Text = ""
46            txtInput.SetFocus
47            'inputString = ""
48            lblMessage.Caption = "The input is invalid" & vbCrLf & _
49                "Please re-enter"
50        End If
51    End Sub
52
53    Private Sub Form_Activate()
54        Call txtInput.SetFocus
55    End Sub
56
57    Private Sub Form_Load()
58        lblTitle.Caption = "This program tests an input and " & _
59            "determines whether it is a valid floating point number."
60        lblInput.Caption = "Enter a floating point number"
61    End Sub
```

The key to the program is testing for all the characters that are acceptable. Line 24 begins the loop that examines the input string one character at a time. Line 27 tests whether each character is in the ASCII range from 48 to 57 inclusive; that is, the character is a numeric character from zero to nine. If the character is in this range, the character is accepted and the loop moves to the next cycle and next character. If the character is not in the specified ASCII range, line 29 tests whether the character is a plus or minus sign. If it is either of these two, the character must also be the first character in the string in order to be accepted. If the character fails the first two tests, a third test is made on line 31, which tests whether the character is the first decimal point. If it is the first decimal point, the character is accepted and the decimalFlag is set to 1. If the decimalFlag has already been set, the character is not accepted.

If the character fails all three tests, the outFlag is set on line 34. Setting the outFlag causes the loop to stop since it indicates an improper input character and there is no point in testing the rest of the characters in the inputString. After the loop has ended, outFlag is tested again to determine which message should be sent to lblMessage. An outFlag that was never set by any of the inputString characters triggers the message indicating a good floating-point number. A set outFlag causes the retry message to be posted and the cursor to return to the txtInput box.

Output of the Visual Basic Program—With Error

```
┌─ Problem8_2 ──────────────── _ □ × ─┐
│                                      │
│   This program tests an input and determines │
│   whether it is a valid floating point number. │
│                                      │
│   Enter a floating point    ┌──────────┐ │
│           number            │ +7.5g3   │ │
│                             └──────────┘ │
│                                      │
│     The input is invalid    ┌──────────┐ │
│       Please re-enter       │   Test   │ │
│                             └──────────┘ │
│                                      │
│   ┌──────────┐      ┌──────────┐     │
│   │  Reset   │      │   Exit   │     │
│   └──────────┘      └──────────┘     │
└──────────────────────────────────────┘
```

Output of the Visual Basic Program—Without Error

```
┌─ Problem8_2 ──────────────── _ □ × ─┐
│                                      │
│   This program tests an input and determines │
│   whether it is a valid floating point number. │
│                                      │
│   Enter a floating point    ┌──────────┐ │
│           number            │ -79.885  │ │
│                             └──────────┘ │
│                                      │
│ The input is a floating point ┌──────────┐ │
│ number with a value of       │   Test   │ │
│        -79.885               └──────────┘ │
│                                      │
│   ┌──────────┐      ┌──────────┐     │
│   │  Reset   │      │   Exit   │     │
│   └──────────┘      └──────────┘     │
└──────────────────────────────────────┘
```

8.3   THE ADVANTAGES OF OBJECTS

Over the past five years structured programming using features of the C programming language has largely given way to object-oriented programming using C++, Visual Basic, and Java. While the logic of structured programming is still important in solving problems and in creating objects, the use of objects can make some problems easier to solve. Problem 8.3 shows how the use of objects can simplify some programming problems.

Monetary values entered by the user pose a particular problem. If the input is accepted by the program as a floating-point number, the program will have a problem if the user precedes the amount with a dollar sign or includes commas for amounts over $1,000. On the other hand, if the value is entered as a string, then addition and multiplication of monetary values create problems.

The solution is to create a new variable type that knows what to do with money regardless of what the user might enter. This new, *smarter type of variable* is a class and the variables themselves that store monetary values are objects or instances of that class.

PROBLEM 8.3   *How can monetary values be handled by a program so that the values are used correctly regardless of the input format?*

The solution to this problem is based on the solution to the floating-point number problem (Problem 8.2). Since the input must be read regardless of whether it contains non-numeric formatting characters or not, the input should be read as a string. The problem will be to extract the value from the string and store it in a floating-point variable that can be used in arithmetic operations. It would also be nice if all monetary values were displayed, neatly formatted, with dollar signs, commas, and two decimal places. In short the solution is to create a very intelligent storage unit for amounts of money that knows how to handle these operations.

Actually the solution to the problem of storage creates a couple new problems. C++ knows how to add and multiply floating-point numbers. If we invent a new class of objects, that we might call Money, C++ does not know how to do arithmetic using these objects and will have to be taught. Fortunately, this is not difficult.

Initial Data: **1.** In order to accommodate any input regardless of format the amount of money must be accepted as a string.

2. In Problem 8.2 we learned how to scan an input for nonnumeric characters. In this case, instead of prompting the user to reenter the data, we will ignore the inappropriate characters.

3. After inappropriate characters are removed, a string can be converted to a floating-point number using the atof() function.

4. The value as a floating-point number must be stored for use in arithmetic operations.

5. Floating point values must be converted into nicely formatted strings for display purposes.

6. A structure variable could be used to store the string and the floating-point value.

7. An object can store both values and store the automatic conversions, string to float and float to display string.

Output: Create objects to store monetary values and show that they can be added and multiplied by a number.

The initial data helps to define the elements of the class that we'll call Money. First, the class must have a character array and a floating-point variable to store the data. Second, there must be a function that will use the string entered by the user and set the input data into the array and the floating-point variable. This data setting function should call two other functions that convert the string into its floating-point value and then convert it back to a string that is formatted with a dollar sign, appropriate commas, and two decimal places.

Since the data is private to each object, there must also be a function that will display the data for the user when requested. Lastly, operations must be defined so that addition and multiplication can be performed on the objects.

The `main()` function of the program will do little more than get the information from the user and demonstrate that it can be added, multiplied, and displayed in a neat format. That is, the `main()` function verifies that the problem of handling money has been solved. The solution to the floating-point input problem was not thought of as an end in itself but a developed unit (read: class) to be used whenever the user is prompted to enter a number. Similarly, the Money class, once it is demonstrated to work correctly, should become part of programs requiring the user to input monetary values.

Pseudocode

  1. Begin class creation.
  2.   Define the class.
  3.   Declare private variables.
  4.   Declare private functions to make conversions.
  5.   Declare functions to communicate with main().
  6.   Declare addition and multiplication operations.
  7.   Define function to set the data in the object.
  8.   Copy user input to private array.
  9.   Call private function to convert string to floating-point number.
10.   Call private function to convert floating-point number to string.
11.   Define function to display private data.
12.   Define function to convert float to string.
13.   Count the number of digits to left of decimal.
14.   Set the first two elements of the array to "$ ".
15.   Isolate digits and place in array.
16.   Place decimal point in array.
17.   Add two decimal places; round if necessary.
18.   Define function to convert to float.
19.   Make a copy of the input string that deletes nonvalid characters.
20.   Use atof() to convert to float.
21.   Define addition operation.
22.   Add the floating-point values from each object and store in temporary object.
23.   Convert floating-point value in temporary object to string.
24.   Return temporary object to be stored in the object holding the sum.
25.   Define multiplication operation.
26.   Multiply the floating-point value by the scalar number and store in temporary object.
27.   Convert floating-point value in temporary object to string.
28.   Return temporary object to be stored in the object holding the product.
29. End class creation.
30. Begin main.

31.   Declare variables and objects.

32.   Prompt for money amount.

33.   Get money and set value in object.

34.   Prompt for second money amount.

35.   Get money and set value in object.

36.   Add the two money values and display sum.

37.   Multiply the sum by five and display product.

38. End main.

Because objects almost take on lives of their own inside the program, describing the flow of the program with a flowchart becomes cumbersome. Generally pseudocode is a more advantageous method for organizing the plan for the program in advance of writing code.

Solution Implemented in C++

```
1    //  Problem 8.3
2    #include <iostream.h>
3    #include <math.h>
4    #include <string.h>
5
6    class Money
7    {
8    private:
9         double amount;
10        char str_amount[50];
11        void convertMoneyToString(void);
12        void convertMoneyToFloat(void);
13    public:
14        Money(): amount(0){strcpy(str_amount,"");}
15        void setMoney(char []);
16        void printMoney(void) const;
17        Money operator + (Money) const;
18        Money operator * (float) const;
19        ~Money(){}
20    };
21    void Money::setMoney (char a[])
22    {
23        strcpy(str_amount, a);
24        convertMoneyToFloat();
25        convertMoneyToString();
26    }
27    void Money::printMoney (void) const
28    {
29        cout << str_amount << flush;
30    }
31    void Money::convertMoneyToString (void)
32    {
```

```
33          double temp = amount;
34          int digits = 0, x, temp_digits, number;
35          while (temp >= 1.0)
36              temp /= 10, digits++;
37          temp = amount;
38          temp_digits = digits - 1;
39          str_amount[0] = '$', str_amount[1] = ' ';
40          for (x = 2; digits > 0; x++, digits--)
41          {
42              number = (int)(temp / pow(10,temp_digits));
43              str_amount[x] = number + 48;
44              temp = temp - number * pow(10,temp_digits);
45              if (temp_digits % 3 == 0 && temp_digits != 0)
46                  str_amount[++x] = ',';
47              temp_digits--;
48          }
49          str_amount[x] = '.';
50          temp = ceil(100000 * temp) / 100000;
51          number = (int)(temp / pow(10,-1));
52          temp = temp - number * pow(10,-1);
53          str_amount[x + 1] = number + 48;
54          number = (int)(temp / pow(10,-2));
55          temp = temp - number * pow(10,-2);
56          str_amount[x + 2] = number + 48;
57          if (temp >= .005)
58              str_amount[x + 2]++;
59          str_amount[x + 3] = 0;
60  }
61  void Money::convertMoneyToFloat(void)
62  {
63          char temp[50] = {0}, *str_amt_ptr, *temp_ptr;
64          str_amt_ptr = str_amount, temp_ptr = temp;
65          while (*str_amt_ptr != 0)
66          {
67              if ((*str_amt_ptr >= '0' && *str_amt_ptr <= '9')
68                  || *str_amt_ptr == '.')
69                  *temp_ptr++ = *str_amt_ptr;
70              str_amt_ptr++;
71          }
72          amount = atof(temp);
73  }
74  Money Money::operator + (Money a) const
75  {
76          Money temp;
77          temp.amount = amount + a.amount;
78          temp.convertMoneyToString ();
79          return temp;
80  }
81  Money Money::operator * (float a) const
82  {
83          Money temp;
84          temp.amount = amount * a;
85          temp.convertMoneyToString();
```

```
86        return temp;
87    }
88
89    void main (void)
90    {
91        Money first, second, third;
92        char input[50];
93
94        cout << "Enter some money                    " << flush;
95        cin.getline(input, 20, '\n');
96        first.setMoney (input);
97        cout << "\nEnter a second amount of money         " << flush;
98        cin.getline(input, 20, '\n');
99        second.setMoney (input);
100       third = first + second;
101       cout << endl << "The total amount of money is          " << flush;
102       third.printMoney();
103       cout << endl << endl
104           << "Five times the total amount of money is   ";
105       third = third * 5;
106       third.printMoney();
107       cout << endl << endl;
108   }
```

In examining the code for Problem 8.3 the critical line is line 21. Here the simple function call to the setMoney() function for each object begins a complex routine that first extracts the value of the string entered by the user and then creates a new string that is formatted correctly for display purposes. Because of the built-in intelligence that is part of the object, the user can enter a monetary value with or without the dollar sign, with or without extra spaces, with or without commas, and even with an embedded errant keystroke. The object will extract a proper value and store it twice, once as a number for doing arithmetic by the convertMoneyToFloat() function, and once as a properly formatted string by the convertMoneyToString() function.

The routine used in the convertMoneyToFloat() function is fairly straightforward. Because C++ already has a function to convert an ASCII string to a float, the only requirement is to create a second string from the user input that contains only valid characters. The while() loop, from line 65 to 71, takes care of creating the second string. Notice there is no need to terminate the second string with a NULL because the string was filled with zeroes when it was created on line 63. The copying routine could have been accomplished without pointers but not as conveniently.

The convertMoneyToString() function is somewhat more complex even though the basic idea should seem familiar. The function is very similar to the one used to convert a floating-point number to binary. In both cases the function begins by searching for the decimal point. The number of digits to the left of the decimal determines the initial divisor used on line 42. This division effectively moves the decimal point to the right of the first digit. Type casting to an integer leaves the single digit that can be converted to a character and stored in the array as the next element after the dollar sign and the space. Line 44 removes the digit from the number, making the second digit the most significant and the process is repeated.

When the decimal point, if there is one, is reached, the period character is placed in the string (line 49) and the digits representing the pennies are determined and placed in the character array. The function of line 50 is not immediately obvious. The binary conversion program demonstrated that most decimal values do not convert evenly into binary. Most decimal conversions result in a repeating bit pattern that is eventually truncated when the storage capacity for the number is reached. This error shows up in the fifteenth significant digit (for double-precision floats) and is usually not a problem. However, after repeated math operations, the error can become significant.

Monetary values require a little more attention to proper rounding. If the value $10,002.80 is entered into the program, the decimal portion remaining by the time line 50 is reached is not .80 but .79999999999. The rounding provided by lines 57 and 58 causes the first nine to be rounded up to zero resulting in a stored number of $10,002.70, which is not correct. Multiplying the truncated decimal by 100,000 yields 79,999.999999. The ceiling function rounds this up to 80,000 and then dividing by 100,000 gives a final result of .80. This corrected value is then converted to characters and stored in the array.

When addition is performed on line 100, a new monetary value is created for the object `third`. In this case the objects that are added are already stored values as floating-point numbers and are ready to be added. The sum is stored in the floating-point variable of `third` and the string needed for displaying the value are automatically created by the addition operation on line 85 by a call to the `convertMoneyToString()` function.

Output of the C++ Program

```
Enter some money                          900
Enter a second amount of money            $    1,234.56
The total amount of money is              $ 2,134.56
Five times the total amount of money is   $ 10,672.80
```

The output shows that regardless of how the amount of money is entered the intelligent object extracts the correct floating-point value and correctly performs addition and multiplication. When the sum and the product have been calculated, the dollar and cents amount is always displayed in standard monetary format.

The program raises certain obvious questions. Can the `Money` object be adapted to know how to perform subtraction and division? Can the `Money` object be adapted to perform conversions into other currencies? It should be clear that these adaptations are simple and have been left to the reader.

There is no need to write a similar program in Visual Basic. Visual Basic already contains a special variable type for handling currency.

PROBLEM 8.4   *The most common letters in English have been determined but what are the most common words?*

Problem 7.6 expanded the letter frequency problem so that an entire file could be examined instead of a small string entered by the user. Reading a large file to find the frequency of each letter provided more reliable information about which letters occur more often in English. It raised the question of which are the most common words found in a large, randomly chosen English text.

The solution would seem to be a combination of the logic of the letter frequency problem and Problem 4.4 that identified words in a string. In modifying the solution to Problem 4.4, a file would take the place of the input string and, as the individual characters are read into the program, the words would be identified and stored. The real difference between counting the number of times a word occurs and the number of times each letter occurs is that there are many more words in English than there are letters. It is this difference between the problem that has been solved and the problem at hand that should be the point of focus (Rule 15).

The problem is one of data storage. In the letter frequency problem there were only 26 counters needed, one for each letter. In isolating the words in Problem 4.4 the amount of text was limited to 20 words. In a large file the number of different words is quite difficult to guess. If the program begins by reserving space for too few words the program may terminate inappropriately when the array limit is exceeded. On the other hand, reserving millions or hundreds of millions of bytes of memory when the file to be examined is small is certainly a waste of resources.

The solution is to not reserve any memory for the data in advance, that is, at the time the program is compiled. Instead the operating system should be asked for whatever memory is required *at runtime*. This is called dynamic memory allocation. If a small file with few words is read, little memory is used. If a large file is read, the program will request exactly the amount required for the program to do its job.

To map out the plan for solving the problem it will be useful to make an initial rough outline in pseudocode to determine what needs to be done, what we already know how to do, and what work is left to be done.

1. Get a file name from the user and open the file, as in the solution to Problem 7.6.

2. Read in the characters one at a time, also as in the solution to Problem 7.6.

3. Identify word groupings as in the solution to Problem 4.4.

4. Each word found in the text should be compared to a list of previously discovered words. If the word is found in the list, the counter for that word should be incremented. If the word is not on the list, a new object should be created to store the word.

5. Sort the stored information with the more common words listed first so the information is more usable. This can be done with a bubble sort as in the solution to Problem 4.7.

Except for item 4 there is nothing new in this problem. The solution is merely a composite of work already done.

The objects required to store the data are extremely simple, consisting of an array to store a new word and an integer to keep a count of how many times the word is found in the file. Functions are also required to get the information into and out of the object. Each time a new word is found a new object can be created *at runtime*. The

C++ keyword new handles the negotiations with the operating system for space to store the object.

Pseudocode

1. Begin class creation.
2. Define the class.
3. Declare private variables.
4. Define public functions to get data into and out of private variables.
5. End class.
6. Declare global pointers for the new objects.
7. Begin main.
8. Declare and initialize variables.
9. Prompt user for file name and open file.
10. Get initial character.
11. Begin loop to get characters.
12. Get another character.
13. If the first character is a letter
14. Store the letter in the word array and increment array counter.
15. Set the flag that indicates a word is started.
16. If the first character is an apostrophe or hyphen and the next character is a letter
17. Store the character in the word array and increment array counter.
18. If not a valid character and the word flag is set
19. Reset counters and word flag.
20. Call the object-creating function.
21. Test to ensure array of object pointers is not overrun.
22. If so, message to user and stop getting words.
23. Copy second character to first character.
24. End loop when EOF is found.
25. Display elapsed time message.
26. Call the sort function.
27. Close the file.
28. Delete new objects.
29. End main.

30. Begin object function.

31.   Declare and set static variable to count new words.

32.   Declare and initialize variables.

33.   Run loop to test word against all previous words.

34.   If match is found, increment that word's counter.

35.   If match is not found, use new to create a new object and set word and counter.

36.   Return word counter for use in display routine.

37. End function.

38. Begin display function.

39.   Run loop for as many cycles as the word count.

40.   Display word and count for each stored word.

41. End function.

42. Begin sort function.

43.   Declare and initialize variables.

44.   Sort objects using bubble sort.

45.   Display time for sort.

46.   Call display function.

47. End function.

Again a flowchart could be constructed but it would be quite large and by covering several pages would add more confusion than clarity to the solution of the problem.

Solution Implemented in C++

```
1    //  Problem 8.4
2    #include <iostream.h>
3    #include <fstream.h>
4    #include <string.h>
5    #include <iomanip.h>
6    #include <conio.h>
7    #include <time.h>
8    #include <stdlib.h>
9    #define LIMIT 15000
10
11   class Words
12   {
13   private:
14       char word[20];
15       int count;
16   public:
17
18       Words(){}
19       void new_word(char a[])
```

```
20      {   strcpy(word, a);    count = 1;                      }
21      void increment_count(void)
22      {   count++;                                            }
23      void display(void)
24      {   cout << setw(19) << word << setw(7) << count << endl;  }
25      char * get_word(void)
26      {   return word;                                        }
27      int get_count(void)
28      {   return count;                                       }
29      ~Words(){}
30   };
31
32   Words *Wptr[LIMIT];
33   void display(int);
34   int object_function(char []);
35   void sort (int);
36   int main(void)
37   {
38       char name[50], letter, letter2, word[20];
39       Words a;
40       int counter, word_counter = 0, letter_counter = 0, word_flag = 0;
41       long start, end, total = 0, unique = 0;
42       cout << "This program opens a file and counts how many "
43            << "times each word appears"
44            << endl << "     in the file. " << endl
45            << "Enter the name of the file to be opened . . " << flush;
46       cin.getline(name, 49,'\n');
47       cout << endl;
48       ifstream incoming(name);
49       time(&start);
50       incoming.get(letter);
51       do
52       {
53           incoming.get(letter2);
54           if (letter >= 'A' && letter <= 'Z' || letter >= 'a' && letter <= 'z')
55           {
56               word[letter_counter++] = letter;
57               word_flag = 1;
58           }
59           else if ((letter == 39 || letter == '-') && letter2 >= 'a' &&
60                   letter2 <= 'z')
61               word[letter_counter++] = letter;
62           else if (word_flag == 1)
63           {
64               word[letter_counter] = 0;
65               letter_counter = 0;
66               word_flag = 0;
67               total++;
68               word_counter = object_function(word);
69               if (word_counter == LIMIT - 1)
70               {
71                   cout << "The word count exceeded " << LIMIT << endl;
```

```
72                    break;
73                }
74            }
75            letter = letter2;
76        }while(!incoming.eof());
77        time(&end);
78        cout << endl << "Reading the data required " << end - start
79                << " seconds" << endl;
80        cout << "Total words = " << total << "    Unique words = "
81                << word_counter << endl;
82        sort(word_counter);
83        incoming.close();
84        for (counter = 0; counter < word_counter; counter++)
85            delete Wptr[counter];
86        return(0);
87  }
88
89  int object_function(char a[])
90  {
91        static int word_counter = 0;
92        int counter, new_word_flag = 1;
93        char *ptr;                                  // ptr change
94        if (a[0] == '-')                            // ptr change
95            ptr = &a[1]   ;                          // ptr change
96        else
97            ptr = a;
98        for (counter = 0; counter < word_counter; counter++)
99            if (stricmp(ptr,Wptr[counter]->get_word()) == 0)  // change a to ptr
100           {
101               Wptr[counter]->increment_count();
102               new_word_flag = 0;
103               break;
104           }
105       if (new_word_flag == 1)
106       {
107           Wptr[word_counter] = new Words;
108           Wptr[word_counter]->new_word(ptr);            // change a to ptr
109           word_counter++;
110       }
111       return word_counter;
112 }
113
114 void display(int number)
115 {
116       int counter;
117       for (counter = 0; counter < number; counter++)
118       {
119           cout << setw(4) << counter + 1;
120           Wptr[counter]->display();
121           if ((counter + 1) % 22 == 0)
122               if (getch() == 27)
123                   return;
124       }
```

```
125 }
126 void sort(int number)
127 {
128     Words temp;
129     int x, flag = 1;
130     long start, end;
131     time(&start);
132     while (flag == 1)
133     {
134         flag = 0;
135         for (x = 0; x < number - 1; x++)
136             if (Wptr[x]->get_count() < Wptr[x + 1]->get_count())
137             {
138                 temp = *Wptr[x];
139                 *Wptr[x] = *Wptr[x + 1];
140                 *Wptr[x + 1] = temp;
141                 flag = 1;
142             }
143     }
144     time(&end);
145     cout << endl << "The sorting took " << end - start << " seconds" << endl;
146     display(number);
147 }
```

Because the Words class is quite simple, the functions were defined inside the class definition, bypassing the use of prototypes. This is a common practice when the body of a function can be written on one or two lines. There are two functions to place information into an object (new_word() and increment_count()), two functions to retrieve the information (get_word() and get_count()), and one to display the information (display()) after the word list has been sorted.

There is an upper limit to the number of objects that can be created by the program. That limit is set by the number of pointers that have been defined for the objects. In this program the value of the LIMIT is set by the define statement on line 9. The pointers themselves were created as global variables on line 32. The pointers are needed because as the new C++ keyword obtains memory space there must be a way to refer to that space. The new keyword returns an address for the memory that must be stored in an already existing pointer. Care must be taken not to overrun the array of pointers. Line 69 detects the cycle when the last pointer is used, displays a message to the user, and breaks out of the input loop.

It should be noted that the restriction set by declaring a limited number of pointers at the beginning of the program could be avoided. By using a linked list or any of several container classes defined in the Standard Template Library the pointers themselves could be generated at runtime. However, these techniques are well beyond the scope of this text.

The body of the do/while loop that begins on line 51 is nearly identical to the code in the solution to the word count problem (Problem 4.4). It performs the same function but in this case the input and output are different. The characters read are drawn from a file rather than a string. After a word has been isolated, instead of storing the word in an array of words, the object_function() is called.

It is the job of the `object_function()` to scan the list of words already found and do one of two things. If the current word is found in the list, the `increment_count()` function for that object is called. If the word is not found, new memory is reserved for a `Words` object, a pointer is assigned to that memory space, and the `new_word()` function associated with that object is called to store the word in memory and set the `count` for the object to one.

The `sort()` function is a bubble sort routine. It sorts the objects based on the value stored in the `count` variable. When the sorting is complete, `sort()` calls the `display()` function to display the word's rank in the ordered list, the word itself, and the number of times the word occurs. An extra feature that has been added to the `display()` function is the bailout option. Rather than have the entire list of words, that will likely number in the thousands, scroll off the screen, the program stops after each set of 22 words, lines 121 and 122. Any key except the escape key displays the next set of 22. The escape key causes the program to exit.

The important item to note is that there is very little in the program that is new. The dynamic allocation of memory and the use of an array of pointers to objects to name the newly reserved memory are new. The file reading, the word isolation, the bubble sort, the display, and the manipulation of objects have all been done in previous programs.

There is one other new feature that deserves mention. It is a matter of house-keeping rather than logic. The loop on lines 84 and 85

```
84        for (counter = 0; counter <= word_counter; counter++)
85            delete Wptr[counter];
```

uses the `delete` keyword to release the memory that was reserved by the `new` keyword. Ideally the memory would be released when the program ends and the destructor function (`~Words()`) executes. This does not always happen and the memory may continue to be reserved until the computer is rebooted.

Output of the C++ Program

```
This program opens a file and counts how many times each word appears
    in the file
Enter the name of the file to be opened . . 2city.txt

Reading the data required 63 seconds
Total words = 136282    Unique words = 10251

The sorting took 44 seconds
   1              The   8021
   2              and   4980
   3               of   4007
   4               to   3474
   5                a   2936
   6               in   2593
   7               It   2031
   8              his   2009
   9                I   1942
  10             that   1911
  11               he   1836
  12              was   1773
```

13	you	1400
14	with	1311
15	had	1297
16	as	1162
17	her	1044
18	at	1033
19	him	976
20	for	960
21	on	923
22	not	855

The file opened was the complete text of *A Tale of Two Cities* by Charles Dickens. The book contains 136,282 total words. Of that total there are 10,251 different words. As each character was read into the program, it was examined to determine whether it belonged to a word. Each word that was discovered was compared to every word in an ever-growing list that eventually contained over 10,000 words.

After the scan a decision was made as to whether the word was new or if an existing word's count should be incremented. This was done for 136,282 words in a little over one minute. Equally amazing is the sorting of a list of 10,251 words in 47 seconds. These times give some indication of the power that a personal computer makes available to the problem solver. The amount of work to be done is often irrelevant. All that is needed is a plan and a way to tell the computer what to do.

Solution Implemented in Visual Basic

ClsWord.cls - File containing the class definition

```
1    Private word As String
2    Private count As Integer
3
4    Public Sub new_word(ByVal a As String)
5       word = a
6       count = 1
7    End Sub
8
9    Public Sub increment_count()
10       count = count + 1
11   End Sub
12
13   Public Sub display(ByRef list As ListBox, ByVal num As Integer)
14      Dim str, str1 As String
15
16      str = Space(5)
17      RSet str = Format(num)
18
19      str1 = Space(30)
20      RSet str1 = word
21      str = str & str1
22
23      str1 = Space(10)
24      RSet str1 = Format(count)
25      str = str & str1
```

```
26       list.AddItem (str)
27  End Sub
28
29  Public Function get_word() As String
30      get_word = word
31  End Function
32
33  Public Function get_count() As Integer
34      get_count = count
35  End Function
```

Problem8_4.frm - File containing VB code

```
36  Option Explicit
37  Private Const LIMIT As Integer = 15000
38  Private WordArray(LIMIT) As clsWord
39
40  Private Sub cmdCount_Click()
41      Dim name, letter, letter2, word, one_line As String
42      Dim counter, word_counter, letter_counter, word_flag As Integer
43      Dim startTime, endTime As Long
44      Dim fileNbr As Integer
45      Dim lineLen As Integer
46      Dim ctr, count As Integer
47      Dim letterAsc, letter2Asc As Integer
48
49      name = txtFileName.Text
50      count = 0
51      If name = "" Then
52          Exit Sub
53      End If
54
55      fileNbr = FreeFile
56      name = App.Path & "\" & name
57      Debug.Print name
58      Open name For Input As #fileNbr
59
60      startTime = Timer
61
62      Do While Not EOF(fileNbr)
63          Line Input #fileNbr, one_line
64          one_line = one_line & " "
65          lineLen = Len(one_line)
66          If (count + 1) Mod 50 = 0 Then
67              endTime = Timer
68              lblTime.Caption = "Reading -- " & _
69                      Int(endTime - startTime) & " Sec."
70              DoEvents
71          End If
72          count = count + 1
73          For ctr = 1 To lineLen
74              letter = Mid(one_line, ctr, 1)
75              letterAsc = Asc(letter)
76              If ctr + 1 <= lineLen Then
77                  letter2 = Mid(one_line, ctr + 1, 1)
78                  letter2Asc = Asc(letter2)
```

```
79              End If
80              '      Map upper case to lower case
81              If letterAsc >= Asc("A") And letterAsc <= Asc("Z") Then
82                  letterAsc = letterAsc + 32
83                  letter = Chr(letterAsc)
84              End If
85
86              If letterAsc >= Asc("a") And letterAsc <= Asc("z") Then
87                  word = word & letter
88                  word_flag = 1
89              ElseIf (letterAsc = 39 Or letterAsc = Asc("-")) And _
90                      letter2Asc >= Asc("a") And _
91                      letter2Asc <= Asc("z") Then
92                  word = word & letter
93              ElseIf word_flag = 1 Then
94                  word_flag = 0
95                  word_counter = object_function(word)
96                  word = ""
97                  If word_counter = LIMIT - 1 Then
98                      Call MsgBox("The word count exceeded " & _
99                          Format(LIMIT), vbOKOnly + vbInformation)
100                     Exit Do
101                 End If
102             End If
103         Next ctr
104     Loop
105
106     lstOutput.Clear
107     lstOutput.Text = "Total Words = " & word_counter
108     sort (word_counter)
109     Close #fileNbr
110 End Sub
111
112 Public Sub display(ByVal number As Integer)
113     Dim counter As Integer
114
115     For counter = 0 To number - 1
116         Call WordArray(counter).display(lstOutput, counter + 1)
117     Next counter
118 End Sub
119
120 Public Function object_function(ByVal a As String)
121     Static word_counter As Integer
122     Dim counter, new_word_flag, length As Integer
123     Dim letter As Byte
124     new_word_flag = 1
125
126     If Mid(a, 1, 1) = "-" Then
127         length = Len(a)
128         a = Mid(a, 2, length)
129     End If
130     For counter = 0 To word_counter - 1
131         If a = WordArray(counter).get_word Then
132             Call WordArray(counter).increment_count
133             new_word_flag = 0
134             Exit For
```

```
135        End If
136     Next counter
137
138     If new_word_flag = 1 Then
139        Set WordArray(word_counter) = New clsWord
140        WordArray(word_counter).new_word (a)
141        word_counter = word_counter + 1
142     End If
143     object_function = word_counter
144 End Function
145
146 Public Sub sort(ByVal number As Integer)
147     Dim temp As clsWord
148     Dim x, flag As Integer
149     Dim startTime, endTime As Long
150     Dim message As String
151     message = lblTime.Caption
152     flag = 1
153     startTime = Timer
154     Do While flag = 1
155        flag = 0
156        For x = 0 To number - 2
157           If (x + 1) Mod 200 = 0 Then
158              endTime = Timer
159              lblTime = message & vbCrLf & _
160                 "Sorting -- " & Int(endTime - startTime) & " Sec."
161              DoEvents
162           End If
163           If WordArray(x).get_count < WordArray(x + 1).get_count Then
164              Set temp = WordArray(x)
165              Set WordArray(x) = WordArray(x + 1)
166              Set WordArray(x + 1) = temp
167              flag = 1
168           End If
169        Next x
170     Loop
171     display (number)
172 End Sub
173
174 Private Sub cmdReset_Click()
175     txtFileName.Text = ""
176     lstOutput.Clear
177 End Sub
178
179 Private Sub cmdExit_Click()
180     Unload Me
181 End Sub
```

The logic of the C++ and the Visual Basic programs is very similar. There are some differences in the implementation. In the C++ program characters are read one at a time from the file and words are built by identifying characters that delimit words. In the Visual Basic program information is read from the file line by line (line 63) and words are identified in the input line. The second difference is in the way strings are handled. The C++ program used C–style strings identifying individual characters with a pointer and an index variable. The string objects of the Visual Basic program are manipulated using the Mid() function.

Output of the Visual Basic Program

8.4 RECURSION

Recursion is a powerful problem-solving technique involving recursive functions. A recursive function is a function that calls itself. Both C++ and Visual Basic allow this interesting behavior for all functions with the exception of main() in C++ programs. On the surface the technique would seem to be self-defeating. If a function calls itself, then the second execution of the function will call the function for the third time. The third execution of the function will again call the function for the fourth time, and so on indefinitely. The breaking of this cycle is obviously quite important and occurs in the base case. Once the base case is reached, the program begins to back out of each function call.

A concrete example will make the technique clearer.

PROBLEM 8.5   *Calculate the factorial of any integer from 1 to 170.*

Consider generating the value of five factorial (Rule 8—The Concrete Example Rule).

$$5! = 5 \times 4 \times 3 \times 2 \times 1 \quad \text{or}$$
$$5! = 5 \times 4!$$

Five factorial can be calculated if the value of four factorial is known. Similarly, four factorial can be calculated if the value of three factorial is known. This observation leads to the two conditions that are necessary for the use of the recursive technique.

Rule 17   The Recursion Rule

A problem can be solved recursively if:

1. The final step or the base condition is known.
2. The first step of the problem leads to exactly the same problem but one step closer to the solution.

The amazing feature of this technique is that the intermediate steps do not need to be considered. In fact, the number of intermediate steps required is usually irrelevant so long as the base case is reached eventually.

In the case of generating factorials the first step is known. The factorial of any number is the number multiplied by the factorial of one less than the number, or $n! = n \times (n - 1)!$. Executing step 1 leaves the same problem of finding the value of a factorial but it is the factorial of $n - 1$ rather than n. That is, the problem is one step closer to the base case. The base case itself is simple $1! = 1$.

$$5! = 5 \times 4! \qquad\qquad n! = n \times (n - 1)!$$
$$4! = 4 \times 3! \qquad\qquad (n - 1)! = (n - 1) \times (n - 2)!$$
$$3! = 3 \times 2! \qquad\qquad (n - 2)! = (n - 2) \times (n - 3)!$$
$$2! = 2 \times 1! \qquad\qquad (n - 3)! = (n - 3) \times (n - 4)!$$

$1!$ is the base case   ...until the base case is found

The typical structure of a recursive function is based on an if/else condition. If the base condition is reached, return the base case value. In all other cases do something that involves another call to the recursive function and return a value. Returning values is typical but, as we will see in Problem 8.6, not always necessary.

Initial Data: **1.** The user will supply the number whose factorial value is needed.

2. The factorial operation is known.

3. The routine for calculating factorials fits the requirements for a recursive technique.

Objective: Calculate the factorial of any integer from 1 to 170.

Pseudocode

1. Begin recursive function.
2.   If the base case is reached.
3.   Return the base case value.
4.   Otherwise.
5.   Multiply number by the value returned by recursive function.
6.   Return the product.
7. End function.
8. Begin main.
9.   Declare variables.
10.   Begin loop.
11.   Prompt user and get input.
12.   If <Esc> is entered, end the loop.
13.   Convert input string to integer.
14.   Test whether integer is in proper range.
15.   If not, continue.
16.   Call recursive function.
17.   Display answer.
18.   End loop.
19. End main.

Flowchart

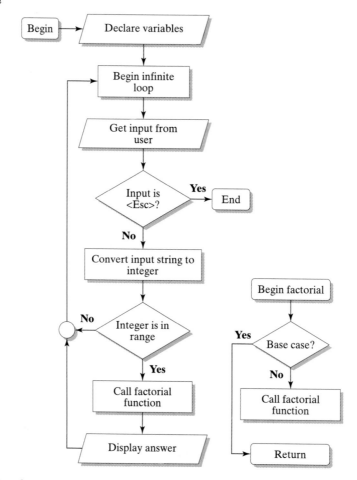

Solution Implemented in C++

```
1    //  Problem 8.5
2    #include <iostream.h>
3    #include <stdlib.h>
4
5    double factorial (int num)                    // the recursive function
6    {
7         double ans;
8         if (num == 2)
9             return 2;
10        else
11        {
12            ans = num * factorial(num - 1);   // call to recursive function
13            return ans;
14        }
15   }
```

```
16   int main (void)
17   {
18       int number;
19       double answer;
20       char input[10] = {0};
21       cout.precision(15);
22       cout << "This program generates factorials. Hit <Esc> to quit"
23               << endl;
24       while (1)
25       {
26           cout << endl << "Number a number from 1 to 170 --   " << flush;
27           cin.getline(input, 8, '\n');
28           if (input[0] == 27)
29               break;
30           number = atoi(input);
31           if (number > 170 || number < 1)
32           {
33               cout << endl << "Number out of range" << endl;
34               continue;
35           }
36           cout << "                                " << number
37               << "! = " << flush;
38           answer = factorial (number);
39           cout << answer;
40       }
41       return (0);
42   }
```

Of course, finding a method for calculating factorial values is not quite a real-world problem in itself. More likely this solution would be used as a function in a larger program that required the calculation of factorials. It is also true that in this case the factorial values could be calculated with a simple loop and without using recursion. The simpler function was used in the calculation of sine function values using MacLaurin series expansions in Chapter 2. The advantage of using recursion in calculating factorials is that the problem represents a simple example of a technique that can be difficult to implement. Problem 8.6 will use recursion to create a simple solution to a problem that is quite difficult to solve without recursion.

Lines 8 and 10 hold the key to making the factorial function work. If the test on line 8 is true, then the base condition has been reached and the first factor in the factorial is 2 as the program backs out of the recursive functions. The test on line 8 could have been written as if (num == 1). This would have worked but the function would have been called one extra time for the purpose of adding a factor of one to the factorial. Since one is the multiplicative identity, this would serve no purpose.

If the base condition hasn't yet been reached, the code on line 12 executes. Notice that the return statement was not reached before there was a new call to the factorial function. Only after the base condition has been found does line 13 execute for each call to the function. When the program has backed out of each call to the function, line 38 can be completed, storing the value for the factorial in the variable answer.

Output of the C++ Program

```
This program generates factorials. Hit <Esc> to quit

Number a number from 1 to 170 --    6
                                    6! = 720
Number a number from 1 to 170 --    17
                                    17! = 355687428096000
Number a number from 1 to 170 --    170
                                    170! = 7.25741561530799e+306
Number a number from 1 to 170 --
```

The output correctly shows that $6! = 6 \times 5 \times 4 \times 3 \times 2 = 720$. Seventeen factorial requires 15 digits to write, making it the largest factorial that can be expressed without using exponential notation. Double-precision, floating-point variables can only store numbers to 15-digit precision. The largest magnitude that can be stored in a double-precision, floating-point variable is approximately 308 powers of 10 making 170! the largest factorial that can be calculated.

Solution Implemented in Visual Basic

```
1    Option Explicit
2
3    Private Sub cmdExit_Click()
4        Unload Me
5    End Sub
6
7    Private Sub cmdGenerate_Click()
8        Dim answer, number As Double
9        number = CDbl(txtInput.Text)
10
11       If number > 170 Or number < 1 Then
12           Call MsgBox("Number out of range", vbExclamation, "Project7_5")
13           lblOutput.Caption = "Re-enter the number"
14           Call txtInput.SetFocus
15       Else
16           answer = Factorial(CDbl(txtInput.Text))
17           lblOutput.Caption = number & "! = " & answer
18       End If
19   End Sub
20
21   Private Sub Form_Load()
22       lblTitle.Caption = "This program generates factorials"
23       lblInput.Caption = "Enter a number from 1 to 170"
24   End Sub
25
26   Private Function Factorial(ByVal number As Double)
27       If number = 2 Or number = 1 Then
28           Factorial = number
29       Else
30           Factorial = number * Factorial(number - 1)
31       End If
32   End Function
```

Output of the Visual Basic Program

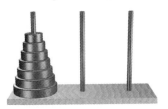

PROBLEM 8.6   *Solve the Tower of Hanoi problem for any number of pieces.*

The Tower of Hanoi is a children's game based on a legend that traces to India. The game involves a stack of disks and three posts on which they can be stacked. The objective is to move the stack from the first post to the third. There are only three rules to the game. Only one disk may be moved at a time, a larger disk can never be placed on top of a smaller disk, and a disk may never be placed anywhere except on one of the posts.

The objective for the problem solver is to create a simulation of the game that will indicate each move that must be made on the way to winning the game. Clarity is critically important. Each element of the game must be labeled so it can be referred to by the program. The posts should be numbered so the stack starts on post 1 and will be transferred to post 3. Post 2 can be used as a temporary holding position. The disks are numbered from one to the number of disks entered by the user. According to the legend, a group of monks in India were charged with moving 64 disks to the new location. Hopefully the user will enter a smaller number. The disks should be named so disk one is the smallest disk and the rest are numbered in succession until the bottom of the stack is reached.

If the disks are to be moved, it is also necessary to describe where a disk is, where it is going, and where it might stop temporarily along the way. These names are relative to where the disk is at the moment. The positions, for the sake of clarity, should be named start, end, and temp but which post each term refers to will be constantly changing for each disk as the game is played.

There are two possible opening moves. Disk one either moves to post two or to post three. Which move is correct is unknown. However, there is one critical move that is known at the beginning of the game. At some point the largest disk must move from post one to post three. For this to happen all other disks must be sitting in order on post two. This provides enough information to begin.

Initial Data: **1.** The number of disks will be entered by the user.

2. The disks can only be moved one at a time.

3. A larger disk can never be placed on top of a smaller disk.

4. At some point in the game the largest disk must be moved from post one to post three.

5. For the move in step 4 to be possible all the disks must be sitting in order on post two.

6. When the largest disk is moved, the `start` position will be post one, the `end` position will be post three and the `temp` position will be post two.

Output: Determine what moves should be made to eventually get all the disks onto post three in their proper order.

Step 5 is the tip-off that a recursive function might be useful. At some point in the game all of the disks except the largest must be on post two. Assume for the moment that there are five disks (Rule 8—The Concrete Example). Getting the top four disks to post 2 would be the solution to the game if there were one less disk than the five that are postulated (and post 2 was the target position). However, to get to this point disk four would have to move to post two implying that the other three disks are on post three in their proper order. Continuing this logic, at some point disk three would move to post three implying disks one and two are on post two. But before this could happen disk two would have to move to post two, indicating that the first move of the game should be disk one to post three.

This drilling-down effect is precisely the method used in the recursive factorial function in the solution to Problem 8.5. Notice that the move of disk one to post three was dependent on the fact that there were five disks. The first move would be different if there were six disks. The number of disks will control how many times the recursive function calls itself.

In this problem we have the two necessary conditions for a recursive solution:

1. The final step or the base condition is known.

The disks are numbered 1 to *n* where *n* is the number entered by the user. The objective is to get disk *n* on to post three. To do that it is necessary to determine where to place disk one. Moving disk one is the base condition.

2. The first call to the function leads to exactly the same problem but one step closer to the solution.

On the way to moving five disks to post three it was necessary to move the first four disks to post two. This represents the $n - 1$ condition or, in other words, exactly the same problem but one step closer to the solution.

This solution was not obvious on first approaching the problem. It becomes recognizable as the problem is examined in an attempt to be clear about the mechanics of the game. This leads to the observation that certain points in the game must occur on the way to a solution.

If the first three moves of a hypothetical game are recorded, we might find disk one moving from post one to post three; disk two moving from post one to post two; and disk one moving from post three to post two. This suggests a nomenclature for the moves themselves. If a move is made from post one to post three, identifying the disk is unnecessary. The move will always be made by the top disk. Only the names of the start and end positions must be noted.

However, it is important to keep track of what disk is on which post and where it is going. This is the information that must be passed to each iteration of the function. Specifically, the arguments for the function should be the disk number, the start position, the end position, and the temp position. The first time a disk is moved the start position will be post one. On subsequent moves its position will have to be known.

The play that is determined by the recursive function should be thought of as consisting of rounds. A round is complete when a new stack is complete. Round one is a single move of disk one to post three and requires only one move. Round two creates a stack of two disks on post two and is completed after the third move. The third round creates a complete stack on post three after seven moves. The creation of complete stacks continues until the entire stack of disks is moved.

The description of the initial stack begins with the largest disk or disk n. However, to make the first move it is necessary to tunnel down through the recursive function until the base case is found that moves disk one. This is equivalent to tunneling up through the stack from disk n to disk one. The second round requires the movement of disk two to post two and a second move of disk one. This is accomplished as the program backs out of the recursive function and executes the next to last level. Similarly, round three is accomplished at the third last calling of the function.

There are as many rounds of play as there are levels to the recursive function and the number of levels is equal to the number of disks chosen by the user. This is enough information to allow the writing of the pseudocode.

Pseudocode

1. Begin recursive function.
2. If the disk number is one (base case).
3. Move disk one from its current position to the end point, i.e., display the move of disk one from its `start` point to its end point.
4. Else
5. Make a new call to the recursive function, reversing the end and temp values for each call. (Remember the analysis of the five-disk stack. Disk five was moved to post three. Disk four was moved to post two. Disk three was moved to post three. Notice that the value for end must alternate between posts two and three. This will eventually determine the correct initial end point for disk one, which is where the game begins.)
6. After the base case for each level, back up one more level and display the first move.
7. Tunnel back down to the base case, making the rest of the moves for the current round.
8. End when the round for disk *n* is complete, i.e., the program has backed out of every level created.
9. Begin main.
10. Get the number of disks from the user.
11. Call the recursive function.
12. End main.

The beauty of recursive functions is that they can take intricate logic and hide it from the programmer. The programmer only needs to know how to make the first step and the base condition. The result is very short, elegant code.

Solution Implemented in C++

```
1    //  Problem 8.6
2    #include <iostream.h>
3    #include <iomanip.h>
4    #include <math.h>
5
6    int move = 1, round = 1;
7    void hanoi ( int n, int start, int end, int temp)
8    {
9        if (n == 1)
10       {
11           cout << setw(3) << move++ << "   " << start << " --> "
12               << end << endl;
13           if (move == pow(2,round))
14               cout << endl;
15       }
16       else
17       {
```

```
18              hanoi(n - 1,start,temp, end);
19              if (n > round)
20                  round = n;
21              cout << setw(3) << move++ << "  " << start <<  " --> "
22                  << end << endl;
23              hanoi(n - 1,temp, end, start);
24          }
25  }
26
27  void main(void)
28  {
29      int start = 1, temp = 2, end = 3, disks;
30      cout << "Enter the number of disks in the tower of Hanoi . . ";
31      cin >> disks;
32      hanoi ( disks, start, end, temp );
33  }
```

The difficult element in writing the code is the list of arguments for each function call. On line 24 the number of disks, the first argument, indicates how many times the function will call itself until it reaches the base case. The rest of the arguments are the start, end, and temp values. When the function calls itself on line 12 tunneling to the base condition, the start value is the same but the temp and end values are reversed. Line 15 is less obvious. In this set of function calls, the post where the disk was placed temporarily becomes the starting point and the end is the final destination of the disk in the current round.

The arrangement of the output data into columns that follows is slightly awkward to build into the program and is a product of post editing by a word processor. The extra lines that have been inserted after each round are a product of the program and are achieved by lines 13, 14, 19, and 20. The variable round tracks the end of the round by noting the maximum disk value as line 18 backs away from the base case. Every round will end with an execution of the base case but the converse is not true. Every execution of the base case does not indicate the end of a round.

It is necessary that round is a global variable. If round is declared locally, it will be created and set to one every time a new iteration of the function is called and destroyed each time a function ends.

Output of the C++ Program

```
Enter the number of disks in the Tower of Hanoi . .   6
  1  1 --> 2          8  1 --> 3        16  1 --> 3        25  1 --> 3
                      9  2 --> 3        17  2 --> 1        26  1 --> 2
  2  1 --> 3         10  2 --> 1        18  2 --> 3        27  3 --> 2
  3  2 --> 3         11  3 --> 1        19  1 --> 3        28  1 --> 3
                     12  2 --> 3        20  2 --> 1        29  2 --> 1
  4  1 --> 2         13  1 --> 2        21  3 --> 2        30  2 --> 3
  5  3 --> 1         14  1 --> 3        22  3 --> 1        31  1 --> 3
  6  3 --> 2         15  2 --> 3        23  2 --> 1
  7  1 --> 2                            24  2 --> 3        32  1 --> 3
```

33	2 --> 3	41	3 --> 1	49	1 --> 2	57	2 --> 3
34	2 --> 1	42	3 --> 2	50	1 --> 3	58	2 --> 1
35	3 --> 1	43	1 --> 2	51	2 --> 3	59	3 --> 1
36	2 --> 3	44	3 --> 1	52	1 --> 2	60	2 --> 3
37	1 --> 2	45	2 --> 3	53	3 --> 1	61	1 --> 2
38	1 --> 3	46	2 --> 1	54	3 --> 2	62	1 --> 3
39	2 --> 3	47	3 --> 1	55	1 --> 2	63	2 --> 3
40	2 --> 1	48	2 --> 3	56	1 --> 3		

It can be proven but observation will suffice to indicate that for a given number of disks the number of moves required is two raised to the power of the number of disks minus 1 or moves = $2^{\text{No. of Disks}} - 1$.

According to legend, a group of monks in India were required to move a stack of 64 disks from one location to another under the rules described earlier. When the task of moving the disks is completed, the world will end. If the monks began moving disks 100 years ago and are able to move one disk per second, how much time does the world have left? The problem is left as an exercise for the reader.

Solution Implemented in Visual Basic

```
1    Option Explicit
2    Private fmove As Integer
3    Private fround As Integer
4    Private Sub hanoi(ByVal n As Integer, ByVal start As Integer, _
5              ByVal finish As Integer, ByVal temp As Integer)
6
7        If n = 1 Then
8            lstOutput.AddItem (fmove & "      " & _
9                start & " --> " & finish)
10           fmove = fmove + 1
11           If fmove = 2 ^ fround Then
12               lstOutput.AddItem (" ")
13           End If
14       Else
15           Call hanoi(n - 1, start, temp, finish)
16           If n > fround Then
17               fround = n
18           End If
19           lstOutput.AddItem (fmove & "      " & start & _
20               " --> " & finish)
21           fmove = fmove + 1
22           Call hanoi(n - 1, temp, finish, start)
23       End If
24   End Sub
25
26   Private Sub cmdCalculate_Click()
27       Dim disks As Integer
28       Dim start As Integer
29       Dim finish As Integer
```

```
30        Dim temp As Integer
31
32        disks = CInt(txtInput.Text)
33        start = 1
34        finish = 3
35        temp = 2
36        fmove = 1
37        fround = 1
38        Call hanoi(disks, start, finish, temp)
39   End Sub
40
41   Private Sub cmdExit_Click()
42        Unload Me
43   End Sub
44
45   Private Sub Form_Activate()
46        txtInput.SetFocus
47   End Sub
48
49   Private Sub Form_Load()
50        lblInput.Caption = "Enter the number of disks in the tower of Hanoi"
51   End Sub
```

Output of the Visual Basic Program

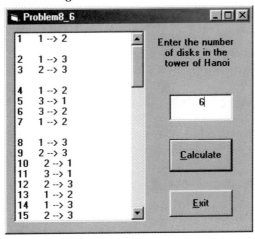

PROBLEM 8.7   *A traveling salesman intends to visit many cities. In order to minimize time and expense he needs to know the shortest path that connects all the cities. Determine the shortest path for any number of randomly chosen cities.*

Problem 8.7 is the general form for the limited traveling salesman problem introduced in Chapter 5. In the original problem the salesman would visit exactly five cities. In the more general form the number of cities is not known until the program is executed.

Compared to the previous recursion problems, finding a minimal distance is considerably more practical. The factorial problem provided a simple example of recursion but the problem could have been solved by a simple loop. The solution to the Tower of Hanoi was far easier using recursion, but the problem itself was somewhat artificial.

On the other hand, minimum distances problems have real-world applications. To be generally useful the solution to the traveling salesman problem must accommodate a variable number of nodes. Unfortunately, the original solution to the problem is not so easily adapted to fit the more general problem. The traveling salesman solution relied on a series of nested loops. The number of loops depended on the number of cities. To accommodate more cities the number of nested loops would need to be changed. This means altering the source code of the program and recompiling the program, a process that is not only error prone but impractical. For convenience a portion of the code for Problem 5.3, the limited traveling salesman problem, is reproduced.

```
69   for (x = 1; x < MAX_CITIES; x++)
70       for (y = 1; y < MAX_CITIES; y++)
71       {
72           if (x == y) continue;
73           for (z = 1; z < MAX_CITIES; z++)
74           {
75               if ( z == x || z == y) continue;
76               total_distance = 0;
77               for (w = 1; w < MAX_CITIES; w++)
78               {
79                   if (w == x || w == y || w == z) continue;
80                   total_distance = cities[0].dis_to_cities[x].distance +
81                       cities[x].dis_to_cities[y].distance +
```

```
82                              cities[y].dis_to_cities[z].distance +
83                              cities[z].dis_to_cities[w].distance +
84                              cities[w].dis_to_cities[0].distance ;
85                      if (total_distance < winner)
86                      {
87                          winner = total_distance;
88                          path[0] = 0, path[1] = x, path[2] = y, path[3] = z;
89                          path [4] = w;
90                      }
91              }
92          }
93      }
```

The general case requires that the program drill down through a variable number of constructions that would perform the same function as the nested loops. As each level of the drilling down is accomplished, one more node on the path is recorded, bringing the program closer to the complete path. After the order of a variable number of cities is recorded, the distances from city to city can be summed and the shortest recorded.

The path itself can no longer be stored in variables such as x, y, and z. Instead the order of the nodes must be saved in an array that itself places a maximum number of cities for which the program can be used. This limit should be stored as a constant and used as a known value throughout the program. Redefining the constant would allow for a larger number of cities; however, there is a practical limit to the number of cities. The number of cities determines the number of paths that must be checked. For n cities the number of possible paths is $(N - 1)!$. Twenty cities implies 121,645,100,408,832,000 possible paths for the computer to check.

The code for each nested loop in the limited solution is nearly the same and leads one step closer to the end point, i.e., a complete path. The only difference is in checking previous nodes to prevent duplications (lines 72, 75, and 79 in the preceding code). When the path is complete, the distance traveled is calculated and, if it is shorter than the previous shortest path, it is stored. The calculations on the completed path represent the base case and a recursive function would appear to be useful in the general solution.

Many of the elements of the limited solution can be reused. The data structures that store the data and the functions that set the data, make the calculations, and display the results are nearly the same in the general solution. The most apparent difference is the need for global variables. In the limited solution the nested loops and the calculations were part of the main function, making local variables viable. In the general solution each iteration of the recursive function must have access to the structure variables and the array that stores the path. These could be passed on from function to function but the code becomes rather messy.

Since much of the code from the limited traveling salesman solution is reused, there is little reason to write pseudocode for most of the program. Only the recursive function is described next.

Pseudocode

  1. Begin recursive function.
  2. Create the base case if the level of called functions is equal to the number of cities.
  3. Begin loop to sum the distances from city to city.
  4. Create running sum of distances from city in path to the next city.
  5. End loop at the second last city (the data structure for each city contains the distance to the next city).
  6. Add in the return trip from the last city to the start city.
  7. If the trip distance is less than the current shortest distance
  8. Store the trip distance as the shortest distance so far.
  9. Copy the path that produced the shortest distance into a holding array.
  10. Display the current path if necessary for troubleshooting.
  11. End base condition.
  12. Create operations to drill down to the base case.
  13. Begin loop to place each city in the current path element based on level.
  14. Set the path element to the current city value.
  15. If the city number is found in any previous path element
  16. Move on to the next city.
  17. Increment level number as the program drills down to the end of path.
  18. Call the recursive functions.
  19. Decrement level number as the program backs out of recursive functions.
  20. End when all cities have been used.
  21. End the current iteration of the function.
  22. End the function and return to main.

It is important to place each new city in its proper place in the path array. This can be accomplished by using a variable to track how many times the function has called itself. With each call to the function, another city number is placed in the path array. The `level` variable referred to in steps 17 and 19 of the pseudocode serves this purpose. This variable also needs to be global in order to count the function calls.

Solution Implemented in C++

```
1    //  Problem 8.7
2    #include <iostream.h>
3    #include <math.h>
4    #include <iomanip.h>
5    #include <string.h>
6    #include <time.h>
7    #define MAX_CITIES 20
8
9    struct data                    // Data structure to store distance to a
10   {                              //     named city
```

```
11        char name[40];
12        double distance;
13    };
14    struct location           // Data structure to store location of cities
15    {                         //     and distances to all other cities
16        char name[40];
17        double latitude, longitude;
18        data dis_to_cities[MAX_CITIES];
19    };
20                // Global variables accessed by all recursive functions
21    location cities[MAX_CITIES];// = {{"Cincinnati",39.1.84.5}.
22        {"Atlanta",33.8.84.4},{"Charleston",32.8.80.0},
23        {"Boston",42.3.71.0},{"Denver",39.8.104.9},
24        {"Rochester",43.2.77.6},{"Chicago",42.0.87.7},
25        {"Oklahoma City",35.5.97.5},{"Annapolis",39.0.76.5},
26        {"Philadelphia",40.0.75.1},{"St. Louis",38.8.90.8}
27        {"Detroit",42.4.83.1}};//,{"Tampa",30.1.82.1}};*
28    int path[MAX_CITIES] = {0}, level = 1, winning_path[MAX_CITIES],
29    int path_counter = 0;
30    double total_distance, winner = 1e7;
31    long start, end;
32                              // Function prototypes
33    location set_data (void);
34    void calculate_distances(int);
35    void final_display (int);
36    void display(int);
37    void copy_path(int);
38                              // Recursive function
39    void get_route(int places)
40    {
41        int x, y, flag;
42        if(level == places      // Base case
43        {
44            total_distance = 0, path_counter++;
45            for (x = 0; x < places - 1; x++)    // Running sum for
46                              //    total_distance
47                total_distance +=
48                    cities[path[x]].dis_to_cities[path[x + 1]].distance;
49            total_distance +=
50                cities[path[places - 1]].dis_to_cities[0].distance;
51            if (total_distance < winner)
52            {
53                winner = total_distance;
54                copy_path(places);
55                //display(places);   // Display each new shorter path
56            }
57        }
58        else
```

```
59            for (x = 1; x < places; x++)
60            {
61                    path[level] = x;
62                    flag = 0;
63                    for (y = 1; y < level; y++)
64                        if (x == path[y])
65                            flag = 1;
66                    if (flag == 1)
67                        continue;
68                    level++;    // level tracks the number of times the
69                    get_route(places);     // function calls itself
70                    level--;
71            }
72  }
73  void main(void)
74  {
75      int places = -1;
76      cout.setf(ios::fixed|ios::showpoint);
77      cout.precision (2);
78
79      do
80      {
81          places++;
82          cities[places] = set_data();
83
84      }while (cities[places].name[0] != 0 && places < 19);
85      time(&start);
86      calculate_distances (places);
87      get_route(places);
88      time(&end);
89      final_display(places);
90  }
91  void copy_path(int places)
92  {
93      for (int x = 0; x < places; x++)
94          winning_path[x] = path[x];
95  }
96  location set_data (void)
97  {
98      location c;
99      cout << "Enter the city name . . " << flush;
100     cin.getline(c.name, 39, '\n');
101     if (c.name[0] == 0)
102         return c;
103     cout << "   Enter the latitude    " << flush;
104     cin >> c.latitude;
105     cout << "   Enter the longitude   " << flush;
106     cin >> c.longitude;
107     cin.ignore (1, '\n');
```

```
108     return c;
109 }
110 void calculate_distances(int places)
111 {
112     int start, destination;
113     for (start = 0 ; start < places; start++)
114         for (destination = 0; destination < MAX_CITIES; destination++)
115         {
116           cities[start].dis_to_cities[destination].distance =
117               sqrt(pow(cities[start].latitude -
118               cities[destination].latitude, 2) +
119               pow(cities[start].longitude -
120               cities[destination].longitude, 2)) * 69;
121           strcpy(cities[start].dis_to_cities[destination].name,
122               cities[destination].name );
123         }
124 }
125 void final_display (int pla)
126 {
127     cout << "The shortest route is " << winner << " miles" << endl
128         << "    and goes from " << endl;
129     for (int x = 0; x < pla; x++)
130         cout << setw(40) << cities[winning_path[x]].name << " to " << endl;
131     cout << setw(40) <<cities[0].name <<   endl
132         << path_counter <<" paths were searched in " << end - start
133         << " seconds " <<endl;
134 }
135 void display(int pla)
136 {
137     cout << "The current shortest distance is " << winner << endl;
138     cout << "The path is " << cities[0].name << endl;
139     for (int x = 1; x < pla; x++)
140         cout << "   " << cities[path[x]].name << " "
141               << cities[path[x - 1]].dis_to_cities[path[x]].distance;
142 cout << endl;
143 }
```

In this general version of the program most of the function calls have been pro-
totyped and defined after the main() function. Only the get_route() function was
defined ahead of main() to give it prominence as the new function in the program.

Several lines of code are not obvious and deserve comment. Since one city number is placed in the path array per function call, the level variable can be used as a sub-
script to properly place the city number in the array. This is done on line 61. Once this
is done, the for() loop beginning on line 63 tests whether the current city number is
found in the previous elements of the array. If it is found, it means that the city has already been visited and that particular route should be discarded. The continue command on line 67 tells the program to move on and use another city in that position before
the recursive function is called. This ensures that only distances for valid paths are calculated in the base case.

Line 55 contains a commented out call to a display function. This function has been included as a typical troubleshooting technique. Each time a new shortest path is calculated the length of the path is displayed along with the cities in the path. The use of the `path_counter` variable, set on line 44 and displayed on line 132, is also included for troubleshooting purposes. For *n* cities the number of valid paths is $(n-1)!$. Actually there are *n*! valid paths; however, every path has $(n-1)$ duplicates. The path 1, 2, 3, 4, 5 for five cities is the same path as 2, 3, 4, 5, 1. Only the starting point has changed. This means that any city can be used as the starting point and `cities[0].name` is always the same. Therefore, for *n* cities there will be *n* shortest paths, all of them identical except for the starting point. The duplicates can be ignored and a definite start city used for every path.

The notation for referring to the distances between cities can be confusing.

```
48    cities[path[x]].dis_to_cities[path[x + 1]].distance;
```

The variables, such as the preceding one found on line 48, involve both nested structures and nested arrays. The city is identified by its number, which is stored in the `path` array. The `dis_to_cities` also is an array of data structures and needs to choose the next city in the path or the $x + 1$ element in the `path` array.

Output of the C++ Program

```
Enter the city name . .    Cincinnati
     Enter the latitude     39.1
     Enter the longitude    84.5
Enter the city name . .    Atlanta
     Enter the latitude     33.8
     Enter the longitude    84.4
Enter the city name . .    Charleston
     Enter the latitude     32.8
     Enter the longitude    80.0
Enter the city name . .    Boston
     Enter the latitude     42.3
     Enter the longitude    71.0
Enter the city name . .    Denver
     Enter the latitude     39.8
     Enter the longitude    104.9
Enter the city name . .    Rochester
     Enter the latitude     43.2
     Enter the longitude    77.6
Enter the city name . .    Chicago
     Enter the latitude     42.0
     Enter the longitude    87.7
Enter the city name . .    Oklahoma City
     Enter the latitude     35.5
     Enter the longitude    97.5
```

```
Enter the city name . .   Annapolis
    Enter the latitude     39.0
    Enter the longitude    76.5
Enter the city name . .   Philadelphia
    Enter the latitude     40.0
    Enter the longitude    75.1
Enter the city name . .   St. Louis
    Enter the latitude     38.8
    Enter the longitude    90.8
Enter the city name . .
The shortest route is 5341.88 miles
and goes from
                            Cincinnati to
                             Rochester to
                                Boston to
                          Philadelphia to
                              Annapolis to
                             Charleston to
                                Atlanta to
                         Oklahoma City to
                                 Denver to
                              St. Louis to
                                Chicago to
                              Cincinnati
3628800 paths were searched in 20 seconds
```

If one more city is added to the route and the program is run again, the runtime increases to 239 seconds, or nearly 4 minutes, and the number of paths is 39,916,800 (assuming the program is running on a Pentium III, 450 MHz). This raises the question of how long it would take for the program to calculate the shortest path connecting the maximum number of 20 cities. The answer is simple to compute with a calculator by following the Units Rule (Rule 2) and listing the initial data.

Initial Data: **1.** 12 cities indicate 11! possible paths.
  2. 11! paths require 239 seconds to search for the shortest path.
  3. 20 cities indicate 19! possible paths.

$$\frac{239 \text{ sec}}{11! \text{ paths}} \times \frac{19! \text{ paths}}{1} \times \frac{1 \text{ min}}{60 \text{ sec}} \times \frac{1 \text{ hr}}{60 \text{ min}} \times \frac{1 \text{ day}}{24 \text{ hr}} \times \frac{1 \text{ year}}{365.24 \text{ days}}$$
$$\approx 23{,}000 \text{ years}$$

Actually the time is not directly related to the number of paths and 23,000 years is more properly a lower limit. On the other hand, as Douglas Adams has pointed out, if you have to wait 23,000 years for the answer, you will likely forget the question. The more relevant issue is that brute force has limits as a problem-solving technique. Readers with computer time to spare might want to try 14 cities.

Solution Implemented in Visual Basic

```
1    Option Explicit
2    Private level, places As Integer
3    Private path(0 To 19) As Integer
4    Private winning_path(0 To 19) As Integer
5    Private total_distance, winner As Double
6    Private start, finish, temp As Single
7    Private cities(0 To 19) As location
8    Private path_counter As Long
9
10   Private Type data
11       name As String
12       distance As Double
13   End Type
14
15   Private Type location
16       name As String
17       latitude As Double
18       longitude As Double
19       dis_to_cities(0 To 20) As data
20   End Type
21
22   Private Sub cmdCalculate_Click()
23
24       Call calculate_distances
25       start = Timer
26       Call get_route
27       Call final_display
28   End Sub
29
30   Private Sub cmdEnter_Click()
31       Dim c As location
32       If txtCity.Text = "" Or txtLongitude.Text = "" Or _
33           txtLatitude.Text = "" Then
34           Call MsgBox("Invalid input", vbExclamation, "Problem8_7")
35           Exit Sub
36           Call txtCity.SetFocus
37       End If
38
39       Call set_data(c)
40       cities(places) = c
41       places = places + 1
42       txtCity.Text = ""
```

```
43          txtLatitude.Text = ""
44          txtLongitude.Text = ""
45          Call txtCity.SetFocus
46     End Sub
47
48     Private Sub cmdExit_Click()
49          Unload Me
50     End Sub
51
52     Private Sub Form_Load()
53          lblLatitude.Caption = "Latitude"
54          lblCity.Caption = "Enter city name"
55          lblLongitude.Caption = "Longitude"
56          lblTitle.Caption = "This program calculates the path that will " & _
57               "have the shortest distance between a number of given cities."
58          lblAnswer.Caption = "Cities entered "
59          level = 1
60          winner = 10000000#
61     End Sub
62     Private Sub get_route()
63          Dim x, y, flag As Integer
64
65          If level = places Then
66               total_distance = 0
67               path_counter = path_counter + 1
68               If (path_counter + 1) Mod 10000 = 0 Then
69                    temp = Timer
70                    lblTime.Caption = "Processing time" & vbCrLf & _
71                         Int(temp - start) & " seconds"
72                    DoEvents
73               End If
74               For x = 0 To places - 2
75                    total_distance = total_distance + _
76                         cities(path(x)).dis_to_cities(path(x + 1)).distance
77               Next x
78
79               total_distance = total_distance + _
80                    cities(path(places - 1)).dis_to_cities(0).distance
81               If total_distance < winner Then
82                    winner = total_distance
83                    Call copy_path
84               End If
85          Else
86               For x = 1 To places - 1
87                    path(level) = x
88                    flag = 0
89                    For y = 1 To level - 1
```

```
90                      If x = path(y) Then
91                          flag = 1
92                      End If
93                  Next y
94                  If flag <> 1 Then
95                      level = level + 1
96                      Call get_route
97                      level = level - 1
98                  End If
99           Next x
100     End If
101
102 End Sub
103 Private Sub copy_path()
104     Dim x As Integer
105
106     For x = 0 To places
107         winning_path(x) = path(x)
108     Next x
109 End Sub
110
111 Private Sub calculate_distances()
112     Dim start As Integer
113     Dim destination As Integer
114
115     For start = 0 To places - 1
116         For destination = 0 To 19
117             cities(start).dis_to_cities(destination).distance = _
118             Sqr(((cities(start).latitude -
119               cities(destination).latitude) ^ 2) + _
120             ((cities(start).longitude -
121               cities(destination).longitude) ^ 2)) * 69
122             cities(start).dis_to_cities(destination).name = _
123                 cities(destination).name
124         Next destination
125     Next start
126 End Sub
127
128 Private Sub set_data(ByRef c As location)
129     c.name = txtCity.Text
130     If c.name = "" Then
131         Exit Sub
132     End If
133     c.latitude = txtLatitude.Text
134     c.longitude = txtLongitude.Text
135
136     lblAnswer.Caption = lblAnswer & vbCrLf & c.name & _
```

```
137            "     " & c.latitude & "     " & c.longitude
138 End Sub
139
140 Private Sub final_display()
141     Dim x As Integer
142     lblAnswer.Caption = ""
143     lblAnswer.Caption = "The shortest route is " & _
144         Format(winner, "#.##") & " miles."
145     lblAnswer.Caption = lblAnswer.Caption & vbCrLf & _
146         "The path is " & "." & vbCrLf
147
148     For x = 0 To places - 1
149         lblAnswer.Caption = lblAnswer.Caption & "        " & _
150             cities(winning_path(x)).name & " to" & vbCrLf
151     Next x
152
153     lblAnswer.Caption = lblAnswer.Caption & "and back to " & _
154         cities(0).name & vbCrLf & vbCrLf & path_counter & _
155         " paths were searched"
156     finish = Timer
157     lblTime.Caption = "Program Completed in" & vbCrLf & _
158         Int(finish - start) & " seconds"
159 End Sub
```

The Visual Basic program has been neatly divided into logical units. The code associated with a click of the Enter command button beginning on line 30 handles the error checking and the passing of the user information to the proper user-defined data types via the set_data() function on line 39. It also keeps a count of the number of cities that the user has entered.

The calculation of all the intercity distances is the job of the calculate_distances() function on line 111. This function used the user-entered data to calculate all the city-to-city distances that will be needed to determine path lengths. Of course, in a real-world problem this would be replaced by the actual distances between nodes regardless of whether the routes were straight, arched, or crooked.

The real organizational work is concisely written in the code for the Calculate command button on lines 22 to 28. In sequence the intercity distances are calculated; all possible paths are determined and their distances calculated; and the results are presented to the user by the final_display() function.

The meat of the program begins on line 62 with the get_route() function. This is the recursive function that will call itself as many times as necessary to connect all the cities with paths that include all nodes but never any node twice, except for the starting city, which also must be the ending city. Like all recursive functions it contains the $n - 1$ case, which contains the call to itself (line 96); and the base case routine, which calculates the path distance after the whole path has been determined beginning on line 65.

Output of the Visual Basic Program—Data Entry

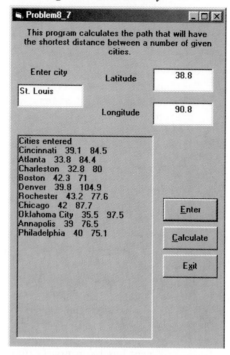

Output of the Visual Basic Program—Calculated Path

CHAPTER 9

Epilog

9.1 RULE ZERO

The purpose of this text has been to answer one single question, "What do I do?" When confronted with a problem, a problem that is novel, a problem whose solution has never been taught in any class, how do you get started? There is no general formula that can be used in a plug-and-chug fashion that applies to all problems. Instead the previous eight chapters have presented approaches that can be used to attack the unfamiliar problem.

There is one more rule. It isn't an approach for finding solutions to problems and shouldn't be listed with the other rules that lead toward that goal. On the other hand, it may be the most important rule because it is the starting point of every solution.

> **Rule Zero   Start! Write something down! Try something!**

This rule has been left until the end because without the other rules there is no starting point, nothing to write down, nothing to try. What should be tried when facing a new problem?

Rewrite the problem.

List the information available.

Draw a picture.

Think of a concrete example.

Limit the problem.

Look for repeated operations.

Examine the units.

Try working the problem backward.

Try to guess at the answer.

Try to brute force your way to an answer.

Try a simulation.

Create an object.

Try recursion.

But do something.

Staring at the problem will not solve it. Wishing it would go away will not solve it. Deciding that it is unfair that you were given the problem to solve will not solve it. If there are things that you will have to learn in order to solve the problem, go learn them. If there is information that you will have to gather in order to solve the problem, go get it. But do something.

Life is a place of incredible variety and there is not nearly enough time to take a class to learn to solve each of the problems that eventually cross everyone's path. It is necessary to develop the skill and background for dealing with novel problems that are challenging and stretch our abilities as problem solvers.

The problems in this text were designed to illustrate that there are many problems that appear difficult but are within the abilities of the creative problem solver. The area of a trapezoid was found without the aid of a formula. Probabilities were determined without performing any probability calculations. Infinite summations were calculated without any advanced mathematics. The area under a curve was found without learning integral calculus. The problems in Chapters 7 and 8 showed that with simple rules, a little bit of experience, and the power of a personal computer even problems of considerable complexity are manageable.

The important rule is to start. Do not worry about pursuing a plan that fails to lead to a solution. This can happen (repeatedly). Start again. Some problems are difficult and refuse to fall apart at the first effort. Start again. Sometimes the solution will seem out of reach because your background in physics, economics, mathematics, or information handling is inadequate. Go learn what you need to know and start again.

Good luck.

Appendix A

Rule 1   The Clarity Rule

    1. Be clear about what information you have to work with.

    2. Be clear about what information you are trying to discover.

Rule 2   The Units Rule

Pay attention to units. If the unit of measurement is kept with each number, the mathematical operation to be performed will be apparent without the knowledge of any formula. Correct operations will lead to units that cancel. Incorrect operations will lead to units that compound and confound.

Rule 3   The Picture Rule

Whenever possible draw a picture.

Rule 4   The Working Backwards Rule

Instead of working from the beginning of a problem asking what is the first step toward the end, start at the end and ask what is needed to perform the last step. From there examine what is necessary for the second to last step and work toward the beginning.

Rule 5   The Repetition Rule

When approaching a problem look for repeated operation. The number of times the operation is repeated is usually irrelevant.

Rule 6   The Clarity in Loops Rule

When a problem involves repeated operations, be clear about which operations are repeated and belong inside the looping structure and which operations occur only once and should be outside of the loop.

Rule 7   The Limit the Problem Rule

When a problem is too difficult to solve consider limiting the problem to find a special case solution.

Rule 8   The Concrete Example Rule

When examining a general problem it is often more illuminating to work with a specific instance. An example with numeric values is always easier to understand than the general case.

Rule 9   The Successive Approximation Rule

When an exact solution is too difficult to calculate, an approximate answer of arbitrary accuracy can often be found by adding terms that make a partial solution come ever closer to the true solution.

Rule 10   The Strategic Guessing Rule

1. Make a reasonable initial guess.
2. Check the accuracy of the guess.
3. Repeatedly refine the guess until the desired accuracy is achieved.

Rule 11   The Functions Rule

As problems become more complex it becomes increasingly important to divide the logic into smaller units that solve individual parts of the problem. These units correspond to programming functions.

Rule 12   The Brute Force Rule

When all else fails try examining all possible solutions in a systematic manner.

Rule 13   The Self-Consistency Rule

If a statement is assumed to be true and then leads to a conclusion contrary to some known fact, the original assumption must be false. If a statement is assumed to be false and leads to a conclusion contrary to some known fact, the original assumption must be true. All real world scenarios must be self-consistent.

Rule 14   The Probability Rule

When probabilities or odds need to be calculated, brute force can usually be applied by simulating the scenario and counting how many times the event of interest occurs.

Rule 15   The Approximation Rule

Look for approximations that simplify a problem but do not appreciably affect the accuracy of the solution.

Rule 16   The Expanding the Scope Rule

When generalizing a solution to encompass a greater range, greater complexity, broader conditions, or greater utility, focus on the differences between the conditions when the solution works and the new conditions.

Rule 17   The Recursion Rule

A problem can be solved recursively if:

1. The final step or the base condition is known.
2. The first step of the problem leads to exactly the same problem but one step closer to the solution.

Appendix B

Determining the general equation for an ellipse requires starting with the definition of an ellipse. An ellipse is a geometric figure made up of points that satisfy the condition that the sum of the distances from two fixed points to every point on the ellipse is constant. Those two points are called the foci of the ellipse.

If the distance between F_1 and F_2 is called F then the coordinates for F_1 is $(-F/2, 0)$ and the coordinates for F_2 is $(+F/2, 0)$.

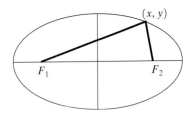

The length of the line from F_1 to (x, y) is

$$\left[\left(x - \frac{F}{2}\right)^2 + y^2\right]^{.5} = L_1$$

The length of the line from F_2 to (x, y) is

$$\left[\left(x + \frac{F}{2}\right)^2 + y^2\right]^{.5} = L_2$$

The combined length L is

$$\left[\left(x - \frac{F}{2}\right)^2 + y^2\right]^{.5} + \left[\left(x + \frac{F}{2}\right)^2 + y^2\right]^{.5} = L$$

Simplifying this equation involves little more than squaring the binomial and canceling identical terms from both sides of the equation.

$$\left[\left(x - \frac{F}{2}\right)^2 + y^2\right]^{.5} = L - \left[\left(x + \frac{F}{2}\right)^2 + y^2\right]^{.5}$$

$$\left(x - \frac{F}{2}\right)^2 + y^2 = L^2 - 2L\left[\left(x - \frac{F}{2}\right)^2 + y^2\right]^{.5} + \left(x - \frac{F}{2}\right)^2 + y^2$$

$$x^2 - xF + \frac{F^2}{4} + y^2 = L^2 - 2L\left[\left(x + \frac{F}{2}\right)^2 + y^2\right]^{.5} + x^2 + xF + \frac{F^2}{4} + y^2$$

At this point several terms will cancel leaving

$$L^2 - 2L\left[\left(x + \frac{F}{2}\right)^2 + y^2\right]^{.5} + 2xF = 0$$

$$2L\left[\left(x + \frac{F}{2}\right)^2 + y^2\right]^{.5} = L^2 + 2xF$$

Squaring both sides of the equation and canceling produces

$$4L^2\left[\left(x + \frac{F}{2}\right)^2 + y^2\right] = L^4 + 4L^2 + xF + 4x^2F^2$$

$$4L^2x^2 + 4L^2xF + 4L^2\frac{F^2}{4} + 4L^2y^2 = L^4 + 4L^2xF + 4x^2F^2$$

$$4L^2x^2 + L^2F^2 + 4L^2y^2 = L^4 + 4x^2F^2$$

Rearranging terms and factoring

$$4L^2x^2 - 4x^2F^2 + 4L^2y^2 = L^4 - L^2F^2$$

$$4x^2(L^2 - F^2) + 4L^2y^2 = L^2(L^2 - F^2)$$

Dividing by the right side of the equation and canceling

$$\frac{4x^2(L^2 - F^2)}{L^2(L^2 - F^2)} + \frac{4L^2y^2}{L^2(L^2 - F^2)} = 1$$

$$\left(\frac{2}{L}\right)^2 x^2 + \left(\frac{4}{L^2 - F^2}\right)y^2 = 1$$

At this point the algebra is complete and the only item left is to interpret the results. The length L is the same length as the major axis. This means that $L/2$ is equal to a, which is half the major axis. The coefficient of y^2 is a little harder to see without a picture.

At the vertex $(b, 0)$, $L/2$ is the length of the hypotenous of a right triangle. $F/2$ is the base of that triangle. According to the Pythagorian Theorem the third sides is $(L^2 - F^2)/4$.

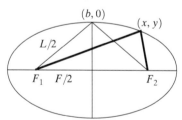

Substituting into the derived equation gives

$$\left(\frac{2}{L}\right)^2 x^2 + \left(\frac{4}{L^2 - F^2}\right)y^2 = 1$$

$$\frac{x^2}{a^2} + \frac{y^2}{b^2} = 1$$

Appendix C

Appendix C provides the calculations for finding the area of the semiellipse used in the basketball court problem (Problem 6.6). The integral calculus gives an exact solution that can be compared to the simulation that was programmed in Chapter 6.

The general equation for an ellipse is

$$\frac{x^2}{a^2} + \frac{y^2}{b^2} = 1 \quad \text{or}$$

$$y = \left(b^2 - \frac{b^2}{a^2} x^2 \right)^{.5}$$

Substituting 30 feet for the major axis and 20 feet for the minor axis gives

$$y = \left(20^2 - \frac{20^2}{30^2} x^2 \right)^{.5} \quad \text{or}$$

$$y = 20 \sqrt{1 - \left(\frac{x}{30} \right)^2}$$

Integrating over the major axis produces

$$I = 20 \int_0^{30} \sqrt{1 - \left(\frac{x}{30} \right)^2} \, dx$$

The integration can be set up for integration by parts by making the substitution $x = 30 \cos u$, $dx = -30 \sin u \, du$. With new limits the integral is

$$20 \times 30 \int_{\pi/2}^{0} \sqrt{1 - \cos^2 u} (-\sin u) du = 20 \times 30 \int_0^{\pi/2} \sin^2 u \, du$$

Using integration by parts,

$$\int \sin^2 u \, du = -\sin u \cos u + \int \cos^2 u \, du = -\sin u \cos u + \int 1 - \sin^2 u \, du$$

$$\Rightarrow 2 \int \sin^2 u \, du = -\sin u \cos u + \int du$$

so

$$I = 20 \times 30 \int_0^{\pi/2} \sin^2 u \, du = 20 \times 30 \left(\frac{1}{2} \right) \left(-\sin u \cos u \Big|_0^{\pi/2} + \int_0^{\pi/2} du \right)$$

$$I = 20 \times 15 \left(-0 + 0 + \frac{\pi}{2} - 0 \right) = 150\pi$$

150π is the area under the curve for the semiellipse or the area between the curve and the x-axis. Including the lower half of the semiellipse (the area below the x-axis) doubles the area or the area of the semielliptical basketball court equals 300π square feet.

Appendix D

Appendix D contains the calculations for a theoretical value for the odds of winning a game of craps. The starting point for the solution is listing the probabilities for rolling each of the possible values that can be rolled with two dice. This list represents a large part of the initial information of the problem.

Value	Combinations	# of Combinations	Probability	
2	1-1	1	1/36	1/36
3	1-2; 2-1	2	2/36	1/18
4	1-3; 2-2; 3-1	3	3/36	1/12
5	1-4; 2-3; 3-2; 4-1	4	4/36	1/9
6	1-5; 2-4; 3-3; 4-2; 5-1	5	5/36	5/36
7	1-6; 2-5; 3-4; 4-3; 5-2; 6-1	6	6/36	1/6
8	2-6; 3-5; 4-4; 5-3; 6-2	5	5/36	5/36
9	3-6; 4-5; 5-4; 6-3	4	4/36	1/9
10	4-6; 5-5; 6-4	3	3/36	1/12
11	5-6; 6-5	2	2/36	1/18
12	6-6	1	1/36	1/36

From the table it is clear that there are 36 possible, equally likely combinations of two dice. Dividing the number of combinations that will result in a given number by 36 gives the probability that a certain outcome will occur when the dice are rolled.

The probability of winning the game is the sum of the probabilities for all the winning rolls. The winning rolls are:

1. Rolling a seven on the first roll.
2. Rolling an eleven on the first roll.
3. If a number other than 7, 11, 2, 3, or 12 is rolled on the first roll, the game is won if that number, called the point, is rolled a second time before a seven is rolled.

The first two winning possibilities are simple to calculate. A seven occurs, on the average, one time out of six roles or 16.66666667 percent of the time. More accurately, the percentage is a repeating decimal with the string of sixes extending indefinitely. Similarly, there are two chances out of thirty-six that an eleven will occur, or an eleven will be rolled 5.55555556 percent of the time. Again this is a repeating decimal with the fives extending indefinitely. Therefore, the odds of a first-roll win are eight chances in 36 or 22.22222222 percent of the time. Once more, this is a repeating decimal.

The odds of winning on subsequent rolls require the examination of several individual cases. Consider the case in which a four is rolled on the first throw. The odds of rolling a four are one in twelve. If a four is rolled, for the rest of the game there are only two numbers that matter. If another four is rolled, the game is won, and if a seven is rolled, the game is lost. All other numbers produce no result and another throw is required.

Since four (the point) and seven are the only relevant rolls, there are nine possibilities that will end the game. Three of the nine have a value of four and produce a win; six of the nine have a value of seven and lose the game. Therefore, the odds of winning the game by rolling a four on the first roll and another four before rolling a seven are:

$$\frac{3}{36} \times \frac{3}{9} = \frac{1}{12} \times \frac{1}{3} = \frac{1}{36} = .02777777\overline{7} = 2.7777777\overline{7}\%$$

If five is the point, there are four chances in thirty-six of rolling the initial five. The odds for matching the five before rolling a seven are four chances in ten. The calculations are:

$$\frac{4}{36} \times \frac{4}{10} = \frac{1}{9} \times \frac{2}{5} = \frac{2}{45} = .04444444\overline{4} = 4.4444444\overline{4}\%$$

If six is the point there are five chances in thirty-six of rolling the initial six. The odds for matching the six before rolling a seven are five chances in eleven. The calculations are:

$$\frac{5}{36} \times \frac{5}{11} = \frac{25}{396} = .06313131\overline{31} = 6.313131\overline{31}\%$$

The calculations for winning on an eight are the same as those for winning on a six because there are five chances in 36 for rolling an eight. Similarly, the odds of winning on a nine are the same as for a five and the odds for winning on a ten are the same as for winning on a four.

The probability of winning is the sum of:

Seven on the first roll	16.666667%
Eleven on the first roll	5.555556%
Making point on four	2.777778%
Making point on five	4.444444%
Making point on six	6.313131%
Making point on eight	6.313131%
Making point on nine	4.444444%
Making point on ten	2.777778%
Total	49.292929%

If the fractions are added instead of their decimal equivalent, the answer is found to be a repeating decimal of 49.29$\overline{29}$% with the 29 repeating indefinitely.

It should be noted that the result of 49.2928% for the simulation on page 000 compares extremely well to this theoretical value.

Appendix E

Dec	Hex	Char		Dec	Hex	Char	Dec	Hex	Char	Dec	Hex	Char
0	0	NUL	(null)	32	20	SPACE	64	40	@	96	60	`
1	1	SOH	(start of heading)	33	21	!	65	41	A	97	61	a
2	2	STX	(start of text)	34	22	"	66	42	B	98	62	b
3	3	ETX	(end of text)	35	23	#	67	43	C	99	63	c
4	4	EOT	(end of transmission)	36	24	$	68	44	D	100	64	d
5	5	ENQ	(enquiry)	37	25	%	69	45	E	101	65	e
6	6	ACK	(acknowledge)	38	26	&	70	46	F	102	66	f
7	7	BEL	(bell)	39	27	'	71	47	G	103	67	g
8	8	BS	(backspace)	40	28	(	72	48	H	104	68	h
9	9	TAB	(horizontal tab)	41	29	)	73	49	I	105	69	i
10	A	LF	(NL line feed, new line)	42	2A	*	74	4A	J	106	6A	j
11	B	VT	(vertical tab)	43	2B	+	75	4B	K	107	6B	k
12	C	FF	(NP form feed, new page)	44	2C	,	76	4C	L	108	6C	l
13	D	CR	(carriage return)	45	2D	-	77	4D	M	109	6D	m
14	E	SO	(shift out)	46	2E	.	78	4E	N	110	6E	n
15	F	SI	(shift in)	47	2F	/	79	4F	O	111	6F	o
16	10	DLE	(data link escape)	48	30	0	80	50	P	112	70	p
17	11	DC1	(device control 1)	49	31	1	81	51	Q	113	71	q
18	12	DC2	(device control 2)	50	32	2	82	52	R	114	72	r
19	13	DC3	(device control 3)	51	33	3	83	53	S	115	73	s
20	14	DC4	(device control 4)	52	34	4	84	54	T	116	74	t
21	15	NAK	(negative acknowledge)	53	35	5	85	55	U	117	75	u
22	16	SYN	(synchronous idle)	54	36	6	86	56	V	118	76	v
23	17	ETB	(end of trans. block)	55	37	7	87	57	W	119	77	w
24	18	CAN	(cancel)	56	38	8	88	58	X	120	78	x
25	19	EM	(end of medium)	57	39	9	89	59	Y	121	79	y
26	1A	SUB	(substitute)	58	3A	:	90	5A	Z	122	7A	z
27	1B	ESC	(escape)	59	3B	;	91	5B	[	123	7B	{
28	1C	FS	(file separator)	60	3C	<	92	5C	\	124	7C	|
29	1D	GS	(group separator)	61	3D	=	93	5D	]	125	7D	}
30	1E	RS	(record separator)	62	3E	>	94	5E	^	126	7E	~
31	1F	US	(unit separator)	63	3F	?	95	5F	_	127	7F	DEL

Index

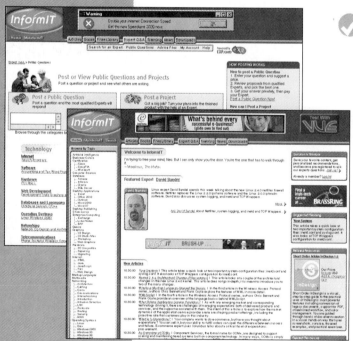